Islam is a world-wide religion embracing many cultures and nations, comprising today nearly 900 million persons. Muslims believe that God (Allah) revealed to the Prophet Muhammad guidance for proper conduct in this world and salvation in the next. These revelations are contained in the Muslims' scripture, the Qur'an. From modest beginnings in Mecca fourteen centuries ago, Islam spread rapidly throughout the Middle East and then into southeast Asia. This book is the story of the Muslims' beliefs and practices as they developed during the formative period. Separate chapters are devoted to a description of the sacred law (the *shari'ah*), theology, and mysticism. Attention is given also to the beliefs and practices of the important Shi'ah minority of Muslims. The story comes down to the present day, recounting the period over the last two centuries during which Muslims have been challenged by Western hegemony and have sought to establish a modern sense of self-identity. This comprehensive, wide-ranging and up-to-date treatment of one of the world's most dynamic and vital religions constitutes essential reading for all those interested in Islamic history and culture.

AN INTRODUCTION TO ISLAM

The Ka'bah in the center of the Great Mosque, Mecca

AN INTRODUCTION TO ISLAM

DAVID WAINES

Senior Lecturer in Islamic Studies,
Department of Religious Studies,
Lancaster University

CAMBRIDGE
UNIVERSITY PRESS

PUBLISHED BY THE PRESS SYNDICATE OF THE UNIVERSITY OF CAMBRIDGE
The Pitt Building, Trumpington Street, Cambridge, United Kingdom

CAMBRIDGE UNIVERSITY PRESS
The Edinburgh Building, Cambridge CB2 2RU, UK
40 West 20th Street, New York, NY 10011–4211, USA
10 Stamford Road, Oakleigh, VIC 3166, Australia
Ruiz de Alarcón 13, 28014 Madrid, Spain
Dock House, The Waterfront, Cape Town 8001, South Africa

http://www.cambridge.org

First published 1995
Reprinted 1996, 1998, 2000

Printed in the United Kingdom at the University Press, Cambridge

A catalogue record for this book is available from the British Library

Library of Congress Cataloguing in Publication data
Waines, David.
An introduction to Islam / David Waines.
p.   cm.
Includes bibliographical references.
ISBN 0 521 41880 1 (hardback) – ISBN 0 521 42929 3 (paperback)
1. Islam   1. Title.
BP161.2.W29   1995
297–dc20   94–9439   CIP

ISBN 0 521 41880 1 hardback
ISBN 0 521 42929 3 paperback

Contents

Plates

The Ka'bah in the center of the Great Mosque, Mecca (photograph by Abdelaziz Frikha) *frontispiece*

(between pages 172 and 173)
Scripture: the Word of the One

Acknowledgments

Many persons over the years have contributed to the making of this book. C. J. Adams, as both teacher and friend, has always been an unfailing source of support and encouragement. More immediately, friends and colleagues have contributed by generously offering their comments and criticisms on various chapters as the book was in preparation. P. Williams, S. Rose, A. Aslan, A. Compton, and H. Lupton all read early chapters, which encouraged me to believe that I might be on the right track. Most or all of the typescript was scrutinized by my colleagues in the Instituto de Filología, CSIC, Madrid: M. Marín, M. Fierro, and M. García-Arenal, who, with G. Gil, helped me avoid various pitfalls. I have also benefited from the expertise of I. R. Netton of Exeter University and M. K. Masud of the Islamic Research Center, Islamabad. The staff of the library of the ICMA, Madrid, dealt with my myriad requests with courtesy and good humor. A special word of thanks is owed to S. Clarke, whose meticulous comments on the whole text improved it immeasurably. A. Wright as editor and P. Marsh as copy-editor have both shown great care and attention to the book's preparation. P. Auchterlonie very ably compiled the index. J. Clayton of the Department of Religious Studies, Lancaster University, was involved at the beginning and at the end of the project. To them all, and to my students, from whom I have learned much over the years, my gratitude.

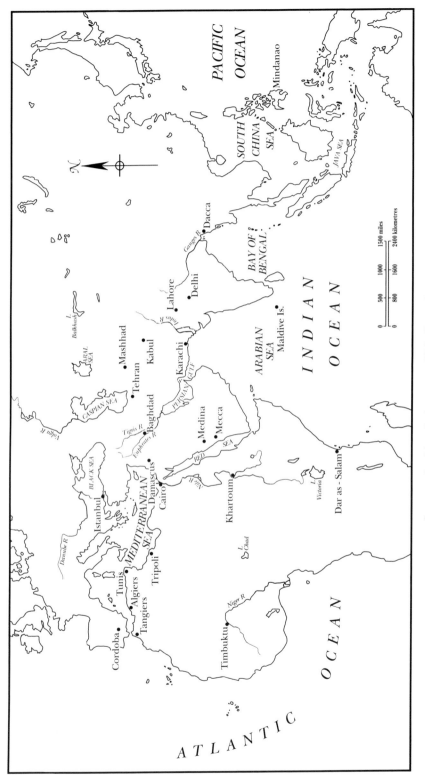

Some major historical centers of Muslim cultures

Introduction

Religion is not a thing, but a happening, and it is people who make things happen. From modest origins in Arabia in the seventh century CE, the universal community of Muslims today comprises around 850–900 million persons living in almost every country in the world. Muslims form a majority of the population in more than forty countries and are the third largest community numerically after Christianity and Buddhism. Playing with statistics can highlight some interesting features of the community's composition. In the Maldive Islands, for example, the population is 100 percent Muslim but contributes only 200,000 souls to the global total. In China Muslims are only 1.43 percent of the population but constitute more than 15 million persons. In the republics of the former Soviet Union, Muslims are 17 percent of the total, or 46 million in all. Pakistan came into being as a Muslim state in 1947 with the partition of British India into two independent countries; and, although Muslims today are only 11 percent of the population of the Indian state, they number more than 80 million people. Until Pakistan broke up in 1971, with the eastern wing forming the separate Muslim state of Bangladesh, it was the largest Muslim country in the world. That honor now belongs to Indonesia, whose 80 percent Muslim population numbers 125 million persons. In the Jewish state of Israel, some 12 percent of the population is Muslim. In the past thirty years, as yet tiny but increasingly important communities of Muslims have emerged in the nations of Western Europe and North America; while they are chiefly composed of immigrants from the major Muslim countries, there are also conversions occurring within the host communities.

Arabic, belonging to the Semitic family of languages, is the language of Muslim scripture, the Qur'an. It is spoken today by more than 150 million Arabs of the Middle East, but the written language (as distinct from the various Arabic dialects) can be understood by educated Muslims everywhere. The languages most widely spoken by Muslims, however, belong to the Indo-Aryan branch of the Indo-European family which includes Persian and Urdu. Turkish- and Turkic-speaking peoples make up another major linguistic group of Muslims. In all some three hundred ethnic and/or linguistic groups, either wholly or partly Muslim, have been identified in a recent world ethnographic survey.[1]

Considering the variety of Muslim peoples and cultures it would not seem possible to speak of the Muslim World in the singular. True, there exists an ethnic, linguistic, and geographical diversity among the peoples who call themselves Muslim. At the same time, there is a sense in which Muslims belong, as do Christians, to a world-wide community. This is called the *ummah* in Arabic, which, in the modern world, indicates a trans-national and cross-cultural loyalty shared by Muslims everywhere. When we ask upon what Muslim loyalty is focused, one answer could be the Lord of the Worlds, something with which a Christian or Jew would have little difficulty in identifying. More precisely, the answer would be that all Muslims share in the possession of a scripture which they hold to be the very words the Lord of the Worlds, Allah, revealed to his Messenger or Prophet, Muhammad, as guidance for his people and all humankind. In this sense the *ummah* is one universal community of the faithful. When, however, one looks at the manner in which various Muslim cultures within the *ummah* have related to their scripture, the Qur'an, it is not surprising to find a persistent pluralism of views and customs expressed in these many cultures throughout history. And then, one individual's understanding of scripture will produce a shade of meaning different from another's. The jurist reads the text for a purpose different from that of the mystic, although each is approaching Allah in a search to understand the divine will. It is in this sense that religion is a happening. It is the way individuals singly or, more commonly, in like-spirited association, contribute to the rich historical complex of a developing religious culture.

The present treatment of Islam is divided into two sections. The first two parts are a thematic presentation of the foundations, the fundamental teachings and practices of Muslims which were elaborated during the community's formative period of about five centuries. The

---

[1] The data given here are taken from the second edition of *Muslim Peoples: A World Ethnographic Survey*, ed. Richard Weekes (2 vols., Westport, Conn.: Greenwood Press, 1984).

connecting thread in the story throughout these chapters is the various ways in which Muslim scholars have explored revelation and the experience of their Prophet, Muhammad. The word *islam* means "the willing and active recognition of and submission to the Command of the One, Allah." People who practice that are *muslims*. They, the scholars and the ordinary faithful, are the ones who have made the community happen. Since only the scholars' works have survived to the present, however, it is their contribution which naturally receives our attention. Folk beliefs and practices which have been rationalized as Islamic do not form part of the story, important as they may be for understanding popular Islamic piety. The third part deals with the community's progress through the long transition it has experienced over the past two centuries to the present. The story is incomplete because the transition appears to be still underway.

In another sense, the story is incomplete throughout, for the material employed is inevitably selective. Notes have been kept to a minimum and used chiefly to indicate the sources of quotations in the text from classic works by Muslim authors in English translation; occasional secondary sources, books and articles, which have helped in developing the story are also mentioned. Two principles have guided selection of the books for further reading: only works written originally in English, or English translations from other languages, are cited, and only, with the exception of a few reprints, if they were published in 1970 or later. The attentive reader will discover that I have not always followed my own guidelines, but owing to the dramatic increase in studies on Islam in recent years, some constraints were necessary.

Part of the recent interest, especially among Western scholars, has centered upon problems surrounding the origins and early formation of Islam. For this reason, the reader is directed to the excursus on works by Western scholars dealing with Islamic origins. As this is an introduction to Islam, it seemed more appropriate to present the Qur'an and the Prophet Muhammad as Muslims might recognize them, rather than as others have described them. The Glossary, which can be consulted for quick reference, contains most of the technical terms mentioned in the text. For simplicity's sake, all diacritics have been omitted with the exception of the *ain* (') and the *hamza* ('), and even these have been omitted from commonly known dynasties (e.g. Abbasid) and place names (e.g. Iraq); to the purists I offer apologies in advance.

Finally, there are two major encyclopaedias which are indispensable. One, authoritative but somewhat less technical, is *The Encyclopedia of Religion*, ed. Mircea Eliade (16 vols., London: Collier Macmillan, 1987); the other, which is still in progress, is the specialized *Encyclopaedia of Islam*, new ed. (Leiden: E. J. Brill, 1960–). *Index Islamicus* is the essential multi-volumed bibliographical source for articles and books dealing with the Muslim world: articles appearing between 1906 and 1955 were compiled by J. D. Pearson (Cambridge: W. Heffer, 1961); books and articles appearing between 1981 and 1985 were compiled by G. Roper in two volumes (London: Mansell, 1991). There are volumes covering the intervening years.

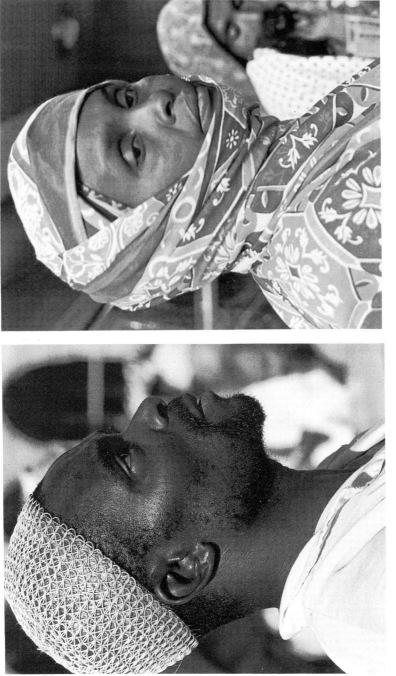

1. Africa

2. Africa

3. Central Asia

4. Saudi Arabia

5. Ferghana Valley, Turkestan

6. Uygur girl embroiders a traditional cap

7. Chinese Muslims in Quanzhou greet travelers retracing the trade routes which brought Islam

PART I

Foundations

CHAPTER I

"There is no god but Allah . . ."

TIME, ETERNITY AND THE GODS

The religious and moral values of the ancient Arabs are mirrored, however partially, in the verses of their poets. Among them was Zuhayr b. Abi Salma, who flourished in the last days of paganism before the emergence of Islam in central Arabia in the seventh century. Toward the end of a long and often turbulent life he recorded these cautionary words in a famous ode:

> Do not conceal from
> Allah whatever is in
> your breasts hoping it
> may be hidden. Allah
> knows whatever is
> concealed.[1]

Zuhayr was reflecting upon the attempts of conciliators to terminate an eruption of inter-tribal bloodshed. Traditional accounts portray these conflicts, the so-called *Days of the Arabs*, as a common feature of Arabian society of the period. His warning to each side in the conflict was to enter an agreement in good faith, for the inevitable consequence of deception would be punishment of the betrayer.

The poet's reference to Allah (*al-ilah* = the God) contradicted neither his pagan values nor the poem's pessimistic pagan ethos. Elsewhere he remarks,

> It is evident that men perish,
> they and their property, but I do not
> see *Time* perish. I see nothing that
> remains and is eternal against events
> except the rooted mountains and the
> sky and the countries, and our Lord,
> and the days that are counted and the
> nights.[2]

7

Time or *dahr* was the pre-Islamic poets' frequent term for the impersonal agent of a preordained destiny, fate or death against which there was no shield or bargaining. Human life and artifacts were acknowledged as inconstant, destroyed by time at their appointed moment. Yet certain natural phenomena resisted its destructive force. In the poet's contemplation of this contrast, he verges upon the abstract notion of eternity: for the mountains, sky and God as well did resist time. Each was eternal. It was a tentative step toward embracing the idea of a single, unique eternal entity.

On the eve of the rise of Islam, the god Allah found a place within the pagan Arabs' world view. It was the god in whose name Zuhayr's younger contemporary, the Prophet Muhammad would first address his kinfolk in Mecca and later his followers in Medina, where the embryonic Muslim community was nourished. The poet's perception of Allah, however, was not the Prophet's. The two were alike in name but not in substance; it was the Prophet's message which would displace the pagan conception of Allah, providing a dramatic departure from the cultural-religious norms of his day and marking a new era in the configuration of the religious map of the Middle East.

In pagan eyes, Allah was the "High God"; neither the sole object of worship nor indeed the sole existent god, he merely stood above, or apart from, all other tribal divinities. Nevertheless, he played a particular role in pagan life. First, as the giver of rain, he ensured the sustenance of life for the inhabitants of this arid desert and steppe region of the earth. Then, as the guarantor of oaths, he was regarded as crucial to the binding nature of agreements, tribal or individual, sworn in his name; violation of such an oath was deemed a grave offense, as it involved serious consequences for social peace and order. In a somewhat vague way, too, Allah was viewed as the creator of the heavens and the earth, although in general no moral conclusions seem to have been drawn from this regarding an individual's behavior and future well-being. On this point, Zuhayr perhaps represented a transitional viewpoint, as he warned in his ode of divine punishment for violation of the treaty agreements. The more widespread attitude toward Allah may be judged from another of his attributes, namely as the god to whom one turns in the event of immanent danger, such as a storm at sea. Once rescued from danger, the pagan responded not by acknowledging gratefully Allah's mercy and power, but rather by reverting to worship of the familiar graven images of the tribal cult.

Thus in matters of daily concern, Allah occupied a particular place, but alongside other gods in the Arabs' pantheon.

Tradition records that the city of Mecca, birthplace of the Prophet Muhammad, was an important center of pagan worship in the peninsula. Allah was lord of the central shrine, a cube-like structure called the Ka'bah; he was said to have three daughters, called al-Lat and al-Uzzah, both astral deities, and al-Manat, a goddess of fate. In or around the Ka'bah the representations of more than three hundred gods were housed. One of these, said to be the greatest of them all, was called Hubal, a bulk of red agate in the form of a man whose right hand had been severed and replaced by one of gold. In Mecca, as within sacred enclaves elsewhere in the peninsula, tribal quarrels and the spilling of blood were forbidden during four months of the year, and gatherings of clans from near and far seasonally transformed the city into a kind of divine supermarket. Sacrificial offerings to the gods and accompanying festivities were also good business for those charged with the maintenance of the shrine and providing the services to meet visitors' needs. The guardians of the shrine were drawn from Muhammad's own tribe of Quraysh. Other shrines existed elsewhere but none seemed to match Mecca's reputation. In addition, portable gods were borne by nomads on their migrations while trees, rocks, springs or other natural features were locales in which lesser spirits were believed to reside. The veneration of ancestors had, in some cases, led to their elevation to deities.

The gods were consulted on various matters of domestic and other concerns: setting the date for marriage, confirming the parentage of a child, and the settlement of a quarrel all fell within the purview of the gods' advice, as did seeking the most propitious moment to embark upon a journey. Their help was also sought for rain or for assistance in battle against a rival tribe. Divining arrows were shuffled and "read" for the answers to requests. Yet as much as advice was sought, it was not always accepted with good grace or gratitude. One petitioner sought a god's approval for avenging his father's murder. He received the negative arrow, and responded in a poem condemning the god's decision as hypocritical. Another petitioner offered a sacrifice to an idol, a red human-shaped rock jutting out from a black mountainside, hoping that punishment would befall a tribesman who had violated the idol's sanctity. When nothing happened, the petitioner renounced all idols and embraced Christianity. When he heard Muhammad preach his message, he converted to Islam. The evidence, such as we have it, suggests that the relation of man to his gods was less one of pious fear and awe than a deference born of time-worn habit and custom; a habit, perhaps, that was wearing out. Soothsayers were also consulted and other omens, such as the particular flight of a raven, were taken as guides to daily decisions.[3]

The afterlife held neither special terror nor concern for the Arab. His or her understanding of eternity (*khulud*) was simply the span between birth and death, one's own experience of life. Death brought man to the grave, a pit of permanent settlement, not in the sense of an eternal lodging, but in the negative sense of a place from which wandering at will as one had done in life was no longer possible. This prospect did not, however, inevitably breed a crippling pessimism. The harshness of existence, its vicissitudes, were countered in part by a defiant individualism displayed in a hedonistic attitude to life and in part by a confidence in the survival of the tribe and its way of life through the seed of one's loins. In this homocentric world view, the pagan Arab bowed first to the force of oral tribal tradition (*sunnah*) rather than to the power of the gods. The moral universe of the *sunnah* centered upon the notion of *muruwwah*, variously rendered as "virtue" and "manliness," expressions of which were captured in acts of bravery, generosity, loyalty, vengeance, and the like. Correct conduct was measured by conforming to the ways of the ancestors, and the upholding of tribal honor. Aberration from the code could be punished by ostracism; and without a tribe one had no name and was a virtual non-being. Justice was thus neither guaranteed nor administered by God or the gods, but rather by the tribal chief and elders and the ever-present threat of retaliation against injury.

". . . AND MUHAMMAD IS THE MESSENGER OF ALLAH"

Into this world Muhammad was born. In the case of each of the great revelatory religions, the central figure of the tradition, for example Moses, Jesus, or Muhammad, has left no personal account of his reflections, intentions, and activities. There exists no spiritual diary to reveal what each was really about. Instead, what the modern reader has received in the case of each religion is a rich tapestry of tradition, itself the product of many generations of embroidering, crafted with pious and meticulous care, laying bare God's design for humankind. It is for the modern observer, then, to appreciate the finished fabric in his or her own way.

There are two major sources for our knowledge and understanding of Muhammad's life and mission. To Muslims they are of different nature and value. The first is scripture, the Qur'an, the collection of revelations from Allah to Muhammad delivered to him through the agency of the angel Gabriel. The second is a vast body of material extant in the form of sayings and anecdotes which comprise the later community's collective memory of the Prophet and his companions. Scripture is strictly regarded as the living word of Allah, and the Prophet the medium by which the word was communicated. Muhammad, however, was not only the bearer of Allah's message, but also its first interpreter, in the conduct of his daily affairs among his followers. Tradition in this sense, therefore, represented the community's subsequent efforts to capture and record, to comprehend and transmit the full significance of this prophetic-revelatory event. By its very nature, scripture could not provide raw biographical data of the Prophet's life, whereas Tradition, as one might expect, provides a proliferation of data, albeit at times confusing and conflicting in detail. Nevertheless, both the message and the messenger are the foundation stones over which the edifice of Islamic culture was eventually erected, each necessarily supporting the other by way of illumination and elucidation. This is perhaps nowhere more evident than in the earliest biography of the Prophet to have come down to us, the work of Muhammad ibn Ishaq (d. 151/770), which has survived in the recension of his editor Abd al-Malik ibn Hisham (d. 213/828 or 218/833). It fuses together elements of both scripture and Tradition and forms the convenient basis of the following compressed account. No more than the main events of the Prophet's life will be known with certainty. The biography, however, does contain two marked transformations: first, Muhammad's encounter with God, and second, the formation under his leadership of the nascent community of believers. Both gave Muhammad's followers of subsequent generations the dramatic plot with which to illustrate their beliefs and the model upon which to found their thought. In the simplest terms, the significance of his life in the Islamic tradition cannot be underestimated.

Tradition places the date of Muhammad's birth in Mecca around 570 CE. Orphaned at an early age, he was raised first in the family of his grandfather and then by an uncle, Abu Talib. As a young man he became manager of the trading enterprise of a widow, Khadijah, whom he subsequently married. Among the surviving children of the union, their daughter Fatimah became the best known and revered,

as the wife of Muhammad's cousin 'Ali, Abu Talib's son, and the
fourth successor to leadership of the community after the Prophet's
death.

Approaching his fortieth year, Muhammad, who had taken to
performing lengthy retreats to a nearby mountain, experienced the
call to mission. According to Ibn Ishaq, it came in the form of a vision
while Muhammad slept in his retreat. The angel Gabriel appeared to
him from Allah and ordered him to "Read!," a command which had
to be repeated twice. Muhammad experienced a sensation of
suffocation, as though he were close to death, and then he responded,
repeating the following words:

> *Read in the name of your Lord who created,*
> *Who created man of a clot of blood.*
> *Read! Your Lord is the most beneficent,*
> *Who taught by the pen,*
> *Taught Man what he knew not.*   (96:1–5)

The angel vanished, and Muhammad awoke feeling as though the
words had been engraved upon his heart.[4] They were the first of the
revelations which, over the next two decades, guided his life as the
Messenger (*al-rasul*) and Prophet (*al-nabi*) of Allah.

Despite his own premonitions that a religious experience might
befall him, Muhammad's initial reaction to this visitation was fear
that he was possessed of some spirit, or merely "inspired" in the
manner of the poets. Comforted by Khadijah and supported by 'Ali,
Muhammad overcame his distress and accepted the "troublesome
burden," as Ibn Ishaq called the mantle of prophecy, adding that
Muhammad felt himself both irresistibly compelled and yet as surely
guided by a powerful force wholly outside himself.

Muhammad identified this force as Allah, who addressed him
through the agency of the angel Gabriel. But it was not the same
Allah, the "High God" of Zuhayr the poet. As further revelations
came to him, Muhammad slowly disclosed to his kinsmen a portrait of
a god unlike the deities of a pagan Arab's experience, although he
would probably have recognized that Jews or Christians of his
acquaintance spoke of their own God in similar terms.

At the same time there are traces of incipient discontent within
pagan Arab religious culture. Muslim tradition cites a number of
individuals called *hanif*s who, some time before Muhammad commenced his mission, had begun to seek a religious alternative to the

prevailing practice of idol worship. The problem with the idols was that they were of no account. Ibn Ishaq describes the *hanifs'* dismissal of the idols as objects which could neither "hear, nor see, nor hurt, nor help." The term *hanif* also occurs several times in the Qur'an, although no instance yields a firm contextual definition of the word. The presence of these individuals, however few in number they may have been, likely indicates an emerging search for a more secure religious anchor point which was not *naturally* provided by the earlier monotheistic models. There were Jewish communities in the peninsula to the north of Mecca and Christians to the south, although they were probably little more than tiny islands of insecure converts in the wider sea of paganism. When they were faced with a growing awareness of the effete character of their own gods, therefore, the impulse may simply have been to elevate the High God of a waning pagan Arab tradition into the Supreme Unique Being of the new.

On the other hand, metaphors drawn from the common Arabian scriptural pool may be found in other contexts in which the word *hanif* occurs. It is, significantly, associated with the prophet *Ibrahim* (Abraham). Of all the messengers mentioned in scripture whom Allah commissioned at various moments throughout history, Muhammad seems to have resembled the ancient patriarch most in his career (2:124ff., 135ff.; 10:105). Both suffered trials and opposition because of their profound conviction in the existence of one, omnipotent God, a belief which resulted finally in their bringing down the helpless idols worshiped by their peoples. Muhammad's mission was, in this sense then, to restore the *Hanifite* faith of the patriarch who, in effect, is seen as the first *muslim*, meaning one who commits the act of submission (*islam*) to the One God to the exclusion of all other deities. When, in the Qur'an, Ibrahim's Lord demanded this of him, he replied *I have surrendered myself* (aslamtu) *to the Lord of all the worlds* (2:131). And Muhammad elsewhere makes the identification explicit: *my Lord has guided me onto a straight way through an ever-true faith, the way of Ibrahim, the* hanif, *who was not of those who ascribe divinity to aught beside Him* (6:161).

The parallel between the prophets Muhammad and Ibrahim, as reflected in the Qur'an, was the seed which nourished the view that the historical community of Islam represented both a concordance with and departure from the previously established monotheistic faiths of Judaism and Christianity. Each has a scripture of its own revealed from the same divine source as that which now addressed the

Prophet Muhammad. For this, Jews and Christians are called Peoples of the Book. Moreover, the prophets of the Torah and the Jesus of the Gospels are celebrated in Islamic tradition as belonging to the same chain of divine activity which manifests a guiding role over the course of history. Muhammad in Islamic tradition is viewed as the final prophet in the chain, linking him thereby with Ibrahim. At the same time, however, Ibrahim was *neither a Christian nor a Jew* (3:67) in the Qur'anic phrase, but simply a *hanif* and one who had surrendered himself (*muslim*) to Allah. He had, by the act of destroying the idols, acknowledged the One Supreme God. Muhammad's mission, therefore, was to restore that pristine *islam* which had subsequently become distorted or neglected by other peoples to whom the message had been brought. This is the import of the Qur'anic command, conveyed through Muhammad, to *set your face steadfastly towards the [true] faith, as a* hanif, *and be not among those who ascribe divinity to others beside Allah* (10:105).

Ibn Ishaq relates that Muhammad did not immediately proclaim his message in public. Rather, he disclosed it at first only to a group of committed followers. The reactions of his Meccan audience to being ordered by Allah to publish his message and to turn away from the polytheists (15:94) are evident from hints provided in scripture.

Muhammad spoke in the name of Allah, to the Meccans a deity at once familiar and yet now somehow different. Allah swore oaths in the name of common daily objects and phenomena of nature: *By the dawn!* (89:1), *By the heaven and the morning star!* (86:1), *By the figs and olives!* (95:1) in just the same manner as Meccans would have concluded deals and obligations, solemnly swearing in the name of their High God, "By Allah!" He was the creator of the heavens and earth and all therein; as the giver of rain he was the sustainer of life and he rescued from danger those who prayed to him for deliverance of their imperiled lives (29:61–65; 31:25ff.). All this was commonplace and reassuring.

Allah, who guided his Prophet, claimed more: first as having an intimate relationship with each individual as his or her creator from a mere clot of blood, then as his or her guide through life and finally as the one who reclaimed that life and judged it. This was a claim to power and sovereignty from a god who could not be "seen" and "spoken to" as an idol, but was only visible and present through his "signs" (*ayat*) in nature, and in humankind itself. More disturbing to the Meccans' perception, because of its implications, was the claim of this god to raise up the dead at some moment of cosmic cataclysm and usher them before the throne of judgment. At this moment the individual's life would be weighed for its moral value and then rendered either an eternal reward or punishment.

First, the notion of raising the dead appeared absurd. The Meccans scoffed, *That [which is ahead of us] is but our first [and only] death, and we shall not be raised to life again. So then, bring forth our forefathers [as witnesses], if what you claim is true!* (44:35–36). Next, the idea of a judging god seemed to lift the execution of justice out of the hands of the tribal elders and make the norms of the *sunnah* irrelevant. Indeed, the very idea of the tribe as the individual's protector and repository of honor was challenged: *Say: Who is there who will protect you from Allah, if He intends evil against you, or intends mercy towards you? They will not find for themselves apart from Allah, either patron* (wali) *or helper* (33:17; also 29:22). Then the prospect of an eternal afterlife over which this god was also sovereign was too much to contemplate. The Meccans could be heard exclaiming, *There is only our life in this world; we die and we live and nothing destroys us but Time* (dahr). To which Allah rejoined, *They have no sure knowledge of this, but only mere conjecture . . . Say: Allah creates life in you, then causes you to die and gathers you at the day of resurrection* (45:24–25). Their pagan omens were rejected as useless. In the Qur'anic parable the earlier prophet Salih had warned his people of Thamud in northern Arabia that all their auguries, that is, their destinies, were in the hands of Allah (27:47). Meccans acknowledged that whereas only fate dealt blows of ill fortune, they had confidently assumed that their wealth and good fortune were of their own making and thus that pride of achievement, even if excessive, was justified. Now, however, Allah demanded they recognize that everything, good and ill fortune, came from him. Little wonder that the Meccans' first response to Muhammad was to dismiss him as a mere "poet" for whom the affliction of fate also lurked (52:30).

MECCAN OPPOSITION

Meccan incredulity and mockery, however, turned slowly to anger. Their kinsman's god, Allah, was not just vying for precedence over their other gods, a proposition that might have been negotiated. He was claiming absolute uniqueness. The command to Muhammad was stark in its simplicity: *Say: Allah is One. Eternal. He neither begets nor is begotten* (112:1–3). This was not negotiable.

Finally, a deputation went to Muhammad's uncle, Abu Talib, to lay their complaints before him. In Ibn Ishaq's words their message was, "O Abu Talib, your nephew has cursed our gods, insulted our religion, mocked our way of life and accused our forefathers of error; either you must stop him, or let us get at him."[5] Here the memory of tradition recalls that Muhammad's mission posed a threat not only to Meccan religious values but also to its tribal norms embodied in the *sunnah*. Possibly worship of the idols had undergone a gradual process of decline, or had merely become a matter of customary routine lacking in religious vitality. In this case, the truth hurt Meccan sensibilities. *Say: Have you considered what you call upon apart from Allah? Show me any part of the earth that they have created; or have they a share in the heavens?* (46:4). And again, theirs are *gods who have created nothing but are themselves created!* (25:3). Therefore, economic motives may be suspected to lie behind the city elders' complaints against Muhammad: the shrine of the Ka'bah with only one god, they would reason, could not possibly have the same attraction for potential pagan pilgrims as the present edifice housing hundreds of idols.

The Meccans' further, and possibly primary, concern was that Muhammad's message appeared to question the honor of their ancestors and thus their total way of life, in sum, the tribal *sunnah*. They charged him with dividing the people against themselves and, in the manner of a sorcerer, of separating "a man from his father, or from his brother, or from his wife, or from his family."[6] It was asking too much to abandon the ways of the ancestors without replacing them with something as secure and familiar (5:104; 7:28; 31:21). Moreover, the summons to acknowledge one god, Allah, together with a call for a moral transformation of society some took as an insult, including the privileged segments of Meccan society. The summons contrasted the gods who have *created nothing but are themselves created, who neither harm, nor benefit, who have power neither over life, nor death nor over the resurrection* (25:3) with the all-embracing sovereignty of Allah. Moral reform covered the just treatment of the disadvantaged, of orphans, mendicants, the poor and hungry, debtors, widows, wayfarers and slaves; in short, it required a sense of social responsibility (90:13–16; 24:33). In a deeper and more important way it also meant locating oneself as an individual in a proper relationship with Allah. Rather than being rebellious by professing a sense of one's *self-sufficiency* or self-importance owing, for example, to a status gained by wealth, one should acknowledge that all possessions are Allah's bounty, for which gratitude, not arrogance, must be expressed (96:6–8).

Meccan opposition to Muhammad increased in proportion to the growing clarity of the message he expounded, and from fear of its impact upon their lives. Allah was the One, All-Powerful but Compassionate and Merciful deity. Evidence of Allah's nature were the innumerable "signs" of his power and beneficence: the creation of the heavens and the earth; the generation of man; animals, vegetation, crops and fruit and their various uses; the alternation of night and day, the sun, moon, and stars, the revival of parched land, the mountains and the sea and so on. One of Allah's "signs" was the resurrection (30:40), which went together with judgment, followed by reward and punishment. Judgment meant that actions in this world bore significance and consequences for the life to come; actions were no longer relevant only to the immediate tribal context, such as the consequences of murder or robbery governed by the moral system of vendetta. The conclusion was simple to draw: the threat to the Meccans' way of life was the replacement of the *sunnah* of their forefathers with the *sunnah* of Allah (48:23).

Inducements of wealth, power, and prestige failed to deflect Muhammad from his purpose, according to Ibn Ishaq. Demands for miracles to prove the veracity of his message met only with the simple response, *Exalted be my Lord, I am but a mortal, a messenger (of God)* (17:93). Indeed, the impasse seemed inevitable. Scripture records the examples of previous messengers sent to their peoples to warn them to serve only One God. Such was Hud, who brought the message to his people 'Ad. They disbelieved and were finally destroyed by a wind which blew for seven nights and days and wiped out everything except their buildings (46:24). Even when a miracle was produced, as in the case of Salih, the result was still stubborn disbelief of his people, called the Thamud, who were destroyed by an earthquake or a thunderbolt which left them prostrated in their dwellings (11:61–68). And drawn from the common scriptural pool are the parables of Noah and Lot, whose peoples were also punished by God for their disbelief. Muhammad's confrontation with his people in Mecca, therefore, was simply confirmation of the experiences of earlier messengers. The lesson was there for the learning, but, as Ibn Ishaq reports, the Meccans' hostility intensified to the point that Muhammad's own clan of Hashim became the target of a prolonged boycott by other sections of the Quraysh, while his followers from all clans were pressured to recant. Two of his major supporters then died, his wife Khadijah and his protective uncle, Abu Talib. Amidst ever-mounting difficulties the time was fast approaching to consider alternatives to remaining in Mecca. This was chiefly for the sake of his own small band of followers, but he perhaps also departed with a sense of foreboding for the fate of his kinsmen, who he feared might also taste the wrath of his god.

THE COMMUNITY OF MEDINA

Several days' journey to the north of Mecca, along the route to Syria, lay the oasis settlement of Yathrib. In Islamic tradition it was renamed Medina, short for the expression "City of the Prophet." Muhammad had been invited there by some of its inhabitants to act as arbitrator or judge in a bitter feud between rival factions. The year was 622 CE when Muhammad and his followers left Mecca for Yathrib in small groups over several weeks. This migration (*hijrah*) marked more than a change of fortune for Muhammad. The event is celebrated in the tradition as the commencement of the Islamic era, the year of the founding of the Muslim community (*ummah*) in Medina, which was to become the vehicle for realizing the will of Allah on earth.

Muhammad's Meccan followers who emigrated with him to Medina were known as *Muhajirun*; those who invited him were called *Ansar* or "helpers." These latter, from among the pagan Arab tribes of Aws and Khazraj, had abandoned their former ways and accepted Muhammad's message. For the rest, Muhammad's task was both to arbitrate disputes and bring some semblance of stability to the town. This meant dealing with the remaining pagan elements of the Aws and Khazraj and their townsmen, confederates among the clans of Jews or Judaized Arabs. In a series of pacts, but recorded by Ibn Ishaq as a single document, a number of reciprocal obligations were agreed between the Prophet Muhammad, his followers and the Jews "in the name of Allah, the Compassionate, the Merciful." They were to form one community (*ummah*) to the exclusion of all others, presumably ruling out the pagan elements who were nonetheless free to join if they accepted the Prophet's message. The Jewish elements were to retain their own faith and property and to enjoy the same peace as all believers in God and the Last Day. Yathrib (as it was then still called) was declared a sacred enclave (*haram*), and a couple of formulae, repeated in several of the pacts, were invoked as a central theme underlying them all: "Observation of one's undertakings eliminates treachery" and "Allah is (surety) for what is most avoided of covenant breaking and what is most honoured in the observance of what is contained in this sheet."[7] These pacts were heavily laden with the tribal values of Muhammad's day. Their novelty was the circumstances in which they were being employed, namely an attempt to forge a community which cut across tribal blood lines but submitted to the final arbitration of Allah and his Prophet (*nabi*), Muhammad; for in the terms of one of the agreements, "If any dispute or controversy likely to cause trouble should arise, it must be referred to Allah and to Muhammad, the apostle (*rasul*) of Allah. Allah accepts what is nearest to piety and goodness in this document."[8]

Although circumstances confronting Muhammad in Medina were new, he nevertheless continued to preach the essence of the Meccan message he had been ordered by Allah to bring to all: God's essential unity, his power and guidance over the *heavens and earth and all that is between them from* creation to the final judgment is reiterated throughout the Medinan period together with continued emphasis on social and economic justice (2:177). Moreover, Muhammad repeated his concern for Medinans who only grudgingly accepted his leadership and even rejected his message. Reassurance on this score arrived in the form of a revelation (6:33–35) that it was not he, Muhammad, whom they repudiated, but Allah, in whose hands their fate ultimately lay.

Ibn Ishaq, however, draws attention to an important consequence of the new situation. Muhammad in Mecca had acted as a missionary to his pagan kinsmen, having been ordered only "to call men to Allah and to endure insult and forgive the ignorant." The Medinan situation demanded other measures to keep the nascent Muslim community intact, secure from external threat or sabotage from within, and the Prophet was now commanded to "fight and protect himself against those who wronged them and treated them badly."[9] This was first reflected in scripture, adds Ibn Ishaq, where *Permission is given to those who fight because they have been wronged . . . those who have been driven from their homes without right only because they said "Allah is our Lord"* (22:40–41). This applied specifically to the Quraysh of Mecca, whose sustained and often openly bitter opposition had finally forced Muhammad and his followers from their own city. Scripture elsewhere compares their plight to that of Moses and his people under the tyranny of the Egyptian Pharaoh (28:4–5).

At this juncture, however, there was emerging an aspect of a more general world view where the believer, supported by Allah, stood against the ungrateful disbeliever (*kafir*) and the hypocrite (*munafiq*) who only feigned adherence to the truth. *Allah is the Protector of the believers; He brings them out of the darkness into the light. And the unbelievers – their protectors are the idols, that bring them forth from the light into the darkness deep; those are the inhabitants of the Fire, therein dwelling forever* (2:257). Compared with the power of Allah, the One Omnipotent God, the idols seemed to offer little real protection for a society which was, so to speak, God-less. Yet believers were exhorted as well to struggle against the forces of unbelief and those who responded bartered *the life of this world for the life to come; for to him who fights in the way of Allah whether he is slain, or is victorious, We shall in time grant a mighty reward* (4:74). The struggle did not have a religious sense alone, for it included fighting with a sense of social justice on behalf of the feeble and the weak (4:75). Moreover, the one who fights with his possessions and his life is better than the one who remains at home (4:95).

At the very moment of establishing the community in Medina (as distinct from leading a movement in Mecca), Muhammad became responsible for defending it from external assault and internal dissension or subversion. If necessary, Muhammad would take the struggle into the Meccan heart of paganism itself. The intermittent raids, skirmishes, and occasional battle over the next few years between Muhammad's supporters among the *Muhajirun* and the *Ansar*, and the Meccans in league with their Medinan allies, were the formative experiences of the nascent Muslim community. The virtue of the enterprise, molded by historical encounter and divine command, was, however, confirmed in the end by its triumph.

Ibn Ishaq recounts the signing of an armistice in the sixth year of the *hijrah* (628 CE) ending hostilities between the Quraysh of Mecca and the Prophet's community. The event is known as the Day of Hudaybiyah. It was a face-saving device for all concerned. The Meccans were wearied of their prolonged struggle against Muhammad. As a diplomatic gesture he did not insist on using his title Messenger of Allah in the document and agreed to delay performing the pilgrimage to Mecca until the following year, in order that it could not be said that Muslims had humiliated the Meccans by a forced entry into the city. In yielding, however, the Prophet had in effect secured the capitulation of his staunchest enemies and in the eighth year of the *hijrah* (630 CE), the Muslim occupation of Mecca was complete. Ibn

Ishaq describes the end of pagan Mecca, marked by the destruction of the idols of the Ka'bah, on which occasion Muhammad recited the Qur'anic verse *The truth has come and falsehood has passed away* (17:82).

Two years later, during the pilgrimage season of the year 10/632, Muhammad made a final public address to his community. It concluded with these words: "Know that every Muslim is a brother to every other Muslim and that you are all now one brotherhood; it is not lawful for any one of you to take anything belonging to his brother unless it is willingly given to you. So do not wrong yourselves!"[10] A few weeks later, following a brief illness, the Prophet died in Medina. His tomb in the city he had made his own is visited by pilgrims to this day.

THE PROPHET IN TRADITION

These highlights of the Prophet's life, drawn from the wealth of detail provided by Ibn Ishaq, are, in effect, scripture seen through the eyes of the evolving tradition of the community. Scriptural allusions were given a time and place in the fleshed-out version of the Prophet's story, and slowly Muhammad's portrait began to reflect the veneration of the early Muslim generations for their Prophet. On the evidence of the Qur'an, Muhammad's opponents had vilified him as a sorcerer, a madman, an impostor, and had mocked his failure to produce a miracle confirming his role such as previous messengers. For all that, Muhammad was a mere mortal, and his own self-image was that of a humble warner and bearer of Allah's message: *I do not say to you "I have the treasures of Allah with me," nor do I say "I know things beyond human perception," nor do I say, "I am an angel." I follow only that which is revealed to me* (6:50; and also 11:31). Or again, *it is not within my power to bring benefit to, or avert harm from, myself, except as Allah may please. And if I knew that which is beyond the reach of human perception, abundant good fortune would surely have fallen to my lot, and no evil would ever have touched me. I am nothing but a warner, and a herald of glad tidings to a people who will believe* (7:188). Yet, as Allah and his angels blessed the Prophet, so believers were summoned to bless him and follow his guidance (33:56). This did not, however, entail worshiping him. The community, in its grief and shock, had to be reminded of this at the moment of his passing. When it was suggested that he was, in fact, still alive and would return, a leading companion, Abu Bakr, was moved to admonish, "If anyone worships Muhammad, Muhammad is dead; if anyone worships Allah, He is alive, immortal."[11] To which he added the following verse: *Muhammad is but a messenger; other messengers have passed away before him. If he then dies or is killed would you turn about on your heels?* (3:143).

On the other hand, this did not deny valid expressions of veneration, and these increased by degrees in the generations following his death, becoming part of the community's living memory of him. Ibn Ishaq records, for example, that even before his summons to prophetic office Muhammad had sensed certain indications of its immanence, when the stones and trees addressed him as a prophet during his lonely vigils on Mount Hirah. Indeed, Muhammad's future role is said to have been foretold by numerous signs, including his mother, Aminah, hearing a voice which announced she was carrying the lord of his people. The opening lines of *surah* 94, *Have We not opened up your heart and lifted from you the burden that had weighed so heavily upon your back?*, are explained as an allusion to the incident of an assault upon the child by two white-cloaked men, or angels, who ripped open his belly and cleansed his heart with snow as a ritual of symbolic purification preparing the young Muhammad for his call.[12] Further, tradition relates the foreknowledge possessed by Jewish rabbis and Christian monks from their scriptures that a prophet was to come from among the Meccans. Even pagan soothsayers, who had been visited by spirits with reports of the news, and who thus had advance notice of the coming event, found their hints unheeded by the people until the time arrived.

One of the most poignant examples of tradition acting as the handmaiden of scripture is the interpretation of the verse *Glory be to Him Who transported His servant by night from the sacred mosque to the furthest mosque, whose precincts We blessed, that We might show him some of Our signs* (17:1). This is taken to refer to the Prophet's night journey (*al-isra'*) in the company of the angel Gabriel, from the Ka'bah in Mecca to the temple in Jerusalem where he led in prayer a gathering of a number of the earlier, long deceased, prophets of God. From there Muhammad ascended into the heavens and the presence of the Lord, where the five daily prayers of the faith (which continue today) were explicitly instituted. The true nature of this experience prompted differing opinions among the Prophet's own companions and later generations of Muslim thinkers; was it a *bodily* journey or a *spiritual* one, and if the latter, was it experienced as in a dream or was it the Prophet's *soul* or *spirit* which had been transported, in the manner of the journey after death? Ibn Ishaq, who himself had no doubt that the experience was genuine, reports that realist-minded, skeptical Meccans dismissed the claim as absurd because everyone knew that the caravan journey from Mecca to Jerusalem took two months there and back! Even some of Muhammad's supporters lost faith, if only for a time, upon hearing this story.[13] While many accept the story simply as a miraculous event, the enduring importance in the tradition of the night journey and the ascension (*al-mi'raj*) is its evidence of the spiritual perfection of Muhammad as a true prophet of God.

The portrait of the Prophet Muhammad is multi-faceted, the parts greater than the whole, but in sum it has provided Muslims an exemplary model to revere, venerate, and attempt to emulate in their own lives, both in its more mundane, socio-political, and in its spiritual dimensions. Tradition, therefore, not only saw the Prophet's biography mirrored in scripture, but recorded every feature of his life which could be recovered from the collective memory of the community. As we shall have occasion to consider later, these efforts preserved the Prophet's *sunnah*, that is his practices and procedures in word and deed, which became, together with scripture, the main sources of the religious law of Islam.

The very process of elaborating the Prophet's life from its scriptural foundation of course points to the primary role of scripture itself in the Islamic faith. The revelations which Muhammad continued to receive over some twenty years were of such importance that they were, according to the traditional account, collected soon after the Prophet's death and set down in the form in which we have the Qur'an today.

THE WORD OF ALLAH

The Qur'an is not easy to read and comprehend, either in the original Arabic or in translation. This is due in part to its apparently arbitrary structure and organization. There is no chronological order of material, and its 114 chapters or *surahs* are arranged chiefly by length, the longest appearing at the beginning of the book. Nor is there any explicit thematic order to the material; instead there is frequent repetition throughout of a number of leitmotifs. It is not essentially a narrative text in the sense that the scriptures of the Hebrew Bible and the Gospels are largely collections of stories; rather, the Qur'an may more accurately be described as aphoristic, being a collection of pithy statements expressing the wisdom and will of Allah.

Scripture understood in its original sense means "something written" (Latin, *scriptus*). When the term is applied to the Qur'an, an important point is missed about its nature, namely its predominantly oral character. The very word *qur'an* itself means "recitation," and what Muslims regard as the enduring miracle of its beauty stems, in part, from the experience of listening to the word of God recited by the human voice. Tradition records the Prophet's saying to his community that they should "Beautify the Qur'an with your voices, for the beautiful voice increases the beauty of the Qur'an."[14] Recitation of the holy text is an art form like the calligraphic designs in mosques derived from it. Recitation of the Qur'an during prayer, according to another saying of the Prophet, is even "more excellent than fasting which itself is a protection against hell."[15]

Scripture lives orally in the Muslim's daily routine to the present day. Parts are included in the daily prayers. It is recited at night in the mosques during the ritual fasting of Ramadan, one section of the book for each of the thirty days of the month. Every festive or formal event, such as the signing of a wedding contract or the paying of condolences to a deceased's family, will be accompanied by passages recited from the Qur'an. Words from the sacred text are whispered into the ear of a newborn child and at the moment of a person's death. Certain of the very shortest *surah*s are recited for special purposes: number 112, describing Allah's incomparable eternal Oneness, finds its way into prayers and litanies of praise and is said to have been described by Muhammad as equivalent to a third of the whole Qur'an; numbers 113 and 114 are recited in order to fend off evil; the final verses of the second *surah* form a prayer of forgiveness, while the famous "Throne Verse" beginning, "Allah, there is no god but He, the Living the Eternal" (2:255) may be recited at bedtime so that a heavenly guardian will remain with the sleeper until morning.

LORD OF CREATION

A special place is held by the opening *surah*, called the *Fatihah*, as an obligatory element in prayer ritual. Of itself it also constitutes a prayer to be repeated and reflected upon, as it is said to contain, in condensed form, the fundamental principles expressed throughout the Qur'an. The following is the rendering of its seven verses by the late Muhammad Asad:

1. In the name of God [Allah], the Most Gracious, the Dispenser of Grace: 2. All praise is due to God alone, the Sustainer of all the worlds, 3. the Most Gracious, the Dispenser of Grace, 4. Lord of the Day of Judgement! 5. Thee alone do we worship; and unto Thee alone do we turn for aid. 6. Guide us the straight way, 7. the way of those upon whom Thou hast bestowed Thy blessings, not of those who have been condemned [by Thee], nor of those who go astray.

Exegetically, the passage may be understood in the following manner: Allah is the sole source and sustainer of life, who alone is worthy of worship and praise. He is Lord of the cosmic drama from the beginning of time at the act of creation, to the end of time, on the Day of Judgment. From beginning to end of the drama humankind requires his guidance, without which the individual or entire communities would go astray, as indeed has been the case in human experience. Guidance has been provided by Allah in history through the agency of his prophets, the bearers of his blessings and his command, sent to warn their peoples of the perils of straying from the straight path.

Central to the Qur'an, therefore, is Allah. This must naturally be the case as scripture itself is regarded as his own immutable utterance; his earlier prophets, Moses and Jesus, and revelations indicate the continuum of his activity in human history which culminates in the final judgment to which all are summoned. The importance of belief in each of these elements as preparation for salvation is concisely expressed in a verse which comes as close as possible to a credal statement of the faith: *for he who denies God, and His angels and His revelations and His messengers and the Last Day, has indeed gone far astray* (4:136; also 2:285). The angels are included since it is through them that Allah conveys his revelations to the prophets – in Muhammad's case the angel Gabriel.

Allah's own self-portrait, as it were, is hinted at in the verse *Allah, there is no deity save Him; His alone are the beautiful names* (20:8). In addition to his essential Oneness, there are his attributes of perfection, described as the beautiful names. Drawn from the Qur'an, they were later compiled into a list of ninety-nine names and used as a basis for meditation. Frequently verses in the Qur'an end with a rhyming pair of these names, such as *al-'alim al-hakim*, the Knowing, the Wise.

These attributes were later to be the subject of debate among scholars who strove to understand and explain the very *nature* of Allah, and by extension the nature of humankind's relation with him. From scriptural references he is, in an apparent paradox, both utterly transcendent and yet as near to one as his own jugular vein. He is merciful and compassionate (an appellation with which all but one of

the *surah*s commences). Yet he can be severe in retribution. He guides
whom he wills and leads astray whom he wills. Yet he will leave a
person to that which he or she has chosen for himself or herself. Or
more explicitly, *Allah does not change men's condition unless they change their
inner selves; and when Allah wills people to suffer evil, there is none who could
avert it* (13:11). It could be said that the Qur'an does not reveal Allah,
but rather his *will* for all creation. This debate will occupy our
attention later on. Suffice it here to note that all these attributes may
be collapsed into Allah's majestic omnipotence, understood as a
property in which are embedded infinite justice and mercy. It will be
recalled that it was this quality of "omni-ness" which marked off the
Prophet's Allah most sharply from all other deities of the pagan
pantheon, including their "High God."

LORD OF HISTORY

A further quality of Allah was communicating his will to humankind
through the missions of the prophets. This role as the God of history
is recounted in several places in the Qur'an.[16] The stories of the
prophets all have a similar structure: God sends to every people a
messenger who warns them to worship God alone; the warning is
disregarded, and God destroys them in some spectacular fashion.
The stubborn opposition Muhammad encountered from the Meccans
was therefore unexceptional. The stories reflect a darker side of the
human condition, the ease of man's unreflective clinging to a
mistaken sense of his own self-interest. As a consequence, a general
truth is offered, that to *those who give the lie to Our messages and scorn
them in their pride, the gates of heaven shall not be opened; and they shall not
enter paradise any more than a twisted rope can pass through a needle's eye*
(7:40).

In the broadest sense there is no distinction between one prophet
and another, as each had acknowledged Allah alone and had
voluntarily submitted to him. The word employed in this context is
by now familiar: the prophets were all *muslimun*, those who had
surrendered themselves to Allah (2:136). This meant that biblical
protagonists such as Moses and Jesus were ranked along with others,
like Hud the legendary prophet sent to his people 'Ad, and Salih, who
appeared to the historical people of Thamud, both figures drawn
from indigenous Arab tradition. In this Qur'anic view of monotheistic
history, the prophetic mission of Muhammad was not simply the

continuation of the Jewish and Christian religious traditions, but the culmination of all previous revelations from Allah. This could be understood to imply that Muhammad's message simply confirmed all previous revelations.

In the Qur'an, however, Muhammad is described as the Seal of the Prophets (33:40), which tradition has interpreted to mean the last of the prophets. Viewed in this light, the Qur'an is perhaps best seen as a mirror of the contemporary popular religious milieu of western central Arabia, which comprised an amalgam of low traditions, a kind of common pool of pagan and Judeo-Christian beliefs and practices, many of which probably bordered on the heretical. For example, both Jews and Christians are criticized for certain views, the former for holding that *'Uzayr* (Ezra) is the son of God (9:30), the latter for their belief that Jesus and Mary are both deities (5:116); such unorthodox views would appear to have been part of the pool of popular notions associated with these faiths in Muhammad's day. The era is described in Islamic tradition as the "age of ignorance" (*al-jahiliyyah*). The term occurs in the Qur'an, not as a past period of time, but rather as a dynamic psychological state of mind being challenged by the new moral force of Muhammad's message. This sense is captured in the following verse: *Whereas they who are bent on denying the truth harboured stubborn disdain in their hearts – the stubborn disdain [born] of ignorance* (al-jahiliyyah) *– Allah bestowed from on high His [gift of] inner peace upon His Apostle and the believers and bound them to the spirit of God-consciousness* (48:26).

This stubborn disdain applied equally to Jews, Christians, and pagans. The view was later expressed in Islamic tradition, based upon the evidence of scripture, that following the deaths of their founding prophets, Jews and Christians alike allowed their scriptures to become altered, consequently distorting and corrupting the original revelation. Each community regarded itself as the exclusive possessor of God's word. Thus: *And [both] the Jews and Christians say, "We are Allah's children and His beloved ones"* (5:20). Or *the Christians say, "The Christ* (al-masih = the Messiah) *is the son of Allah"* (9:30). In another instance, Jews and Christians each claimed exclusively for themselves the God-given grace of salvation and privileged entry into paradise (2:111); moreover, each party, citing their respective scripture, charged the other with false truths (2:113). This led to Muhammad being cautioned and advised: *never will the Jews be pleased with you, nor yet the Christians, unless you follow their own creeds. Say: "Behold, the guidance of Allah is the only true guidance"* (2:120). The gates of paradise would open to those alone who acknowledged this simple proposition.

Finally, the God of creation and of history is the God of the Last Day. Eschatological judgment is implied in Muhammad's message from the beginning: *surely man becomes grossly overweening whenever he believes himself to be self-sufficient: for behold, to your Lord all must return* (96: 6–8). The climax of history when the present world comes to an end will be marked by a cosmic upheaval (81:1–14) followed by the gathering of all humankind before Allah the Judge. As the details of this picture became clearer to the Meccan pagans, their incredulity was evident: *What? When we are dead and become dust and bones, shall we indeed be raised up? And our forefathers of old?* (37:16–17; also 50:2–3 and 34:7). Together with their skepticism of bodily resurrection was bewilderment at the notion that behavior in this world could have consequences beyond the present, let alone in a world to come. *There is nothing beyond our life in this world, for we shall not be raised from the dead* (6:29). Their error lay in believing that man was self-sufficient, lord of his own domain, an attitude which bred overweening pride, even in the face of a blind and arbitrary fate.

Here the message of the Qur'an may be seen to operate on two levels, the particular and the universal. The former describes the pagan milieu of Muhammad's day. While there existed a clear antagonism between pagan moral ideals and those expounded by Muhammad, there is no wholesale, indiscriminate rejection of them depicted in the Qur'an.[17] Rather, many of the Arab virtues of *muruwwah* like generosity, courage, loyalty, veracity, and patience were assimilated, but recast in a purer form and deflected away from the authority of the tribal *sunnah* toward the new moral order under the sovereign guidance and command of Allah.

Take, for example, the virtue of generosity. As an act of chivalry, Arabs deemed it proof of genuine nobility; the more extravagant and impulsive the act, the more enhanced one's honor became. The poet Zuhayr had expressed the idea simply: "Whoever makes of generosity a shield for his honour makes honour grow. But whoever does not guard himself from blame, will be blamed."[18] The Qur'an, on the other hand, condemned all acts which stemmed from vainglory and pride.

O you who have attained to faith! Do not deprive your charitable deeds of all worth by stressing your own benevolence and hurting [the feelings of the needy], as does he who spends his wealth only to be seen and praised by men, and believes not in Allah and the Last Day . . . Such as these shall have no gain whatever from all their [good] works; for Allah does not guide people who refuse to acknowledge the truth. (2:264)

Thus, although generosity *is* recognized as a virtue, it ceases to be so if it is ostentatious and thoughtlessly wasteful, intended only to magnify one's reputation for nobility. The proper course is to *believe in Allah and His Messenger, and spend on others out of that which He has made you trustees: for those of you who have attained to faith and who spend freely [in Allah's cause] shall have a great reward* (57:7). True generosity, therefore, is an act founded upon piety; expending from one's means in the way of Allah is to acknowledge gratefully his goodness for the provision of all one possesses. True nobility reaps its reward from Allah in the life to come. In the Qur'anic moral order, nobility contrasts sharply with the pagan virtue, for now *the noblest of you in the sight of Allah is the one who is most deeply conscious of Him* (49:13).

On a universal level, the Qur'an addresses not merely Muhammad's audience but all humankind; or, from another viewpoint, the wider audience is implied throughout, Muhammad's listeners being a specific example of general *jahiliyyah*-mindedness. The tone here is prescriptive, designed less to inform the mind than to reform the soul. Throughout, the Qur'an portrays the moral dualism of the human character; this in turn gives rise to a moral struggle creating the tensions necessary for creative action by humankind.

When Allah expressed his intention of placing humankind on earth as his vicegerent, the angels in their dismay predicted that it would only spread corruption and bloodshed (2:30). Their prediction seemed justified as Adam succumbed to the temptation of Satan (Iblis) and disobeyed Allah's command not to eat fruit from the tree of eternal life (2:35 and 20:120). Once Adam sincerely repented his act, Allah forgave him. In the Islamic tradition as distinct from the Christian, the human race did not thereafter bear the burden of original sin, thus requiring a savior to redeem it. Left to his own frail devices, however, humankind would falter and, without signposts to guide it, lose its way. And so Allah's last words to Adam before he took up his abode on earth were that, despite his banishment, *there shall, none the less, most certainly come to you guidance from Me; and those who follow my guidance need have no fear and neither shall they grieve; but those who are bent on denying the truth and giving the lie to Our messages – they are destined for the fire and therein shall they abide* (2:38–39).

The world is therefore populated broadly by two groups of people, those who believe (*mu'min*) in Allah and follow his guidance and those who reject it in their ingratitude (*kafir*). *He it is who has created you: and among you are such as deny this truth* (kafir), *and among you are such as believe* (mu'min) *[in it]. And Allah sees all that you do* (64:2). Despite Allah's assurance to Adam of his guidance, reiterated in history through the agency of his prophets, there was, nevertheless, a powerful force ever at work attempting to subvert man's discernment of good and evil. This force is the artful seduction of Satan, the only angel among the heavenly host to refuse to acknowledge Adam's superiority and bow down before him (2:34). In what way, then, was Adam superior to his temptor? Satan follows his nature as seducer *naturally*, this being his assigned role in the creator's scheme of things. Man, on the other hand, *ought* to follow his nature, which is to accept the sovereignty of Allah and the wisdom of his guidance. To accept the contrary ultimately is to act unjustly against oneself (7:23). Moral responsibility and accountability, therefore, belong to each individual. The final goal for each will be either the reward of paradise or the punishment of the fire; the potentialities and the penalties offered are equally immense.

RITUALS, EXHORTATIONS, AND INJUNCTIONS

In pursuit of the path toward salvation, the Qur'an commands the performance of certain acts which have become the emblems of the faith and the expressions of communal identity. The instructions for each of these so-called "Pillars" of Islam are sparse in detail. The institutions of prayer and alms giving sometimes appear together in the same context (13:22; 9:54). Fasting is prescribed so that the faithful "might remain conscious of God" and is associated with the month of Ramadan, the time when the Qur'an is believed to have been first revealed (2:183–184). Pilgrimage to Mecca is to be performed; but if for some reason the believer is prevented from performing it, another act of worship, fasting or giving alms, may be offered in its place, the object again being "God-consciousness" (2:196). Each of these four rituals is subsumed under the main "pillar" or emblem of the faith called the *shahadah*, the witnessing that *There is no god but Allah* and *Muhammad is the Messenger of Allah* (49:19;

48:29) These phrases sum up the prophetic-revelatory event in Islam, and the rituals themselves draw their essential meaning from it, that is, as the performance of obedient acts of service (*'ibadah*) to and worship of the One God.

While the Qur'an is primarily a text of religious and moral principles and exhortations embodying the will of Allah, it cannot be described as a compendium of laws. Nevertheless, there are injunctions of a legal nature contained in it, many of which reflect the period of Muhammad's construction of a religious based community in Medina. On matters of dietary concern, for example, believers are enjoined to *partake of what is lawful and good on earth* (2:168; 16:114), including food allowed to Jews (3:93) and Christians. The Prophet was instructed to broadcast the exceptions: *In all that has been revealed to me, I do not find anything forbidden to eat, if one wants to eat thereof, unless it be carrion, or blood poured forth, or the flesh of swine – for that, behold, is loathsome – or a sinful offering over which any name other than Allah's has been invoked* (6:145; also 5:3). Intoxicating beverages (treated together with games of chance) were apparently at first regarded as simply more harmful than beneficial (2:219), but later condemned as one of the works of the devil, who sought to sow rancor and enmity among the community, causing it to turn away from prayer and the remembrance of Allah (5:90–91). Matters of business are touched upon in the prohibition of usury, and the recording of commercial transactions (2:282) so as to avoid later confusion and misunderstanding. The existence of the institution of slavery is acknowledged in the Qur'an, while at the same time believers are urged by their belief in Allah and the Last Day to create the conditions of its ultimate dissolution. True piety involves the care for society's disadvantaged, including *freeing human beings from bondage* (2:177; also 24:33). Finally, a number of passages deal with the general area of family law, including subjects of marriage, divorce, and inheritance. As these and other matters raise questions requiring somewhat fuller treatment, they will be left until later for discussion.

Scripture comprises Allah's will or command in both letter and spirit, although the one may not always be clearly distinguished from the other. For example, the penalty for the act of stealing could scarcely be plainer: *Now as for the man who steals and the woman who steals, cut off the hand of either of them in requital for what they have wrought, as a deterrent ordained by Allah; for Allah is mighty, wise* (5:38). Clear as the letter of this command is, the question arises what tradition made of it when scholars pondered the fullness of its meaning, or dwelt upon its implications in the light of the spirit of the text as a whole. Another well-known textual example is the subject of polygyny, which permits men to take up to four wives. The letter of the law, as it were, is plain; the underlying spirit, however, appears to qualify the permission, namely that *if you have reason to fear that you might not be able to treat them with equal fairness, then [only] one . . .* (4:3), which is followed later in the same *surah* by the verse *And it will not be in your power to treat your wives with equal fairness, however much you may desire it* (4:129). Why in this case did the letter prevail in practice over the spirit? These and other related matters will be dealt with later.

The Islamic religious tradition, like others, is the community's acceptance of the challenge of a divinely revealed authority. It is an attempt on the part of believers to stand before the Almighty, to comprehend and in the end to cope with the the burden of his, at times, unfathomable demands. By definition tradition is a cumulative and collaborative process. Untold numbers of individuals contributed to the process of rendering meaningful the life of the believer within the community and that of the community in the world at large. It is the story of this enterprise which will be related in the following chapters.

CHAPTER 2

Tradition in the making

The first generations of Muslims lived through extraordinary times. In less than a century after the Prophet's death in 10/632, the community's twin birthplaces of Mecca and Medina had become the religious centers of a far-flung patchwork of dominions stretching west across North Africa and into the Iberian peninsula[1] and to the east as far as the Great Wall of China. The famous scholar Muhammad b. Jarir al-Tabari (d. 310/923) traced the course of Muslim expansion in his *History of Prophets and Kings*. In the year 92 of the new Muslim era (710 CE), he records how some 12,000 troops crossed from North Africa into al-Andalus and fought hard "until God killed the Christian king Roderick." This marked the beginning of a Muslim presence in the peninsula which lasted eight hundred years, until it was finally reconquered for the church in Rome. In 96/714, again according to al-Tabari, there occurred in the East a brief encounter between a delegation of Muslims and "the ruler of China." No enduring Muslim presence, however, resulted from this exchange. Indeed, the first short session between the Muslims and the emperor's courtiers seems only to have left the latter bemused at their guests' appearance. Clad in simple white domestic garments, sandal-footed, and perfumed with musk and ambergris, the Arabs conveyed the impression to their Chinese hosts that they were women! A Chinese account of these encounters records the Muslims' arrogant behavior in refusing to prostrate themselves before the emperor, a gesture of submission which Muslims could make only before Allah. Apart from the occasional enclave of Muslim Arab and Persian traders on Chinese territory, an indigenous Chinese Muslim community did not emerge until many centuries later. For the moment, however, rich though the contacts and exchanges were in these early decades between Muslims and varied ethnic-religious communities throughout the Middle East and North Africa, the Great Wall of China in the east remained more than a mere physical barrier shutting out the new Muslim order.

Islamic tradition began to set down its own roots in the fertile cultural soil of these regions during the period of rapid expansion north, west, and east of the Arabian peninsula. Tradition constituted a complex response to a number of inter-related challenges. Foremost, in a strictly religious sense, was the challenge of the prophetic-revelatory event. What did the divinely revealed message and the life of its Messenger mean in detail, and how was each source relevant to the new community's daily concerns? These were questions which took time and immense effort to answer.

In the process, concerted and deliberate inquiry and debate contributed its measure to the growth of tradition. So, too, did violent dissent. Not surprisingly, therefore, tradition reflects the currents and counter-currents of the myriad points of view which went into its making. Moreover, tradition mirrored the challenge confronted by the community in its continuing experience of the founding event. That is, the community continued to reinterpret the event from different perspectives in changing historical circumstances and different cultural locales. Thus, while the prophetic-revelatory event itself can be said to have *transformed* both history and the lives of subsequent generations of Muslims, at the same time the emerging tradition was being *moulded* by the impact of history upon the community.

In this chapter only a rather impressionistic picture of this tradition-in-the-making can be attempted. Despite much recent effort given to questions of the origins and early development of the complex phenomena which comprise the tradition, modern scholarship is as yet far removed from any consensus as to how, when, where, and why the tradition developed as it did. Probably we shall never know with any comfortable degree of certainty the details of "what really happened" during, say, the first Islamic century. This has not prevented the more adventurous spirited from venturing, cautiously or boldly, into the minefield of the Arabic source material bearing upon the period. The reconnoitre, however, has left few entirely unscathed. While this state of affairs is grist for the specialist's mill, the interested non-specialist reader cannot be expected to share the expert's apparently suicidal enthusiasm.[2] Thus in the story that follows, some of the more important signposts will be charted for the period under present consideration, that being roughly the first two to three centuries of the community's existence. This will be done, it should be said, from the safety of the sidelines rather than by plunging again through the minefield.

The first two "generations" or classes of Muslims are remembered in the tradition by their relationship to the Prophet. The Companions of the Prophet (*sahabah*) were the men and women who lived, worked, and fought beside him in his lifetime. They included those who led the community after his death. Abu Bakr was the first Caliph or successor to Muhammad, followed by 'Umar, 'Uthman, and then 'Ali. This generation of leaders oversaw (from 10–41/632–661) the opening stage of Muslim expansion in regions well beyond the Arabian peninsula, although in many areas Muslim rule would not be firmly consolidated for some decades to come. In mainstream Muslim historical works, these leaders became known as the Rightly Guided Caliphs (*al-khulafa' al-rashidun*), a term which implied not only model leadership of justice and prudence but also a golden-age model community. Yet, this same generation of Muslims also witnessed, as well as exhilarating successes, the first traumatic shocks of internal division and conflict.

The second "generation" was logically called the Successors (*tabi'un*) to the Prophet's Companions. Many lived to between the years 81–107/700–725, the oldest of them dying even later. Thereafter, succeeding generations received no special label of merit, although individuals who, until the present day, claim descent (*ashraf*) from the Prophet have enjoyed a certain dignity within their local communities.

The lands and peoples brought under Muslim rule were in the trust of the Caliph, who governed through cadres of political and military personnel, a task which included, of course, the fiscal control of these territories and subjects. The administrative details of Muslim rule do not, however, form part of the present account. It is germane to note here that the course of development of Islamic tradition was unlike that of either Judaism or Christianity in one important respect. Jews had received the Covenant from God well before experiencing its fulfilment in the earthly kingdom of Israel; much of the characteristic ethos of the tradition was nevertheless implanted in Jewish thought *after* the loss of terrestrial power, a loss which then had to be accounted for and rationalized by the rabbis. Christians for their part had struggled against centuries of imperial pagan power until the

Emperor Constantine converted to the faith and changed their worldly fortunes; but much of what characterized Christian thought had already been formed during a long period of the community's political impotence. Islam, on the other hand, grew swiftly from a tiny central Arabian commonwealth to an empire of international compass, confident in its own divine commission to rule. From the beginning Muslims were charged with the grave task to *Obey Allah, and obey the Messenger and those among you who have been entrusted with authority* (4:59), and, as historical circumstances favoured their enterprise, the experience of power and domination shaped much of what became characteristic in the tradition.

THE QUEST FOR KNOWLEDGE

The individuals who dedicated themselves to tradition building undertook activities in which each laboriously mined one or more of the numerous rich shafts of knowledge embedded in the pro-phetic-revelatory event. Some of this labor, but by no means all, was carried out by the Muslims of these first two generations. The mining process was known as "the quest for knowledge" (*talab al-ʿilm*), the persons engaged in the activity were the "people of knowledge" (*ahl al-ʿilm*, or *ʿulamaʾ*). An individual was known as an *ʿalim*, referring in its crudest sense to a person possessing a degree of knowledge (*ʿilm*) of the Qurʾanic revelation and the life of the Prophet Muhammad as well as the contributions of the best known of his Companions. In other words, knowledge essential for the proper worship of Allah and of life in society. Even knowledge extracted from sources outside the community, from Jews, Christians, and the like, was initially firmly embraced. From the second/ninth century onward, experts in separate disciplines directly related to scripture and the Prophet emerged; and, in addition to their creating auxiliary sciences to support these primary concerns, they collectively contributed to the elaboration of Islamic doctrine and practice. At the same time, it must be stressed that the intellectual output of these centuries was not confined to religious matters. Numerous Muslim scholars, with their training in the religious sciences as well, devoted their lives to a range of other disciplines including philosophy, medicine, astronomy, and mathe-matics. Their labors, indeed, constituted a crucial pool of knowledge inherited by Europe through Latin translations from these Arabic treatises from the fifth/eleventh century.

The motives behind the urgent desire to accumulate knowledge of a particularly religious nature are not difficult to imagine. As one prominent scholar among the Successors, Abu Bakr b. 'Abd al-Rahman b. al-Harith (d. 93/712), is reported to have put it, the purpose of knowledge was to gain honor, to strengthen one's faith and to win favor with the ruling Caliph in order to serve him. The individual's motivation could also have been found in revelation. There, the incessant refrain was that true knowledge was knowledge of religious insight, even a mark of faith itself: *Allah will exalt by many degrees those among you who have attained to faith and those who have been given knowledge* (58:11). There was in addition the wider pragmatic consideration of the *ummah*'s needs. In the historical confrontation of the new community with the older, established religious communities of Jews and Christians, knowledge of its own founding experience was essential to confirm the faith of its own flock, to tackle internal dissent considered dangerous to the community's welfare, and to fend off challenges from the others. The body of knowledge was potentially vast, albeit finite, encompassing as it eventually did a formidable range of religious sciences. Polymaths there were, but only the rare scholar of exceptional gifts could possibly be acclaimed an expert in nearly *every* discipline. In any case, as theologians later concluded, no one could possibly know *everything* about Allah. Indeed, what was more important, as we have already seen, was to understand and then obey the *will* of Allah. For the average Muslim layman of some cultural pretension and social standing, religious education and learning covering at least *some* knowledge of scripture and tradition was deemed essential. The rest, the unlettered masses, had access at least to the recitation of the Qur'an and the tales of the story-tellers.

The pursuit of knowledge began informally among individuals or families which, by the time of the Caliphate of 'Umar b. 'Abd al-'Aziz (99–102/717–720), had taken on all the aspects of a fairly well-developed movement. One event of particular importance prior to this period had been, of course, the successful collecting of the Qur'an into a single canon completed, according to the traditional Muslim account, during the Caliphate of 'Uthman (23–35/644–655). This left many problems unresolved, for example the meaning of unfamiliar terms or obscure passages, the occasion of individual revelations, and the elucidation of matters of legal or theological importance. Next, the Caliph 'Abd al-Malik (66–86/685–705), one of the most outstanding leaders of the Marwanid branch of the Umayyad Caliphate

(41–132/661–750), decreed Arabic as the official language of the chancellory. This move helped ensure that Arabic, as the language of both God and government, would in time displace other contemporary idioms of high culture (such as Greek) in favor of the new *lingua franca*. This official act may have helped stimulate the study of the Arabic language, for grammars and lexicons clearly served the religious purpose of aiding understanding of scripture as well.

The repository of religious knowledge was the collective mind and memory of the Prophet's Companions in Mecca and Medina. Through mutual contacts among the Companions themselves and with others, information on the prophetic-revelatory event was exchanged and slowly disseminated. Such contacts and exchanges were not confined to these two centers alone. Some Companions moved to other cities in the burgeoning Muslim dominions as the political fulcrum shifted from central Arabia to Damascus in Syria under the Umayyad dynasty. Indeed, the growth of Islamic culture is intimately connected to the urban centers throughout the community. Some, like Damascus, Alexandria and Cordoba, had venerable histories of their own, while others, such as Kufah, Basrah, and Baghdad in Iraq, Fustat (Cairo) in Egypt, and Qayrawan in Tunisia were creations of the new order. Most were initially military outposts which gradually became transformed into centres of cultural creation and dissemination. Everywhere teaching was undertaken in places of worship, the mosque (*masjid*), or else in a scholar's private home, where he would meet with a small circle (*halqah*) of students. Instruction, originally given by a Companion or Successor, who were chiefly Arabs, with increasing frequency became the charge of persons among the rapidly growing body of converts to Islam, eager to spread the knowledge they themselves had recently acquired.

THE "RIHLAH" AND THE PILGRIMAGE

A chief feature of this process was the institution of the *rihlah*, the journey undertaken by student-scholars in search of persons, wherever they were to be found, reputed to be sources of information. Journeys were embarked upon in the spirit of a saying attributed to Luqman, the pre-Islamic sage who had advised his son to "sit with the learned men and keep close to them. Allah gives life to the hearts with the light of wisdom as He gives life to the dead earth with the abundant rain of the sky."[3] The practice may have been rooted in the cultural and spiritual stirring among the Arabs prior to Islam as stories of *hanifs* tell how some "roamed the earth" in search of true knowledge of God. In his biography of the Prophet, Ibn Ishaq tells of delegations of tribesmen received by Muhammad during his lifetime who were instructed in certain matters of the faith which they in turn imparted to their own people.[4]

The following story, preserved in one of the major third-/ninth-century collections of Traditions, appears in keeping with this pattern of searching for knowledge. A man from Medina journeyed one month's distance north to Damascus seeking out the Companion Abu Darda', who was known to transmit a certain tradition from the Prophet. When the man found him seated in the *masjid* and explained his purpose, Abu Darda' quoted the Prophet, who said,

For one who travels a road in search of knowledge, Allah will have him travel one of the roads of Paradise. Angels will lower their wings, approving the seeker of knowledge, while those in the heavens and the earth, and the fish in the depths of the sea, will seek pardon for the man of learning. The excellence of the learned over the devotee is like that of the full moon over the other stars. The learned (*'ulama'*) are the heirs of the prophets. The prophets bequeathed neither dinar nor dirham but rather knowledge; so he who receives it, obtains an abundant portion.[5]

This saying of the Prophet incidentally illustrates a problem of historical interpretation inherent in the sources. It may indeed reflect the general sense, if not the precise wording, of something a Companion remembered the Prophet having said; in the light of the corresponding emphasis on the importance of knowledge in scripture, it would not be surprising for the Prophet to have expanded upon the theme. There may be, on the other hand, reasons for suspecting that the saying is entirely the product of a later period, or perhaps merely the object of tampering: for example, the phrase "The learned are the heirs of the prophets" could be construed as an insertion by a later hand to justify a status in Islamic society of the *'ulama'* above that of the Caliphs. Much effort and ingenuity has been expended by scholars on trying to distinguish the genuine from the false in such sayings. What is important to recognize in any event is that within the tradition itself, Muslims in general will defend such prophetic sayings as genuine, or will accept them at worst as pious frauds, important nevertheless for the spiritual edification of the community.

Other famous Companions were sought out for their knowledge, including the Prophet's cousin 'Ali b. Abi Talib (d. 40/661) and his uncle Ibn 'Abbas (d. 68/687), and even closer members of his family like his wife 'A'isha (d. 58/678) were consulted. An early extant compilation of Traditions, that of al-Tayalisi (d. 203/818), cites material from some six hundred Companions, suggesting that the initial pool of knowledge was by no means small, even if not every person was approached.

The career of the scholar Makhul al-Shami, who died sometime toward the end of the first century, illustrates another aspect of the development of religious culture in this early period. Born in Kabul in the province of Sind (present-day Afghanistan), he traveled extensively gathering religious learning and then settled in Damascus, where he issued legal opinions (*fatawa*) and transmitted his collected material to other students and scholars. It is said that he never lost his foreign accent when speaking Arabic. Makhul was part of the ever growing number of non-Arab converts (*mawali*) from the outlying provinces making their mark on the emerging religious culture of Islam. A marked change in *Muslim society* was in motion: from a conquering stratum of Arabs who happened to be bound together by Islam, it was perforce becoming a society of Muslims who happened to use the Arabic tongue and adhere to certain aspects of the Arab heritage.

Another major institution which served as a point of exchange and dissemination of knowledge was the annual pilgrimage to the holy shrine at Mecca. The Meccan scholar Ibn Jurayj (d. 150/767) enjoyed a double advantage. He received at home scholars from various parts of the Islamic domains and traveled himself to the Yemen, where he taught others. The pilgrimage, in this sense, has not altered its function over the centuries to the present day. By the close of the first century, therefore, the pool of transmitters, drawn from most corners of the expanding community, had become concentrated in several major regional centers: Medina and Mecca in central Arabia, the Yemen, Damascus, and Homs in Syria, Basra and Kufa in Iraq and Egypt. In al-Andalus, where neither Companion nor Successor had set foot, this development necessarily occurred at a later period.

TRADITION ("HADITH") IN THE TRADITION

How this body of knowledge was transmitted from one generation to the next is still a matter of unresolved debate. Almost certainly both oral and written methods were employed for transmitting it from the beginning. However, as opposition had early been expressed against the recording of religious knowledge (apart from the Qur'an), the written form probably took longer to become firmly established (perhaps toward the end of the second/eighth and early third/ninth century) than would otherwise have been the case without opposition. When, with time, the system of transmission reached maturity, a number of technical terms were employed to distinguish different methods: for example, the *'ard* method meant that a student who had received a work from his teacher either by dictation or from an authenticated manuscript would read his newly completed manuscript back to the teacher for correction; then there was the *mukatabah* method, where a manuscript of a work received by correspondence was copied; the *munawalah* method meant that manuscripts changed hands without an accompanying oral reading; finally, the *ijazah* method meant that a teacher would provide a certificate that a particular student was permitted to transmit his master's material, regardless of the methods by which the student acquired them. No method, however, guaranteed perfect accuracy of transmission, or indeed prevented the appearance in circulation of forgeries, whether committed from purely pious motives or not.

A single Tradition is called a *hadith*, literally a story, anecdote, or narrative of an event. The same term applies also to the entire corpus of Tradition literature. Each Tradition in its classically accepted form was supposed to have two components, the substance of the Tradition (*matn*) or the point it conveyed, and a chain of transmitters (*isnad*) listing the persons allegedly responsible for handling it as far back as the original source, whether a Companion, a Successor, or the Prophet himself. Two examples will illustrate the form a *hadith* could take. Both are taken from a work called the *Kitab al-Muwatta'*, compiled by the Medinan jurist Malik b. Anas (d. 179/795), which contains many Traditions. The first, which is traced back to a decision of a Companion of the Prophet, became technically known as an *athar*.

{A} Malik informed us that al-Zuhri reported from Sa'id b. al-Musayyab to the effect that: {B} Nufay'a, a slave of Umm Salamah, had as a wife a free woman against whom he uttered a double-divorce formula. The husband sought a legal opinion on the matter from 'Uthman b. 'Affan, who said that the wife had thus become forbidden to him.[6]

The *isnad* {A} cites two persons, the famous collector of Traditions Ibn Shihab al-Zuhri (d. 124/742), and Sa'id b. al-Musayyab (94/713), a man reputed for his expertise in legal matters. The *matn* {B} of the Tradition involves an instance of the divorce formula "I divorce you," uttered twice by a man against his wife. The normal procedure required a triple utterance of the phrase "I divorce you" for a divorce to be considered legally absolute. But as the man concerned was a slave, the Caliph 'Uthman (d. 35/655) who was responsible for the legal opinion (*fatwa*), declared that the double-divorce formula was sufficient for the marriage union to be severed absolutely. It seems that Nufay'a regretted his impulsive act and, wanting his wife back, sought the Caliph's opinion, hoping that he had not irrevocably dissolved his marriage! In the period before legal terminology became fixed, however, *hadith* was applied alike to sayings of the Companions, the Successors and the Prophet himself.

The second Tradition is an example of what technically is called a prophetic *hadith* (*hadith nabawi* or *hadith al-nabi*).

{A} Malik informed us that Ibn Shihab reported from Abu Bakr b. 'Ubaydallah from 'Abdallah b. 'Umar that the Apostle of Allah (May the blessings and peace of Allah be upon him) said: {B} Whenever any of you eats, let him do so with his right hand, and drink as well with it, for the devil eats and drinks with his left hand.

The *isnad* again cites al-Zuhri of the previous chain of authorities and includes also 'Abdallah, the son of the second Caliph 'Umar. 'Abdallah, a Companion famed as a traditionalist and a man of high moral qualities, died in 73/693. Unlike the previous Tradition, this *matn* does not appear, from today's vantage point, to concern a matter of law but rather of table manners or etiquette. As it deals, however, with the seductions of the devil, Allah's dissident angel, it expresses the need for awareness of their danger. Both Traditions were therefore regarded as part of the *religious* law of Islam, about which more will be said in the next chapter. The source of this second Tradition is unimpeachable, the Prophet himself; hence the formulaic expression of respect which follows each mention of his name or title in Malik's work. It represents the strictly non-scriptural or Prophetic dimension of the prophetic-revelatory event, that is, the *prophetic* word as distinct from the *divine* word.

In the previous Tradition, 'Uthman might have decided the matter of divorce according to prevailing custom, or he could have based his decision upon how he believed the Prophet *would* have acted had he still been alive. Either way, his decision was understood to constitute part of the community's new dispensation, which one was obliged to obey. These two *hadith*s constitute but a minute fraction of Traditions slowly being excavated throughout the first and second centuries by dint of the labor of hundreds, possibly thousands, of persons pursuing the same quest for knowledge.

Early Islamic tradition knew another, special, type of *hadith* which stood part way between the Qur'an and Traditions of the type just described. This was called the *hadith qudsi*, or divine saying. It was a pronouncement from Allah reported by the Prophet, but which did not constitute part of scripture itself. Few of them had any relevance to matters of strictly legal or creedal importance, but concerned rather the believer's spiritual life and his or her proper relationship to Allah. They tended to be didactic in nature, as indeed were many *hadith*s transmitted from either the Prophet or his Companions. As a source of inspiration guiding an individual's faith, divine sayings were particularly favored in the mystical piety of the Sufis. The following two related and representative examples of divine saying stress the unbounded mercy of Allah: "the Messenger of Allah said: When Allah completed creation, He wrote in His book which is with Him above the Throne, 'Truly, My mercy overcomes My wrath.'" And again, "the Prophet said: Allah says, 'The angels have interceded, the prophets have interceded and the faithful have interceded; there remains only the Most Merciful of the merciful to intercede.'" Thus the Qur'an, the divine sayings and the prophetic *hadith* form a continuum of revelation in which divine and prophetic authority cannot easily and simply be isolated one from the other.

The study of scripture in its broadest sense included a concern for grammar and the Arabic lexicon and the collection of sayings of the Prophet, his Companions and Successors, but these were only a few of the areas of inquiry conducted by Muslims from the earliest period. Their appearance as fully developed disciplines of course occurred later. Another group of individuals who contributed to the enrichment of nascent Islamic culture comprised the popular preachers (*mudhak-kirun*) and story-tellers (*qussas*), although this last term was taken to include the others as well.[7] Some *qussas* are reported to have been appointed to the position of religious judge (*qadi*).

Their activities, like those of other teachers, centered upon the mosque, relating stories of an edifying nature drawn from a wide range of sources, at times elaborating upon Qur'anic allusions, at others employing Christian and Jewish material directly, or else recasting such tales and pre-Islamic stories in an Islamic idiom. It is true that criticism of story-tellers was, from time to time, leveled by some who accused them of, among other things, a lack of proper religious knowledge and moral rectitude, membership of sectarian groups, and in general engaging in practices considered to be innovations (*bid'ah*), since story-telling had allegedly not been sanctioned in the times of the Prophet or his Companions. Many of the charges were true of some, but not all, story-tellers. A scholar's rebuff stung one story-teller to respond in a manner which also contained an embarrassing grain of truth. A noted Iraqi jurist, Shu'bah (d. 160/776), once dismissed a story-teller from his presence saying "We do not relate Traditions to the *qussas*!" To which the story-teller rejoined, "Why not? Scholars receive Traditions from us the width of a hand span and stretch them into a cubit!"[8] Despite the strictures, story-tellers remained important as public communicators to popular audiences of educated and uneducated people alike.

The purpose of the *qussas* was, by means of narrating and interpreting stories of the pious people of old, to instill in their audiences a sense of awe in the majesty of Allah and the blessings he has bestowed upon them and to arouse in them a desire for his promised rewards. In this sense, they continued one aspect of the Prophet's mission (4:64; 88:21; 51:55). If the *qussas* performed this task with dignity and with a serious goal in mind, well and good, but if only for cheap theatrical effect, their performances were liable to censure. Moreover, according to the view of a sixth-/thirteenth-century scholar, only a learned person (*'alim*) was capable of properly fulfilling this task, since he could be questioned by his audience on any subject relating to religious matters. An ascetic temperament was important, too, in order to set a good example to the people.[9] Clearly, not every story-teller met these standards. Personal probity was an essential quality of all scholars, for the "errors of the learned" could lead to confusion and disorder. This danger was explained by the Medinan story-teller and early Christian convert Tamim al-Dari (d. ca. 40/661), who said that "when a learned man (*'alim*) commits a sin before the people, they imitate him; but while he might repent his action, they continue to follow his sinful way."[10] The same man is reported to have advised a friend to "take from your religion something for yourself and give to it something of yourself, so that you might achieve in worship what is within your capability."[11] In these words of personal advice there seems to lie a deeper truth about the historial reality: a community of individuals, each accepting the new dispensation as he or she finds it, while at the same time bringing to it his or her own understanding and experience. Both sides slowly and subtly emerged affected by the exchange.

SCHOLARSHIP AND POLITICS

In the foregoing we have followed some of the factors which brought about the formation of a broad group of learned persons, known collectively as *'ulama'*, who throughout succeeding centuries became responsible for the reproduction and dissemination of religious knowledge in the *ummah*. They were, in other words, the carriers and custodians of the literate memory of Islamic culture. If they appear at first to have been an amorphous, disparate body, they were probably just that. They were, however, united from the first in purpose, namely to bring to full light the mysteries concealed in the prophetic-revelatory event. Later, together with the growth of diverse and specialized subject areas of religious knowledge, the *'ulama'* as a body became socially differentiated. They represented neither the state itself nor society; rather, different group of scholars held positions in both.

Nevertheless, those trained in the religious law eventually did achieve greater status and wealth than the others, such as Qur'an readers or preachers in mosques. The legal profession too, however, was socially and economically stratified. Notwithstanding these developments, Islamic society never produced a clerical hierarchy or, indeed, a formal priestly office of any kind. There is no direct parallel between Muslim religious authorities and the offices of bishop or rabbi. It has often been said that church and state were united in Islamic culture, but since no institution like a church ever existed, it was pointless to invent a distinction between the two. On the personal level, recognition of an individual's religious status was simply that he or she appeared to be a good Muslim, the more so when he or she was scholarly, pious, and ascetic. The sense of community, fostered and nourished by the *'ulama'*, became the effective and affective bond between individuals.

While performing their tasks of discovery, or rather recovery, of religious knowledge, the *'ulama'* never shrank from engaging in polemics amongst themselves or against other religious communities; nor did they eschew involvement in campaigns of political dissent, for the realm of the political was merely an extension of the religious, as the Prophet's own life had exemplified. Every member of the *ummah* was affected in one way or another by the traumatic consequences of the murder of the third Caliph, 'Uthman (d. 35/655). 'Ali b. Abi Talib succeeded him but was soon embroiled in a bitter quarrel with 'Uthman's nephew, Mu'awiyah, the governor of Syria. When 'Ali's own support failed him, ensuring his downfall, Mu'awiyah succeeded as Caliph in 40/661 and founded the Umayyad dynasty, which survived until 132/750.

The conflict, or trial (*fitnah*), as Muslim accounts describe it, was explicitly political, but was nevertheless fraught with religious implications for the community. Henceforth, the *ummah* would be divided by rival visions of salvation. The majority, although with varying degrees of commitment, sided with the Umayyad victors and forged the mainstream of Islamic culture, which finally emerged as Sunni Islam. The losers, who had sided with 'Ali, became identified with an ethos which sustained them through their centuries-long status as a religious minority. A modern scholar has described this ethos as "an attitude of mind which refuses to admit that majority opinion is necessarily true or right, and – which is its converse – a rationalised defense of the moral excellence of an embattled minority."[12] These became known as the Shi'ah, from the phrase *Shi'at 'Ali*, the faction of 'Ali. One way in which their differences with the majority may be seen is in the manner historians with Shi'ah sympathies dealt with the pre-*fitnah* period of the Caliphate. Abu al-'Abbas al-Ya'qubi (d. 284/897) uses the word "Caliphate" for the period of 'Ali's rule alone, simply describing the "days" of the previous three rulers Abu Bakr, 'Umar, and 'Uthman. For the Shi'ah, there was only one Rightly Guided Caliph. Another point which would, in time, separate the

Sunni from the Shi'ah was the view each had of its past. For the Shi'ah the most exemplary generations of their history were those of their leaders, 'Ali's descendants the *imams*, of whom the majority of Shi'ah accepted twelve in all. The line ended when the last *imam* vanished toward the end of the third/ninth century. Sunnis, on the other hand, viewed the generations of the Companions and Successors collectively as the "pious ancestors" (*salaf*) of blessed memory.

More radical than either the Sunni or Shi'ah, however, were a group which had at first been among 'Ali's supporters and later abandoned his camp when he agreed to submit his dispute with Mu'awiyah to an arbitrator; they became known in Islamic history as the *Khawarij*, or the Kharijites, a name which was virtually synonymous with rebellion against established authority. One of their doctrines, which was at once theological and political, was that a person who had committed a grave sin was thereby excluded from the community; from this they could regard themselves as the "people of paradise" and all others as the "people of hell." Although their initial impact upon the course of historical events in time waned, some of their ideas and attitudes have never entirely lost their attraction. Muslim groups which the Western media are fond of labeling indiscriminately "fundamentalist" could trace their inspiration to the early Kharijites.

In any event, each group to emerge from the conflict between 'Ali and Mu'awiyah found its supporters and detractors among the *'ulama'*, and within each group also there were shades of opinion ranging from moderate on certain matters to extreme on others. Each faction could take comfort in a saying attributed to the Prophet that his community would never agree upon an error, believing it applied exclusively to its own party. The Sunni majority of the community, however, found the correctness of its course sanctioned in another Tradition attributed to the Prophet in which he foresaw his people becoming divided into seventy-two sects, only one of which, implicitly themselves, would achieve salvation.

Sunni *'ulama'*, therefore, who required and welcomed the political protection of the Caliphs while at the same time resisting any attempt by them at overt control or manipulation were engaged, in the decades following the *fitnah* of 40/661, in defining community membership and how its members should conduct themselves, including the Caliphs themselves.

PROPHETIC PARADIGM AND THE INNOVATOR

A concept employed in this exercise of self-definition was the *sunnah*, from which the label "Sunni" is derived. Literally the word means "path" or "beaten track," and in pre-Islamic times referred to the ways of the ancestors which formed the basis of each tribe's identity and pride. As a term for tribal custom it bore a normative force, that is, the path which the tribe *ought* to follow to preserve its honor and pride intact.

In the Qur'an the word occurs in the sense of established practice or a course of conduct (15:13), although in the context of scripture *sunnah* takes on a religious coloring which is absent within the homocentric world view of the pre-Islamic Arab (33:38, 62). In the Islamic Tradition literature, the term *sunnah* appears in reference to the Prophet. One famous *hadith* relates that when Muhammad sent his companion, Mu'adh b. Jabal, as a judge to the Yemen, he asked Mu'adh how he would arrive at his decisions. Mu'adh replied that he would first consult the "Book of Allah" and if he found no solution there, he would refer to the *sunnah* of the Prophet, and finally, if that too failed, he would use his own judgment (*ra'y*).[13]

On the face of it, this *hadith* appears anachronistic. For one thing, the Qur'an was not complete until Muhammad's death and was only collected together a generation later; moreover, the term *sunnah* was initially used to apply to the precedent of the Companions as well as that of the Prophet; and finally, the use of *ra'y* seems to have become widespread among Muslim judges at the beginning. *Ra'y* was the personal discretion or sound opinion of a judge (*qadi*) who, while taking scripture, *sunnah*, and local practice into account, did not feel compelled to cite these explicitly in his decision. None of this is particularly surprising. On the other hand, the concept of the *sunnah* referring specifically to the Prophet and the *sunnah* or acknowledged practice of his Companions were probably taken together in a general and abstract sense to mean the path the community as a whole was following under the Prophet's leadership. This in turn was understood to refer to direct guidance during his lifetime and to the community's memory of it after his death. It was the labors of the early generations of *'ulama'* which slowly supplied the content of this general notion as the tradition was taking shape.

However, it was perhaps not until near the end of the first century that judges began to introduce into their decisions, in addition to the continued use of *ra'y*, *sunnah* of the Prophet supported now by some of the available *hadith* from which a point of law could be deduced. Within another generation, or two at the most, the *'ulama'* had more or less succeeded in restricting the meaning of *sunnah* to the normative conduct of the Prophet alone. In reality, of course, the Prophetic *sunnah* as latterly defined contained data from the period of his Companions and Successors. By this time the *hadith* and *sunnah* had become, as technical terms, practically synonymous, the former being the vehicle or carrier of an example of the Prophet's conduct. Nevertheless, Traditions from the Companions and Successors (*athar*) continued to play an important role, but secondary to those accepted as genuine prophetic *hadith*. The detailed picture of this overall development, however, is still the subject of much debate.

Adherence to the *sunnah*, in the sense of prophetic precedent, defined one's full membership of the majority Sunni community. The ordinary believer was able to conduct his or her day-to-day activities observing the required rituals of faith but without the need to be acquainted with the minutiae of the *sunnah*'s content. Few paid heed to occasional lapses. Realistically, only the *'ulama'* as a body had access to the full content of the *sunnah*. A Muslim's standing could be severly tested, however, if some felt that his or her *public* bearing in matters of ritual, belief, or accepted custom lacked the approved prophetic precedent. In this event, such behavior was judged an innovation or *bid'ah*.

Books on *bid'ah* began to appear. The earliest extant example of this genre was compiled by one Muhammad b. Waddah al-Qurtubi (d. 287/900), descendant of a non-Arab who had been purchased and then freed as a convert to Islam by his master.[14] Born in the city of Cordoba in al-Andalus, Ibn Waddah journeyed to the East on two occasions, visiting Mecca and Medina as well as the major cities of Egypt, Syria, Palestine, and Iraq. His lifetime coincided with the period in which the prophetic Traditions were being scrutinized for their authenticity and gathered into enormous collections which eventually would be acknowledged as the canonical works of sound *hadith*. Ibn Waddah's short treatise on innovations, therefore, ranks among the efforts of the *'ulama'* to reach some consensus on the community's beliefs and practices and thereby protect it from internal corruption.

One theme of Ibn Waddah's work is the lament that the community had fallen upon corrupt times. It was a cry heard before and often to be repeated throughout the centuries. He quotes two earlier masters to the same effect. Asad b. Musa (d. 212/827), whose defence of the faith earned him the epithet of "lion of the *sunnah*," claimed that fighting innovation was more important than performing the obligatory rituals of prayer, fasting, and pilgrimage. Then, Sahnun b. Sa'id al-Tanukhi (d. 240/854), from Qayrawan in present-day Tunisia, described the followers of the *sunnah* in his own day as but "a single shining star in a night of deepest darkness." The cause was simple: innovations creeping into the beliefs and practices of the faithful. The Prophet is said to have warned his people of the moment when they would be overcome by "an intoxication of ignorance and a love of the present life such as would distract you from contemplation of the next."

Ibn Waddah nowhere defines *bid'ah* and one is left to deduce its meaning from the contexts of the Traditons he cites. An innovator is one tempted by the devil, who allows his passions to rule his life, who searches for fame and fortune and performs his devotional acts with an exaggerated display of humility. Certain specific rituals are reviled as innovations, many of which are related to prayer: the use of the rosary, raising the voice and hands during prayer, alterations in the accepted formula summoning the faithful to prayer, transforming places visited by the Prophet into sanctuaries for worship, and celebrating non-Islamic festivals like the Persian New Year (*nawruz*). Groups which held certain "false" ideas according to the "people of the *sunnah*" were to be shunned, especially those with notions affecting what may be broadly called political theology. Ibn Waddah only mentions certain groups by name, such as the Murji'ites, the Qadarites, and the Mu'tazilites, it being assumed that the particular beliefs he was condemning were too well known to require discussion. They will be treated in a later chapter.

Despite drawing the line between the good Muslim and the innovator in this manner, the concept of innovation was cloaked in ambiguity. Its application, therefore, was necessarily inconsistent or arbitrary, and it was this characteristic which gave ample scope for polemical debate. On the other hand, an innovator was condemned neither as an unbeliever (*kafir*) nor as an apostate (*murtadd*). He remained among the believers so long as he continued to pray in the direction of Mecca. No specific punishment for the innovator in this world is recommended, although torment in the next is deemed inevitable according to the warning that Allah does not accept an innovator's repentance. In the here and now, the good Muslim best avoids the innovator's company. Walking with a Christian, it was said, was better than being seen in the company of a corruptor of the faith. This attitude reflects the absence of (in addition to a priestly hierarchy, already mentioned) a central ecclesiastical body with the powers to debate and legislate on matters of faith and to judge and execute in matters heretical. The ordinary person charged with innovation in the Islamic context was best dealt with by pressure applied within his or her local community acting under the general injunction to "command the good and prohibit the reprehensible." Cases brought to the attention of the court almost invariably involved persons of social standing and often mirrored political intrigues of the moment. Charges of "free-thinking" (*zandaqah*) and of atheism, or public vilification of the Qur'an and the Prophet, were uncommon but treated more harshly.

The Muslim attitude to *bid'ah* in Ibn Waddah's day may best be summed up in the tradition he cites attributed to the Prophet that "a person does not create a *bid'ah* in Islam without abandoning a *sunnah* which was better than it." The tone is factual but realistic. The community was warned against the danger of innovation. Nevertheless, some innovations were accepted and absorbed into the community's practice. The most famous example, perhaps, is the celebration of the Prophet's birthday (*mawlid*), introduced in Egypt during the fifth/eleventh century.[15] Originally a Shi'ah festival, Sunni celebrations were held in Syria and Iraq in the following century. The famous Egyptian scholar Jalal al-Din al-Suyuti (d. 911/1505) wrote a lengthy defense of the practice in which he cites the opinion of an earlier chief justice who said that

> The legal status on the observance of the *mawlid* is that it is an innovation which has not been transmitted on the authority of one of the pious ancestors from the first three centuries. Despite this, it comprises both good things as well as the reverse. If one strives for good things in the practice thereof and the opposite is avoided, it is a good innovation (*bid'ah hasanah*).[16]

Opponents were concerned about people's possible lewd behavior expressed in overeating, dancing, and singing during the celebrations. From a certain "official" viewpoint, this and other manifestations of "popular" piety were judged regrettable. The community, nevertheless, never ceased to persevere in its quest to recapture the spirit of the prophetic golden age. At the same time, scholars conceded that only the Prophet's intercession with Allah on the Day of Judgment could restore the purity of the early days. Later authors on innovation continued to condemn "aberrations" from the *sunnah* in their own day. At the same time, they often remained silent about innovations from previous periods, such as the use of the rosary or "worry beads," which meanwhile had become widespread practice.

CONVERTS AND "DHIMMIS"

While the *'ulama'* fashioned the shield of the *sunnah*, and forged the sword of *bid'ah*, the community of Muslims was steadily growing in number in almost every region where the first Arab armies had secured their conquests. Natural growth among the conquerors would account for a portion of this increase, but most important was the increase in the rate of conversion to Islam from among the subject peoples. The *'ulama'* themselves were well represented by non-Arab converts. The rate was not uniform across the different Muslim regions. Over many generations Muslims remained a minority in some or at best a bare majority in other areas they governed, and it is not possible to speak of a "mass Islamic society" until some four hundred years after the Prophet's death.

As rulers of others Muslims had to define the relationship of their community to those non-Muslim peoples under their control. The general principle underlying these relations was that since Muslims alone had accepted the obligations of living the Muslim way, they had, therefore, to shoulder responsibility for the whole of society. For this purpose the religious law, elaborated by the *'ulama'*, defined members of the minority religious communities as having the status of *dhimmi*, or protected person. This term embraced most importantly Jews, Christians, and Magians (or Zoroastrians), but also applied to Samaritans and even idolaters and fire-worshipers (and much later, Hindus as well), who were included as a matter of expediency so long as they were not resident in the Arabian peninsula, the birthplace of the community in Mecca and Medina.

The status of *dhimmi* guaranteed a person's life, property, and religious practices, under the supervision of their own religious leadership, in return for payment by every male adult of a poll-tax or *jizyah*, which was lifted in the event of his conversion to Islam. This tax was the real mark of subjugation, a common medieval practice toward minority religious communities, and may have acted as a stimulus to conversion in order to avoid its social stigma, even though the financial burden was not great. Indeed, the preservation or improvement of one's social status or prestige was probably the single most important cause of conversion during the first centuries of Islam. For example, members of the defeated Iranian army and landed aristocracy retained their prestigious roles in the new order by conversion, while many from the lowest ranks in society found themselves socially and perhaps economically better off than before. We have already encountered individuals who, through their own or a forefather's conversion, entered the community and succeeded in achieving a reputable role for themselves among the *'ulama'*. Examples of forced conversion exist, despite the clearest scriptural prohibition (2:256) against such practice, but in any case appear to have been rare. The incidence of persecution of non-Muslim religious minorities was largely the result of the arbitrary policies of rulers and/or rapid deterioration of the economy, factors which just as often created harsh conditions also for the ruler's own Muslim enemies.

The conversion process finally reached the point when it was possible to speak of a *Muslim* society, and the conversion curve began to level off. Even then significant communities of Jews and Christians, in particular, remained in parts of the Muslim domains like Iraq, Syria, and Egypt, which at one time or another had been former provinces of the diminished Byzantine state and the defunct Sassanian Empire of the Persians. We know little of the nature of daily contacts between Muslims, Jews, and Christians through this long period of transition down to the turn of the fifth/eleventh century.

APOLOGISTS AND POLEMICISTS

There is, however, evidence of contact of another kind, namely one community's perception of another preserved in contemporary religious apologetics and polemics. These reflect the views of literate defenders of their respective faiths rather than idle gossip in the market place. For all that, they resonate with the passionate convictions of committed persons living in a period when the promise of salvation or fear of its loss bore an urgency which modern civilization has obliterated from its memory.

The monk John of Damascus (d. 136/753) had prior to his church calling worked in the bureaucracy of the Umayyad Caliphs. He later wrote an apologetic work for Christians, to help strengthen and preserve their faith under the experience of Muslim rule. As a means to that end, he dealt with some aspects of Islam, providing answers for Christians to questions of faith which seem to have arisen from actual encounters with Muslims. Muhammad, he believed, had derived his ideas from a Christian heretic. Then, pretending to be God-fearing, Muhammad "spread rumours that a scripture was brought down to him from heaven. Thus having drafted some pronouncements in his book, worthy only of laughter, he handed it down to his people in order that they may comply with it." John perceived weaknesses in the Muslim's faith compared with his own. Unlike Christ's mission, the coming of Muhammad had neither been foretold nor testified to in scripture by the earlier prophets. Muslims call Christians polytheists (*mushrikun*), as they believe Christ to be both the Son of God and God. The appropriate response, says John, is that in the Qur'an Christ is referred to as both Word and Spirit, and hence Muslims should not scold Christians alone for associating another deity with God! He concludes that the Qur'an in fact confirms the divinity of Christ, for "if the Word is in God, then it is obvious that he is God as well."

John's familiarity with parts, if not all of the Qur'an, despite his faulty understanding of it from a Muslim perspective, nevertheless provided a more sophisticated argument by comparison with certain Christian polemics expressed in the next century from beyond the Byzantine frontier in the capital, Constantinople. Here the language employed was cruder and the tone more violent. The objective, too, was entirely different: first, to answer for the humiliating defeat of Byzantine's forces and seizure of its former provinces by Muslims, and second, to touch the hearts of Christian converts to Islam and bring them back into the fold.

Nicetas (d. ca. 300/912), a teacher at the court in Constantinople, composed a refutation of the Qur'an, destined to became an enduring classic in the Christian controversy against Islam. Of the Qur'an he asserted "there is one thing that must be stressed about this coarse booklet, and it is this: its author knew, in his raving, that this mythical and barbarous belief that he had fabricated could never be accepted by Christians and Jews: consequently he plundered the divine prophecies found in the Divine Scriptures." Of Muhammad, Nicetas had little better to say than that "he was by nature perverse and talkative, or rather stupid and bestial, a coward too, quick to anger, distrustful and arrogant . . . as to right judgement and clear thought, his speech is entirely lacking of them."[17]

It was not, however, this kind of polemic with which Muslim

scholars had to contend within the boundaries of their own community. Increasingly in their day-to-day contact with Christians and Jews, Muslims were obliged to supply solutions to theological questions which, in the immediate aftermath of the conquests, they had not needed to confront. John's defence of Christ's divinity, *based upon the Qur'an*, could not go unchallenged. Muslims had acknowledged Jesus as a prophet of Allah and conceded, too, his virgin birth. But Jesus himself, they said, had been neither slain nor crucified (2:157–158) but rather had been elevated by Allah into the realm of his special grace, a position that (from his writings) John was well aware of. From the Muslim point of view, they had generously met the Christian more than half way, and felt they did not deserve the dismissal of their Prophet as a heretic and their scripture as a collection of "idle tales," to quote John once again.

Thus, one aspect of the development of the Muslim community as a community of faith (as distinct from a conquering elite) was the role played by the convert in his new faith. A consequence, for example, of the growing numbers of Christian converts was perhaps linked to the growing veneration of the Prophet. The portrait of him as a mere human, alluded to in scripture and confirmed by many *hadith*s on his earthly affairs, gave way to the glorious Tradition in Ibn Ishaq's biography, cited in the previous chapter, of Muhammad's night journey to Jerusalem, where he prayed in the company of the prophets, and his ascension into heaven and the presence of Allah. This Tradition seems to have fulfilled a spiritual need. Ibn Ishaq's Sunni version was later retold by the Shi'ah, where 'Ali played a part in the drama along with the Prophet; poetic versions cast in terms of Sufi mystical spirituality also became renowned. The parallel with the Resurrection of Jesus notwithstanding, Muslims were able to maintain correctly their denial of Jesus' divinity, while not committing the equal blasphemy of raising the Prophet to the rank of a deity.

During the formative period of four to five centuries following the death of the Prophet, Muslim sources record debates between the *'ulama'* and Christians and Jews. The authenticity of the debates may be doubted, but not their purpose. A central concern was to establish proofs of Muhammad's mission by appealing to the scriptures of "the Peoples of the Book," where his coming was alleged to have been foretold.

In one such encounter, the Shi'ah leader (*Imam*) 'Ali al-Rida (d. 203/815) questioned the Jewish exilarch and the Christian patriarch in Baghdad concerning references in the Torah and the Gospels which, he claimed, foretold the Prophet's coming. 'Ali asked both to confirm the presence of a passage in Isaiah which said, "O people, I see the form of a rider on the ass clothed in a raiment of light, and I see the rider on a camel with a brightness like that of the moon." The two men agreed it was so said. Then 'Ali asked the patriarch whether the following prophecy appeared in the Gospel of John when Jesus spoke, saying, "I am going to my Lord and your Lord, and the Paraclete will come. He it is who will witness to me about the truth as I have witnessed to him . . . and he it is who will expose the evil deeds of the peoples and who will shatter the designs of the unbelievers." The patriarch agreed it was so said. The conclusion was, therefore, that Isaiah had prophesied Jesus' riding upon an ass and Muhammad upon a camel, while mention of the Paraclete by Jesus was construed as a reference to the Prophet as well. The method of searching for biblical quotations, whether real or spurious, was a common means of validating the beliefs of any particular faction.

Beside the main point of the debate, establishing the scriptures' forecast of the Prophet's coming, it may have had an underlying purpose in inter-Muslim polemics. That is, it would illustrate the *Imam*'s formidable knowledge of and special insight into the scriptures of the "Peoples of the Book." It would thereby have supported the Shi'ah view of the unique spiritual nature of their *Imams* as against the more worldly figures of the Sunni Caliphs. Moreover, if the debate itself is imaginary rather than real, it is possible that the ideas it contained were circulated by persons unknown who possessed a close knowledge of the Torah or the Gospels, that is, converts from Judaism and Christianity employing their own scriptural knowledge in the service of their new faith.[18]

On a more mundane level, however, Christians and, to a lesser extent, Jews and other sects did present a challenge to Muslims in their evolution toward establishing a dominant religious culture. This was another side of the problem seen by the *'ulama'*, who urged upon the faithful a proper observance of the *sunnah* and decried the introduction of innovation. The brilliant essayist al-Jahiz (d. 256/869) penned a polemic on how to refute the Christians, particularly those of Iraq, among whom he lived, in response to official alarm at their influence upon the vulnerable Muslim masses. The epistle was intended to provide Muslims with answers to Christian objections to Islam. Al-Jahiz also conveyed the impression that the *'ulama'*'s worries about the community's spiritual health were justified. He wrote, "a cause for the admiration accorded by the masses to the Christians is the fact that they are [government] secretaries and servants to kings, physicians to nobles, perfumers, and money changers." The Christians' high standing in Muslim society, on the other hand, was unfortunate for other reasons as well. Al-Jahiz notes their filthy habits: they were uncircumcised, did not purify themselves after sexual intercourse, and ate pork. Coupled with this was their pursuit of arguments with Muslims pointing out contradictory statements in the *hadith*, their weak chains of authority, and the ambiguous verses of the Qur'an. These questions they would take up with weak-minded persons or those without staunch faith, causing in them perplexity and confusion. And worse, says al-Jahiz acidly, it was a tragedy that every Muslim regarded himself as a master dialectical theologian (*mutakallim*), worthy and capable of debating with an atheist![19] Al-Jahiz concludes his essay stating that Christian doctrines were themselves impossible to comprehend, especially the concept of divinity, inasmuch as no two Christians, whether Nestorian, Melchite, or Jacobite, could agree on what it meant. From his point of view, though, the appeal of Christian doctrine was not a threat to Islam so much as the corrupting influence of individual Christians upon impressionable Muslims of half-hearted faith, the very problem which concerned the *'ulama'*.

A second "refutation" of the same period was written by the famous physician and man of culture 'Ali b. Sahl b. Rabban al-Tabari (d. 241/855). Al-Tabari was a Nestorian Christian who, at the age of seventy, converted to Islam. The main theme of his refutation of Christianity was that it could not be true since Jesus is in one and the same aspect both creator and created. This position could not be sustained within a genuine monotheistic faith since confusion arises as to whether Jesus *is* God or a second God; moreover, Jesus seems to contradict himself, claiming both that he is God and that he was sent by God; and how could God the Father be creator of all and Jesus uncreated? Al-Tabari's argument, doubtless written with sincerity, may help explain his conversion. As a Nestorian, he possibly saw Christ very much as Muslims perceived him, as a man used or sent by God, that is, a prophet. In any event, the line of thought pursued by al-Tabari was followed up by later Muslim writers. It contributed to drawing the line between Muslim and Christian belief with greater clarity, by focusing upon the crucial question of the nature of God/Allah while underwriting Muslims' own belief, supported by their scripture, that Jesus was a prophet in the same cosmic chain culminating in and completed by Muhammad.

Despite polemical outbursts in the relationship between Muslims and their Christian subjects, there are examples of acceptance as well. In a Tradition from the Prophet he is given to say that

> If anyone testifies that there is no God but Allah alone, who has no partner, that Muhammad is His servant and messenger, that Jesus is Allah's servant and messenger, the son of His handmaid, His word which he cast into Mary and a spirit from Him, and that paradise and hell are real, Allah will cause him to enter paradise no matter what he has done.[20]

In another Tradition a Companion, Abu Hurayrah, reported that the Prophet said, "Except Mary and her son, no human being is born without the devil touching him, so that he cries out because of the devil's touch."[21] Such Traditions may have helped ease the entry of ordinary Christians into the Muslim fold, but to churchmen they were danger signals of potential defeat.

The Muslim community, through triumph and failure, was coming of age. The conquests had altered the political, linguistic, and religious map of the Middle East and beyond. Arabization and Islamization went hand in hand as the new culture took shape. The *'ulama'* played out their roles as the chief agents and architects of the transformation within the burgeoning urban centers where the new religious sciences and learning flourished. Islam had displaced the paganism of its birthplace and now rivaled and surpassed the older scriptural faiths in their own places of birth.

But triumph was purchased at a price. The pristine community of Medina and Mecca suffered division in the great *fitnah* between 'Ali and Mu'awiyah. The first century was peppered with revolts of disgruntled Shi'ah and Khawarij. The early second century witnessed a major convulsion as the Umayyad Caliphs were all but annihilated by the family of Abbasids claiming legitimacy to the Caliphate on the basis of kinship with the Prophet. The center of power shifted with them, from Damascus to Baghdad in Iraq, but any real unity under the Caliphate was soon challenged. An Umayyad refugee restored the family's political fortunes by founding a dynasty in al-Andalus (300–418/912–1027). The province of Egypt secured a strong measure of autonomy under the Ikhshidid dynasty (324–359/935–969) before falling in the mid fourth/tenth century to the Shi'ah dynasty of the Fatimids (359–567/969–1171). By establishing a rival Caliphate, it posed the greatest threat to the Sunni authorities in Baghdad. However, even in the heartland of the Abbasid domains, Baghdad and Iraq had fallen under the effective control of the Buyid family (334–373/945–983) of Shi'ah mercenaries who also controlled large areas of western Persia. Further east, many of the Persian districts supported lines of native hereditary governors. Unlike the Fatimids of Egypt, however, these dynasties, including the Buyids, were content to wield power as vassals of the Abbasid Caliphs, despite their decline from the earlier days of glory.

Amidst the political upheavals, Islamic culture nevertheless sustained its growth toward maturity. Rival positions on a myriad of religious matters still existed. At the same time a coherently rich and varied religious culture was coming into being and signs of future growth were already at hand. Arabic, the language of revelation, continued to hold the dominant position as the medium of religious learning. Yet on the eastern fringes of Islamic domains, in Khurasan, Transoxania, and Khwarazm, the absolute primacy of Arabic was beginning to be challenged during this same period. Here literary expression in (New) Persian was asserting itself, almost exclusively at first in epic or lyric poetry. There were important prose contributions of a religious nature, however, such as an original Qur'an commentary in Persian and a translation from the Arabic of al-Tabari's monumental exegesis. Theological works in Persian of a polemical nature appeared in this period as well. The Persians differed from other Islamized peoples, like the Berbers of North Africa, in possessing a culture strong enough to adopt the new faith yet retain its own distinctiveness. Even the Turkish dynasty of the Ghaznavids (384–432/994–1040), whose eastern dominions stretched from modern-day Tehran to the Ganges valley in India, became thoroughly Persianized in their cultural interests, although it would not be long before the first works in the Turkish language would also appear. Islamic culture's remarkable capacity was being and would continue to be demonstrated – absorption and adaptation – while remaining true to a vision of salvation focused upon the submission to the will of a One, Unique, and Omnipotent deity, Allah.

8. The Prophet's Mosque, Medina

9. The Koh Pan Yi Mosque, Thailand

10. Main Gateway of the Friday Mosque, Fatehpur Sikri, India

11. Village Mosque in Mali

12. The Ruimveldt Jamaat Mosque, Guyana

13. Panfilov Mosque, Kazakhstan

14. Cristo de la Luz, Toledo

15. Mihdar Mosque, Tarim, Yemen

16. The Ahmediye (or Blue) mosque, Istanbul

17. Jami' mosque, Qavzin, Iran

PART 2

Islamic teaching and practice

CHAPTER 3

Divine will and the law

THE DIVINE SOURCES

The most impressive and characteristic monument in the religious culture of Islam is the *shari'ah*. This is the expression of the *will* of Allah manifested in his guidance of Muhammad and preserved by the community in their scripture, the Qur'an. The will of Allah, the sole metaphysical reality, was both eternal and immutable. Allah had not, however, disclosed his will solely through the medium of revelation, but also through the deeds and sayings of the Prophet Muhammad. Once the text of scripture had been established, the attention of the *'ulama'* turned to the community's affairs under the Prophet, for Muhammad had been ordered to guide his followers saying to them, *if you love Allah, then follow me, and Allah will love you and forgive you your sins; and Allah is forgiving, a dispenser of grace* (3:31).

A keynote of the Muslims' faith is implicit here. This is the emphasis upon direct human responsibility before Allah. Each individual who personally chooses to obey him directly confronts the divine will expressed in the *shari'ah* and strives to conduct his or her life according to that imperative. This is without the aid of either an intermediary or some manner of collective responsibility. The essence of the obligation to Allah is to act as his vicegerent on earth, ordering the good and forbidding wrong (3:104 and 3:110). In other words, it is a duty to accept responsibility for the establishment of proper public order. The law, as the concrete expression of Allah's will and guidance, is therefore central to the individual and collective Muslim identity. It constitutes the sole blueprint for the good society. Muslims, of course, hold that adherence to the law is demanded of Muslims alone. By implication, however, it is also believed that the same law provides the securest way for all peoples to conduct their lives. This is so because the will of the One Creator is one for all.[1]

From the two fundamental sources of scripture and the Prophet's deeds and sayings (*sunnah*), the *'ulama'* derived the law (*fiqh*), first by establishing rules and procedures which developed as the science of jurisprudence or the "roots of the law" (*usul al-fiqh*). Here discussion will focus upon the classical theory of the law as formulated within the Sunni community. The Shi'ah (who will be treated fully in a later chapter) and the Kharijite minorities equally accepted the primacy and immutability of the *shari'ah*, although each differed from the Sunnis in its method of understanding the divine will.

In very general terms, the two basic sources were scrutinized in minutest detail for their essential meaning. Scholars employed all the tools of analysis available to them. These included philological examination of the Qur'anic text and determining the reliability of *hadith* reports from the Prophet through study of their chains of transmission (*isnads*). Exegetical activity, albeit unsophisticated by later standards, commenced from earliest times and reports attributed to the Prophet's cousin 'Abdallah b. 'Abbas (d. 68/688) were handed down, covering the entire Qur'anic text. Much of the work of the first scholars centered upon an examination of the language of the Qur'an, since in scripture Allah declared that *We have sent it down as a discourse* (qur'an) *in the Arabic tongue so that you might encompass it with your reason* (12:2). Building upon efforts of the previous century, Ma'mar b. al-Muthanna (d. 210/825) and his contemporary Yahya b. Ziyad al-Farra (d. 207/822) each produced commentaries governed chiefly by lexical and syntactical considerations. The apex of this scholarly trend, however, was achieved by Muhammad b. Jarir al-Tabari (d. 310/923), the famed historian whom we encountered at the beginning of the previous chapter. His monumental work (of thirty published volumes), which proceeded verse by verse through the whole Qur'an, embraced every conceivable aspect of investigation: from variant readings of the text to the definitions of rare or unusual words and phrases, from varying interpretation of legal and theological issues to an account of historical and legendary allusions in the text.

By means of this collective, scholarly enterprise, an approximate understanding of the will of Allah was ultimately achieved. Already the process assumed rational investigation, whether in the exegesis of scripture or in judging the greater moral fitness of one *hadith* transmitter over another. In the sphere of judges' (*qudah*, s. *qadi*) application of the law, other aspects of reasoning, inherent from the beginning, were used as well. Discretionary or sound opinion (*ra'y*) has been mentioned in the previous chapter. When a judge exercised his discretion to extend the ruling in one case to another by virtue of a common element shared by the two, the process was known as analogical deduction (*qiyas*). An early term meaning approval or preference (*istihsan*) was employed when a judge's opinion reflected some measure of public interest or convenience. Moreover, the notion of consensus (*ijma'*) could apply to the anonymous agreement on points of the law among scholars of a particular locale or of a given generation.

The problem was further complicated by the need to account for the variety of local customs in the lands outside Arabia proper brought under the control of Muslim authority. Many of these practices were simply rationalized in Islamic terms, justified by means of argument from the basic sources. This intellectual effort, which is implied in each of the technical terms just noted, was described broadly as *ijtihad*. Literally meaning "exertion" or "effort," it was the term applied to a jurist's deduction of a point of law from the sources, or to his attempt to find a link between them and local practice. The expert who performed this task was a *mujtahid*. The law finally embraced two broad sets of relationships, the first being the spiritual relationship between Allah and humankind (*'ibadat*) and the second, the normative relationship between one human being and another (*mu'amalat*). Both were believed to be governed by the guiding will of Allah.

THE SCHOOLS AND THEIR MASTERS

In the elaboration of the law and its methods, a place of special merit is accorded to four scholar-jurists (*fuqaha'*, s. *faqih*; also *mujtahid*) who were recognized as the founders of the Sunni legal schools (*madhahib*, s. *madhhab*). Together these four schools comprise the Sunni understanding of the *shari'ah*. Important data and the occasional telling anecdote concerning each of these outstanding figures were recorded by the author of one of the most famous biographical dictionaries of the medieval Islamic period. The genre itself is an important original contribution to the historical development of Islamic literature. In his work, Ibn Khallikan (d. 681/1282) included notices of over eight hundred eminent men and women from every region and walk of life in the Muslim community. In the following accounts, he describes these scholars as his contemporaries perceived them.

Abu Hanifah

The earliest was Abu Hanifah (d. 150/767), after whom the Hanafi *madhhab* is named. He was a non-Arab native of Kufa in Iraq, whose father had been born a Muslim, but whose grandfather had been a freed slave. Ibn Khallikan casts doubt on the claims of Abu Hanifah's disciples that he had personally known some of the Prophet's Companions. He was recognized, moreover, as a man of the highest qualities: learned, a performer of good works, remarkable for his self-denial, humble spirit, devotion and pious awe of Allah. He was a cloth merchant by trade.

The Abbasid Caliph al-Mansur appointed him to the post of judge (*qadi*) in Baghdad, an order Abu Hanifah refused for fear that he would be unable to execute the terms of the religious law unimpeded by political interference. This was not an uncommon attitude for the '*ulama*' of the time to adopt; either their hands were tied by the exercise of political power and preference, or less scrupulous members of the judges' fraternity were prepared to discredit their posts and play their masters' game. In the face of the Caliph's anger, Abu Hanifah declared himself unfit for the post. "You lie! you are fit!," shouted al-Mansur. "You have now decided in my favor," retorted Abu Hanifah; "is it lawful for you to appoint a liar as *qadi* over those whom Allah has confided to your care?" Abu Hanifah suffered the punishment of the pious, a prison cell.[2] Almost none of Abu Hanifah's writings has survived. He was apparently a noted exponent of analogy (*qiyas*), and in the later development of his school "preference" (*istihsan*) continued to be recognized where the strict application of analogy could have led to undesirable results. Two of his disciples, Abu Yusuf (d. 182/798) and Muhammad al-Shaybani (d. 189/804), recorded his teachings in their own works, adding their own commentary where they disagreed with the master. Abu Yusuf, unlike his teacher, did accept the post of chief *qadi* of Baghdad during the later reign of the Caliph Harun al-Rashid (d. 193/809).

Malik b. Anas

The second jurist was the younger Medinan contemporary of Abu Hanifah, Abu 'Abdallah Malik b. Anas, who died in his eighties in 179/795. The Maliki school of law is named after him. Ibn Khallikan records this thumbnail sketch of his appearance: he was a tall, well-attired man of ruddy complexion with a balding forehead, who neither shaved his moustache nor dyed his grey hair. Malik had a profound devotion for the Traditions of the Prophet, which he would only transmit in a state of ritual purity, after having performed his ablutions, so that he could feel the import of the Prophet's words as he repeated them to others.[3] His major work, the *Muwatta* (meaning the *Trodden Way*, that is, the agreed practice, or *'amal* of Medina), is the earliest surviving textbook of law (*fiqh*). It contains some two thousand Traditions (*hadith*). The arrangement of the book is by legal topic, beginning with the prescribed rituals of prayer, fasting and the like and ending with chapters on sales and credit. In this way he covers the two relationships mentioned above, that of man's ritual obligations (*'ibadat*) to Allah and the normative behavior between individuals in society (*mu'amalat*). He often refers to the Qur'an and the Prophet's *sunnah*, as well as to the old Medinese lore and practice which he took for granted were the uncorrupted ways of the early Muslims and, indeed, of Muhammad himself. Malikis also used the legal method of having regard for the public interest. Later Malikis extended the Medinan concept of "local practice" (*'amal*) to the judicial practices of other localities.

Al-Shafi'i

The next jurist of the quartet was, among his contemporaries, the most influential of them all, although fewer Muslims were to follow his "school" than the others. Abu 'Abdallah Muhammad b. Idris al-Shafi'i, a descendant of the Prophet's tribe of Quraysh, was born near Gaza in Palestine. He commenced his study of the law in Mecca before moving to Medina, where he became a student of Malik, who was impressed by the young man's talent and precocious progress. Two years' study in Baghdad, where he met disciples of Abu Hanifah, preceded a further move to Cairo, where he died in 204/820, aged fifty-four. From him the Shafi'i school of law derives its name.

Ibn Khallikan, who was himself a Shafi'i, notes that his accomplishments in the religious sciences were unmatched by anyone of his day, and that he was also an expert in poetry. He was, it is said, destined for greatness. His mother, while carrying him, dreamed that the planet Jupiter issued forth from her womb and proceeded to Egypt, where it fell, a portion of its rays touching every city on earth. Experts in dream interpretation (*mu'abbirun*) declared that the mother would give birth to a learned man who would communicate his knowledge to the people of Egypt alone, but whose influence would spread to other countries.[4] As is often the case with such forecasts, the course of events proved it correct.

Al-Shafi'i's legal production was extensive and systematic. He is said to have written more than one hundred books, some of a polemical nature on various aspects of the law. The single most important work is his comprehensive treatment of the roots of the law, simply entitled *The Epistle (al-Risalah)*.[5] It was, indeed, the first treatise of its kind. Later jurists debated the finer points of the theoretical structure erected by al-Shafi'i, but few challenged the validity of his overall thesis.

In general, he refined and systematized the legal thinking of his predecessors, including Abu Hanifa and Malik, seeking to reduce the range of differences in the theoretical approach to the law. Typical, too, of his thought is the rigorous application of philological distinctions and linguistic arguments to his analysis of scripture and Traditions. His starting point was to insist that the whole of the *shari'ah* could in principle be derived from the Qur'an, which itself provided the necessary indications for the development of a methodology of the law. This ensured that the law (*fiqh*) would reflect the human confrontation with the divine, the very basis upon which the community was founded.

More crucially, and in a departure from Maliki and Hanafi views, he insisted that the concept of *sunnah* be narrowed. That is, the practice of the community *under* the Prophet's direct leadership and inspiration following his death should now be taken to mean simply the practice *of* the Prophet himself. Prophetic *hadith* alone would be considered the sole authoritative source of the *sunnah*. The proof of origin must be explicit in a Tradition's sound chain of authorities (*isnad*) regressing from the last narrator to the Prophet himself. In this manner al-Shafi'i perhaps hoped to eliminate innovation (*bid'ah*). He could not, however, have been entirely secure in this hope. A "sound" *isnad* could be attached to Traditions already in circulation whether or not they originated with Muhammad. Moreover, the pious could weld "sound" *isnads* to new traditions in the genuine belief that whatever was of real value for the community at large must have been uttered by the Prophet as Allah's agent.

Next to the Qur'an and the Prophet's *sunnah*, al-Shafi'i recognized as the third root of the law strict analogical reasoning (*qiyas*). This meant that analogy must be firmly based on the two material sources of the law, the Qur'an and the *sunnah*. Here he hoped to eliminate or severly restrict the use of the jurists' discretionary opinion based on *ra'y* or *istihsan*.

Finally, he adopted as the fourth root the general consensus (*ijma'*) of all Muslims on essential matters of the law. The Muslim community as a whole, he argued, could not be ignorant of a ruling given by Allah and the Prophet.

We accept the decision of the public because we have to obey their authority, and we know that wherever there are sunnas of the Prophet, the public cannot be ignorant of them, although it is possible that some are, and we know that the public can neither agree on anything contrary to the sunna of the Prophet or on an error.[6]

This principle continued to be held by the Sunni majority as a description of itself. However, in terms of its formulation as a root (*asl*, pl. *usul*) of the law, later legal theorists adopted the position that consensus meant the unanimous and infallible agreement of the Sunni scholars (*mujtahidun*) alone, and not of the entire community. Later scholars of the Shafi'i school also accepted this position. It seems that in practice this resulted in a practice al-Shafi'i had not perhaps intended. That is, the scholarly consensus of each of the four schools was henceforth able to interpret Prophetic Traditions in the manner most appropriate to its own needs.

What has been described in modern studies as the "classical theory" of Islamic law comprised the following four roots or principles: the Qur'an, the *sunnah* of the Prophet as contained in recognized Traditions, the method of reasoning by analogy (*qiyas*), and the consensus (*ijma'*) of scholars of the community. Much of this final theory, as we have seen, was due in no small measure to the efforts of al-Shafi'i's powerful mind, whose theories and arguments extended, as foretold, well beyond the frontiers of Egypt where he composed them. He did not invent the four principles of the law, but rather systematized and crystallized the several elements which had already existed albeit not always in easy juxtaposition.

This was al-Shafi'i's legacy. Not all scholars, however, were satisfied with his doctrine as it stood, or even as it was modified, despite his underlining the importance of Traditions from the Prophet as the second source of the law. Those who were utterly dedicated to Traditions preferred to reduce the use of reason to an absolute minimum. They chose instead to base a point of doctrine entirely on the plain text of a *hadith* from the Prophet. But, as their opponents were quick to point out, the dedicated traditionist would rather argue from a weak Tradition than employ a strong analogy.

Ahmad b. Hanbal

The eponym of the last legal school is, by contrast to al-Shafi'i, identified with the greatest traditionist scholar of his time. Ahmad b. Hanbal was born in Baghdad and died there in 241/855. While he is regarded as a theologian and a jurist as well, most of his works are collections of Traditions. Like many before him, he traveled widely in Iraq, Syria, and the Yemen, but acquired his main training in Mecca and Medina. Ibn Khallikan claims that he knew a million *hadith*s by heart.

His major surviving work is a collection of Traditions, numbering around thirty thousand, arranged according to the name of the first transmitter cited in the *isnad*, from the first Caliphs and Companions to those from different Tradition centers, like Kufa and Basrah. Hence it is called a *musnad* (from *isnad*)-type collection, an awkward arrangement unless one does indeed know the Traditions by heart. It was possibly deliberately intended to be distinguished from Malik's *Muwatta'* and other collections of Traditions which were arranged by legal topic.

Like Abu Hanifah before him, he fell foul of the Caliph's wrath. In this case it was over the vexed and explosive theological question of whether the Qur'an was "created" or "uncreated." Rationalist theologians, backed by Caliphal authority, attempted to force judges to accept their doctrine of the Qur'an's createdness. Ibn Hanbal vigorously defended the view of its essential *un*created nature and suffered beating and imprisonment for his stubbornness. After two years in prison, he was allowed the restricted freedom of his home, where he conducted private classes in the study of Traditions, and eventually he regained a public post as professor. The period is remembered in the sources as the *mihnah* or trial, and Ibn Hanbal is acclaimed the star defense witness against willful and arbitrary political power.

He was consulted by ordinary people on a wide range of matters pertaining to the correct conduct of life and this activity is reflected in his work on *Legal Questions* (*Masa'il*). He did not, like al-Shafi'i, compose a work on the principles of the law. His views, however, can be deduced from his writings. He argued that the Qur'an must be understood in its literal sense, without resort to allegorical interpretation, and that all Traditions from the Prophet regarded as sound in his time comprised the unquestioned second source of the law. He did nevertheless recognize that in order to resolve contradictions between *hadith*, to reconcile divergent views, and to draw deductions from them, some minimum degree of personal judgment was required. The third source of the law he regarded as the legal opinions (*fatawa*) of the leading Companions, since they were best placed to understand and practice the Prophet's *sunnah*. Finally, he regarded *ijma'* as meaning the general consensus of a truth based upon the Qur'an and the *sunnah*.

Ahmad b. Hanbal's fame, enhanced by official punishment which conferred upon him a badge of honor in the eyes of many, had reached such heights that when he died huge crowds of men and women attended his funeral. A significant impact was apparently also made on the conversion curve, for Ibn Khallikan reports that 20,000 Jews, Christians, and Magians became Muslims that same day! As befitted his popular image, he was buried in the martyrs' cemetery in Baghdad, which became a place of visitation by the pious. Ibn Hanbal stamped his mark upon his school: a passionate devotion to the *hadith* of the Prophet as opposed to those, like the Hanafis and the Shafi'is, whom he regarded as bestowing a suspiciously dangerous emphasis upon human reason in the deduction of the law. Ibn Hanbal's attachment to the Prophet's example is said to have been mirrored in his practice of dyeing his hair light red. And, since he knew of no Tradition stating that Muhammad had ever eaten watermelon, he avoided partaking of this fruit as well.

These four preeminent figures form an unbroken chain in the view of later Sunni scholarship. Al-Shafi'i had been a student of Malik and Ahmad b. Hanbal a student of al-Shafi'i; and to complete the circle, Abu Hanifah is said to have died the very day al-Shafi'i was born!

THE TRADITION COLLECTORS

Scholars were still aware in the decades after Ibn Hanbal's death that within the expanding pool of Traditions in general, there existed forgeries. Others were simply considered weak or unreliable. Criticism of *hadith* was the inevitable response. Books were written dedicated to the subject of deliberately fabricated *hadith*, called *mawdu'at*. Another response contributed to the growth of a separate discipline connected with the emergence of the biographical dictionary. *Hadith* criticism involved the scrutiny of persons appearing in the chains of authority and an assessment of their individual moral probity as transmitters of Traditions. Not everyone passed the test.

One of the most important of the these dictionaries to appear in the period after al-Shafi'i and Ahmad b. Hanbal was compiled by Muhammad b. Isma'il al-Bukhari (d. 256/870). He had begun to learn Traditions at the age of ten. During his extensive travels to gather them he is said to have met more than a thousand persons from whom he received *hadith*s. While still a young man in Medina he began his dictionary and catalogued all those whose names were known to him and who appeared in the *isnad*s of the prophetic *hadith*s. It included over 3,500 names. He chose not to pass judgment on the worth of each transmitter. Instead, he noted the persons from whom each had received Traditions and those to whom each had passed them on. In any case, it was an invaluable research tool for the later preparation of his major collection of Traditions, which took him sixteen years to complete. It was a work of devotion in the literal sense. He reduced an assembled mass of 600,000 Traditions to around 2,750 (not counting repetitions). Before entering a single one in his book, notes Ibn Khallikan, he performed the ritual ablutions and prayed. Al-Bukhari's collection is known as a *musannaf*, that is, the Traditions are arranged by subject matter, and embraced all of the important topics required in the study of the law. Indeed, it covered topics which were not part of the *fiqh*, for example, Allah's creation of the world, paradise and hell and Qur'anic commentary.

In the century following his death, the work was already acknowledged by the community as one of the two "canonical" collections of its kind each containing the Traditions of recognized authoritative transmitters. The other collection, also a *musannaf*, was prepared by his contemporary, Muslim b. al-Hajjaj (d. 261/875). Together, these two collections contain more than 5,500 traditions (not taking repetitions into account) all judged to be sound (*sahih*).

The half-century between al-Bukhari's death and the turn of the fourth/tenth century was a period of feverish activity on the part of Tradition collectors. Four other collections were compiled in this time, all of the *musannaf* type, although none achieved quite the status as the first two. These were the works of Ibn Majah al-Qazwini (d. 273/887), Abu Da'ud al-Sijistani (d. 275/888), Muhammad b. 'Isa al-Tirmidhi

(d. 279/892), and Ahmad b. Shuʿayb al-Nasaʾi (d. 303/915).

One of the results of this activity was the emergence of an effective religious homogeneity within the Sunni community. This was achieved, moreover, without the presence or need of either a hierarchical authority or councils and synods to determine the parameters of the community's practice and belief. By the beginning of the fourth/tenth century there were perhaps some five hundred "schools" of law functioning. The number gradually reduced thereafter to the four major schools whose origins we have outlined above.

One of these transient groups was the "school" of Muhammad b. Jarir al-Tabari (d. 310/923), the famous historian and exegete. Another of the failed ventures, however, deserves mention here. At the time the traditionists were compiling their definitive collections, Daʾud b. ʿAli b. Khalaf (d. 270/884) founded the Zahiri school of law. Born in Kufa, Iraq, he became a professor in Baghdad. He is described as a fervent follower of al-Shafiʿi and was known as a man of great piety and self-mortification. The only hint of criticism against him is that his intellect was greater than his learning. His main principle was to rely exclusively on the literal meaning (*zahir*) of the Qurʾan and *hadith*, and to reject the technical methods of legal reasoning, all of which were considered subjective and arbitrary. Against their opponents, who were not slow to point out their use of deduction from a proof text, the Zahiris retorted that its meaning was already *implied* in it. A second principle of the school was that consensus could only properly mean the *ijmaʿ* of the Companions of the Prophet, for it was in their time that real agreement was possible as they formed a circle of members well known to each other. Daʾud's school was eventually excluded from the Sunni consensus, but his thought did prove powerfully attractive to many scholars of later generations, among them the Andalusian Ibn Hazm (d. 456/1065) of Cordoba, one of the most outstanding intellectuals of his century. Far from being a defense employed by the gullible and simple-minded, the literalist approach to the divine will is marked, in the case of Ibn Hazm and many others to the present day, by a profound appreciation of the limits of reason together with a pious passion for eternal verities which were believed to reside only in the word of Allah.

Furthermore, in the field of the law the fourth/tenth century reflected the entrenchment of the traditionists who were subsequently able to monopolize the education of young jurists in the mosque (*masjid*). They also succeeded in excluding their opponents, rationalist theologians of the kind who had persecuted Ahmad b. Hanbal, from this institution of learning. The *musannafs*, by virtue of their organization by topic, created easy access to the amorphous body of Tradition, study of which formed part of the legal curriculum.

REGIONAL DISTRIBUTION

The later geographical spread of the four major schools of law may be briefly noted here. The Hanafi *madhhab* remained strong in Iraq, where it began, and Syria. Early on it moved eastward to Afghanistan and the sub-continent of India. The British encountered the Hanafi school during their long sojourn in India, and a number of Hanafi treatises were translated into English for use by British administrators in their dealings with the Muslim population. It also achieved exclusive recognition in the territories of the Ottoman Empire, which tottered to its demise during the First World War. The Maliki *madhhab*, on the other hand, spread westward from Medina through Egypt, to almost the whole of North Africa, and to Central and West Africa, where there still exist significant Muslim communities. It was also the predominant school in al-Andalus down to the Christian reconquest of the Iberian peninsula. The Shafi'i school originated in Cairo, where the tomb of its founder is still preserved. It exists in Egypt today, in parts of Arabia and East Africa, in some regions of central Asia and some coastal areas of India. Its major presence, however, is in Indonesia, Malaysia, and the remainder of southeast Asia. The Hanbalis had a slower start than the other schools partly because they were perceived for a time more as a theological school of traditionists than a *madhhab*. Indeed, apart from its two main centers of activity, Baghdad and Damascus, it experienced a period of decline until its fortunes were restored by the revival movement of Muhammad b. 'Abd al-Wahhab (d. 1201/1787) in Arabia, which has led in the present century to the school becoming officially recognized in the state of Saudi Arabia.

METHODS OF THE JURISTS

The scholars who elaborated the detailed rules of procedure by which the law could be determined were the jurists (*fuqaha'*, s. *faqih*), the experts in *fiqh*. The literature produced by or for them comprises the most substantial output of any field of Islamic culture. Each school eventually compiled its own compendium of legal rules, generally multi-volumed works covering the fields of *'ibadat* and *mu'amalat*. Jurisprudence was divided into studies on the sources of the law (*usul al-fiqh*) and those dealing with more specialized subjects of the law's application (*furu' al-fiqh*), such as marriage, divorce, inheritance (*fara'id*), religious endowments (*awqaf*, s. *waqf*), legal devices (*hiyal*), and so on. Scholars produced works dealing with the administration of justice, market inspectors' manuals, legal documents, comparative works on the differences between the various schools, bio-bibliographical dictionaries on the members of the separate schools, handbooks for judges, and more. These works are too numerous and technical for even a survey of the material not to be burdensome for the reader. It would seem more pertinent to highlight some of the definitions and methods jurists employed in reaching an understanding of the law. In this manner some appreciation of the complex nature of Islamic law may be gained.

Legal capacity is vested in every person by virtue of his or her dignity as a human being, but a person possessing full legal responsibility (*mukallaf*) must be of sound mind and have reached the age of majority. Thus the insane and small children are wholly incapable, while others may be judged to be deficient in some way in their capacities.

Next, the content of the law comprises the commands, prohibitions, or other permitted acts which are incumbent upon a legally responsible individual. The *mukallaf* is not obliged to act on another person's behalf. Nor can he or she be judged guilty if forced against his or her will to commit a prohibited act or if, conversely, he or she is prevented from fulfilling a command.

To reiterate, the source of all law is Allah. His will is known to the *mukallaf* either directly from revelation or indirectly by means of inference and deduction. *Judgement rests with none but Allah alone* (6:57). Some scholars found the authority for each of the *sources* of the law, as described above by al-Shafi'i, alluded to in the following verse: *O you who have attained to faith! Pay heed to Allah* [the Qur'an, as Allah's revealed word] *and pay heed to the Prophet* [the *sunnah*] *and those from among you who have been entrusted with authority* [consensus, *ijma'*, of the religious scholars]; *and if you are at variance over any matter, refer it to Allah and the Prophet* [analogy, *qiyas*, on the basis of decisions that follow from these sources], *if you believe in Allah and the Last Day. This is best for you and best in the end* (4:59). At this point, however, scholars held different views as to how his will was to be precisely identified and deduced.

Disputes centered upon the problems, familiar also to Christian and Jewish scholars, of whether right or wrong conduct can be known by human reason independently of revelation and whether there is any essential conflict between the judgments of reason and those of God. The general Muslim position historically on these matters has been that since human reason is liable to error and, moreover, liable to produce a multiplicity of conflicting views leading to confusion and corruption, the only certain basis for discerning right from wrong is to follow what Allah has decreed. At the same time, one must keep in mind that owing to the compelling urgency of the divine command, no effort is to be spared in comprehending it. The exercise of such effort (*ijtihad*) became an obligation upon the entire community. It was facilitated by the Tradition which stated that *ijtihad* conferred upon its practitioner (*mujtahid*) two rewards in the afterlife if his judgment was correct, and one if it was wrong.[7] In other words, there was no sin attached to the effort, whatever the result. Even later Hanbali scholars, whose master, Ahmad b. Hanbal, had rejected all but the most minimal degree of personal judgment, accepted the use of analogical reasoning in matters of law. The divine law joins ethical and more strictly legal matters together, thereby encouraging the harmonization of conscience and the law.

The evaluation of actions

This combination of ethics and the law is the characteristic style of Islamic legislation expressed in the five values or qualifications (*al-ahkam al-khamsah*), a term and classification devised by the jurists. When an act is assessed as obligatory, it is called *wajib* or *fard*; when it is absolutely forbidden it is assessed as *haram*. In consequence, the performance of an absolute duty is rewarded and its omission punished, whereas the avoidance of plainly forbidden acts is rewarded and their commission punished. Punishments may refer to penalties imposed in this world or chastisement in the next. The remaining shades of values between these two extremes are called: reprehensible (*makruh*) acts, which fall short of outright prohibited ones, their omission, however, being preferable to their commission; recommended or commendable (*mandub*) acts, which are regarded as pious conduct worthy of spiritual merit, but the omission of which does not entail penalty; and finally, permissible (*mubah*) acts, toward which the law is totally indifferent. These categories are nevertheless ethico-religious in character and can be employed in determining the nature of any human act. It is only the extremes of *wajib* and *haram*, however, which incorporate legal commands and prohibitions with their accompanying rewards and punishments.

Commands and prohibitions

Each command and prohibition must be established by a clear, definitive text in the material sources of the law. An example of an obligatory command is fasting which Allah stipulated, saying, *O you who attained to faith! Fasting is ordained for you as it was ordained for those before you, so that you might remain conscious of Allah* (2:183). Obligations are divided into two kinds, the individual (*fard 'ayn*) and the collective (*fard kifaya*). The former apply to every person in the community who is required, for example, to pray, to fast, or to obey parents. The latter obligations are addressed to the community as a whole and are fulfilled so long as some members are always available to perform them, such as saying funeral prayers over the dead, building schools and hospitals, or defending the community from attack. And, as we have noted, the exercise of *ijtihad* was just such an obligation, incumbent upon all qualified jurists when dealing with a new case.

In an explicit prohibition the verb "to forbid" (*harrama*) is often used: *Forbidden to you is carrion, and blood and the flesh of swine* (5:3). As for the second material source of the law, a Tradition preserved in Muslim's collection states that "everything belonging to a Muslim is forbidden [*haram*] to his fellow Muslims: his blood, his property, and his honour."[8] Other prohibitory expressions may be used such as *do not slay* (5:95) or *it is not permissible to you* (4:19).

So far, the examples selected have been straightforward, derived directly from scripture and Tradition. The Qur'an, as the word of Allah, provided jurists with the primary source for determining judgments of certainty in the law, despite the difficulties and disagreements involved in particular points of interpretation.

Tradition presented its own problems, which have been alluded to above in the context of *hadith* fabrication. The corpus of Tradition was treated by jurists, for purposes of defining the law, as a source classified according to the degree of certainty of knowledge provided by different kinds of *hadith*. The highest value was accorded a *mutawatir* Tradition, which had been transmitted via so many

different channels (*isnad*s) that the possibility of its being fabricated
was precluded. From this type *positive* knowledge could be derived.
On the other hand, another type, called a *mursal* Tradition, lacks a
link in the chain of transmission between the Prophet and a Successor.
This places it in a lower order than the first. From these and other
considerations Traditions were classed as either sound (*sahih*), fair
(*hasan*), or weak (*da'if*). Differences between the schools on points of
law, in most cases of a minor nature only, may frequently be traced to
the way each employs, or otherwise interprets, a Tradition cited in
support of a particular issue.

To return to commands and prohibitions. Not every utterance in
the imperative mood may be considered absolute, even where such a
statement appears to be expressed clearly in the Qur'an. There is the
command *take witnesses whenever you trade with one another* (2:282), which
the majority of scholars represent as only a recommendation (*mandub*),
since a sound Tradition illustrates that the Prophet often concluded
sales and purchases without witnesses. Hence if there is accompanying
evidence, either in scripture or Tradition, representing a reliable
commentary on the probable intent of a specific scriptural passage, an
apparent *command* could be interpreted as a *recommendation*.

Another instance is instructive. The scriptural prohibition against
eating the meat of animals which have not been slaughtered in the
name of Allah is clear and forceful: *Eat not of that over which Allah's name
has not been pronounced, for this would be sinful conduct indeed* (6:121 and
5:3). With the exception of Ahmad b. Hanbal, the schools found in
the utterance of the name of Allah, known as *tasmiyah*, a pious custom
rather than a strict necessity. Abu Hanifah held that the *tasmiyah* was
obligatory, but if it had been unwittingly omitted, the meat was still
legal for consumption. Of course, where there existed a real possibility
that the name of another god might have been uttered, the prohibitive
force of the text was adopted by all. The *tasmiyah*, that is, uttering the
expression "In the name of Allah" (*bismillah*, sometimes adding "the
Compassionate, the Merciful," *al-rahman al-rahim*), is widely used in
Muslims' daily lives following a saying of the Prophet that any
significant act undertaken without pronouncing the *tasmiyah* is
deficient. Muslims living today in minority communities, for example
in the European Community or in North America, have tended to
insist upon the stricter application of this formula in the slaughtering
of their food animals. It remains a mark of community identity in an
otherwise non-Muslim environment.

Other actions

Acts qualified as recommended (*mandub*) or reprehensible (*makruh*) incur neither punishment nor moral blame according to most jurists. The Hanafis, however, regard some acts in the latter category as entailing moral blame but not punishment. These are referred to as *makruh tahrimi*, matters which are frankly discouraged but where the evidence required to establish them as *haram* is uncertain. The textual authority for these acts may be an explicit identification of them as such, or the use of an equivalent term as in the Tradition "The most abominable of permissible things in the sight of Allah is divorce."[9]

Permissible acts are optional; they may be performed or not, for they carry no consequences of reward or punishment. The literalist jurist Ibn Hazm in fact considered the categories reprehensible and recommendable as merely two varieties of the permissible. One example of the category is indicated in the scriptural reference to foodstuffs that *today all the good things of life have been made lawful to you* (5:5). Taken in conjunction with the prohibition, mentioned above, against eating carrion, blood, and pork, all foods except these are considered good in the sense of their being lawfully permitted.

On the other hand, even a sinful act committed under compulsion or force of circumstances and without a person's wilful disobedience incurs no guilt and is, in this sense, also a permitted act (2:173). The schools also differ on actions deemed by some to be permissible. Al-Shafi'i and Ahmad b. Hanbal, for example, regard the consumption of horse meat *mubah* (permissible), while Abu Hanifah valued it as *makruh tahrimi*, and Malik simply as *makruh*. The differences are accounted for by the manner in which each adduced its interpretation from scripture, from the particular Traditions employed, or in analogical deduction (*qiyas*) drawn from the texts.

Analogy

Analogical reasoning was an acknowledged rational source of the law. Although the use of reason was considered subservient to revelation by those who employed *qiyas*, it has always had its critics, however limited their impact was upon the evolution of the law. The Qur'an lacked unequivocal authority for the use of analogy, while Tradition suggested that the Prophet may on occasion have resorted to it. Critics of *qiyas* pointed to Allah's own words that *We have revealed to you the Book to make everything clear, and to provide guidance and grace to all* (16:89) and argued that the application of a speculative source of the law simply acknowledged Allah's failure to provide complete guidance. They were also concerned lest analogy would lead to conflicting judgments, confusion, and discord. Supporters of this rational method, however, found their reponse in the Tradition from the Prophet to the effect that differences of opinion in the community were a blessing from Allah. The critics' view did not prevail, but the jurists accepted that the results of *qiyas* obtained only a probable, not an absolutely certain, degree of conformity with Allah's intentions.

Qiyas is the application of a ruling in a case already known, to a new case on which the law is silent, the application made possible by the presence of an "effective cause" (*'illah*) or common denominator shared by both cases. One example is the ruling on the cessation of market activities during the call to the Friday congregational prayer (62:9). By analogy, *all* business and other transactions are included in this prohibition since the same cause (*'illah*) – that is, a diversion from performing the prayer – is said to be common to both situations. The original ruling must be based on the two material sources of the law, although in those instances where the cause may not be evident, the jurist will attempt to identify it by disciplined mental effort (*ijtihad*) in the light of his understanding of the objectives and intentions of Allah's will.

Another example, this time from the Tradition in which the Prophet says, "whoever drinks from a golden or silver vessel, sips hellfire into his stomach."[10] Jurists explored the *spirit* of the law, and by means of analogy extended the application of this saying to embrace the use of luxuries in general, which served to heighten a believer's arrogance and pride. Literalists of the Zahiri school, however, regarded *qiyas* as unwarranted speculation about Allah's intent. They did not look for the cause of a prohibition or its extended application arguing that had the Prophet intended otherwise, he would have said so clearly. They therefore adhered strictly to the *letter* of the Tradition, prohibiting drinking but not eating from such vessels. Both methods were valid, as both were based upon scriptural authority. Or rather one could say, each approach to the texts was sound psychologically and consistent in itself, given the common goal of seeking an understanding of the divine will. One side may have felt it had achieved greater certainty of understanding than the other. But *rationally* each side would have had to concede that it could never *know* that for sure.

In any event, analogy was not applied wholesale to every pronouncement of the texts, because identification of the "effective cause" of a ruling was not always possible. Discovery of the "effective cause" was more straightforward in practical matters of daily concern (*mu'amalat*), whereas details of the rituals (*'ibadat*) were generally not thought to be the proper area for the application of analogy. Their real *'illah* was known only to Allah.

Another area in which jurists have been reluctant on the whole to use analogy is penal law. Among the schools, the Hanafis were most concerned because the "effective cause" in these cases could not be identified with certainty. These include offenses against religion, that is, acts which have been explicitly forbidden or sanctioned by punishments in the Qur'an. These are theft, unlawful intercourse, drinking wine, highway robbery, and false accusation of unlawful intercourse, or of one's parentage. The punishments (*hudud*, s. *hadd*) for these are laid down, depending upon the crime, as either death, severing of the hand or foot, or flogging. The punishment of flogging for wine drinking is not stipulated in the Qur'an but is found in the *sunnah*.[11] For the male or female thief, on the other hand, punishment is stipulated as the cutting off of a hand (5:38). Here, as in the other *hadd* punishments (with the exception of false witness), there is a strong tendency among jurists to limit the application of the punishments, an attitude itself based upon a Tradition which states that it is "better to err on the side of leniency than on the side of severity."[12] The religious nature of theft is seen in the role of repentance, expressed in the very next verse: *But as for him who repents after having done wrong, and makes amends, Allah will turn towards him [in grace] for Allah is forgiving, a dispenser of grace* (5:39). Thus, if the thief were to return the stolen object before a charge was brought against him, the *hadd* punishment would not be carried out. Moreover, narrow definitions of the act of theft, of what constitutes stolen goods and so on, have the effect of limiting the application of the *hadd*, so that in practice, punishments are enacted under a different aspect of the law which renders the culprit liable to the discretionary punishment of a judge. The religious nature of the law is again underscored in that imprisonment is not regarded as a punishment but rather a means of bringing about an offender's repentance.

Consensus

Finally, the fourth root of the law, consensus (*ijma‘*), shares with analogical reasoning the characteristic of being a rational proof. Support for its use was found in scripture, where Allah warns that *anyone who splits off from the Messenger after the guidance has become clear to him and follows a way other than that of the believers, We shall leave him on the path he has chosen and land him in Hell* (4:115). The verse did not convince all scholars that it was intended as a reference to *ijma‘*. Its evident meaning was simply a warning against disobedience to the Prophet, who, moreover, had himself provided no interpretation of the verse as a reference to consensus. The most commonly cited Tradition in support of consensus is the famous saying "My community shall never agree on an error."[13] Again, conscientious scholarly opinion pointed out that the *hadith* was not reliable (*mutawatir*) and the Qur’an on this point was unclear.

There were several other Traditions cited to justify consensus, each of them having similar weaknesses. Yet there can be no doubt that the notion of *ijma‘* in some sense existed from quite early times. To what constituency it referred, the whole community, the Companions, religious scholars as a class, or just those of a particular locality, and whether it was regarded from the beginning as infallible opinion are subject to debate. The need felt by all thoughtful believers for a continuing human authority to bind the community together, especially in the aftermath of the grave internal political crisis between the Caliph ‘Ali b. Abi Talib and his Umayyad rival, Mu‘awiyah, was possibly the compelling religious reason for its emergence as a dynamic concept. The community turned naturally to itself as a source of authority to unite the faithful under a common body of doctrine and law.

Later juristic theorists argued that the various Traditions adduced in support of consensus were authenticated by their common meaning, if not in their precise wording, and the customary understanding of them by scores of scholars over the course of time.

The universality which al-Shafi‘i appears to have wanted to claim for consensus proved impossible to achieve. There is a hint, however, that he may have intended to confine consensus to obligatory duties alone as he regarded it as unrealistic to expect consensus on all other matters as well.[14] Even defining *ijma‘* as the *unanimous* agreement of legal scholars (*mujtahidun*) in any period after the Prophet on any matter of religion was bound to point to an unattainable ideal. In reality, consensus, more often than not, represented either the agreement of a majority only or else an absence of disagreement. That is, *ijma'* occurred when a jurist looked to preceding generations of legal scholars for agreement upon a currently held opinion. This he could determine by the absence of dissenting voices against it in the past. Once a doctrine or opinion was embraced by consensus, say by means of *qiyas*, it moved from the realm of a probable legal judgment to one of certainty, irrevocable and binding on succeeding generations. Consensus then also became an authority in itself, providing a precedent upon which later judgments could be based. It is in this sense regarded as infallible according to the Prophet's declaration that "my community shall never agree on an error." Consensus could not be abrogated by either scripture or Tradition, but equally, it could abrogate neither of them.

Consensus has been seen as a conservative instrument in the preservation of the religious heritage but at the same time it has also reflected, despite continuing polemics, the tolerant coexistence of rival scholars' views in the changing historical circumstances of the community. It was quite common, for example, to have a jurist of one school write a commentary on, or prepare an abridgement of, a work of legal theory penned by a jurist of another school. It is fair to say that differences among scholars or the four schools of law are regarded by Muslims themselves as simply different manifestations of the same divine will. Their views overall, therefore, constitute an essential objective unity.

In addition to the four roots or sources of the law, Islamic jurisprudence recognized other subsidiary principles. Some had been present from the earliest attempts at law making, juristic preference or equity (*istihsan*) among them. Another was custom (*'urf*), meaning the collective practice of a large number of people. Where this did not contravene the principles of the law, it was regarded as valid. Its acceptance was founded upon scripture where Allah states that he has not laid upon believers any hardship in religion (22:78). This was understood to mean that hardship would be caused if approved prevailing custom was totally ignored in legal matters where there was no explicit conflict with the material sources. Custom could be accommodated and assimilated through interpretations based on the exercise of *ijtihad* in cases determined by preference, public interest, and even consensus.

CONTINUITY AND CONTENT

The masterplan of legal theory devised by the architects of the second/eighth to fourth/tenth centuries had resulted in a profound understanding of the contents of the material sources. A massive corpus of positive law derived from them, believed to reflect the divine will, was also produced. The blueprint suited the conditions of society of the day, but adjustments and fine-tuning to the plan were required as time passed and new problems arose. Whatever solutions were found to meet new situations, later jurists remained aware of their obligation to confront the material sources of the law in the same spirit as their great predecessors, even if few thought they could emulate their pioneering achievements. Our understanding of developments in the law during the period between the fourth/tenth and tenth/sixteenth centuries (indeed, to the beginnings of the modern period in the twelfth/eighteenth century) is, admittedly, still tentative. Recent research suggests, however, that the still widely held view that Islamic law in its post-formative period was a stagnant institution divorced from social realities and change must be abandoned, or at least dramatically revised.[15]

One development in legal theory was the concept of public welfare (*istislah* and its derivative *maslahah*) discussed among jurists during the fifth/eleventh century and later.[16] This was intended to deal with matters which would protect the objectives of the law which were described as the preservation of religion, life, reason, family, and property. It was assumed that the basic purpose of the law was to secure people's welfare, and ways of achieving this were legion as society's needs changed according to time and circumstance. The very premise of *maslahah* was a tacit challenge to the uncompromising nature of some of the extant body of positive law. The notion was admittedly debated in a climate of controversy, and only jurists of the Maliki and Shafi'i schools seem to have succeeded in developing a convincing theoretical basis for it. Nevertheless, it is worth noting that the concept of *maslahah* was to become the point of departure in the thinking of many modern Muslim legal reformers.

THE GATE OF "IJTIHAD"

The growth of positive law was also assured through the continuing activities of the *mujtahid*s, the jurists qualified to deduce the law from the sources by their own efforts (*ijtihad*). The *mujtahid* freely exercised his skills, answerable only to Allah. "Islam's insistence on rewarding the jurisconsult in the Hereafter, regardless of the result, dramatized the importance of this supreme function . . . and put a precious premium on the exercise of *ijtihad*."[17]

In contrast to the *mujtahid* was the *muqallad*, who was a jurist who followed or "imitated" the decisions of his predecessors without question or resort to his own individual *ijtihad*. Scholarly concern had been expressed from the sixth/twelfth century about whether the community could survive in the absence of *mujtahids* and whether any indeed still existed. On the one side there were those who claimed *mujtahids* were not only present at the moment but would always need to be so, as they were the only persons qualified to inform the community and the rulers on matters lawful and unlawful, especially when new situations arose. From this viewpoint, *muqallads* could only be entrusted with the transmission of their predecessors' doctrines, which might not always be appropriate when circumstances changed. On the other side of the debate, some argued that the community obligation (*fard kifaya*) to sustain *ijtihad* could be lifted without consensus lapsing and the community falling into error. Others of a more pessimistic turn of mind claimed that over time the law would inevitably deteriorate and lawyers become extinct.

The debate perhaps expressed the anxiety of jurists in both camps over developments which slowly emerged with the rise and spread of new institutions of learning, the colleges of law or *madrasah*s, founded in the fifth/eleventh century. Unlike the mosques, which were privately established and funded by religious endowment (*waqf*) to train jurists for the benefit of the entire community, the new colleges were government sponsored and founded to provide administrative personnel. When the government began to employ its own jurists on a wide scale, this marked an interference with the *mujtahid*'s free and unfettered practice of providing legal opinions. The government-hired jurist was often suspect, regarded by some as a man whose opinions had been bought by those in power. As a consequence, the *mujtahid–muqallad* divide possibly reflected the views of those who respectively rejected and those who accommodated themselves to the new developments of the *madrasah* system. In any case, the so-called "closure of the gate of *ijtihad*," discussed by scholars from the seventh/thirteenth century, was never accepted by consensus of all the schools. Although there does seem to have been a relative decline in the number of recognized *mujtahid*s after the tenth/sixteenth century, the practice never became extinct, and the call for *ijtihad* was vigorously resumed by premodern Muslim reformers. Future research on the detailed developments of the law in this long period of seven or eight centuries will eventually clarify these problems and some, if not all, of the questions remaining.

LEGAL OPINIONS ("FATAWA")

An illustration of these developments may be seen in a transformation in the office of the *mufti*, a specialist in religious law who was competent to give an authorative opinion (*fatwa*) to a person seeking a solution to a problem. The change involved the qualifications a *mufti* was supposed to possess. Opinion among fifth-/eleventh-century jurists concurred that a *fatwa* must be delivered by a qualified *mujtahid*. By the ninth/fifteenth century jurists claimed that there then existed a consensus legitimizing the *fatwa* of a *muqallad* as well. This represented a decline in the qualifications formerly required. A *muqallad* was not trained in the exacting techniques for rendering a sound argument by analogy. He needed only to search among the works of renowned jurists of the past for a "ready-made" solution to a given problem. *Fatwa*s neverthless continued to be delivered, and the collections of *responsa* of celebrated jurists remain an important juridical source for the legal and social history of Islamic society.

As a legal opinion, a *fatwa* is intended to elucidate a point of law brought to the *mufti* by a member of the public or by a government-appointed judge (*qadi*) whose duty it was to try a case before him. As an opinion, the *fatwa* is not binding upon anyone. Unlike the *qadi*'s judgment, a *fatwa* is not enforceable unless a judge follows its advice. The *qadi* may seek opinions from several *mufti*s before arriving at his decision. Legal opinions (*fatawa*) could cover any aspect of the law, be they straightforward matters of belief and ritual or convoluted issues involving contracts or inheritance. Two examples from totally different periods, places, and social contexts will have to suffice as illustrations of this institution.

Ahmad b. Muhammad b. Ziyad was appointed *qadi* of Cordoba in 291/903. The court sessions were held in the central mosque, which is still the most famous and prominent monument in the city today. One day while the court was in session a woman of the Christian *dhimmi* community entered and solemnly proclaimed to the assembly that she denied the divinity of Allah, for Jesus was himself God, and that Muhammad's claim to prophethood was fabricated. This was tantamount to declaring false the Muslim's profession of faith expressed in the words "There is no god but Allah and Muhammad is the Messenger of Allah." The jurists present were asked for their opinion on the matter, and they unanimously agreed that the woman had willfully committed the crime of reviling Allah and the Prophet, for which the penalty was death.

As the *fatwa*s were only advisory, the sources do not inform us whether the *qadi* acted upon the jurists' opinion. The woman's behavior would seem bizarre, deliberately courting death as she did, unless hers was a spontaneous act epitomizing the spirit of an earlier generation of Christians in al-Andalus who sought martyrdom as an expression of revolt against their Muslim masters. The *qadi* in the same opinion goes on to make further observations related to what could be said in respect of the Prophet. If a Muslim, Jew, or Christian were publicly to deny Muhammad's prophethood or curse him, and this were brought to the *qadi*'s attention, the penalty would be the same as the Christian woman in this case presumably did suffer. It was, on the other hand, acceptable for a *dhimmi*, a Christian or Jew, to say that Muhammad had not been sent to them and that they had their own prophets in Jesus and Moses. It was not acceptable for them to claim that their religion was better than Islam.[18] The *fatwa* deals with a contemporary concern, relations between the dominant Islamic culture and minority religious communities, a matter which could have led to grave disturbances of the public order.

The second *fatwa* belongs to the present century. It involves the case of a Beduin *shaykh* from a sedentary tribe in the region of Jerusalem–Bethlehem who had unintentionally divorced his wife. In his request for an opinion, the *shaykh* explained that he had lost his temper over his brother's intention to marry a woman of whom the *shaykh* did not approve. "The groom shall not marry the bride; she shall not enter my house," he had sworn, emphasizing his seriousness by making an oath to dissolve his own marriage should his brother's intentions be fulfilled. The couple defied the *shaykh* and the woman entered her husband's house, which he happened to share with the *shaykh*. The condition of the *shaykh*'s divorce had been met, and he now sought the means of extracting himself from his unforeseen and unwanted predicament.

The *qadi* of the district court applied the law of the Hanafi school which attached no importance to intent in divorce. This meant that the court would uphold the divorce (even accepting that the *shaykh* had sincerely not intended it) and he could only recover his wife if she married again, however temporarily, and was divorced from her second husband. The *shaykh* then sought remedy in a decision from an independent, private, *mufti* of established personal authority who belonged to the Shafi'i school, which recognizes the element of intent in the utterance of the divorce formula. The *shaykh* obtained his *fatwa* as evidence of a still valid marriage, although the decision was not confirmed or registered with any state institution. This solution, involving an area of personal law, was seen by most as a fair judgment in a situation which could have led to greater grief, had the full rigors of the Hanafi school been enforced on this particular point of law.[19]

Apart from the specific circumstances illustrated by individual *fatwa*s, the extant collections of these documents collectively reflect the complexity of Muslim societies. They show, moreover, the way the theoretically unchangeable law could be adapted over the centuries to changing practices and how imperceptibly judicial evolution might be accomplished.

*Fatwa*s continue to be published to the present day, their purpose being to guide concerned Muslims on various matters of the faith which they may encounter in their everyday life. The traditional question and answer procedure has, naturally, been modernized by all the facilities of the age of the electronic media. The Saudi Arabian weekly magazine *al-Dawa*, founded by the late Muhammad b. Ibrahim Al al-Shaykh, carries a section of *fatwa*s in response to readers' queries, provided in the main by the respected legal scholar 'Abd al-'Aziz b. 'Abdallah b. Baz. The former head of the al-Azhar mosque-university in Cairo, the late Mahmud Shaltut, published a collection of his *fatwa*s dealing with "problems facing the contemporary Muslim in his daily life." These bring together his responses made over many years via the radio and newspapers to queries from concerned believers. They embrace most of the subject matter found in the classical works on positive law: questions of doctrine, religious ritual, custom and innovation, matters concerning family and personal status, financial and business arrangements, drinking, drugs, and smoking. The purely modern nature of the book, however, is found in the inclusion of the topics of space travel and the relationship between Islam and communism.[20]

RELIGIOUS OBSERVANCES

The scope of the law, as we have already had occasion to note, encompassed two fundamental relationships, one between the creator and his vicegerents on earth, the other between human beings themselves. It will also be recalled that actions were judged according to a five-fold ranking of obligatory, forbidden, reprehensible, recommended, and permissible.

The first relationship is spelled out in the Muslims' obligatory duties to Allah as an expression of their submission to his will, and of their gratitude for the plenitude of gifts he has bestowed upon them. These are called the duties of worship or *'ibadat*. They are often referred to as the Five Pillars of Islam, comprising the ritual observances of prayer, fasting, alms giving, and performance of the pilgrimage which together are embraced by the simple profession of faith, the *shahadah*, "There is no god but Allah and Muhammad is the Messenger of Allah."[21]

Prayer

Prayer (*salat*) is performed five times a day facing the holy shrine at Mecca. The times are at daybreak, just after noontime, mid-afternoon, sunset, and evening, and worshipers may perform the prayer in whatever place they find themselves at the appointed moment. In large cities like Cairo, the call to prayer at daybreak shatters the slumbering stillness of one's own neighborhood, the voice of the muezzin seeming to echo across the city as it is joined by the call of other muezzin summoning the faithful to their first duty of the day:

> *Allahu Akbar! Allahu Akbar!*
> I bear witness that there is no God but Allah . . .
> I bear witness that Muhammad is the messenger of
>   Allah . . .
> Come to prayer, come to salvation . . .
> Prayer is better than sleep . . .
> *Allahu Akbar! Allahu Akbar! La ilaha illa-lah!*

The human voice in Islam plays the role in the summons to prayer of the bell in Christianity and the horn in Judaism. Prayer is preceded by ablutions that cleanse the hands, mouth, face, and feet and a declaration of intent to perform the ritual with sincere solemnity; this establishes a "covenant from Allah" to forgive the supplicant's sins, which then fall from him as do "leaves from a tree."[22] A Tradition from the Prophet states that, "When my people are called together on the Day of the Resurrection, their foreheads and hands will bear the bright marks of their ablutions."[23] Prayer in common has greater merit than in isolation, according to another Tradition.[24] In either case, prayers are said to be witnessed (17:78) by the angels at any time of day or night.[25] The noon prayer on Fridays was specified as a special congregational prayer in the main mosque following a scriptural injunction (62:9) and an explanation from the Prophet that this day would distinguish Muslims from Jews and Christians, whose special days were Saturday and Sunday.[26] It is on this occasion that a sermon (*khutbah*) is delivered in which the preacher traditionally included a prayer of well-being for the ruler, and then expounded his message based on a Qur'anic verse and frequently focused on a topic of current concern to his audience.

Alms

The giving of alms (*zakat*) is mentioned in scripture along with prayer (9:11). It is not regarded as charity but rather as an act of purification, a means of distributing a portion of the wealth of the rich among the disadvantaged in the community, or to the less fortunate members of one's own family. Giving is better than receiving, or, in the metaphor of Tradition, "the upper hand is better than the lower hand."[27] Scripture warns against those who amass fortunes and fail to spend from them assisting others (9:34–35). Building upon a Qur'anic allusion (3:180), Tradition paints a graphic picture of the punishment awaiting the niggardly offender on the Day of Judgment. A python, wrapping itself around his victim's neck and about to devour him, will say, "*I* am your wealth, your treasure!"[28] The Prophet tells the tale of a man who had on consecutive days given alms to a thief, a prostitute, and a rich man. It came to the man in a dream that the acts in themselves were good. The thief and prostitute might be persuaded by his gesture to abandon their trades, while the rich man might see in the act one worthy of imitation and would give to others "a portion of that which Allah had given him."[29] The *zakat* traditionally could be paid in different forms, either in cash or kind, the latter meaning a proportion of a herd of animals or, for example, of a date crop.

Fasting

Fasting (*sawm*, or *siyam*) is prescribed during the month of Ramadan, the ninth month of the Islamic calendar. During the hours from sunrise to sunset, those adults whose health permits are required to abstain from food, drink, and sexual relations. "When Ramadan begins," said the Prophet, "the gates of heaven are opened, the gates of hell are locked and rebellious devils enchained."[30] The month is important as a period of reflection and spiritual discipline, of physical endurance and sharing with others, and in a *hadith qudsi*, Allah said that "fasting is done for My sake and I give reward for it. One abandons his passion and his food for My sake."[31] Toward the end of the month there occurs the Night of Power (*laylat al-qadar*), during which the Qur'an was first revealed to Muhammad. "Whoever prays during this night in true faith and hope will be pardoned his previous errors,"[32] the Prophet is recorded to have said. The rigors of Ramadan may best be appreciated by recalling that the Islamic calendar is lunar and hence the fasting month shifts eleven days forward each year and is therefore observed in all seasons of the year, summer and winter. Fasting may be interrupted on a journey, and menstruating women do not fast. A pregnant woman likewise is excused from fasting if she fears harm may come to the unborn child. The Prophet was aware of the demands on the body required by the fast, for in another Tradition he says, "The odour of the mouth of one who fasts is to Allah as a perfume more fragrant than musk."[33] Ramadan begins and ends with the sighting of the crescent moon, and the month concludes with one of the two major religious celebrations of the Muslim calendar, the feast of the breaking of the fast (*'id al-fitr*). The occasion is marked by the exchange of visits and gifts in a spirit of joyousness and the distribution of special alms in a spirit of thanksgiving. Fasting may also be performed as an act of expiation for certain offenses like a broken oath.

Pilgrimage

The final and most complex ritual duty is the pilgrimage (*hajj*). At least once in a believer's lifetime, providing the necessary means are available, the journey to Mecca is performed in the twelfth and last month of the year, Dhu al-Hijjah. It is based on scripture (2:196; 3:97), as are all the rituals: the Prophet said that the most meritorious form of *jihad*, literally struggle for the sake of Allah, was the pilgrimage piously performed. Moreover, it "removed poverty and sin as a blacksmith's bellows removed impurities from iron."[34]

The pilgrim enters the sanctuary of the Ka'bah in Mecca in a state of ritual purity (*ihram*) clad in two plain white pieces of cloth, indicating the equality of all believers before Allah. The unity and universality of the community is reflected in the pilgrims' gathering together from every corner of the globe. Over several days a number of acts are performed as part of the pilgrimage, most having been incorporated from similar pre-Islamic practices. These include the circumambulation of the Ka'bah, the sacred house originally built by the patriarch Abraham; the procession between the hills of Safa and Marwa, commemorating Hajar's desperate search for water for her son; the stoning of three pillars where Ibrahim (Abraham) is said to have been tempted by the devil not to sacrifice his son; and a visit to the plain of Arafat, where the pilgrims stand in repentance before Allah, on the spot where the Prophet Muhammad is said to have preached his farewell message of peace and harmony to all people. The pilgrimage concludes with the second of the major Muslim celebrations, the feast of the sacrifice (*'id al-adha*), or the Great Feast. The sacrifice of animals and the distribution of the meat to the poor are performed not only in Mecca but throughout the world wherever Muslims celebrate away from the holy city itself. The Traditions are replete with details of the way the Prophet performed the rites at the various stages of the pilgrimage, details replicated in the compendia of legal rules of the different schools of law.

Each of the four specifically ritual obligations has an informal, non-obligatory expression as well. In terms of legal valuation, they would be considered recommended acts conferring merit upon the performer but no punishment in the event of their omission. For example, a private, personal invocation to Allah is called *du'a* and can be uttered at any time, without the accompanying performance of ablutions and prostrations. There are also special prayers said at the times of the feasts of Ramadan and the pilgrimage. A form of meritorious but non-obligatory alms is called *sadaqah*. Fasting outside the month of Ramadan is also recognized as worthy of merit so long as it is not excessive. A form of pilgrimage to Mecca may be performed at any time of year, outside the pilgrimage season, and is called the *'umrah*; a number of the rituals essential to the *hajj* are not conducted on these occasions. In all, prayer, alms, fasting and pilgrimage combine the Muslim's acknowledgment of his or her submission and obedience to the will of Allah, and comprise his or her deepest expression of gratitude for his bounty.

This primary axis of the Muslim's religious life, the vertical God–man relationship, is accompanied by a second, horizontal axis, man's relationship with his fellow man. In the law this is referred to as the *mu'amalat*. If the believer has established a proper relationship with Allah in the first sense, it is believed that his or her conduct in the day-to-day world of, say, family life and business will create the conditions for the achievement of the Muslims' vision of the ideal blueprint for society in the second. The scope of these social laws is too broad for even a summary. Some, such as the *hudud* punishments, have already been mentioned, and so the following account will touch briefly only upon the most important remaining areas.

SOCIAL RELATIONS

Undoubtedly the family lies at the core of Islam's social laws, just as it is the basic unit in all Muslim societies. Laws related to the family include those touching upon marriage, divorce, inheritance and bequests, the rights of children and relatives, and finances. The patriarchal nature of Muslim societies was not a characteristic created or invented by Muslim scripture. Patriarchies were widespread in the Middle East prior to the rise of Islam, and some of their values were preserved within the new religious culture, chiefly in the way some jurists interpreted the material sources of the law. This was despite the revolutionary thrust of the new faith to create a solidarity of believers to supersede that of the tribe.

A clear example is the case of polygyny. The Qur'an explicitly allows a man to have up to four wives at one time (4:3). This was not intended as an encouragement to do so, but rather as a means of restricting the prevailing central Arabian custom of unlimited polygyny, for the same verse urges that if each wife could not be treated equally, then only one was permitted. This was the position of the majority of early jurists. An exception was allowed, perhaps curiously, by the literalist school of the Zahiris. The Qur'an was taken by them to encourage the act of marriage, a single *continuous* union, not a series of them. The predominant view had scriptural basis which conformed to existing patriarchal norms, although there is no way of determining how common was the practice. It is not until very recent

times, when these norms have weakened or are under challenge, that
Muslim reformers have argued on the basis of another verse in the
same chapter (4:129) that Allah's real intention had been to impose
at least a *moral* restriction on plural marriages or to eliminate
polygyny altogether.

Marriage and divorce

Marriage (*nikah*) is a civil contract concluded by an offer and
acceptance between two qualified parties before two witnesses. It is in
practice not a union of two individuals so much as a contract between
two families. Marriage arranged by families or guardians is traditional,
and while this custom may be widely accepted and almost always
irresistible, the majority of jurists are agreed (with the exception of
al-Shafi'i) that an adult woman cannot be forced into a union against
her wishes. A majority also hold that the bride should be assisted (but
not compelled) by a guardian in her choice although the Hanafites
argue that the woman has complete freedom in this matter too. The
question of suitability of the prospective partners may also be raised,
since the relationship between the two families contracting the union
should allow for the greatest possible agreement between them.

There exist certain impediments to marriage such as the prohibition
between a man and a woman of certain degrees of blood relationship
as specified in the Qur'an (4:22–23). Marriage is also forbidden
between two persons suckled by the same milk-mother, as jurists held
that this form of nourishment is like that given to the embryo in the
womb by the natural mother. Lastly, marriage between a Muslim
and someone from a community other than those possessing a
revelation is invalid. Jews and Christians, as Peoples of the Book, are
therefore acceptable, but a Muslim woman may not marry either
unless the man converts.

The bride receives a dowry (*mahr*), according to the contract, paid
to her directly by the husband, the agreed amount forming part of her
personal property over which the husband has no legal right. The
custom of the wife furnishing the house may still be the prevailing one
in Muslim countries, although it is the legal responsibility of the
husband to do this. In return for the husband's support, meaning the
provision of the necessary food, clothing, and shelter, the wife's
obedience and care of the home are expected by the husband. In the
contract of marriage it is possible for the woman to stipulate that her

husband should take no other wife, or that she may secure the prior authorization (*tafwid*) to divorce herself from her husband should she choose to do so.

The roles of husband and wife are perceived as complementary, reflecting their different capacities and dispositions in conformity with the values of traditional patriarchal society. Since the man acts in the public sphere of the market place and government, his experience gained thereby means that in legal affairs the testimony of one man is equal to that of two women. The woman acts within the private sphere of the home, managing it and raising the children, which includes their moral training. By virtue of the husband's total financial responsibility for the family, the wife is regarded as his subordinate (2:228). As a couple, on the other hand, both are equally responsible before Allah to lead their lives virtuously. This is made clear in the Qur'anic verse (33:35) said to have been revealed when the Prophet was challenged by a woman to explain why it appeared that Allah only addressed the men of the community.

The termination of a marriage is regarded by law as an abomination in the sight of Allah, and arbitration is counseled when serious difficulties arise. *And if you have reason to fear that a breach might occur between a married couple, appoint an arbiter from among his people and one from hers; if they both want to set things aright, Allah may bring about their reconciliation* (4:35). The gravity of the act is said to be reflected in the requirement that a wife must be divorced by her husband not once, but three times to make it irrevocable. That is, if a husband utters the divorce formula, "I divorce you," once only, there follows a three-month waiting period (*'iddah*) before it becomes effective in order to give the parties a chance for reconciliation and also to see whether the wife is pregnant. If the husband reconsiders, he may take his wife back and life continues as before, although he is deemed to have committed one divorce. After a third divorce of this nature, the marriage is irrevocably severed. If the formula is pronounced once in each of three successive months, the couple may reconcile during this period, but if this is not achieved by the end of it the divorce is also final. A divorce absolute means that a husband may not marry his wife again unless she has meanwhile married another man and subsequently been divorced.

The most problematic form of divorce (and perhaps the most common) occurs when a man utters the divorce formula three times at once. It is legally valid, although considered an innovation (*bid'ah*) and therefore sinful. This is clearly a further example of the powerful influence exercised by patriarchal values on the religious norms of the faith. Thus, with certain exceptions, unless the contract of marriage stipulates the conditions whereby a woman may divorce her husband, it is always the husband's right to initiate the process. The main exceptions are that the wife may sue for a divorce in the *qadi*'s court in the event of her husband's impotence or insanity.

Inheritance

Concomitant with the importance of laws governing marriage and divorce are those of inheritance. The Qur'anic injunctions assured that the rights of individual members of the immediate family were strengthened over against the prevailing tribal practice in which women were generally excluded from inheritance. According to Islamic principles, two-thirds of the estate of the deceased was reserved for inheritance, and the final third set aside for payment of debts and the making of bequests. The property was distributed among near kin, so that its concentration in the hands of one person was unusual. The portions inherited by different heirs were assigned according to their assumed need, the male being granted in most cases double the female's portion and the children together inheriting more than the surviving parent. And finally, for these purposes relationship through the mother was placed on the same level as relationship through the father, although the portion each received was different. The heirs stipulated in the Qur'an (4:7-11), among them wives, daughters, sisters and grandmothers of the deceased, were thus entitled to an assured share of the estate before the inheritance devolved to the nearest male relative.

The market

Beyond the confines of the household lay the world of the market place. Business and commerce, too, were areas of concern to the jurists, and the objective of good public order was as important to them as justice and harmony in the home. The market inspector (*muhtasib*) was a government-appointed officer who, along with his assistants, was charged with a range of duties encompassed in the Qur'anic phrase "to command the good and forbid wrong." These duties included ensuring that vendors employed true weights and measures for the goods they sold, that cheating in the quality of a product did not occur (or if it did, could be punished when detected), that cooked or baked goods were properly prepared in market stalls with good ingredients, and that no one offended against public morality.

The inspectors' handbooks provide a valuable and lively source of information concerning the daily operations of a medieval market place. An eighth-/fourteenth-century Egyptian handbook instructs concerning sausage-makers that their shops are best placed near the *muhtasib*'s booth, "for the frauds practiced in connection with them are numerous. Only clean, sound and fat meat from the sheep should be used. Other meats are used fraudulently. The *muhtasib* must order the cooking pans to be changed at intervals." The same work states that it is in the public interest that butchers should not combine together in order to fix prices for their goods.[35] An earlier manual from sixth-/twelfth-century Seville in al-Andalus censured a matter of evident moral concern (whether real or imaginary), namely that Muslim women should not be permitted to enter churches because priests were thought to be libertines, fornicators, and sodomites. It would be better, the handbook adds, if Catholic priests married as they did in eastern Christianity, and those desiring this end should be encouraged to do so![36]

The Islamic world down to premodern times had developed its own international common market in which goods moved long distances along trade routes linking one urban center to another. To facilitate the movement of goods commercial techniques were devised by the jurists, notably those of the Hanafite school. Partnerships of a general or limited kind, a variety of investment forms, and legal credit arrangements which did not violate the prohibition of usury produced a versatile set of commercial instruments which functioned not only in trade but also in the industrial sector, combining the production and distributive sides of manufacture. The conclusion to a recent study of these commercial techniques observes that "Some of the institutions, practices and concepts already found fully developed in the Islamic legal sources of the late 8th century (C.E.) did not emerge in Europe until several centuries later."[37]

''DHIMMIS'' AND SLAVES

Islamic law by definition was the law applied to and followed by Muslims. Not everyone, however, who lived in Muslim societies was a member of the dominant faith. One category of non-Muslim has already been mentioned in the previous chapter, that is, members of the *dhimmi* communities, chiefly Jews and Christians, who lived under treaties of protection with their Muslim rulers. Apart from the main feature of their subjugation, payment of the poll-tax or *jizyah*, these communities possessed legal autonomy and control over their own religious jurisdictions. Muslim law interfered in their internal affairs only where its own direct interest was concerned. For example, in penal law the *dhimmi* was not liable to the *hadd* punishment for drinking wine (forbidden only to Muslims) but was liable in the case of theft; or again, the *dhimmi* was protected against the false accusation of unchastity in a similar manner to the Muslim. While a Muslim and a *dhimmi* could not inherit each other's property, the granting of legacies or gifts was not prohibited. In the law of property, contracts, and obligations the Muslim and *dhimmi* were virtually equal, although neither could enter certain forms of commercial partnership with the other.

A second category of person, the slave, was not recognized by the law as fully responsible as a free Muslim. The institution of slavery has been described as belonging more to family law than to the law of property.[38] That is, the law reflects the virtually exclusive use of slaves in the domestic household rather than in productive sectors of the economy such as agriculture or mining. A slave was either born to his or her station or was a non-Muslim who fell into captivity, most often as a consequence of war. Slaves were also purchased by Muslim rulers, and trained and employed as elite military guards loyal solely to the person of the sovereign. In many cases this policy led to slave elites becoming the rulers in effect, for, once they had converted to Islam, their former slave status was no stigma or impediment to power.

In the religious sense, therefore, the slave was considered a person with certain rights, but, as his or her master's subject, he or she was not regarded as fully responsible. For example, a slave could marry, even a free man or woman. But he or she was liable to only half the penalty of a free person for the crimes of drinking wine and the false accusation of unchastity. A child born to a free man and his concubine was considered free when the owner acknowledged the child as his own; the mother likewise becomes free upon her owner's death. The treatment of slaves is placed on the same plane as that of one's kin (2:177). The manumission of a slave belongs to the category of recommended act, either as a religious expiation (*kaffarah*) or as a voluntary gesture. Expiation may be offered in this manner when one Muslim inadvertently kills another (4:92) or breaks an oath (5:89). Otherwise the slave may purchase his or her own freedom by instalments in agreement with his or her owner. Thus, while the law acknowledged slavery as such, it stipulated that the slave's condition must not be intolerable and implied that slave ownership was not a badge of the truly pious (2:177). As we have had occasion to notice in the previous chapter, early generations of Muslim scholars contained some notable figures who were either freedmen themselves or were the sons or grandsons of freedmen.

THE CALIPHATE

The '*ulama*' who elaborated the methods and details of the law as outlined in this chapter described in their voluminous and varied works society and the individual believer's life regulated by divine will. The scholars also created a doctrine of leadership (*imamah*) of the community which, for convenience, may be called the theory of the Caliphate (*khilafah*).

The Muslim community (*ummah*), it was held, had for a brief time achieved the goals set for it by divine command. This was during the Prophet's lifetime and the period of the Rightly Guided Caliphs, the first four successors who had governed the community's affairs for three decades after the Prophet's death. Thereafter, decline from the state of pristine perfection set in when political strife (*fitnah*) split the community and the Caliphate reverted to natural kingship under the Umayyad dynasty. The fundamental cause of this deterioration was accounted for by the community's drift from the "straight path" governed by Allah, owing to human imperfection and vulnerability to the blandishments of Satan.

Jurists continued to argue nonetheless that since "religion and temporal power are twins," the *khilafah* is required by divine law (4:59), and not by the dictates of reason. The Caliph was to be appointed by an informal council of electors who would then acknowledge the ruler on behalf of the community. The precise number and identity of the electors, however, remained a moot point. Scholars then produced a utopian picture of the qualifications a Caliph must possess and the duties he should perform. He must be just, have adequate knowledge to enable him to decide on points of law, be of sound physical and mental state, be a descendant of the

Prophet's tribe, the Quraysh, and finally, possess the ability to defend the domains of Islam (*dar al-islam*) from external threat and internal rebellion.

This last provision entailed the Caliph's ability to discharge the call to *jihad*, or holy war, a duty (*fard kifayah*) the jurists described as sufficiently fulfilled when performed at least by a certain number of Muslims. Furthermore, the world was divided, according to the jurists, between *dar al-islam*, the domains under Muslim rule, and the rest which are not, namely the domains of war (*dar al-harb*). Theoretically, this implied a constant state of war with the non-Muslim world which in reality proved impossible. For periods relations between Muslims and their Christian opponents in Byzantium or in al-Andalus remained static, neither full peace nor open war prevailing.

Likewise, political realities throughout Islamic history have shown that society acquiesced to the rule of whoever wielded effective power, such as a military commander, whether the Caliph's role was reduced to a fiction and the divine law was violated or vindicated. In these cases, although the *'ulama'* acknowledged political realities as swiftly as anyone, they continued to uphold and sustain the utopian character of the Caliphate. They saw themselves as the expositors of the prophetic message and the will of Allah to which even the Caliph, like every ordinary believer, was ultimately subject. For the *'ulama'*, acceptance of a government's functional legitimacy did not mean they granted it doctrinal legitimacy.

Moreover, despite the utopian program of the *'ulama'*, the system of law in practice under the Caliphate and later successor states combined both the decisions of the judges based upon the *shari'ah* and the edicts of the rulers themselves or their ministers and deputies, the provincial governors. A complementary court was established with much wider powers than the judge's (*qadi*) court, to review wrongs (*mazalim*) committed by government officials against ordinary subjects which involved a host of financial and administrative matters not touched upon in detail by the religious law (*fiqh*). Hence the system of law which the community experienced on a day-to-day basis was not the *shari'ah* pure and simple but rather a dual network emanating from divine and secular sources. For example, land law and land tax were based upon local practice so that interpretation varied from one place to another and over time. Later, using juristic notions of social necessity and public interest, rulers began to create their own laws, effectively increasing the scope of state law. The two, divine law and state law, inevitably interacted in the sense that the decisions of one court could influence decisions in the other and local practice and custom could be used as sources for decisions in both the *qadi*'s and the *mazalim* court.

Law is a mirror of society. By the end of the fifth/eleventh century Islamic society had reached maturity. Throughout these first five centuries of growth, the evolution of Islamic law reflected a degree of pluralism and religious heterogeneity which was possibly more ingrained than in any other contemporary society. Muslims by now constituted a majority everywhere within their domain of rule, and the community itself comprised a multiplicity of ethnic groups, Arabs, Turks, Berbers, and Iranians. The *dhimmi* communities of Christians and Jews, despite conversions from their ranks, remained in significant numbers. They participated in most social groups other than the army, owing to the prohibition against their bearing of arms. These included the merchant class, the crafts, government bureaucracy, and even agriculture. They were, however, regarded as socially and religiously inferior to Muslims, who alone were fully responsible (*mukallaf*) according to the religious law. The *dhimmi*'s monotheism was regarded as a corrupted version of the pure Abrahamic faith to which Islam was the genuine heir. The prophets Moses and Jesus had communicated the same message from their Lord to their peoples. It was, in Muslim eyes, only later generations of their followers which had distorted and misrepresented the message in the divine word. In practice, however, as Peoples of the Book the Christian and Jewish *dhimmi* communities were not rigidly marked off from the majority Muslim society in the same way that Jews, for example, experienced marginalization in Christian societies of Europe.

By the year 1100 CE two recent events caused Christians and Muslims to encounter each other in a manner neither had previously experienced nor were wholly prepared for. Christian armies from Europe, the *dar al-harb*, conquered lands of the *dar al-islam*. In Syria and Palestine the age of the Crusades was marked by the triumphal fall of Jerusalem in 1099, and in the Iberian peninsula the capture of Toledo in 1085 was the signal for the reconquest of Muslim al-Andalus. In the East, the Crusader kingdoms eventually collapsed and Jerusalem was permanently recovered in 1244, a reverse which owed much to the warrior skills of the Muslim commander, Saladin, in the previous generation. In the West, however, al-Andalus was irretrievably lost to Christian rule as the final outpost, the Muslim kingdom of Granada, fell in 1492, an event which eventually led to the expulsion of Muslims from the whole of the peninsula.

During these centuries of prolonged crisis, Muslims experienced for the first time subjection to an alien religious power, something the law and the great jurists had never contemplated. In both eastern and western regions, the method of takeover by Christian forces of Muslim cities generally determined the subsequent treatment of their inhabitants. Conquest by assault led to slaughter and enslavement, while siege leading to surrender resulted either in exile of the population or its subjection to Christian rule. The conditions of Muslim subjection were in many ways similar to those of the *dhimmi* in Muslim lands: religious liberty and certain property rights guaranteed, coupled with restrictions such as a ban on all outward manifestations of the Muslim faith; restraints on sexual and social relations between Muslim and Christian, social distance between the communities being further enforced by the requirement that Muslim attire was distinct from that worn by the Christian to ensure immediate recognition and the avoidance of intimacy.

Medieval attitudes to enslavement and sexual defilement were manifestations of a deeper conflict of theologies between the Christian and Muslim faiths, differences which linger to the present, if only in a muted way. To the Christian, Jesus was the Son of God and Savior. Muhammad was contemptuously dismissed as "a villainous dog," as the expression would have it in both vernacular and theological contexts. The sublime Christian symbol contrasted with the vile and absurd of the Muslim. The Muslim, on the other hand, was naturally wounded by this libel of his or her Prophet. Moreover, since he or she honored Jesus as one of the prophets sent by Allah, the Muslim was equally perplexed by the Christians' obstinate clinging to an idea of their God which explicitly contradicted Allah's description of himself as *The One God, Allah the Eternal, Who begets not and neither is He begotten, Who is without peer* (112:1–4). For Allah to have a son was also an absurdity and an infamy in the Muslim's eyes. It is, therefore, the appropriate moment to turn the discussion toward a consideration of some aspects of the nature of Allah and his relationship with his creation in the discourse of Muslim theology.

CHAPTER 4

Theology: faith, justice, and last things

FAITH AND COMMUNITY

Some scholars labored to construct a logically consistent methodology of the law and to elaborate the detail and scope of its coverage. Others, working upon the same raw data, strove to define the nature of belief and to find answers to questions concerning the nature of Allah. These answers were, in turn, relevant to questions concerning the individual's freedom of action in this world and fate in the hereafter. The beginnings of these inquiries in the second half of the first/seventh century are not easily distinguished from the first tentative steps taken in a number of other disciplines which came to comprise the Islamic sciences; in one way or another, these sciences were concerned with the facts and context of the prophetic-revelatory event and with grasping its meaning and implications for correct belief and proper action in the post-prophetic period.

A famous *hadith*, included by both al-Bukhari and Muslim in their collections, recounts an incident in Muhammad's lifetime as narrated by 'Umar b. al-Khattab, later to become the community's second Caliph after the Prophet's death. 'Umar said:

One day when we were with Allah's messenger, a man with very white clothing and very black hair came up to us. No mark of travel was visible on him, and none of us recognized him. Sitting down beside the Prophet, he said, "Tell me, Muhammad, about *islam*." He replied, "*Islam* means that you should testify that there is no God but Allah and that Muhammad is the Messenger of Allah, that you should observe the prayer, pay the *zakat*, fast during Ramadan, and make the pilgrimage to the Ka'bah if you have the means to go." The man said, "You have spoken the truth." We were surprised at his questioning Muhammad and then declaring that he spoke the truth. The man then said, "Now tell me about belief (*iman*)." Muhammad replied, "*Iman* means that you should believe in Allah, his angels, his Books, his messengers, and the Last Day, and that you should believe in the Decree

103

of both good and evil." The man then said, "Now tell me about perfection (*ihsan*)." Muhammad replied, "It means that you should worship Allah as though you saw him, for he sees you though you do not see him."

The stranger then left the company and Muhammad informed them it had been the angel Gabriel, come to instruct them in matters of their religion.

We shall return to the last part of the Gabriel Tradition at the end of the chapter. For the moment, we can examine the relationship of the two terms *islam*, "submission," and *iman*, "faith," which is expressed in a passage in the Qur'an. When some Bedouin Arabs claimed to have become believers, they were told by the Prophet, *You have not attained to faith; instead say "We have submitted," for faith* (iman) *has not yet entered your hearts* (49:14). What seems to be implied here is that rustic desert Arabs who had professed allegiance to the Muslim community under Muhammad and its God, Allah, had not yet achieved by this act an inner state of faith. Their submission (*islam*), while accepted by the Prophet, did not mean that their hearts had been touched and transformed.

THE KHARIJITES

The scholars who scrutinized the sources in their search for answers to what it meant to be a Muslim (a person of *islam*) or a believer (a person of *iman*) did not pose their questions in the peaceful seclusion of the cloister or private study, but rather in the traumatic aftermath of communal conflict. It has already been observed that within a generation of the Prophet's death, the question of the leadership of the community had become the focus of a bitter schism. The fourth Caliph, 'Ali b. Abi Talib, became locked in struggle (*fitnah*) with his governor of Syria, Mu'awiyah b. Abi Sufyan, over the former's alleged failure to bring to justice the murderers of Mu'awiyah's uncle, the third Caliph, 'Uthman. During the Battle of Siffin in 37/657, 'Ali agreed to arbitration of the conflict in the customary tribal fashion, and swiftly lost the support of a segment of his followers who fiercely insisted that human arbitration should never supplant the clear judgment of Allah (12:40). From these events, various factions of Kharijite ("secessionist") activists and rebels emerged. They condemned as unbelievers 'Uthman and 'Ali and all involved with them. Wherever extreme Kharijite rebels were able by force to expel or eradicate what they perceived to be society's sinful elements, the "true" path to salvation was declared possible only within the security and isolation of their own armed camps. Other less fanatical groups who continued to live in the community's midst in general held that a grave sinner (*fasiq*) was an unbeliever deserving ostracism in this world and eternal damnation in the next. By attempting to identify who was not a believer, they took the view that faith was irrevocably impaired by sin. The sinner was labeled an unbeliever (*kafir*) or idolator (*mushrik*), worse by far than either a hypocrite (*munafiq*), Christian, or Jew.

For the first time in the community's experience the question of *bona fide* membership was raised in a stark, albeit unsophisticated manner. In Kharijite eyes, the unbeliever, or perhaps better the "wrong-believer," was the enemy within, a so-called "Muslim" who professed *islam* but who was judged to be a grave sinner (*fasiq*). Faith without works was anathema to the Kharijites. "Whoever does not *do* what Allah commanded him to do, nullifies his own *work* and *belief*; and whoever nullifies his *work* is a man without *belief*, and a man without belief is no other than a *kafir*."[1] And what was a grave sin? Everyone, Kharijite and opponent alike, agreed that polytheism was the worst. *Allah does not forgive the ascribing of divinity to aught beside Him, although He forgives anything short of that* (4:48). Beyond that, however, some Kharijites indicated the Qur'anic crimes of fornication and theft. Whatever the offense, the conclusion was the same. The sinner forfeited his or her claim to be a believer and to membership in the Muslim community. Only by repenting and joining the "true" camp of the Kharijites could the sinner have his or her faith renewed. A Tradition, possibly intended to refute their views, has the Prophet observe that a Muslim's faith could not be tested by splitting open his or her heart to uncover the motive for submission.

The readiness with which the Kharijites were prepared to utter *takfir*, that is, to declare someone a *kafir*, was countered by other Traditions condemning their rigid stance. For example, the Prophet is recorded as saying that there were three things which belonged to the very root of faith and which protected an individual from censure and chastisement: first, one who professed that there is no God but Allah must not be molested; second, a person who committed a sin must not be declared an infidel (*kafir*); and third, for the mere commission of some act or other, one could not be excommunicated from Islam.[2] Again, the Prophet is said to have told his companion Abu Dharr that whoever died believing that there was no God but Allah would enter paradise. Abu Dharr asked, "Even if he commits fornication and even if he steals?" and the Prophet confirmed that this was so.[3]

Not only in Tradition, but also in the broader currents of early Muslim society, Kharijite intransigent idealism was challenged. Following repeated Kharijite rebellions and their defeat by government forces, the extremist character of the movement moderated in time. (One sub-group, the 'Ibadiyyah, which originated in Basrah, Iraq, has managed to survive peacefully until the present day in Oman, East Africa, and North Africa.) The Kharijite question "Who is *not* a believer?" shocked the community into pondering the broader problems of self-definition, which in turn stimulated the process of theological debate and writing. The matter was of some urgency. In the century following the first *fitnah*, during the rapid expansion of Muslim rule over non-Muslim territories, political dissent within the ruling Muslim stratum posed a threat to Muslim control over the larger dominions. Moreover, dissent expressed in religious terms increased the need to elaborate and consolidate a coherent expression of faith and the law which could stand the stresses of the *ummah*'s transformation from its Meccan-Medinan heartland into an international faith community. In one sense, what was at stake was the continued success of the very mission of the Prophet himself.

THE MURJI'ITES

The initial response to the Kharijites came from a loosely related group of scholars and their followers referred to as the Murji'ites. The name bore a political coloring, meaning the "suspension of judgment" on the question of whether a particular person, including the Caliph, was a believer or a *kafir*. This could only be a matter for the judgment of Allah. The name also had a theological nuance where Murji'ite views on the essential structure of belief were concerned. Belief came to be understood by Muslim scholars as comprising three factors: *tasdiq* (*bi'l-qalb*), or the assent, avowal of the truth by the heart; *iqrar* (*bi'l-lisan*), or verbal confession of the truth by the tongue; and *'amal* (*al-ta'at*), acts of obedience or good works. The Murji'ites accepted sinners as members of the community (in contrast with the Kharijites) and they also "postponed" the importance of works to a secondary rank after assent by the heart and verbal confession. It was, therefore, sufficient to have in the heart a knowledge of Allah and his messenger(s), accompanied by a love for and submission to him, and then to acknowledge this inner state verbally. It was a theory which stressed intent or motivation and can be seen to be implicitly supported by the tradition from Abu Dharr cited above. Works were not necessarily the fruit of faith or an expression of it, but rather complementary or additional to it.

As a response to the political turmoil created by the Kharijites, the Murji'ites' quietism and their desire for the unity and well-being of the community was appropriate. Equally, their doctrine had the practical effect of easing conversion to Islam at a moment when Muslim presence in the new territories needed to be strengthened among the conquered peoples. However, certain extreme Murji'ite views eventually tainted their entire position, and in the third/ninth century it was discredited by the then more confident Sunni majority as a heresy. One such view was that a person had merely to declare his faith publicly to be accepted as a believer in the sight of Allah, even if he harbored unbelief in his heart! Critics of the Murji'ites also claimed that their position encouraged total moral laxity, since works were regarded as unessential or completely irrelevant to belief. One scholar scathingly denounced their doctrine as seeming to justify the feeling that belief remained intact even if one were to have "sexual relations with his own mother and sister . . . drink wine, murder, eat forbidden food . . . neglect ritual worship and the giving of *zakat*. . ."[4] This was in direct contrast to the Kharijites, whose practice of *takfir* was based directly on their judgment of a person's actions. The Murji'ite refusal, however, to countenance expulsion of sinners from the community had a lasting impact on later generations of theologians.

FAITH AND WORKS: HANAFITE VIEWS

The implications of these positions were tackled and worked out during the first two centuries of the Abbasid Caliphate (132–341/750–950), the dynasty which succeeded the Umayyads. Amidst discussions and debates by Sunni scholars, the pendulum of opinion swung between two opposing doctrines. One was associated with adherents of the Hanafite school of law who continued to stress the importance of faith over works. As a result, opponents branded them "Murji'ites." Abu Hanifah (d. 150/767) alluded to the political origins of the inquiry on faith in a letter he wrote to a colleague in which he concluded that "a loss as to works does not involve a loss as to belief, and belief may be attained without any acts." He qualified this by adding "those who face in the direction of Mecca at prayer are true believers and no act of theirs can remove them from faith."[5] Sin in any case was not deemed a disqualification from membership of the community, as the Kharijites had insisted; the offender was simply labeled "a sinful believer." A second document ascribed to Abu Hanifah, but belonging to the next century, spelled out the position on belief, which consisted in

confessing with the tongue (*iqrar*), believing with the mind and knowing with the heart (*tasdiq*). Confession by the tongue alone is not faith, for, if this were so, all the hypocrites (*munafiqun*) would be faithful. Neither does assent of the heart alone constitute faith, for if this were so, all the People of the Book [Christians and Jews] would be faithful.[6]

Works were distinct from faith, and one person could excel another in acts. Moreover, a believer could be exempted from works but never from faith; a menstruating woman, for example, was excused from prayer. Finally, faith was judged to be indivisible. That is, it could neither increase or decrease. Otherwise it would be implied that a person could be both (partially) faithful and an infidel at the same time, which was absurd.

Mu'tazilite views

Among the Hanafites' critics were the Mu'tazilites, of whom more will be said below. They adopted the view that a grave sinner (*fasiq*) was neither an unbeliever (*kafir*) nor a believer (*mu'min*) but belonged to a separate, intermediate category between the two. Nevertheless, a sinner remained a member of the community, just as the Murji'ites and Abu Hanifah had asserted in support of community unity and growth. In his famous commentary on the Qur'an, the later Mu'tazilite scholar al-Zamakhshari (d. 538/1143) concisely defined *iman* in the following manner:

True *iman* consists in a person's being convinced of the truth, then expressing that inner conviction by the tongue, and then confirming it in deeds . . . A person who lacks inner conviction is a hypocrite (*munafiq*), however much one may attest verbally and do good works. Whoever fails to make verbal confession is an unbeliever (*kafir*), and whoever fails to "act" is a sinner (*fasiq*).[7]

Sin included acts of omission (of obligatory duties) as well as acts of commission.

Hanbalite views

The followers of Ahmad b. Hanbal confirmed an opposing position to the Hanafites which stressed the necessary inclusion of works in faith. Not surprisingly, justification was found in the Qur'an and the example of the Prophet's life. One of the earliest defenses of this position has come down to us in the short treatise by one of Ahmad ibn Hanbal's friends, Abu 'Ubayd al-Qasim b. Sallam (d. 224/839).[8] After reminding believers to obey and heed the word of Allah and his Messenger, scripture adds *Believers* (mu'minun) *are only they whose hearts tremble with awe whenever Allah is mentioned, and whenever His signs are conveyed to them, they increase them in faith* (iman) (8:2). The fact that faith could increase is understood by Abu 'Ubayd to mean that while Muhammad preached in Mecca, to confess faith (*shahadah*) was sufficient to be a believer. This simple requirement was seen as a mercy from Allah to help induce hard-hearted pagans to convert. Faith had not yet been "perfected," the point perhaps being made in the Qur'anic quotation cited earlier concerning the rustic desert Bedouin. The religious duties imposed upon the community in the Medinan period subsequently became an integral part of the faith; these duties were additions to the initial state of belief. Opponents, said Abu 'Ubayd, had misunderstood Traditions like the Gabriel *hadith* which seemed to reduce faith merely to a belief in Allah, his angels and Books and so on without reference to essential works. In sum, the structure of faith, according to Abu 'Ubayd, consisted of three factors, intention (*niyyah*), speech, and works. In a second more refined statement, he says that faith can be expressed by various parts of the body; hence knowledge of Allah is the *work* of the heart, confession the *work* of the tongue, and the rituals such as prayer the *work* of the body's limbs. Despite his refutation of the Murji'ite view of faith, Abu 'Ubayd maintained in agreement with them that a Muslim who sins does not lose the name and status of a believer; he is simply not a believer in the full sense of the word.

A much later analysis of the problems implicit in the Gabriel *hadith* was provided by a scholar whose name was synonymous with controversy in his own day but whose reputation has continued to influence the community to the present, especially among those who have been labeled inappropriately in the Western media as "fundamentalist." Theologian and jurist Ibn Taymiyyah (d. 728/1328) succeeded his father as professor of Hanbali law in Damascus. By figuratively crossing swords with rulers of the political establishments of Syria and Egypt and by aiming his polemical skills at scholars of rival legal schools he succeeded in stirring up sufficient enmity against himself to spend several spells in prison. Undeterred by these interludes of forced absence from the public arena, he taught prisoners the basics of Islam and wrote religious treatises, devoting a whole volume of his very considerable output to the question of faith.

Iman, he argued, is inextricably linked to *islam*, the former being the higher concept, embracing the latter in it. The *hadith* transmitted by Ahmad b. Hanbal that "*Islam* is external, whereas *iman* is in the heart" must be understood to mean that the inner state will of necessity be manifested externally and that any such necessary manifestation will conversely point to the inner state of the heart. Faith was not, however, mere assent of the heart (*tasdiq*), but must be accompanied by *works* of the heart like the love of Allah and his Messenger and fear of him. This "psychological" state or act leads perforce to the demand for external acts out of love for what Allah has commanded and prohibited. "Works," properly grasped, begin at the deeper level of the heart and not with the body itself. Hence "works" cannot be excluded from one's understanding of faith. Ibn Taymiyyah also held that faith may vary from one person to the next, since *tasdiq* admits of various degrees. Two persons who know that Allah and his Messenger are true and that heaven and hell are real may nevertheless differ in the strength of their love of Allah and fear of being consigned to hell. *Iman*, therefore, is a very personal and individual affair.

"If Allah wills . . ."

One final point in connection with the nature of faith may be mentioned here, as it anticipates the next section of the discussion. This concerns arguments over the addition to the descriptive statement "I am a believer" the conditional phrase, "If Allah wills (*in sha'a Allah*)." Controversy was widespread as to the precise meaning of the qualifying phrase and whether its use was permitted. Some used it to avoid appearing self-righteous. Others claimed that its use was a confession of doubt concerning one's faith. If, however, the qualification implied a believer's ardent desire to become more perfect in *iman*, then there could be no harm in it.

Rival views on the matter, based in part upon positions drawn from the Qur'an and *hadith*, continued to be espoused as tradition developed. Differences of opinion rested upon whether it was deemed possible to achieve subjective certainty of one's faith or whether faith depended solely upon the will of Allah. An extreme manifestation of this controversy arose when the phrase "If Allah wills" became entwined with a theory of faith which laid exclusive emphasis upon a person's final act in life, which determined his or her destination to heaven or hell. If one died a believer, then it mattered not what one's status during life had been; conversely, a person could die in the state of unbelief (*kufr*) even after having led a life of irreproachable piety. Ibn Taymiyyah voiced the general Sunni understanding, however, that while use of the cautionary phrase was not forbidden, its connection with the "last act" notion of faith was an innovation (*bid'ah*) unsupported by any ancient authority. One could only express the *hope* that Allah in his mercy would confirm at death one's present state of faith.

The debates which centered upon the nature of faith and membership in the community were resolved in due course by a consensus which stressed intensely catholic tendencies. Excommunication of sinners was eschewed in favor of a tolerant embrace of slight differences on matters of detail in the "creed." As the community matured, works were acknowledged as an integral part of faith the core of which lay in the heart. We have already seen a parallel expression of this ecumenical spirit in the coexistence of the four schools of law. Ahmad b. Hanbal preserved a Tradition of the Prophet which said that anyone who called his brother an infidel could equally be smeared with the same epithet.

Problems other than these, however, were inevitably raised as a kind of theological chain reaction was set off by the debates we have just examined on the nature of *iman* and *islam*. One such problem is implicit in the "last act" theory of faith and more explicitly in the Kharijites' fervent emphasis upon works: are a believer's acts created by his or her own free will or determined by Allah alone?

THE NATURE OF ALLAH

In the aftermath of the early politico-religious controversies involving Kharijites and their opponents, debate among a number of informal groups of scholars also turned upon questions concerning the nature of Allah and his relationship with his creatures. The finer points of these discussions often seem arcane to the modern mind. That these discussions were conducted with great passion and vehemence is evident. The protagonists earnestly saw in their own (and, of course, in their opponents') views practical consequences urgently touching upon the life and ultimate salvation of every believer. All were agreed, however, on one matter: the oneness or uniqueness of Allah, repeatedly stressed in scripture, Allah's own portrait of himself. Beyond this agreement, which, it transpired, was also not a simple proposition, differences of emphasis emerged as to the crucial defining attribute of Allah's nature, whether omnipotence or justice (or some other quality or combination of qualities), without which he could not be said to be Allah. These differing emphases, in their turn, reflected scholars' views as to what constitued for them the *primary* source of religious truth and guidance, revelation or reason.

AL-HASAN AL-BASRI AND THE QADARITES

One early center of ferment, both political and religious, was the southern Iraqi city of Basrah, which has already been noted as having Kharijite connections during the first Islamic century. Here there settled one of the century's most distinguished religious figures, al-Hasan al-Basri (d. 110/728), who belonged to the generation of the Prophet's Successors. Born in Medina of a Persian enfranchised slave, al-Hasan made Basrah his home for the greater part of his life. Details of his life are few. He seems not to have belonged to any political faction of his day. Nonetheless, this did not prevent him from holding certain religious views which carried a political sting. He was once asked by a provincial governor whether one was obliged to obey any order issued by the Caliph. Al-Hasan is said to have replied, "Allah outweighs the Caliph, the Caliph cannot outweigh Allah . . . Do not confuse the civil power established by Allah with His religion, for no obedience is due to a creature who disobeys his Creator."[9] He later became an important symbolic figure for many different groups who had little in common with each other. Among the writings ascribed to al-Hasan, which reveal him as a master of the sermon and aphorism, is an epistle drafted in response to a query from the reigning Umayyad Caliph 'Abd al-Malik (66–86/685–705).[10]

The letter is certainly one of the earliest Muslim expositions on the question of *qadar*, or power, understood in the sense of man's control over his own actions. The question had political implications inasmuch as those who held man accountable for his actions (known as Qadarites) saw political leaders responsible for theirs as well. The reigning Umayyad Caliphs, on the other hand, are said to have designated themselves as *God's* Caliphs, appointed by him with combined political and religious authority preordained by *his* power. Sensitive as it clearly was politically, the dispute over free will versus predestination may equally have had its origin in the scholars' contemplation of scripture and the apparently contradictory verses (6:125; 16:93) which were claimed to support one side or the other of the issue. In any event, 'Abd al-Malik beseeched al-Hasan to enlighten him on his position and the sources upon which it was based. When the reply arrived he was left in no doubt that al-Hasan was a dedicated supporter of the Qadarites.

A striking feature of the epistle is the almost exclusive use al-Hasan makes of scripture to support his argument. The discussion of free will, he hints, was a recent development in the community, and his opponents' views stemmed from their misreading of the Qur'an. God had created mankind, he says, solely for the purpose that they may worship him (51:56); none of the pious ancestors had ever denied or quarreled with this notion.

Proceeding from this point he establishes by further quotations that since Allah had forbidden abominations (6:151), he would not then *approve* of someone who had committed wrong; therefore, a person's evil act could not have been *determined* by him but was rather the result of a person's free will to act. Even prophets might err (34:50; 7:23; 28:16). Al-Hasan concludes this part of his epistle reiterating, "Allah would not openly prohibit people from something and then destine them secretly to do it as the ignorant and heedless say. If that were so He would not have said *Do what you wish* (41:40) but he would rather have said, 'Do what I have destined you to do' . . . Guidance is from Allah and error from His servants."[11] Allah's decree or determination (*qadar*) is nothing but his commandments, and he does not command evil.

His opponents, al-Hasan claimed, distort Allah's true intent by quoting such verses as *He leads astray whoever He wishes* (13:27) because they ignore the context of the preceding and following verses. The real sense is clear from another verse, *When they went astray, Allah led their hearts astray* (61:5), meaning that only after a people had disobeyed Allah did he allow their hearts to be led astray. *Allah leads astray the evildoers* (14:27); he does not misguide the doers of good. Or again, how could Allah send a prophet to be obeyed (4:63) and then prevent his people from obeying him? It would be absurd for prophets to rouse in their people a fear of Allah, to exhort them to righteousness, only to have their path blocked by divine decree. This would be a far cry from Allah, his justice and wisdom! Indeed, it is clear from another verse (74:37) that Allah has given man the capacity (*qudrah*) by which he may perform an act or refrain from it. Without choice there can be no morality in Allah's reward or punishment.

Man was free in the moral and religious sense, free in matters of faith and obedience. In the sphere of material existence, however, al-Hasan conceded that Allah's determining power (*qadar*) was certain. Material possessions, a bounty of Allah, are not a matter for boastful rejoicing, and so their diminution or loss should not be a matter for grieving. Rather, the proper response to affliction is patience, for there is security in the belief that *Surely we belong to Allah and to Him we shall return* (2:156).

Drawing this contrast between the moral and material spheres of life, al-Hasan's "hidden agenda" in his letter to the Caliph may possibly have been to sound a warning against the moral laxity he perceived to be prevalent in his day and which could be said to be a logical consequence of an absolute determinist view of Allah. The issues raised in his epistle, however, did not rest there but were the ingredients of important debates that extended over the next two centuries focusing upon how to hold the balance between the need for moral effort and a debilitating trust in Allah.

THE MUʿTAZILITES

We have already noted in the above discussion the presence of a group which dissociated itself from both the Kharijites, who held that sinners were unbelievers, and the Murjiʾites, who maintained that they were believers. The Muʿtazilites took an intermediate position on this matter and called the transgressor a *fasiq*, rather than merely a hypocrite (*munafiq*) in the pietisic manner of al-Hasan al-Basri, who perceived the world to be populated chiefly by Muslims in name and appearance only.

The precise meaning of the name "Muʿtazilite" and the problem of the Muʿtazilites' origins as a speculative theological movement have exercised scholars' ingenuity for some time.[12] It seems likely, however, that the precursors of the movement were to be found in the religious milieu of al-Hasan's adopted home of Basrah among the circle of his pious disciples, one of whom was probably responsible for the doctrine of the intermediate state which the Muʿtazilites later accepted. The legacy of al-Hasan and his successors ensured that Basrah continued as a center of active religious debate, and by the reign of the illustrious Abbasid Caliph Harun al-Rashid (d. 193/809) the Muʿtazilite movement flourished both there and in the capital, Baghdad. The Baghdad branch of the movement enjoyed the singular good fortune of Caliphal sympathy and support for a period of nearly a quarter-century, during which they played an important role in policy-making. Their ascendency was marred by ruthless attempts by the Caliphs to pressure the *ʿulamaʾ* into conformity and make the post of religious judge conditional upon acquiescence to Muʿtazilite doctrine.

Many *ʿulamaʾ* resented not only doctrines they regarded as odious but also the Caliphs' infringement of their singular privilege to formulate doctrine. The Muʿtazilite courtship with power came to an abrupt end early in the reign of the Caliph al-Mutawakkil (232–247/847–861), who had had enough of controversy and swung his support behind their opponents. Although the Muʿtazilites never regained political influence, their intellectual presence was directly felt in subsequent theological disciplines into the fifth/eleventh century and also in related areas like Qurʾan commentary well into the sixth/twelfth century. Some joined the moderate majority of the Shiʿah community, who will be treated in a later chapter. Others, who remained loyal to and fascinated by the explanatory power of reason, became philosophers and attempted to reformulate Muʿtazilite ideas within a different framework. Indeed, their impact upon the mainstream Sunni community was never totally forgotten, for in the present century, certain of their general attitudes, if not all of their doctrines, have reemerged in the guise of Islamic modernism.

Muʿtazilites and "Kalam"

The doctrine of the "intermediate state" was based upon a general attitude that religious truths, that is, belief in Allah's commands and prohibitions, were accessible by the use of reason. This attitude challenged the prevailing view that such truths were confined solely to revelation. Although a place was preserved for scripture in Muʿtazilite theological discussions, scripture's role, in their view, simply testified to the veracity of the claims of reason. From this basic assumption, the Mu'tazilites honed and refined an already existing technique of dialectical argument on matters of theological speculation which they employed in polemics against their opponents within the community, but also in encounters with Christians. The method was called *kalam*, and an exponent of the technique in theology was known as a *mutakallim*, a dialectical theologian. The early role of these individuals seems to have been as ascetic preachers drawn from among the merchants of the markets of Basrah who wore special garb and performed supererogatory acts of prayer and fasting.

The philosopher Abu Nasr Muhammad al-Farabi (d. 340/ 950) neatly distinguished the aims of a jurist from a those of a theologian in his work *The Enumeration of the Sciences*, as follows: "the jurist takes the opinions and the actions stated explicitly by the founder of the religion and, using them as axioms, he infers the things that follow from them as consequences. The dialectical theologian, on the other hand, defends the things that the jurist uses as axioms, without inferring other things from them."[13]

The *kalam* method is found in two complementary styles of argument. The first, possible traces of which may be seen in certain passages of the Qur'an (2:142), appears in the use of the simple defensive formula "if you say . . . then we say." The more developed, sophisticated and aggressive style follows a pattern of argument by which an opponent is questioned on a matter of belief and is then placed on the horns of a dilemma by being offered two mutually exclusive alternatives. Regardless of the opponent's answer, he or she is reduced either to a contradiction or refutation of his or her own position. The method was not only used by the Mu'tazilites and their Qadarite predecessors but by their opponents as well, who quickly appreciated the method's effective cutting edge in demolishing views they held in total contempt. A short, early example of this technique is found in an anti-Qadarite argument which challenges, from a predestinarian viewpoint, their belief that evil acts are man's alone, since they cannot be associated with Allah:

Did Allah will *good* for mankind and then establish Hell for them, or did He will *evil* for them by doing so? If they answer *good*, then they should be asked how that could be when He created Hell knowing there would be no benefit in it, but only harm for them. If they answer *evil*, then they refute their own doctrine.[14]

The question raised by this single point of contention went to the heart of Mu'tazilite theological concerns, the nature of Allah. The

Mu'tazilites were known as "The people of unity (*tawhid*) and justice ('*adl*)," referring to their two central doctrines. Three minor principles were also adhered to by Mu'tazilites, one being the "intermediate state" of a transgressor already mentioned. Of the remaining two, one is linked directly with the nature of Allah. His Qur'anic decrees are a *truthful* promise to the faithful of the reward of paradise and a *just* warning to the infidel and unrepentant Muslim of an abode in hell. The other principle stresses the obligation of every Muslim to promote and defend true faith and good acts and fight against infidelity and reprehensible acts. All three principles are corollaries of the basic assumption that the faithful can rationally know what is obligatory and forbidden and moreover, that reward and punishment are the just deserts of free and accountable human action.

Mu'tazilites: people of unity and justice

One of the two central Mu'tazilite doctrines, Allah's unity (*tawhid*), was aimed against a number of opponents. Implicitly it challenged the popular notion, based upon numerous Traditions which the Mu'tazilites did not hold in high regard, that Allah could be seen by the faithful in paradise. It was directed, too, against simple anthropomorphic interpretation of the attributes or qualities of Allah mentioned in the Qur'an. The Mu'tazilites, therefore, made enemies among the traditionists who clung devoutly to the authentic spiritual value of the prophetic *hadith*; and they embittered those who took Allah's description of himself in the Qur'an as literal and real. The Mu'tazilites were not only concerned with opposing Muslim traditionists within the community. They also perceived the Christian belief in the trinity and Magian dualist views of two eternal, contending forces, good and evil, as external threats to genuine Muslim doctrine which required solid defense based upon reason independently of revelation.

Each of these positions is touched upon in the following phrases extracted from a summary of their doctrine of Allah:

The Mu'tazilites all agree that *Allah is One* (2:158), there is *nothing like him* (42:9) and *he is the Hearing One, the Seeing One* (17:1), and is not a substance or an object or a body ... nor does he move or rest; nor is he divided. He has not parts or atoms or limbs or members ... he is not bound by the limitations of space or time ... nor is he to be compared with mankind, or likened to creatures in any way at all. He is eternally first, antecedent, prior to contingent beings, existent before created things. He is eternally Knowing, Powerful and Living and thus he continues. Eyes do not see him, nor does sight attain to him.[15]

The profusion of negatives in this portrait was based upon the assumption that reason could ascertain the truth of the world's creation in time by an eternal maker. It concluded that Allah, therefore, must be utterly different from all created things. For example, scriptural descriptions of Allah having hands (48:10) and a face could not be accepted in any literal sense. Rather, they had to be interpreted allegorically to mean his grace and his knowledge. Opponents, however, accused the Mu'tazilites of "denuding" Allah, describing him negatively and denying the reality of the attributes by which he described himself in scripture and which were further supported in Tradition.

Other qualities, however, were not expressed in negative terms and were treated differently. "Knowing," "powerful," and "living" were described as eternal and unchangeable qualities subsisting in Allah; these were attributes of essence. On the other hand, attributes of action like "hearing" and "seeing" did not subsist in him and therefore could change by coming into being and ceasing to be without affecting Allah essentially. By analogy, Allah "speaks" as well as hears and sees. The Mu'tazilites concluded, therefore, that since his speech or word is embodied in the Qur'an, it had come into being and was thus "created" just as were time, space and matter. For if the Qur'an were preexistent and eternal, rather than created, this would entail another eternal entity besides Allah, the unique One. And that was a pernicious form of polytheism.

Opponents were outraged. At the time of discussions about the "created" Qur'an, Mu'tazilites were enjoying their honeymoon in power. The doctrine became a *cause célèbre* and featured in a furious political and religious row. At the center of it all was the indomitable Ahmad b. Hanbal, who stoutly refused to submit to the Caliph's strong-arm methods to force a hated doctrine upon 'ulama' who fiercely resisted limitations on their independence to pronounce upon doctrine and the law. Ibn Hanbal and his supporters found scriptural evidence for the Qur'an's preexistence on a heavenly tablet (85:21) whence it was sent down to Muhammad in the month of Ramadan. But the Mu'tazilites saw another problem in this position. The Qur'an contained numerous allusions to historical peoples and events, for example, the prophets Moses, Noah, Salih, and Hud. The claim that the word of Allah was eternal rather than created would, they argued, imply that the fate of all these peoples had been predetermined. That conclusion was directly opposed by the Muʿtazilites' second major doctrine, the justice of Allah.

This doctrine was a continuation of the concerns of al-Hasan al-Basri and the Qadarites. They shared the view in common with the Muʿtazilites that man was the author of his works and was thereby accountable and responsible for choices he made. The Muʿtazilites, however, seem to have laid greater emphasis on protecting the ethical nature of Allah rather than that of man. Evil, injustice, and disobedience to Allah's commands were neither willed nor created by him, but were rather the consequences of man's own free will. Conversely, Allah would be *unjust* if he punished individuals for acts over which they had no control and for which they were not responsible.

Among the clear signs of Allah's goodness and mercy were the prophets sent with revelation to confirm what reason could discover for itself. Consequently, Allah's eternal knowledge meant that he *knew* what a person would do by his or her own activity, not that he would *determine* what people would do by his knowledge. Allah knew that a person would be an unbeliever, but made him or her able to be otherwise. Moreover, when Allah claimed that he had set a seal upon the hearts of unbelievers (2:6), it meant that his act of sealing followed upon a person's unbelief and did not precede or cause it.

Muʿtazilites analyzed freedom as the capacity to perform an act through a series of moments. A formula accepted by many was that "a person is able in the first moment of time to perform an act in the second moment of time. Thus, before the second moment exists, it is said that the act 'will be done' in that second moment. When the second moment existed, it is said that the act 'has been done.'"[16]

These views were challenged not because opponents denied the absolute justice of Allah. Rather they perceived the general Muʿtazilite orientation to contain a threat to painstaking successes in areas of common concern other than theology, such as the law. First was the threat to the status of prophetic Traditions, the importance of which Muʿtazilites tended to play down; second, the rebuff to a more literal but also more widely popular and accessible understanding of the Qur'an; and third, opponents perceived a threat to scripture if reason was ever claimed to be the sole source of religious truth. The traditionist opposition to Muʿtazilite doctrines found a spokesman for its cause in an unexpected quarter, from a former Muʿtazilite who

had experienced "conversion" and had abandoned their ranks. This
scholar was Abu al-Hasan al-Ash'ari, whose works marked a turning
point in the history of Islamic theology.

AL-ASH'ARI

Al-Ash'ari was born in Basrah in the generation after the Mu'tazilites
had fallen from Caliphal grace in Baghdad. Like most young
intellectuals he first studied law, and then he devoted himself to
theology at the feet of the prominent Mu'tazilite al-Jubba'i (d.
303/915). Several versions of his "conversion" have survived as
symbolic if not factual accounts of the experience. They tell in varying
detail of the Prophet's appearance before al-Ash'ari in a series of
dreams. In one, the Prophet urges al-Ash'ari to defend his teachings
preserved in the Traditions, an allusion to Mu'tazilite indifference
toward them. Ash'ari complied and abandoned the study of *kalam* to
devote every moment to acquiring a deeper knowledge of *hadith*. In
another appearance, however, the Prophet rebuked al-Ash'ari for
this course of action, saying "I told you to defend Tradition, not to
abandon *kalam*!" In other words, he was to employ the Mu'tazilites'
own weapon of the dialectic to refute their doctrines. The usually
helpful Ibn Khallikan says of al-Ash'ari that owing to the scholar's
celebrated status he could dispense with writing a lengthy article on
him! He does not mention the conversion experience, but merely
notes the public disavowal in a mosque of his previous beliefs.
Nevertheless, we are told that he was a man of gaiety and humor. He
supported himself from the income of an estate which an ancestor had
made into a religious endowment (*waqf*), and his daily expenses
amounted to 17 dirhems a day. Al-Ash'ari died (324/935) in
Baghdad, and his mausoleum was erected on a plot of land between a
mosque and a public bath situated near the bank of the River Tigris.[17]

Al-Ash'ari showed every respect for the traditionists' great patron
Ahmad b. Hanbal, who, he claimed, had fought against all manner of
innovator, deviator, and skeptic. His own agenda, however, involved
strengthening attachment to Tradition while defending it by the
rational arguments of *kalam*, despite the hostility this sparked off
among Ibn Hanbal's followers. Al-Ash'ari wrote a short work
vindicating the use of *kalam* which, even if it belonged to his earlier
Mu'tazilite period, doubtless informed his later attitude toward
kalam. Opponents of *kalam* asserted that the Prophet and his Companions

had discussed and fully explained all necessary matters of religion. Any other matter not raised by them meant that they were ignorant of it or had not discussed it. In either case there was no subsequent need to explore such questions, certainly not by employing the rational arguments of *kalam*. Against this line of thought al-Ash'ari retorted that the Prophet had also never denied that the questions dealt with by *kalam* should be discussed. It was, moreover, perfectly legitimate for scholars to engage in *kalam* in order to give the uninformed the means of judging these matters for themselves.[18]

The purpose of the broad movement which flourished after al-Ash'ari was to challenge and modify the conclusions reached by the Mu'tazilites. The principle believed to provide the soundest interpretation of scripture and *hadith* was a reading based upon their face value rather than speculation, unless good reason was found to depart from the clear meaning of the texts. Reason should fall under the authority of revelation. The objective, in short, was to steer a middle course between extreme Mu'tazilite rationalism and the more rigid literalism of the traditionists.

Al-Ash'ari on Allah's unity and attributes

On the question of divine unity, al-Ash'ari clung to his key scriptural texts that *there is naught like Him* (42:9) and *none is His equal* (112:4), which the Mu'tazilites accepted, too, as we have seen above. Allah is one, single, and eternal and can in no way be likened to his creatures. From this point of agreement, however, al-Ash'ari did not draw the same conclusions as the Mu'tazilites. As for the divine attributes, he accepted Allah's description of himself in the Qur'an. Thus he said: "If we are asked, 'Do you believe Allah has two hands?' the answer is: We believe it and His words *I have created with my two hands* (38:75) is proof of it."[19] In addition to this scriptural support, he also offered a rational explanation based upon linguistic usage that "hands" cannot be understood allegorically to mean "grace" after the Mu'tazilite fashion. In ordinary Arabic usage (the language of the Qur'an) one cannot say "I have done something with my hands" meaning "with my grace." Nor can the expressions "hands" and "eyes" (54:14) and "face" (55:27) be understood in a crudely anthropomorphic way. Mankind simply cannot fathom these descriptions. They are to be accepted *bila kayfa*, "without questioning how" they all harmoniously form part of Allah's nature. This avoided the risk of attributing to Allah what he had not revealed of himself. Indirectly, the attitude emphasizes the fact that Islam is less concerned with knowledge of Allah's nature than with his law. The sixth-/twelfth-century theologian Muwaffaq al-Din ibn Qudamah (d. 541/1146) stressed this while condemning as irrelevant any interpretation of his qualities, "For we have no need to know the meaning which Allah intended by His attributes; *no course of action is intended by them, nor is there any obligation attached to them* except to believe in them. It is possible to believe in them without the knowledge of their intended sense."[20]

Al-Ash'ari asserted the existence of Allah's hearing and seeing by similar arguments. He did not deny their reality as the Mu'tazilites had done by saying these attributes were changeable and could come into being and cease to be. On the basis of scripture, too, he accepted that Allah will be seen by the faithful on the Day of Judgment because of his words, *Some faces will on that Day be bright with happiness, looking upon their Lord* (75:22–23). He explained the favorite Mu'tazilite text refuting this position, *Eyes do not attain to Him* (6:103), as referring to this world, but not to the hereafter.

He also confirmed the uncreated nature of the Qur'an, citing as proof the famous verse where Allah says: *Whenever We will anything to be, We but say to it "Be!" and it is* (16:40).[21] Since the creator's speech was with him eternally, the Qur'an as his speech must be uncreated. When a Muslim reads, recites, writes, or memorizes the Qur'an, he or she is not thereby "creating" it as Allah creates from nothing. Rather, he or she is merely reproducing the text.

Al-Ash'ari on Allah's omnipotence

As we have seen, the Mu'tazilites were chiefly concerned with protecting the notion of Allah's justice and, therefore, of the freedom of the actions of mankind. Al-Ash'ari, on the other hand, seems to have been primarily dedicated to defending the idea of Allah's omnipotence as creator. This is expressed in the style of a *kalam* argument as follows:

If our opponents say that there are under His authority things He does not will (such as evil), there exist, in that case, things of which He disapproves. They will certainly answer "yes."

Then it may be said to them: Therefore you cannot deny that there are under His authority things the existence of which He forbids. If they make a reply to this, the answer is: Then disobedience exists, whether Allah wishes or forbids it; and that is an attribute of weakness and poverty. May Allah be far removed from that![22]

Belief and the capacity to believe are, therefore, a gracious gift and favor from Allah, that is, a function of his all-determining power. Al-Ash'ari provides the following as one among several rejoinders to his opponents' views:

It may also be said to them: Has Allah power over the grace He gives the infidels so that they may be faithful? Wherefore if they say no, they assert His impotence. May He be far above that! But if they say, "Yes, He has power over it, and *if He gave them grace, they would surely believe*," then they abandon their belief (in man's free will) and believe the truth.[23]

Allah's stated purpose in creating humankind was solely for it to worship him. He has the power to will belief and unbelief, obedience and disobedience. By faith (not reason) one accepts that Allah is as he describes himself in scripture, *bila kayfa*, and that he commands what *rationally* may seem impossible and unjust. Everything is possible for Allah, and faith accepts that justice lies in what he commands. For al-Ash'ari, the fundamental error of the Mu'tazilites lay in their imputing to Allah a *rational* purpose and then in attempting to impose upon him how he must act, namely behaving justly toward his creatures. This was simply to detract from his omnipotence. It could be said that it showed a lack of *faith* in Allah's essential justice, mercy, and compassion.

By protecting the omnipotence of the transcendent, unique, eternal, creator Allah, al-Ash'ari risked painting himself into the corner occupied by extreme determinists, the so-called Compulsionists, who denied that man had any power at all to act. He was, however, aware that the consequences of determinism led to a crippling moral laxity or paralysis. He argued that we are conscious of certain involuntary motions in our bodies like shivering from the cold or a fever over which we have no control. Moreover, we are conscious of the distinction between these and other movements, like our "coming and going," which we perform without any feeling of impotency. In acts like these, he concluded, there is a power created in us, by Allah to perform them. The resulting act is thus "acquired" by us, for which, al-Ash'ari insisted, we are responsible and accountable.[24] Nevertheless, he conceded that Allah creates both the involuntary and the acquired types of act in us. Allah's omnipotence was the converse of mankind's total dependence upon him.

Allah furthermore creates both the evil and the good actions of his creatures, a position denied by the Muʿtazilites, who would not associate evil with a just deity. But al-Ashʿari repeatedly asserts that evil and injustice are not created by Allah for himself but for his creatures. This point seems to mean that *evil* and injustice in the world can only touch humankind as a counterpart of the *good* which Allah commands. The one cannot be known without the presence of the other. Allah does not command evil, although he does create it. In this fashion, too, al-Ashʿari strove to preserve the infinite power of Allah while at the same time underlining the need of his creatures to respond to his guidance in a morally responsible way.

Al-Ashʿari's handling of the "theory of acquisition" (*kasb, iktisab*) caused later scholars unease and some worked to modify his views. The individual required greater evidence of participation in the performance of his or her acts. One proposed solution was that the actor's choice or intention must precede the "acquired" act created by Allah. Another described Allah as the ultimate or remote cause of an act while the individual was its immediate cause. On the other hand, theologians who followed more closely the predestinarian views of al-Ashʿari were, like al-Ashʿari himself, fully conscious that Allah's infinite power infused everything he created, including the moral sphere. Awareness of Allah's omnipotence demanded, therefore, recognition of the necessity of mankind's moral choice and freedom which in the end are guaranteed by his gift of grace (*tawbah*).

THEOLOGIANS AND PHILOSOPHERS

Debates over the nature of Allah, his creation, and the destiny of humankind were not the monopoly of the practitioners of *kalam*. Theologians confined their questions to those raised by revelation. Philosophy in Islam developed out of non-religious sciences, both practical and theoretical, which included logic, ethics, physics, mathematics, music, astronomy, psychology, medicine, metaphysics, and politics. These were the "sciences of the Ancients," so-called because they came to Muslim scholars through the medium of translations of works chiefly from the Greek but also from the Persian Pahlavi and Indian Sanskrit languages. The scope of philosophy, in other words, was universal, dealing with all branches of knowledge. The only limits to the philosopher's exploration were those of reason itself. In his famous *Introduction to History*, Ibn Khaldun (d. 808/1406) observed that while philosophy investigated, for example, the physical and metaphysical worlds in and for themselves, theology dealt with the same subjects only insofar as they served as arguments for the creator of existence itself. Theology was a useful weapon in combating heresy and defending the faith by means of logical argument "so that innovations may be repulsed and doubts and misgivings concerning the articles of faith removed."[25]

Philosophers' descriptions of Allah and his creative acts differed from those of the theologians, including even the Mu'tazilites, who, like the philosophers, had argued their views on rational grounds. Two thinkers, al-Farabi (d. 339/950), whom Muslims called the Second Teacher (after Aristotle), and Ibn Sina (d. 429/1037, known in European thought as Avicenna), whose influence was so profound on later philosophers, more than any others shaped the general character of Islamic philosophy. At the same time, each was conscious of the need for a sound metaphysic which could be seen to bridge the gap between philosophy and the foundations of the new faith, Islam. Their efforts, however, did not dispel theologians' suspicions of the philosopher's enterprise.

Al-Ghazali

The theologian-jurist Abu Hamid al-Ghazali made a concerted attempt to formulate the "proper" relationship between theology and philosophy. He was born in Tus in northern Iran and died there in 505/1111. An adherent of al-Shafi'i's legal thought, he also studied theology, and so prodigious were his talents, says Ibn Khallikan, that even during the lifetime of his famous teacher al-Juwayni (d. 478/1085) he had become one of the most distinguished scholars of the day as his reputation "spread with the caravans to distant lands."[26] The height of his public career came with his appointment as professor of theology in the new *madrasah* founded in Baghdad by the wazir Nizam al-Mulk. There he wrote his treatises on philosophy and attacks against an extreme political manifestation of Shi'ism, the Isma'ilis. Four years later he succumbed to a malady which left him in a state of doubt as to the proper way to pursue and achieve religious truth. He addressed the problem of this crisis and the development of his ideas in a thematic "autobiography" written toward the end of his life.[27] His views of theologians had moderated somewhat from his early days. Nonetheless he held *kalam* to be more a useful tool of defense against heretics than a means of achieving certainty on crucial matters of faith such as knowledge of Allah and salvation. He accepted, on the other hand, the benefits of the philosophers' inquiries into logic, mathematics, ethics, and politics, but had grave misgivings about their treatment of metaphysics. In an incisive polemical treatise entitled *The Incoherence of the Philosophers*, al-Ghazali attacked the views he judged most inimical to faith. He discussed twenty theses in detail, seventeen of which were dismissed as innovations. The remainder, however, he denounced in a more severe legal manner as entailing unbelief. Some fundamental differences between the theologians and philosophers can be illustrated by the three theses al-Ghazali condemned outright: the philosophers' belief in the eternity of the world, their view that Allah could not know the particulars of his creation, and their denial of the resurrection of the body after death. Each side portrays Allah in starkly contrasting terms.[28]

Eternity or creation of the world

First, the theologians held that at some moment in the distant past Allah had created the world out of nothing. To deny this doctrine was to deny Allah revelation. Philosophers, on the other hand, argued that although Allah was the supreme cause of all existence other than his own, creation of the world out of nothing was impossible. The act of creation would mean a change in the nature of Allah, who is, by definition, unchangeable. Metaphorically, creation is like the radiation of the sun's light outward, the sun itself remaining unchanged. In the philosophers' terms, creation is an entirely involuntary emanation from Allah, which he neither wills nor chooses and which no obstacle can prevent. And since Allah is eternally active, the world which proceeds from him must also be eternal. The world was conceived in this scheme as the final link in a hierarchical chain of Celestial Intellects which is itself the effect of this activity. This depiction of Allah, the First Cause or Necessary Being, in the philosophers' jargon, seemed to theologians remote from the Qur'anic paradigm they sought to defend. Allah would never, al-Ghazali insisted, act by necessity of his very nature, but only when and how he willed to do so.[29]

Particulars or universals

The second doctrine which al-Ghazali attacked as entailing unbelief was the philosophers' claim that Allah did not know the particulars of his creation except in "a universal way." That is, he did not know the individual man but only the universal qualities of man in the abstract.[30] This would lead to absurdities, al-Ghazali pointed out. Opponents would be bound to say, for example, that although Muhammad had proclaimed his prophecy, Allah did not know that he had done so; or worse, that Allah could only know of the belief or unbelief of man-in-general but not the particular states or actions of any specific individual. Since the Allah of scripture was clearly concerned with the individual's destiny, the philosophers' position was untenable.

Body or soul

Finally, the philosophers held that as the soul alone was immortal, the resurrection of the body was impossible. Souls do not return to their bodies after death as the theologians believed. Philosophers denied also the physical reality of paradise and hell or, in Qur'anic terminology, the Garden and the Fire. Philosophers, said al-Ghazali, "maintain that these things are mere symbols mentioned for the common man in order to ease his understanding of the spiritual nature of reward and punishment which are superior to those of a physical character."[31] The negation of bodily resurrection, al-Ghazali rejoined, was a denial of Allah's power to execute it.

Belief in these three doctrines, he concluded, is to "accuse the prophets of falsehood, and to consider their teachings as a hypocritical misrepresentation designed to appeal to the masses. And this is blatant blasphemy to which no Muslim sect would subscribe."[32]

Al-Ghazali's polemical judgment of the philosophers was only partially fair. The philosophers conceded that their language differed from that of the theologians. Theological discussion employed symbols and images so that the non-philosopher could easily grasp the essentials of his or her faith. Symbolism, moreover, was a veil to shield the uninitiated from what they were incapable of comprehending. Philosophers were nonetheless convinced that their esoteric conception of Islam was in accord with scripture, since theology and philosophy yielded the same fundamental truths. But they never accused the prophets of falsehood.

For his part, al-Ghazali also judged the masses incapable of grasping the profoundest realities of religious truth. He argued, too, that ordinary believers needed protection from certain notions which could confuse and corrupt their faith. The real tension between theologians and philosophers, however, concerned their different views of the Godhead. The philosophers depicted it as an austere, utterly transcendent, All-Knowing, but essentially unknowable, Mind. Al-Ghazali also defended the concept of Allah's transcendency, in accordance with Qur'anic descriptions which explicitly added the attributes of will, power, speech, hearing, seeing, compassion, and justice. However, he asserted that the Godhead was a more personal Being, more accessible to the comprehension of the ordinary believer.

Al-Ghazali, who had composed his *Incoherence of the Philosophers* in Baghdad, did not have the last word in the dispute with the philosophers. In Cordoba, at the western end of the Muslim world, the philosopher-jurist Ibn Rushd (d. 595/1198, in European thought known as Averroes) also took up the challenge.[33] First, as a scholar of the law, he defended by means of scripture the legal obligation of philosophers, society's gifted few, to pursue their exploration into all existent things as manifestations of divine wisdom. But under no circumstances must the mysteries of existence be disclosed to the masses. Then in a philosophical treatise entitled *The Incoherence of "The Incoherence"*[34] he attacked al-Ghazali's refutation of the philosophers as incompetent and ineffective. The conflict between philosophy and theology was merely apparent rather than real. Ibn Rushd acknowledged that while theology had a role to play, it should be subject to the scrutiny of philosophy in order to fulfill the intent of the divine law, which was to assure the happiness of the whole community.

Disputes between philosophers and theologians died away in the generations after Ibn Rushd, although philosophers continued to explore their own concerns within certain circles of the Shi'ah and the Sufi mystics. For theologians of the Sunni persuasion, like al-Ghazali, the portrait of Allah continued to be drawn directly from the data of revelation rather than speculative reason: the sole creator God, at once transcendent and yet immanent, the supreme Guide throughout history whose will can be known through his prophets and who can be known through the medium of his creation, however imperfect and indirect that apprehension may be. One final feature of the Godhead requires treatment here, inasmuch as it touches upon the last of the three counts of infidelity with which al-Ghazali accused the philosophers, namely corporeal resurrection. The following section deals briefly with Allah as the sole arbiter of man's fate on the Day of Judgment.

LAST THINGS

The philosophers accepted that scripture emphatically affirmed corporeal resurrection, but they denied that this teaching must be understood in a purely literal sense. Theologians like al-Ghazali, on the other hand, asserted that scriptural verses concerning resurrection were unambiguous and did not warrant allegorical interpretation. Tradition, moreover, confirmed that bodily resurrection and the judgment were among the fundamentals of the faith.

Al-Ghazali left an account of the events and process of the afterlife in the final section of his *magnum opus, The Revival of the Religious Sciences*, a work of enduring influence which is studied in the Muslim world to this day.[35] His treatment of eschatology draws naturally upon scripture and the Traditions, of which the latter are often picturesque in detail.

The inevitabilty of the resurrection and the Day of Judgment (although not necessarily its immanence) had been part of the earliest message stressed in the Qur'an. Contemplation of the gravity of the event had implications for the behavior in this world of every believer. Al-Ghazali felt that in his own day the greater part of mankind did not take the Day seriously. He cautioned:

It is part of human nature to deny all that is unfamiliar. If a man had never beheld a snake walking upon its belly like a flash of lightning he would deny the possibility of anything walking without a foot . . . So beware denying any of the wonders of the Day because they fail to accord with the measure of mundane things.[36]

The length and intensity of anticipation of that Day preceding the final judgment itself must be contemplated by all so that "perhaps endurance in the face of sin in your fleeting life in this world may grow easier for you."[37]

When Allah decides that his servant's time has arrived, he sends the Angel of Death to seize his soul. The deceased are questioned on their faith in the grave by two angels of fearful aspect called Munkar and Nakir. The *shahadah* is therefore recited to the dying so the last words they hear are "There is no god but Allah . . ." to ensure that the response to the angels is correct and to foil attempts at seduction by Satan. The questioning does not determine the deceased's final fate but does underline the link between a creature's accountability in this world and recompense in the next.

The Last Day of terrestrial time, heralded by a trumpet blast, is preceded by a period of apocalyptic signs which include the reversal of the natural and moral order of things, for example the rising of the sun in the west and the prevalence of pride over piety, of lies over truth. The end of the world is proclaimed by a messianic figure, sometimes identified with Jesus, who slays the one-eyed anti-Christ, Dajjal, and defeats the enemies of peace and justice, Gog and Magog, who have swept down upon civilization from the north. Then, at the moment prescribed, the four-winged archangel Israfil standing beneath the throne of Allah sounds his trumpet to awaken the dead and assemble the hordes upon a great expansive plain. The Day of Resurrection (*yawm al-qiyamah*) has arrived. Al-Ghazali vividly describes the scene. "The sun's burning and the heat of their breath conjoin with the conflagration produced in their hearts by the flames of shame and fear, and perspiration pours forth from the root of every hair until it flows upon the plain of the Resurrection and rises over their bodies in proportion to their favour with Allah."[38] The "Day" lasts hundreds, even thousands, of years, during which the sun and stars are extinguished and the earth plunged into darkness.

Accounts differ as to the most terrible moment of the Last Day. To some it occurs when oppressors are confronted by those they oppressed, when the angels bear witness to the deeds of all and Allah acts as interrogator at the final judgment. Each person is handed a book of his or her deeds to read, or the deeds are weighed upon the pans of a scale. The final obstacle is a bridge over which the saved traverse and enter the gardens of paradise, while the damned tumble off into the fires of hell. For al-Ghazali the crossing holds the greatest terror, and he seizes upon its description to reiterate his earlier warning that he "who is safest from the terrors of the Day is he who contemplated them most abundantly in this world." The same didactic purpose is expressed in Traditions where the Prophet describes twelve classes of people gathered together on the Day of Resurrection (77:18). Usurers, for example, will emerge from their graves as dogs; those who incited discord among people will appear as monkeys; those who pursued passion and pleasure will be gathered bound hand and foot with their own hair. Each group is identified with those who committed an offense cited in scripture, from stealing the property of orphans to disobeying one's parents, but who did not repent of their actions. The warning to the living is evident.[39]

The division of mankind into the communities of the Garden and the Fire is not the end of the story. Allah in his infinite compassion and mercy permits Muhammad, in the company of all the prophets, to intercede on behalf of sinful Muslims in the Fire and bring them forth to the River of Life and thence into the Garden. Al-Ghazali goes further. Even those who enjoy a good relation with Allah will be given the right to intercede on behalf of their families, kinsmen, friends, and acquaintances. He therefore admonishes the faithful to be zealous in acquiring such favor with Allah. This may be achieved by never belittling an act of obedience or underestimating an act of transgression, but above all "by never despising any human creature, for Allah has hidden sainthood among His bondsmen, and it may well be that the person your eye scorns is one of His Saints."[40] Later theologians saw in the purpose of the Fire a means of purification, a kind of temporary purgatory holding out the prospect that all might eventually enjoy the reward of the Garden.

The events of the Last Day occur as the final act of the cosmic drama which commences with creation and runs through the entire gamut of human history. Every vivid physical detail of the resurrection and judgment underscores the belief that sinful acts may be mitigated by repentence in this life and by intercession in the next. Most crucial of all was Allah's grace, which, for the theologians, was an aspect of his power. The same Arabic word strikingly conveys the dependent but ultimately reciprocal relationship between man and God in this drama: if a sinner sincerely turns away from sin in repentance (*tawbah*), Allah restores him or her to his grace (*tawbah*). Death is an end. Resurrection is a new beginning, the return to Allah as promised in scripture (96:8). To the believer Allah's essential oneness (*tawhid*) is finally revealed and he comprehends the truth of his words, *All that lives on earth or in the heavens is bound to pass away: but forever will abide the face of Allah full of majesty and glory* (55:26).

Theologians like Ibn Taymiyyah understood the concept of perfection (*ihsan*) mentioned in the Gabriel *hadith* as being a degree higher than faith (*iman*) and *islam*. As perfection comprised all of the attributes contained in the other two concepts, it naturally applied to fewer persons who might achieve that rank. Perfection meant, in the words of the Tradition, to "worship Allah *as though* you saw him, for he sees you though you do not see him." The true vision of Allah, according to al-Ash'ari and al-Ghazali among Sunni scholars, was only a reality for the faithful in the afterlife, a possibility the Mu'tazilites had even denied. Al-Ghazali regarded the vision of Allah as the very limit of bliss. Compared to meeting the Lord, all the other delights of paradise were as "those of a beast let loose in a pasture."[41] Within the community, on the other hand, others read the Tradition in a different light. For Muslim mystics, the Sufis, a vision of the Lord was not only possible but desirable as the goal of spiritual perfection in this life. And so we shall turn next to an account of this rich expression of the religious life in Islam.

CHAPTER 5

The way of the Sufi

A MUSLIM ''ROBINSON CRUSOE''

In the famous sixth-/twelfth-century philosophical tale *Hayy b. Yazqan*,[1] the hero first encounters another human when he is fifty. Abandoned as an infant on a remote, uninhabited island off the coast of India, Hayy was raised by a doe foster-mother until her death when he was seven years of age. His initial experience of life was the animals' experience of nature. Hayy was different from the animals, however, by virtue of his gift of reason. The next stages of his life, until he was twenty-one, were spent discovering how to use and control nature for his own purposes.

From there Hayy's thought developed from reflection upon the order of the physical world to unraveling the mysteries of the metaphysical world; from the discovery of his own vital spirit or soul to that of the One Necessary Existent Being, with whom all creation began. Given his innate capacities and his experiences of life, discovery alone was not enough for Hayy. Wisdom seeks more than knowledge.

Seeing that what made him different from all other animals made him like the heavenly bodies, Hayy judged that this implied an obligation on his part to take them as his pattern, imitate their action and do all he could to be like them. By the same token, Hayy saw that his nobler part, by which he knew the Necessarily Existent, bore some resemblance to Him as well. For like Him it transcended the physical. Thus another obligation was to endeavor, in whatever way possible, to attain His attributes, to imitate His ways, and remould His character to His, diligently execute His will, surrender all to Him, accept in His heart His every judgement outwardly and inwardly. Even when He caused harm or pain to his body, even if He destroyed it completely, he must rejoice in His rule.[2]

Hayy attained his goal. From the discovery of the incorporeal, eternal part of himself, he strove toward achieving the highest degree of philosophical and religious insight, and through the contemplation of God, the attainment of happiness, a vision in this life of "goodness, beauty, joy without end, the like of which eyes cannot see, ears hear or human hearts conceive, ineffable, known only by the aware who arrive."[3] He reached his goal on his solitary island first by reason and contemplation and then by his soul's domination of the body. In this state he made his first human contact, with Asal.

Asal had grown up on another island, where the inhabitants followed the teachings of an ancient prophet. He and his good friend Salaman adhered to the laws and precepts of their faith and studied together revelation's description of God, his angels, resurrection and his reward and punishment. The two young comrades, however, accepted their faith in different ways. Asal was prepared to attempt an allegorical interpretation of scripture while Salaman was more concerned to preserve its literal sense and check the free reign of his thoughts. "Still, each of them executed the express commands of the text fastidiously, kept watch over his soul, and fought his passions."[4] The cause of their final parting was that Asal, by nature contemplative, clung to statements in the law proposing a life of solitude and isolation; Salaman, on the other hand, preferred the company of others and saw in the law's focus on the community a protection from the goadings of the devil.

Asal hired a craft to take him to a solitary island where, unknown to him, Hayy lived. For a time their paths did not cross. When the inevitable encounter occurred, it was at first mutually perplexing, except that each intuitively recognized that the other had sought and found the Truth. As a bond developed between them, Asal taught Hayy language and was able to question him about his life on the island. When he heard Hayy's description of beings divorced from the sense-world and his contact with the divine, Asal had no doubt that all the Traditions of his religion about God, the Last Day, heaven and hell were symbolic representations of things Hayy had witnessed for himself. For Asal the eyes of his heart were opened: "his mind caught fire. Reason and tradition were at one within him . . . all his old religious puzzlings were solved, all the obscurities clear. Now he had a 'heart to understand.'"[5]

The author of this classic tale, Abu Bakr Ibn Tufayl, was born near Granada in al-Andalus, and died in Marrakesh, Morocco in 581/1185. The little that is known of his life reveals a man of wide culture, a philosopher, teacher and practitioner of medicine, and adviser to the ruling circle of his day. As a patron of scholars, it was Ibn Tufayl who introduced Ibn Rushd, al-Ghazali's philosophical adversary, to court circles. A critic himself of some of al-Ghazali's ideas, the eastern Muslim nevertheless had a clear influence on Ibn Tufayl.[6]

Ibn Tufayl was a man of the world. He was the opposite of his hero Hayy, who was uniquely born to a life of the solitary ascetic. Nor did the author achieve his awareness of the divine, like that of his hero, by virtue of his unaided, innate reason, but as a Muslim socialized by the values drawn from revelation and the *shariʿah*. Hayy was for Ibn Tufayl, therefore, a pure, abstract ideal. His spiritual goal, namely the emancipation of the mind and spirit, was offered by Ibn Tufayl as the moral ideal for those audacious enough to seek it for themselves.

That goal, however, was attainable by another path. Asal's experience, like that of Ibn Tufayl, was grounded in the religious tradition of his society. Scriptural descriptions of the Truth, although *symbolic*, did not contradict anything in Hayy's experience. Nevertheless, Asal felt impelled to complete his spiritual journey in solitude, although physical withdrawal from society was not a practical choice open to all. Moreover, even fewer are capable, in Hayy's words, of risking self-destruction in order to endure now the painful joy of God's rule. Asal, therefore, is a metaphor for a spiritual elite. Salaman, on the other hand, represents the majority of sincere believers, gratefully acknowledging God and his Prophet and faithfully following his commandments within society here and now, content to await salvation and judgment in the life to come.

Asal and Salaman do not exhaust every type of religious experience. Nor does Ibn Tufayl suggest that they do. His tale is about the potentiality of the human spirit. He presents the unfolding of an intricate moral psychology by which the initiate is guided in his pilgrimage toward purification of the soul. In the Muslim tradition it was ascetics and mystics who, in their different ways, set out upon the path toward fulfillment of their spiritual potential.

VANITY AND REPENTANCE

"Whosoever feels safe from the world is like one who holds a fistful of water and is betrayed by the spaces between the fingers."

This anonymous ascetic's view of the world was widely shared in the early generations of Islam. Persons of ascetic temperament appeared in local communities throughout the newly established

Muslim dominions. Collectively, however, they would best be described at first as a sporadic phenomenon rather than a movement. Within the communty the ascetic's (*zahid*) piety was based upon religious learning and an intense devotion to duties of the faith. Some ascetics were simply indifferent to earthly well-being; others desired to be purged of sinful qualities, avoiding everything which endangered the soul.

Motivations for these attitudes were manifold. One major stimulus to the emergence of asceticism was ironically a consequence of the triumphal expansion of Islam throughout the first century of the community's history. Sensitive souls judged that the rapid spread of Muslim rule had deadened the impact of scripture's warning against the vanities of the world, the sin of prideful self-sufficiency and the promise of judgment to come. For them study of the Qur'an and Traditions was a means to pious self-examination: *O you who have attained to faith! Remember Allah with unceasing remembrance and extol His limitless glory from morn to evening* (33:41–42). The significance of scripture for questions of the law, philology, metaphysics, or dogma was secondary.

The ascetic was essentially "inner-worldly," rejecting neither family nor community but rather maintaining strict control over the pattern of his or her life and behavior in society. Rigorous prayer and fasting beyond what was required by the faith were important tools of the pious life. A monastic regime on the Christian model, however, did not emerge. The ascetic's opposition to the world was psychologically felt, not physically dramatized by withdrawal from it. Scriptural sources did not condone the hermit's isolation or simple celibacy and they could not, therefore, become the norm in Islamic asceticism. Modesty, temperance, contentment with what the divine will offers, and the denial of luxuries were ascetic characteristics. Further, it was necessary not just to avoid what Allah had forbidden (*haram*), but even to abstain from what he had declared lawful (*halal*). Abstinence from sin held no great merit, whereas abandoning the enjoyment of things permitted was conducive to attainment of the proper spiritual state.

Such men and women were believed to possess special gifts. They were capable of receiving from Allah answers to other petitioners' prayers. They could bring rain in time of drought. They touched society's wounds and could humble an unjust governor by invoking Allah's wrath against him. Later sources ascribe to them wondrous feats, always directed at easing the plight of the poor and disadvantaged: a prayer, for example, fetched a mother's long-absent son back to her; a pebble changed into a precious stone, so a poor man could pay off his debts; a fugitive from injustice who had sought refuge with a holy man was made invisible to his pursuers.[7] As instruments of the Lord ascetics were assured of his continuing grace.

Preparation for the active life of the ascetic began with repentance. The Qur'an alluded to certain stages of development. First, it entailed a struggle against the lower soul (*al-nafs al-ammarah*) and its disordered impulses. The soul here was understood in a physical sense to mean "the flesh" together with its allies, the world and the devil. Through remorse at his disobedience and fear of divine chastisement, the penitent had to abandon the sins of which he was conscious with the resolve never to repeat them. As all temptations were gradually overcome, the reproachful soul (*al-nafs al-lawwamah* (75:2)) remained alert to continuing imperfections until the soul at peace (*al-nafs al-mutma'innah*) was finally reached and a state of dis-passion achieved. The soul, having ceased to lust, was now free to love.

Imperceptibly over the first two centuries, individualist piety matured into expressions of mysticism. This transformation was first spawned in the major cultural centers of Iraq and Iran and from there spread eastward and westward. While the simple ascetic life continued to hold its appeal for many, others were attracted by an emerging interest in religious psychology to a different goal, that associated with the Sufis. The direction in which this transformation moved is reflected in the words of the Sufi Abu Bakr b. Jahdar al-Shibli (d. 334/945), who defined asceticism (*zuhd*) anew in Sufi terms as the "turning away of the heart from things to the Lord of things." That is, while the ascetics' path was directed toward securing by means of self-denial and pious works a state of blessedness after death, the Sufis' goal was gaining direct access to knowledge of the eternal by means of contemplation.

SUFISM: MEANING AND METHOD

The word *sufi* means, by general acceptance, a wearer of wool (*suf*), in reference to the coarse garment worn by the early ascetics. The Sufis' distinctive dress was a patched woolen garment known as a *khirqah*, usually blue, the color of mourning. The practice of Sufism, *tasawwuf*, is frequently defined by Sufis themselves in the form of maxims.

"Sufism is to possess nothing, and to be possessed by nothing," runs one version. "Sufism means being at ease with Allah" is another. Or again, "Sufism is not composed of practices and sciences, but it is morals."

'Ali b. 'Uthman al-Hujwiri (d. ca. 467/1075), a native of Ghazna in Afghanistan, wrote a textbook in Persian on the doctrines and practices of Sufism from which these quotations by earlier mystics have been taken. With each maxim he provides an explanatory comment. "Sufism is keeping the heart pure from the pollution of discord" means, he says, that love is concord, the opposite of discord, and the lover has but one duty, namely to keep the commandment of the Beloved; thus, if the object of desire is one, how can discord arise? For the briefest of definitions, "Sufism is good nature," al-Hujwiri offers an even fuller commentary. Good nature is expressed in three ways, he writes, "first, towards Allah by fulfilling His commandments without hypocrisy; second, towards mankind, by paying respect to one's superiors and behaving with kindness to one's inferiors and with justice to one's equals, and by not seeking recompense and justice from mankind in general; and thirdly towards one's self, by not following the flesh and the Devil."[8]

On the face of it, some of these maxims appear to depict the Sufi as no different from any faithful member of the community. Indeed, Sufis do trace their origins back to the Qur'an and the Traditions of the Prophet. These are the foundations of the religious law or *shari'ah* which we examined earlier. The *shari'ah* as the embodiment of the will of Allah touches the domain of daily action in matters both ritual and social. This can be described as the exoteric or outward dimension of the faith. It is the way of Salaman in Ibn Tufayl's tale. Complementary to this is an *esoteric* or inner dimension, the spiritual path of contemplation pursued by Asal and of course Hayy b. Yazqan. Sufis describe it as a path (*tariqah*) or branch leading off the main highway (*shari'ah*). Al-Hujwiri complained that among the aspirants to the Sufi path in his own day there were many impostors who wrongly supposed that the Sufis' outward behavior was everything. "It is the inner flame (*harqah*) that makes the Sufi," he said, "not their religious garb (*khirqah*)." Some Sufis even refused to wear the patched garment on the grounds that Allah knew the true state of the heart. For emphasis al-Hujwiri states that if by wearing the Sufi garment "you wish to show the people that you belong to Allah, should your claim be true, you are guilty of ostentation; and if false, of hypocrisy."[9]

The goal and method of the Sufi path are each derived from scripture and the *sunnah* or exemplary practice of the Prophet. The famous Light Verse is a scriptural parable of the Sufi's quest.

Allah is the light of the heavens and the earth. The parable of His light is, as it were, that of a niche containing a lamp. The lamp is in a glass, the glass shining like a radiant star. A lamp lit from a blessed tree – an olive tree that is neither of the East nor of the West – the oil whereof would almost glow forth of itself even though no fire touched it. Light upon light, Allah guides to His light whom He will. And Allah propounds parables to mankind, for Allah has full knowledge of all things. (24:35)

The Prophet is reported to have said that "to know oneself is to know your Lord."

A modern Sufi scholar has described man's spiritual aspiration as a dual one: to achieve a relative nearness to the divine presence and an absolute nearness or identity with him. This dual aspect is based upon the Qur'anic verse *Allah has promised believers, men and women, gardens that are watered by flowing rivers where they shall dwell immortal, abodes of excellence in the Paradise of Eden. And* ridwan *from Allah is greater. That is the immense attainment* (9:72). Paradise in the ordinary sense is the goal of all believers. For Sufis, Eden is the experiential proximity to Allah without their separate existence being extinguished; *ridwan*, Allah's *acceptance* of the seeker's soul to himself, is the ultimate nearness where duality is extinguished as though Allah has *come in between a man and his own heart* (8:24).[10]

As to the method by which Sufis pursued their goal, the Qur'an also provided significant guidance: *Keep vigil the night long, save a little – a half thereof, or abate a little thereof, or add a little thereto – and chant the Qur'an in measure . . . so remember the name of your Lord and devote yourself with complete devotion. Lord of the East and the West; there is no God but He* (73: 2–4, 8–9). These words, addressed to the Prophet, enjoined a form of worship well beyond what ordinary believers could be expected to follow. A night-time vigil of prayer and scripture reading in addition to the five-times daily ritual prayer was an intense spiritual exercise which came to be practiced by the "seekers" or those who "longed" for the nearness of Allah in imitation of the prophetic example.

The invocation or remembrance of the name of Allah is also mentioned in the above verse (and cited elsewhere in the Qur'an, for example 29:45; 62:10). In Muslim cultures the name of Allah is invoked throughout everyday life in expressions such as *in sha'a Allah*, "if Allah wills," and *al-hamdu li'Llah*, "praise be to Allah." However, the repeated vocal invocation or silent remembrance of the name "Allah," or one of his many other names like *al-Rahim*, "the Merciful," and *al-Ghafur*, "the Forgiver," forms the core of Sufi spiritual gatherings by which Allah can be known experientially and inwardly realized.

Remembrance of Allah is called *dhikr*, the same term commonly given to a Sufi gathering for this purpose. The English Arabist and traveler E. W. Lane witnessed popular performances of these meetings during his sojourns in Cairo, which he described in his *Manners and Customs of the Modern Egyptians*, published in 1836. Not untypical was a night-time open-air gathering of some two dozen men, seated in a circle on reed mats, who began their meeting reciting the first chapter of the Qur'an. This was followed by a chanting of the *shahadah*, "There is no God but Allah," first in slow measure to rhythmic bowing of head and body and then at a quicker pace, next shifting to a different tune while repeating the same words. Singers sang poems of mystical love accompanied by a flute player. The session reached a climax after two hours, with one or more of the participants collapsing in an ecstatic state. The use of poetry, music, and dancing, designed to heighten sensibilities and intensify concentration, was a central feature of Sufi performances from quite early days, although accompanied at first by discussions among authorities as to whether these aids were appropriate to the spiritual path. Such aids persisted, however, and the mystical dance of the Mevlevis or the Whirling Dervishes has attracted the attention of European visitors to Turkey for over two hundred years.

The practice of *dhikr* itself is commended in Traditions of the Prophet, one of which states that "There is a way of polishing everything and removing rust and that which polishes the heart is the invocation of Allah." A divine saying (*hadith qudsi*) states simply, "I am with my servant when he thinks of Me." Another *hadith qudsi* held in special reverence by Sufis records Allah's own description of the possibility of achieving the desired inward state: "My servant does not cease drawing near Me with devotions of his free will until I love him; and when I love him, I am the hearing with which he hears, the sight with which he sees, the hand with which he grasps and the foot with which he walks."

Thus from the Sufi vantage point, each of the obligatory rituals of the faith is valid owing to its inward purpose and meaning. Al-Hujwiri comments, for example, that pilgrimage (*hajj*) is an act of self-mortification whose true object is not to visit the Ka'bah in Mecca but to contemplate Allah. A seeker whose poverty is voluntary does not give alms (*zakat*) but must receive them, not for his own wants, but because he must relieve a fellow Muslim of his obligation. Fasting (*sawm*) during Ramadan or at any other time weakens the lower soul and strengthens the reason until every vain desire is effaced in the manifestation of the Truth; the fruit of hunger, too, is contemplation of Allah. Prayer (*salat*) also is not mere outward form. A tale is told by an early ascetic, 'Abdallah b. Mubarak (d. 181/797), who in his childhood had seen a female ascetic. While at prayer, she was stung forty times by a scorpion without making the slightest effort to prevent it. When he asked her why she had behaved in this way she replied, "Silly boy! Do you think it right that while I am engaged in Allah's business I should attend to my own?"[11]

THE PATH: STATIONS AND STATES

The wayfarer's progress along the path was in the hands of a spiritual guide (*shaykh* in Arabic, *pir* in Persian) who strictly directed the disciple's (*murid*) ascetic practices and meditations. The initiate's so-called apprenticeship could last up to three years before the *shaykh* formally accepted him or her into the group with the presentation of a patched garment. Even following their formal induction, the disciples' sense of personal loyalty to their master continued throughout their lives.

The path was marked by various spiritual stations and states. These were important terms in the Sufis' glossary, but their number and sequence varied from one authority to the next. Terminology was ambiguous, and a single word for a station or state often covered several meanings. The first station was generally agreed to be repentance, marking one's conversion to a new way of life. A maxim concerning this station is attributed to the Sufi Dhu 'l-Nun al-Misri (d. 245/859), who observed that "Ordinary men repent of their sins, but the elect repent of their heedlessness of Allah." This phrase in turn can be explained by the words ascribed to the famous woman mystic Rabi'ah al-'Adawiyyah (d. 184/800), who, in repenting sincerely, said she sought the "pardon of Allah for my little sincerity in saying, 'I ask pardon of Allah.'" Another station common to all accounts of the path was complete trust (*tawakkul*) in Allah. In the manual on Sufism by Abu Bakr al-Kalabadhi (d. 385/995) trust is described as "abandoning every refuge except Allah."[12]

A station (*maqam*) is distingished from a state (*hal*) by al-Hujwiri as follows:

> While the term "station" denotes the way of the seeker, his progress in the field of exertion, his fulfilling the obligations pertaining to that "station," and his rank before Allah in proportion to his merit, the term "state" denotes the favour and grace which Allah bestows upon the heart of His servant, and which are not connected with any mortification on the latter's part. "Station" belongs to the category of acts, "state" to the category of gifts.[13]

Higher stations of the path were patience, gratitude and acceptance. During his progress the seeker underwent changing spiritual states. Al-Ghazali distinguished a station which endures through time from a state which is only temporary. Certain states were expressed in contrasting pairs such as fear and hope; seekers hope they may receive Allah's gifts, but fear they may not owing to their awareness of the abyss between Allah's supreme sovereignty and their own insufficiency in obeying him.[14] The final stages of the path were reached by love and gnosis (interior knowledge, *ma'rifah*). The goal of annihilation (*fana'*) may then at last be achieved. This initially ethical concept which meant the annihilation of one's own attributes gradually came to mean the total extinction of the personality in Allah. The experience of spiritual intoxication transformed seekers who returned to the world of phenomena. They could now continue their journey in Allah, that is, subsisting (*baqa'*) *in* him rather than striving *for* him as before. "Hence, writes al-Hujwiri, all one's actions are referred to Allah, not to one's self, and whereas a man's actions that are connected with himself are imperfect, those which are attached to him by Allah are perfect."[15]

A true description of the experiences of the path and its goal was impossible. The paradigm of the mystics' path was Muhammad's ascent (*mir'aj*) into heaven, alluded to in scripture and elaborated in Tradition as Islamic piety expressed increased veneration of the Prophet.[16] Sufis accepted, however, that ordinary language was inadequate for the task of describing their own journey. Despite this, every major literature of Islamic culture including Arabic, Persian, Turkish, and Urdu contains the poetic jewels of Sufis' attempts to render their experiences intelligible, if only to fellow travelers on the path. It was possible, however, to misinterpret or misrepresent a Sufi's inspired ejaculation of ecstasy as the ravings of an antinomian anarchist. Al-Ghazali had warned in his own spiritual autobiography that any attempt to express the ineffable led inevitably to error. Al-Hujwiri perceptively pin-pointed the real danger of a public utterance of rapture, for the person thus overcome has not the power to express himself or herself correctly. "Besides," he said, "the meaning of the expression may be difficult to apprehend, so that people mistake the writer's or speaker's intention, and repudiate not his real meaning, but a notion which they have formed for themselves."[17]

Such utterances were sometimes interpreted as a blasphemous claim of self-deification. The famous utterance "I am the Truth (*Ana al-Haqq*)" of Husayn b. Mansur al-Hallaj (d. 310/922), where he identified himself by one of the names of Allah, was seen in this light. This and his alleged antinomian attitude ultimately led to a cruel execution by the authorities in Baghdad. Al-Hallaj's martyrdom made a profound impact upon Muslims well beyond Sufi circles. His memory has been preserved through the centuries in literature, religious and secular, a recent instance being the free-verse drama by the late Egyptian poet Salah 'Abd al-Sabur, *The Tragedy of al-Hallaj*.[18] In the modern version, al-Hallaj's life and death are depicted less as a question of religious heresy than a symbol of a pious man's stand against political and social injustice.

In any event, partly as a consequence of al-Hallaj's execution, manuals on Sufi doctrine, terminology, and practice were written in order to correct false impressions Sufis might convey and to deal with other potential dangers. Abu Nasr al-Sarraj (d. 378/988) surveyed some of the errors to which Sufis were susceptible. One was the belief in incarnation (*hulul*). The true meaning of the doctrine that a person leaves his or her own qualities or attributes and enters those of Allah is that "he goes forth from his own *will* and enters into the *will* of Allah, knowing that his will is given to him by Allah and that by virtue of this gift he is severed from regarding himself, so that he becomes entirely devoted to Him." The error rests, says al-Sarraj, in failing to note that Allah's qualities are not identical with Allah as he is in essence and therefore man does not, simply cannot, become divine.

In a later manual, al-Hujwiri offers the following metaphor to clarify a commonplace error associated with annihilation and subsistence, namely that *fana'* was believed to entail loss of the Sufi's essence while *baqa'* meant the indwelling of Allah in man: "The power of fire transforms to its own quality anything that falls into it, and surely the power of Allah's will is greater than that of fire. Yet fire affects only the quality of iron without changing its essence, for iron can never become fire." [19]

Despite the anxiety and anger which an occasional "intoxicated" Sufi like al-Hallaj could cause others (while endangering himself), the Islamic mystical tradition in general shared deep affinities with the piety of the Hanbali traditionists in their mutual emphasis upon Qur'anic meditation and adherence to the prophetic Tradition that good works are the product of a pure heart.[20] Both Sufis and traditionists, although for different reasons, rejected rational deliberations on theological concerns and the use of *kalam*. Nevertheless, the traditionists' devout attitude toward the very letter of the Qur'an and *hadith* did not preclude esoteric interpretation, as witnessed by the earliest commentary on scripture in Persian by the Hanbali Sufi 'Abdallah al-Ansari (d. 481/1089). Furthermore, the respect of the common people was won by many Sufis by the virtues of dignity and purity they preached and mirrored in their own lives, together with the moral assistance they extended to all who brought their problems to them. Tales of the ascetics' and Sufis' marvels, which they did not claim for themselves but which were rather ascribed to them by their followers, reflect the deferential awe of the people.

On the other hand, the Sufis exhibited a spiritual elitism. This can be illustrated by the role Sufis accorded to intuition in the exegesis of the Qur'an. Sufi commentaries were of different kinds, ranging from the usual chapter-and-verse treatment of the entire scripture to shorter expositions of parts of it. Their particular technique of interpretation was known as *ta'wil*, the illumination of the inner meaning of particular verses as distinct from their plain, surface meaning accepted by jurists and theologians. Reaching this inner sense by intuition was a gift granted to those few for whom Allah reserved the deepest level of insight into his revelation.

The earliest continuous Sufi commentary on selected Qur'anic passages was written by Sahl al-Tustari (d. 283/896).[21] Meanings of verses are discussed in both their exoteric and esoteric dimensions. The exegetical method involved interpretation flowing from the impact of the oral recital of the Qur'an upon the Sufi listener, an "encounter event" resulting in mystically inspired speech and sometimes in ecstatic utterances. Symbolism suffuses these spiritual hermeneutics. One simple example is the verse *He has set loose the two seas; they meet one another* (55:19), which in its plain sense refers to salt and sweet water but symbolically can refer to "the spirit and the body" or "this world and the next."

Al-Ghazali, whose debate with the philosophers we have already discussed, left esoteric interpretations of verses from scripture scattered throughout his surviving masterpiece *Revival of the Religious Sciences*, which, moreover, contains a chapter on esoteric interpretation as a necessary complement to the exoteric.[22] He has also left a short work devoted to the interpretation of only two Qur'anic verses, one of which is the Light Verse cited above. There, the Niche, Glass, Lamp, Tree, and Oil are seen as symbols for five classes of the human spirit. The Niche, for example, is a symbol of the sensory spirit of every human while at the highest rank, Oil is symbolic of the transcendental prophetic spirit possessed by the Prophets as well as some Sufi masters, the *shaykh*s, *murshid*s or *pir*s.[23]

THE FRIENDS OF ALLAH

The master–disciple relationship was considered to be the foundation upon which the acquisition of a knowledge of Allah along the path was based. Sufi masters are often referred to in English by the misleading term of "saints." In the absence of both a priesthood and a church in Islam, however, there can be no procedure for the canonization of individuals since there is no authority to validate their sanctification.

Several words designating Sufi masters have been incorrectly rendered as "saint" which more properly have other meanings, such as "elder" for *shaykh*, or "guide" for *murshid*. The commonest expression translated as a Sufi "saint" is *wali Allah*, which means "friend of Allah" in the sense of someone under the care of, or client, of Allah. The term is Qur'anic and can be understood in both an active and passive sense. The best-known instance is *Truly, the friends of Allah* (awliya' Allah) *are those who fear not, nor are they sad* (10:62), because they are especially *protected* by him. There is also the verse *Allah is the friend* (wali) *of those who believe, Who takes them from the darkness into the light* (2:257) because he is the protector of those who worship and obey him.

Divine "friendship" (*wilayah*) is common to all the sincere faithful, while the advanced mystic is the Sufi who has experienced annihilation and subsistence in Allah. It is in this latter sense, al-Hujwiri notes, that the "friends of Allah" are those

whom He has specially distinguished by His friendship and whom He has chosen to be the governors of His kingdom and has marked out to manifest His actions and has peculiarly favoured with many kinds of miracles (*karamat*, s. *karamah*) and has purged of natural corruptions and has delivered from subjection to their lower soul and passion, so that all their thoughts are of Him and their intimacy is with Him alone.[24]

Sufi masters were trained in the same sciences as scholars like jurists and theologians; certainly a sound knowledge of scripture and *hadith* was essential. Nevertheless, al-Hujwiri draws the following distinction between the two groups: "Inasmuch as the scriptural and intellectual proofs of the faith are to be found among the scholars (*'ulama'*), it follows that the visible proof is to be found among the 'friends' and elect of Allah." The master Sufis were therefore the living embodiment of the signs of Allah's truth and of the veracity of the Prophet.

The question of "friendship" was much discussed among Sufis, and there eventually emerged the theory of a hierarchy of ranks among the elite, the highest spiritual authority being called the *qutb*, the "pole" or "axis." The *qutb* was regarded as the center of spiritual energy upon whom the well-being of the world depended, just as a mill wheel turned upon its axis, without which it would not function. Although Allah's "friends" were said to be known to each other, they were veiled by Allah from the common people. Among these governors of the universe of the lowest rank, four thousand Sufis were said to be even hidden from each other and from themselves. Generally it was not known who was the *qutb* of any particular generation, but at times advanced mystics professed themselves to be the *qutb* of their age, while on occasion an individual was acknowledged by others to be that "axis." As one Sufi theorist put it, the "friends of Allah" are the eyes which regard Allah, since they are the eyes through which he regards the world.

THE SUFI BROTHERHOODS

During the lifetime of Ibn Tufayl Sufism had already begun to show signs of transformation from its early spiritual elitism into a movement among the masses. Previously, mystical life had been chiefly confined to the relationship between a master and his few disciples meeting in a mosque or the master's house. The change may have started as early as the third/ninth century when a Persianized Arab, Muhammad b. Karram (d. 255/869), left behind him a strong following in Iran.[25] Their activist asceticism and preaching led to the conversion of many Zoroastrians and other protected (*dhimmi*) peoples. It was the same master–disciple relationship which made it possible for a disciplined structured organization to emerge, at least at the local level, centered upon a purpose built meeting place called in Persian *khanqah*, or lodge. This institution is said to have been introduced by the followers of Ibn Karram. These lodges provided free food and shelter for travelers and the poor and, more importantly, they allowed members of the general public to be absorbed as lay seekers in the Sufi gatherings. Later, masters began to trace their training through a "chain" of teachers going back to the Prophet, often by way of his cousin and brother-in-law 'Ali, who appears prominently in many of these spiritual genealogies.

The Sufi "chain" (*silsilah*) of authority (which functioned much as the *isnad* did for the *hadith*) guaranteed the soundness of the master's teaching and practice, especially on details associated with the performance of *dhikr*. Other regulations were laid down which, like the *dhikr*, varied from one brotherhood to another. These included shaving an initiate's hair, the kinds of food he could consume during the compulsory forty-day retreat, the use of litanies, prayers, musical instruments, and dancing in their meetings, and the general deportment of disciples. The master also invested disciples with the patched garment (*khirqah*) as the sign of their joining the brotherhood. The chain survived and continued with a master's appointment of his successor or *khalifah*, who could be chosen from within his own family.

The appearance within the chain of a charismatic personality could produce a sub-group or new brotherhood of either revivalist or radical tendencies. Moreover, it was possible for a person who sought wide experience and qualifications to belong to more than one brotherhood. The term used for the institutionalized brotherhood was *tariqah*, the same word for the Sufi path as a way of life. The first *tariqah* was perhaps founded by Abu Ishaq al-Kazaruni (d. 963/1035), who, like Ibn Karram, was an activist ascetic and hypnotic preacher. He established a number of *khanqah*s in villages and towns in the west and south of Iran and was also engaged in a campaign of conversion among the Zoroastrian community.

The most famous and widespread of the early Sufi brotherhoods was undoubtedly the Qadiriyyah, whose eponymous ancestor was 'Abd al-Qadir Jilani (d. 562/1166). He was a popular Hanbalite preacher in Baghdad during his lifetime, and his tomb in the city remains to this day a place of pilgrimage for Muslims, especially from India and Pakistan, where the brotherhood spread in the late eighth/fourteenth century. Later still Qadiriyyah lodges were established in Indonesia. 'Abd al-Qadir was subsequently known as the *qutb* or Pole of the East, although in fact his followers were to be found as far west as Morocco while the spread of Islam into West Africa resulted from their influence as well.

Numerous legends circulated about 'Abd al-Qadir, and many other Sufi masters were also credited with marvels and miracles. A familiar theme in Sufi lore was a master's conversion of wrongdoers on the strength of his own example of moral rectitude. The youthful 'Abd al-Qadir is said to have converted an entire robber band which had accosted the caravan in which he was traveling. Mu'in al-Din Chishti (d. 633/1236), whose teachings spread throughout India, likewise secured the repentance of a tyrannical governor and his entourage. These stories had popular appeal among the masses, as did the celebrations marking the anniversaries of masters' deaths. The brotherhoods adapted themselves to every level of Muslim society. The human sympathies of the Sufis touched hearts more easily than mere belief in the compassion of a remote, transcendent Allah and even more than the arcane debates of jurists and theologians. In the same way, frankly un-Islamic elements drawn from the folklore of myriad local cultures throughout the Middle East and south Asia crept into Sufi practices. Veneration of Sufi masters and other popular innovations were condemned by the 'ulama', even by those who were perhaps Sufis themselves, but who could then only turn a blind eye to such practices since they did in fact help to legitimize the spiritual presence of Islam among society's lower and most neglected strata.

Two brotherhoods may be mentioned briefly here, one which became rooted in eastern Islamic lands, the other in the West. Each crystallized around the teachings of masters who died in the seventh/thirteenth century. Both fraternities have survived to the present day, but from their different origins, they developed somewhat different spiritual "styles."

The Chishtiyyah

By the fifth/eleventh century Lahore had become the first center of Persian Muslim culture in northern India. It was the burial place of al-Hujwiri, whose tomb can still be visited today. Over the succeeding three centuries Sufism made a major impact on the continent. Much of this was due to the untiring activities of the Chishtiyyah brotherhood, whose name derives from a local association of seekers from the town of Chisht in modern Afghanistan. Foundation of the fraternity is ascribed to a native of Sistan in Iran, Mu'in al-Din, who took the name of Chishti.[26] He traveled widely, studying with many eminent Sufis, and then journeyed to Delhi, finally settling in Ajmer, where he died. His mausoleum in that city remains today a shrine for Muslim pilgrims and center of a popular cult.

Islam encountered in India a religious culture alien to its own ethos. Hinduism was not founded upon a single prophetic-revelatory event but a whole revelatory tradition. Nor was it based upon worship of a single deity, but a multiplicity of gods and goddesses. Islam nevertheless spread rapidly under the influence of Chishti missionaries, among others. Hindus were attracted by the simple preaching and practice of the love of Allah and the classless atmosphere of the *khanqah*s, where members of the lower castes especially found haven from their own degraded status in society. Important, too, was Chishti willingness to adopt a number of Hindu customs and ceremonials. These included, for example, the controlled breathing techniques and sitting postures of the Hindu yogis and sages. Tolerance and respect for other religions were expressed by the great poet Amir Khusraw (d. 726/1325), a disciple of the equally famous Chishti master Nizam al-Din Awliya' (d. 726/1325), renowned for his teaching of the Sufi way by means of anecdotes. Popular poems and songs composed in local dialects brought the teachings of the fraternity direct to the ordinary villager, while Sufi literature in the vernacular acted as a bridge between Islamic and Hindu mysticism. Chishtis also evinced a deep mistrust of government and refused offers of patronage from rulers and wealthy persons. Spiritual rules ascribed to Mu'in al-Din himself stressed a stern asceticism which forbade the earning or borrowing of money and begging for food. Any surplus of food, money, or clothing acquired by voluntary donation was given away by the following day. For centuries Chishtis remained one of the

most important brotherhoods in India, but they never spread beyond
the confines of the continent.

The Shadhiliyyah

The Shadhiliyyah brotherhood emerged in North Africa. The name
is taken from the village of Shadhilah in Tunisia, where a young
Moroccan ascetic and jurist of the Maliki school of law, one Abu
al-Hasan, settled on the orders of his famous Sufi teacher, ʿAbd
al-Salam b. Mashish (d. 625/1228), who himself was subsequently
known in Sufi hagiography as the *qutb* of the West. Abu al-Hasan,
now known as al-Shadhili, established his first meeting place (in
Arabic, *zawiyah*) in Tunis and later moved to Alexandria in Egypt.
He died in 656/1258.[27]

The doctrine of the Oneness of Allah (*tawhid*) and the spiritual
practice of concentration in "remembering Allah" (*dhikr*) the
Shadhiliyyah shared with other brotherhoods. They were concerned,
too, with the exoteric dimension of Islam, the teachings and practices
of the law and questions of the creed. At the same time they
represented a spiritually reforming attitude against the more
exaggerated formalistic and literalist expressions of the faith. In
addition, they were critical of fraudulent claims made by bands of
wandering ascetics and certain excesses of behavior. Such excesses
included entering a large communal oven while it was in operation in
order to demonstrate Allah's power working within them. The goal of
gnosis (*maʿrifah*) or the attainment of wisdom and purity of soul
emphasized in Abu Hasan al-Shadhili's teachings perhaps set them
apart from the more severe devotionalism and asceticism of the
Chishtis. Their most significant characteristic, however, was that
members could not be distinguished externally from the rest of
society. There were no special insignia of the fraternity, and disciples
neither wore the patched garment nor carried the traditional bowl or
staff. Membership was drawn from all ranks and walks of life, but
especially from the urban middle class, and disciples had to earn their
own livelihood. It was not unusual for scholars and sultans, booksellers
and bureaucrats in Abu Hasan's day to be attached to Sufi masters,
each seeking the appropriate level along the path to suit his
capacities. Meetings were often held in the master's own home. The
Shadhili mark was to lead a sober contemplative life in this world,
and thereby revive the restrained practices of an earlier era of Sufism.

By the time the third *shaykh* of the Shadhiliyyah "chain," Shaykh Ibn 'Ata' Allah (d. 709/1309), had become master of the fraternity in Cairo, it had spread across North Africa into al-Andalus and into Syria and Mecca in the Hijaz as well. Like Abu al-Hasan, Ibn 'Ata' Allah was a learned Maliki jurist. Unlike al-Shadhili, Ibn 'Ata' Allah set down in writing the teachings of the brotherhood, which preserved some of Abu al-Hasan's best-known litanies.

One of his own most important and popular works was *The Book of Wisdom*, a collection of instructive maxims on the spiritual life which also contained a number of brief, personal invocations to Allah. The contents have been well described as "conversation with God and conversation about God." Scholars later wrote commentaries upon the book, which was adopted as a manual by other brotherhoods, while certain sayings became proverbial in Sufi circles. Some present the wisdom of the path in typical and apparently paradoxical form: "You are more in need of His forebearance when you obey Him than when you disobey Him," meaning, according to one of his commentators, that whereas obedience could lead to a spiritually dangerous sense of self-satisfaction, disobedience heightens the awareness of one's need of Allah.[28] On the same subject, Ibn 'Ata' Allah cautions that true obedience entails an awareness that it is a mercy from Allah: "Suffice it as a recompense to you for obedience that He has judged you worthy of obedience."[29] In one of his invocations to Allah, he expresses gratitude with a plaintive query: "My God, how kind You are to me! So what is it that veils me from You?"[30]

Ibn 'Ata' Allah's most celebrated successor was Ibn 'Abbad, who was born in the hilltop town of Ronda in al-Andalus and died in Fez, Morocco in 793/1390. He has been described as the precursor of the famous tenth-/sixteenth-century Christian Spanish mystic St. John of the Cross. Ibn 'Abbad's fame, unlike that of St. John, which centered on his poetry, rested in part upon the widely read commentary he wrote of Ibn 'Ata' Allah's *Book of Wisdom*. Furthermore, important collections of his own sermons and letters have survived which reveal a deep concern to make the mystical vision of the masters accessible to a wider, more popular audience. In his correspondence, he counseled seekers grappling with personal obstacles along the path and on the fundamentals of mystical spirituality in practical, non-esoteric terms. The following brief extracts from two letters to different persons convey something of their author's warmth and caring concern rather than the breadth of his skills as a physician of the soul.

Once Allah has made available to you the understanding I am talking about
and you have immersed yourself in it, yours will be endless devotion and
everlasting proximity to Allah, from which neither exhaustion, nor the ennui
that goes beyond fatigue, nor deception, can keep you – provided you live by
that understanding in all your comings and goings. If you consider all things
as having their being and source in Allah, you will give due gratitude to Him
who has bestowed on you this easy conquest . . . Then you will have felicity
and an excellent place in the next world. (3:14; 13:29)

On the other hand, if you remain blind and deceived and do not sincerely
seek refuge and acknowledge your indigence [before Allah], you will
continue to despise your actual spiritual condition because of a strong urge to
alter your spiritual states. You will detest yourself and grieve over your
negligence and dissipation. If this should happen, you must undertake
devotional works of both heart and body. Such works will point the way on
the Path to your Lord and the malaise you endure will not hinder the Path. A
man of great stature has said, "Travel toward Allah even though you are
lame and broken."[31]

Ibn 'Ata' Allah and Ibn 'Abbad both taught that the summit of the
path was a unity of vision (*wahdat al-shuhud*) in which, by his activity
and conformity of will, the contemplative seeker and the One
contemplated retain their essential identities. This, in other words, is
the relative degree of nearness to the divine presence, according to a
modern Sufi's interpretation of the dual nature of man's spiritual
aspiration, already mentioned above.[32]

The second or absolute degree of nearness, identity with the divine
presence, represents the enduring influence of another strand within
Sufism whose greatest exponent was Muhyi al-Din ibn al-'Arabi (d.
638/1240). Although he founded no brotherhood, his influence has
pervaded the thought of all Sufis to the present day who have
expressed their teachings within a system of mystical philosophy.
Born in the Andalusian town of Murcia, Ibn al-'Arabi journeyed
eastward to perform the pilgrimage and continued his travels in
Egypt, Anatolia (modern Turkey), and Syria, finally settling in
Damascus, where he died. He was a prolific writer; his greatest and
most popular works are entitled *Meccan Revelations* and *The Bezels of
Wisdom*.[33] His intricate and difficult system is built upon the doctrine
of Unity of Being (*wahdat al-wujud*), for which, over the centuries, he
has stood accused by some of heresy, while modern scholars have
debated whether or not it tainted his thought with pantheism or
monism. The problem centers around the question whether creatures

in their actual existence are identical with Allah or are rather reflections of his attributes. Critics perceived in the logic of Ibn al-'Arabi's doctrine a claim that "union" was not a process of the seeker's uniting with the One, but rather that he or she *was* the One already. Followers of his system, however, insisted that unitive fusion (*ittihad*) with Allah was impossible since this would entail the union of two essences, while Allah is himself the only Essence. The doctrine of Unity of Being is supported by another key feature of Ibn al-'Arabi's system centering upon veneration of the Prophet, who assumes the role of the Perfect Man. This is understood in the sense that Muhammad's inner reality embraced all of Allah's attributes, that is, he had realized in himself all the innate possibilities of being, a state which only prophets and the Sufi friends (*awliya'*), like Ibn al-'Arabi himself, had attained.

The Hanbali theologian Ibn Taymiyyah denounced Ibn al-'Arabi's philosophical excesses, but he was stoutly defended by the Shadhili leader, Ibn 'Ata' Allah, who confronted the theologian in public debate in Cairo, charging him and his ilk with reducing Islam to the level of their own understanding. Ibn al-'Arabi's ideas found favor in the Shadhiliyyah brotherhood and in its later sub-groups down to the present century,[34] where notably they have even attracted European converts to Islam.

By the end of the eighth/fourteenth century Sufi ideas and idioms had penetrated all levels of society and every region where an Islamic presence had become established. Dissemination was facilitated by the institutionalization of Sufi beliefs and practices in the brotherhoods and the plethora of their offshoots. As important as the migration of Sufis and the spread of their lodges across the Islamic landscape was the reflection in Sufi literature of the cosmopolitan nature of Islamic culture. Studies of scripture and the law were still written almost exclusively in Arabic, whereas Sufis wrote and sang their poems in nearly every vernacular they encountered. Arabic, naturally, and Persian, by which it was followed closely, were both already the major languages of Sufi expression. Three of Sufism's greatest poets had distinguished themselves in the previous century, namely Farid al-Din al-'Attar (d. 627/1230),[35] 'Umar ibn al-Farid (d. 631/1234),[36] and Jalal al-Din al-Rumi (d. 672/1273).[37] The second of these composed in Arabic, the other two in Persian. In the eighth/fourteenth century, another language – Turkish – began its slow ascent to becoming a third medium of expression in Islamic culture. This occurred in Anatolia, the region to which converted nomadic Turkic peoples from central Asia had migrated and settled. The region would eventually become the heartland of the Ottoman Empire in the centuries following the fall of the Christian Byzantine capital, Constantinople, to Muslim forces in 1453. The greatest Sufi poet in the Turkish language is Yunus Emre (d. 720/1320),[38] whose compositions on mystical love, employing simple diction with traditional prosody, have succeeded in conveying its subject's beauty and complexity to Turkish audiences of every type throughout the ages.

Here we leave the Sufi path of spirituality to explore another dimension of Islamic religious culture, the Shi'ah, to which reference has been made in passing but which now deserves our closer attention.

CHAPTER 6

The way of the Imams

A few weeks before his death, the Prophet Muhammad set out for
Mecca to perform the pilgrimage. This event is known in Islamic
tradition as the Farewell Pilgrimage. On the return journey to
Medina, he and his followers stopped at a place called Ghadir
Khumm. Shaded by palm fronds from the mid-day sun, Muhammad
addressed his companions. He took 'Ali b. Abi Talib by the hand,
raised it before the assembly and said, "Everyone whose patron I am,
also has 'Ali as a patron. O Allah, befriend every friend of 'Ali and be
the enemy of all his enemies; help those that aid him and abandon all
who desert him."[1] Ibn Ishaq does not mention Ghadir Khumm in his
biography of the Prophet. The event is recorded several times,
however, in Sunni Tradition literature, including the account given
here transmitted by the great traditionist Ahmad b. Hanbal.

Muhammad's affection and support for 'Ali were evident to all.
They were cousins and 'Ali was married to the Prophet's daughter,
Fatimah. Muhammad, who had no surviving male heir, is said to
have loved his two grandsons, al-Hasan and al-Husayn, dearly.
Moreover, Ibn Ishaq notes that the youthful 'Ali had been brought
up in Muhammad's care, and was the first male to believe in him and
accept his message.

To many, Ghadir Khumm had no further significance. A small
segment of the community, however, was fiercely loyal to 'Ali. Their
support was sustained in the years after the Prophet's death, during
which three of his companions, Abu Bakr (632–634), 'Umar
(634–644), and 'Uthman (644–656), in turn became leader of the
community as its Caliph or Imam. Each was also related by
marriage to the Prophet and was a member of his tribe, the
Quraysh. 'Ali eventually became leader, although his brief reign

155

(35–40/656–661) was marked by constant turmoil. In any event, about a generation after 'Ali's death, those still loyal to his memory began to interpret Ghadir Khumm in a radical manner. Muhammad, they claimed, had intended 'Ali to become his immediate successor. Therefore, he was viewed by them as the only legitimate and Rightly Guided Imam after Muhammad.

In Islamic history, those who have expressed a special devotion and loyalty to 'Ali are called collectively the *Shi'at 'Ali*, "Ali's faction" or "party," or more simply, the Shi'ah. Gradually, over a period of three to four centuries, they formed a splinter group (*firqah*) within the Muslim community, opposed to many of the doctrines and beliefs of the overwhelming Sunni majority. Today, the Shi'ah comprise about 10 percent of the total Muslim community world-wide. Within this minority, a small group known as the Zaydiyyah are found mainly in the Yemen. Another faction, the Isma'iliyyah, together with its various branches, are located chiefly in East Africa and India.

By far the largest and most important group of Shi'ah, known as the Twelvers or Imamiyyah, constitute a majority in Iran and the southern regions of Iraq and Lebanon; they are also scattered throughout the Gulf States, Afghanistan, India, and Pakistan. It is their story which will occupy our attention in the present chapter, providing an overview of their main beliefs and practices. Sunni and Shi'ah share the prophetic-revelatory event described in the first chapter; they each accept as fundamental Allah's unity and the mission and message of Muhammad, his Prophet. The Twelvers, however, developed a distinctive vision of the foundation and subsequent fate of the Muslim community, and of their own particular role in its future. Sunni and Shi'ah are often labeled respectively "orthodox" and "heterodox." Historically, in the absence of the central authority of a church in Islam, these terms are inappropriate. Any qualified Muslim jurist could condemn as innovation the belief or practice of another group, if it seemed to deviate from the Prophet's practice. Moreover, although it is unlikely that we shall ever know "what really happened" in detail during the community's early years, it is nevertheless conceivable that a minority preserved some kernels of the original tradition while the majority rejected them in the course of rapid Muslim expansion and the consequent internal conflicts experienced. In any event, the story of the Shi'ah begins at Ghadir Khumm.

'ALI AND GHADIR KHUMM IN TWELVER TRADITION

A lengthy account of 'Ali's deeds and sayings has come down to us from the pen of one of the most eminent and gifted early Twelver Shi'ah scholars. Abu 'Abdallah Muhammad b. Muhammad b. Nu'man was known by the honorific title al-Shaykh al-Mufid, "the scholar who brings benefit." Born in Iraq, he studied in Baghdad under Shi'ah and Mu'tazilite scholars, living in the largely Shi'ah quarter of al-Karkh on the west bank of the Tigris. His knowledge of Shi'ah traditions and of dialectical theology was poured into more than two hundred works, including many short polemical pieces. Al-Mufid indeed marked the zenith of an entire era of famous Shi'ah scholars. Two of his teachers were the important Shi'ah traditionists Ibn Qulawayhi (d. 368/978) and Ibn Babawayhi (d. 381/992), and two of his students were the equally prominent Shi'ah scholars the brothers al-Sharif al-Radi (d. 406/1015) and al-Sharif al-Murtada (d. 436/1044). Al-Mufid died in 413/1022 and was buried in al-Kazimayn, the site near Baghdad (now part of the modern city) which became a famous shrine for Shi'ah pilgrims.[2]

By the time of al-Mufid's death, the main features of the Twelver Shi'ah community and its thought were already well established. The basic claim of the Prophet's testament appointing his successor was enriched by colorful legends about 'Ali's personal qualities, while Shi'ah exegetes extracted from scripture interpretations at variance with Sunni views. Al-Mufid's version of Ghadir Khumm in his *Book of Guidance* records that the Prophet had received a revelation concerning 'Ali's succession to the leadership (*imamah*) of the community. Muhammad delayed making the announcement, awaiting the appropriate moment to do so. At Ghadir Khumm Allah spoke again to him, saying, *O messenger, make known what has been revealed to you from your Lord* (5:67), that is, what concerned the succession, for *If you do not do it, you will not have made known His message* (5:67). Muhammad addressed his followers saying, "I have been summoned and it is nearly the moment for me to answer. The time has come for me to depart from you. I leave behind me among you two things which, if you cleave to them, you will never go astray – that is, the Book of Allah and my offspring from my family (*ahl al-bayt*). They will never scatter from you until they lead you to me at the sacred waters of Heaven."[3] The Prophet is then said to have uttered the words cited above from the *hadith* transmitted by Ahmad b. Hanbal. The

Tradition is understood by al-Mufid to mean that 'Ali was divinely ordained as the Prophet's successor. Sunni exegetes, on the other hand, deny that the Qur'anic verse and the relevant Traditions bear the meaning attached to them by the Shi'ah; some maintained that the Prophet was merely trying to boost 'Ali's flagging popularity.

Al-Mufid's portrait of 'Ali may be compared with that of the Prophet by Ibn Ishaq, in the sense that both accounts reflect the veneration of their subjects within the respective Twelver Shi'ah and Sunni traditions. 'Ali is presented as the central pillar of support in the Prophet's mission. 'Ali's virtues and his exploits in the field against the community's enemies are viewed as marks of divine favor ensuring the Prophet's ultimate success. Moreover, the quality of 'Ali's legal decisions was attested to by the Prophet, who was said to have remarked upon his outstanding merit in this field. Significantly, 'Ali's legal decisions delivered during the Caliphates of Abu Bakr, 'Umar, and 'Uthman are recounted by him in a manner which reveals 'Ali's superior judgment in contrast to their weakness and incompetence.

'Ali's precedence over all others demonstrated his entitlement to authority and leadership after the Prophet. Al-Mufid finds scriptural support for this in the following verse, among others: *Is not he who guides you to truth more entitled to be followed than one who does not go aright unless he is guided?* (10:35).[4] Al-Mufid records 'Ali's wisdom in his speeches and maxims. His special relationship with Allah is demonstrated by his ability to perform miracles, a gift Tradition attributes to the Prophet as well. 'Ali transcended human norms, for example in the perfection of his intellect, when he was only some ten years of age. His strength and military prowess were also beyond human norms, and he was able to predict events before they occurred.

Wondrous things happened to 'Ali which have parallels in the biography of the Prophet. Ibn Ishaq relates the tale of the Prophet's coming being foretold by the Christian monk Bahira.[5] Al-Mufid tells the story of a desert hermit who converted to Islam when 'Ali miraculously unearthed a huge rock under which fresh water flowed. "No one knows its place, said the hermit, except a prophet or the trustee of a prophet. He must be a friend of Allah . . . whose sign is the knowledge of the place of this rock and his ability to remove it."[6]

A further reported miracle underlies the reason for a minor difference between the Sunni and Shi'ah food taboos. Once, when the flood waters of the Euphrates threatened to engulf Kufah, 'Ali's main center of support, the populace approached him to deal with the danger. 'Ali approached the rising river and performed his prayers. He called upon Allah's help and, striking the water's surface with his staff, he commanded it to recede. Fish trapped on the bottom were exposed by the sinking waters and some greeted 'Ali as Commander of the Faithful while others remained silent. Astounded onlookers asked the reason for this phenomenon. 'Ali said, "Allah made those fish which were ritually pure speak to me and he kept those silent towards me which were forbidden, impure or worse."[7] The silent ones included eels, a variety of fish without scales, and mud fish. Sunni schools of law permit their consumption, while under Shi'ah law they are prohibited.

Generations of loyal followers transformed the historical figure of 'Ali into a semi-legendary, tragic hero. His life story came to be seen as a long catalogue of trials and tribulations. The Shi'ah, according to al-Mufid, mark the length of 'Ali's true leadership (*imamah*) from the day of the Prophet's death until his own (10/632 to 40/661). For twenty-four years and six months of this time, however, 'Ali was prevented from exercising his rightful authority to administer the laws, owing to the usurpation of the Caliphate by the other Companions. Even during the remaining years of his rule as Caliph, says al-Mufid, 'Ali was confronted by a revolt from a group of the Prophet's Companions, open dissent from Mu'awiyah, then governor of Syria, deviation of others from the faith and even betrayal from among his own supporters. Then, as 'Ali himself is said to have foretold, an assassin's poisoned sword struck him down at the mosque door in Kufah on the night of the 19th of Ramadan. He died on the third day.[8] Today in Shi'ah communities everywhere during the fast of Ramadan, three days of public mourning are still observed to commemorate his death.

AL-HUSAYN, PRINCE OF MARTYRS

Twelver Shi'ah tradition came to see the tragedy of 'Ali's life repeated in that of his son, al-Husayn. Al-Mufid's account of al-Husayn's brave but futile opposition against the new Umayyad Caliph, Yazid, the son of Mu'awiyah, is told with the pathos of a Greek drama. Facing overwhelming odds, al-Husayn and most of his small party, including a dozen or so of his close relatives, were slain in battle at

Karbala, near Kufah, on the 10th of Muharram 61/680.[9] The event is still commemorated in the Shi'ah calendar of martyrs during ten days of mourning known as *'Ashura'*. The immediate aftermath of the event probably marks the time when the idea of 'Ali's divine designation as legitimate leader (*imam*) began to circulate among the early Shi'ah. It was extended to his sons, first al-Hasan, who in fact remained politically passive, and then al-Husayn. Al-Husayn failed to lead the Muslim community, but within Shi'ah tradition he is honored as the first to wear a martyr's crown.

Al-Mufid based his story in the main upon the history of the famous Sunni scholar al-Tabari (d. 310/923), who in turn pieced together his composite account from earlier sources available to him from the late second/eighth century. It is evident that al-Husayn's death was perceived by these early transmitters as a tragedy for the community as a whole. Yazid possessed few of his father's gifts for rule, and al-Husayn was regarded by many as a man of profound piety whose turn had come. As yet an agreed method of selecting the Muslims' leader did not exist, although there was a growing constituency who believed that authority was best handed down through the Prophet's family or someone closely connected with it. In the end, vested political interests supporting Yazid triumphed over the still fresh spirit of religious idealism represented by al-Husayn.

At the same time, the drama unfolded in a climate of foreboding. Repeatedly, friends advised al-Husayn not to venture out against the Caliph's forces, or to trust the support of those "whose hearts might be with him but whose swords were with Yazid." To one such attempt at persuasion, al-Husayn replied that he had received "a vision in which he had seen the Messenger of Allah who confirmed that he had been ordered to do what he was doing whether it went against him or in his favour. They asked him what that vision was. He answered that he had not told anyone of it and he would not tell anyone of it until he met his Lord."[10] To another confidant who pleaded with al-Husayn to hold back, he said, "Servant of Allah, wise decisions are not hidden from me. Yet the commands of Allah cannot be resisted."[11] The Shi'ah perceived the seeming inevitability of al-Husayn's fate as a matter preordained by Allah.

Al-Tabari includes in his narrative reports in which al-Husayn speaks to his followers as the son of Fatimah, daughter of the Messenger of Allah, and in the name of the Prophet's family (*ahl al-bayt*), who are more entitled to leadership of the community than pretenders such as Yazid. Nearing the moment of the fateful battle, al-Husayn learns that most of his pledged support has vanished. To those who remained he preaches

You see what this matter has come to. Indeed, the world has changed, and it has changed for the worse. Its goodness has retreated, and it regards good as bitter. Or, there remain only the dregs, like the dregs in a jar, sordid nourishment like unhealthy fodder. Can you not see that truth is no longer something that men practice and falsehood is no longer desisted from, so that the believer rightly desires to meet his Lord. I can only regard death as martyrdom and life with these oppressors as a tribulation.[12]

Speaking on behalf of his companions, a loyal supporter replies, "We have heard Allah guide your words. If our world were eternal and we could be immortal within it and, if by helping you we must abandon it, then we would still prefer going with you rather than staying in the world."[13]

The Muslim community's conscience was deeply touched by the tragic end to the débâcle at Karbala. Not for the first time had Muslims died at the hands of Muslims. 'Ali's brief but troubled reign had witnessed several bloody clashes. The plight of al-Husayn and his supporters, however, appeared to Muslims of conscience to have been resolved by a crudely excessive display of Caliphal power.

For the Shi'ah, however, the drama at Karbala assumed a deeper spiritual significance. History and legend fused as history became the vehicle for the transmission of religious feelings and ideas. Al-Husayn was not merely a hero who died in battle, but one who died for his love of Allah and to defend his faith. Shi'ah piety, for example, also interprets the blood of al-Husayn as a source of healing. A story related on the authority of the Prophet's family by a twelfth-/seventeenth-century Shi'ah traditionist tells of a Medinan Jew whose daughter was blind and crippled. While seated one evening in a garden under a tree, she heard the mournful call of a bird in the branches above her. The bird had witnessed al-Husayn's death, smeared itself in his blood and flown to Medina to mourn the martyr in his own city. As the disabled young girl's own sorrow responded to that of the bird's, a drop of al-Husayn's blood fell on her eyes and they opened; and, as others fell on her limbs, she became totally cured.[14]

Furthermore, since al-Husayn's martyrdom was believed to have been divinely ordained, Karbala became a symbol of Allah's mercy and justice, through which the redemption and condemnation of mankind are achieved. A modern Shi'ah scholar has explored in detail the redemptive nature of al-Husayn's suffering, first as a struggle in the way of Allah (*jihad*) of right against wrong, justice against falsehood, and second as a means by which the faithful participate in the sorrows of al-Husayn and his family.[15]

THE PASSION OF KARBALA

This latter aspect of the Karbala heritage involved from early Shi'ah times a period of mourning during Muharram commemorating the suffering of their third Imam, al-Husayn, Prince of Martyrs. In Shi'ah communities everywhere today, the '*Ashura*' celebrations draw upon a rich oral and written tradition of lamentation over his death. They are expressed in public processions of mourning, recitations of elegies, and reenactment of al-Husayn's last journey from Mecca and his death, together with his small band of companions, on the desert sands at Karbala. The staging of the series of tableaux (*ta'ziyah*) extending over several days, varies from one Shi'ah community to the next. It may take place in large halls called *Husayniyyat* built adjacent to mosques, or performed in an open area of the village market place. Apart from Muhammad and his family, the cast includes angels and biblical prophets. Heroes and villains of the piece are easily distinguished by their dress and speech. A poet introduces the play and pronounces the eulogy for the dead. Audience participation in the unfolding drama is intense; the activities are viewed as both redemptive and commemorative. In one modern reenactment, a criminal is released from jail and his sentence commuted – providing he consents to play the part of the arch villain, Yazid. During the public street processions, participants beat their breasts and heads with their hands, with swords and even chains. Self-flagellation, often disapproved of by the authorities, is nevertheless a popular expression of mourning for al-Husayn.

A nineteenth-century version of the *ta'ziyah* "passion play" has al-Husayn address his sister on the day of his death:

Trials, afflictions, and pains, the thicker they fall on man the better, dear sister, so they prepare him for his journey heavenward. We rejoice in tribulations, seeing they are but temporary, and yet they work out an eternal and blissful end. Though it is predestined that I should suffer martyrdom in this shameful manner, yet the treasury of everlasting happiness shall be at my disposal as a consequent reward. You must think of that and be no longer sorry. The dust raised in the field of such battles is highly esteemed by me, O sister, as the philosopher's stone was, in former times, by the alchemists; and the soil of Karbala is the sure remedy of my inward pains.[16]

The ultimate purpose of al-Husayn's tribulations is revealed in the final scene of the play, which depicts the raising of the dead at the resurrection. In their terror of the judgment, sinners cry out for Allah's mercy and forgiveness. Muhammad, who has listened to his grandson's tale of suffering, soothes him, saying that his trials have served to forge a strong bond with Allah. In response, al-Husayn calls upon his Lord to forgive those who had acted unjustly toward him and his family. The archangel Gabriel then arrives with a message from Allah to Muhammad, saying,

None has suffered the pain and afflictions which al-Husayn has undergone. None has, like him, been obedient in my service. As he has taken no steps save in sincerity in all that he has done, put the key of Paradise in his hand. The privilege of making intercession for sinners is exclusively his. Al-Husayn is, by My grace, the mediator for all.[17]

And the sinners, upon entering paradise, sing out their joy in unison, "Allah be praised! by al-Husayn's grace we are made happy, and by his favour we are delivered from destruction . . . We were thorns and thistles, but are now made cedars owing to his merciful intercession."[18]

Sorrow and weeping for al-Husayn and his family, therefore, become for the Shi'ah a means of redemption. The *ta'ziyah* drama is also an expression of the community's annual ritual of reintegration, a cementing of its identity, a mark of the endurance of its heritage against the odds, and a renewal of the religious nature of protest against the evil of worldly political power.

MAHDIS AND IMAMS

Karbala was a decisive turning point for the Shi'ah of 'Ali, who now began to emerge more clearly as a religous movement. Nonetheless, as with the majority Muslim community during much of its formative period, the Shi'ah were like a chorus seeking a common melody but singing in discordant parts. An unsuccessful revolt against the Umayyads to avenge the death of al-Husayn was launched in the name of a third son of 'Ali (by a wife other than Fatimah). It built upon the shame felt by those who had only half-heartedly supported al-Husayn, or had even abandoned him to his fate. This son, Muhammad b. al-Hanafiyyah, was proclaimed the *Mahdi*, meaning simply a rightly guided Imam-Caliph appointed by Allah. Here, the idea of divine appointment was an extension of the doctrine, probably developed at this same time, of the Prophet's designation of 'Ali as his successor. 'Ali had in his turn, it was claimed, designated his eldest son, al-Hasan, as Imam after him. Then, in the words of al-Mufid, "The Imam after al-Hasan was his brother al-Husayn [may Allah bless him and his family] through the designation (*nass*) of his father ('Ali) and grandfather [the Prophet] and the testamentary bequest (*wasiyah*) of his brother al-Hasan."[19] Muhammad, however, disassociated himself from the abortive rebellion and died peacefully in Medina some years later (81/700).

The idea of the *Mahdi* nevertheless survived and developed eschatological coloring. Indeed, a group which had backed this same Muhammad believed that he was still alive and in hiding near Medina. At some point in the future he would emerge to destroy his enemies and fill the earth with equity and justice. Throughout the formative phase of the Shi'ah, down to the beginning of the fourth/tenth century, the movement was characterized by a constant swing between recognition of an Imam living in their midst and hope placed in the return of a *Mahdi* from concealment.

The figure of Ja'far al-Sadiq (d. 148/765), a great-grandson of al-Husayn, is central to this development. Although politically quietist, Shi'ah tradition describes him as a charismatic character and regards him as the founder of Shi'ah law, which is based, to a great extent, upon decisions supposed to have been transmitted from him. His Imamate lasted thirty-four years. When he died, some professed him to be in concealment as the awaited *Mahdi*, for he was supposed to have declared, "If one day you were even to see my head rolling down a mountain-side toward you, do not believe anything of it, for I shall always be your lord."[20] Others supported his eldest son, Isma'il, denying that he had died during his father's lifetime. It is to this figure that the Isma'ili sect of the Shi'ah trace their origin. Finally, however, the main body of Shi'ah notables and jurists rallied around, Musa, another son of Ja'far. Musa died in 183/799. One group now claimed that the succession of Imams had terminated and that Musa was himself the awaited *Mahdi*.

THE TWELFTH AND LAST IMAM

This was a new and important idea. The end of the line of Imams did not, however, occur immediately. The eleventh Imam in line from al-Husayn died in 260/873. A period of confusion ensued. The contemporary scholar al-Nawbakhti, member of an important Shi'ah family in Baghdad who died between 300 and 310/912 and 922, described fourteen groups with different views on the question of the succession. The twelfth was a group called the Imamis, whose views corresponded closely with those which finally coalesced to become the mainstream Shi'ah community as we know it today. After the first three Imams, 'Ali and his two sons, the Imams had all to be descendants of al-Husayn, the succession passing from father to son. Moreover, they argued that the earth could not survive without an Imam as "proof" (*hujjah*) from Allah. On the basis of a Tradition from Ali, the Imamis held that should the world be for one moment without an Imam, whether visible and known or concealed like a sword in its scabbard, it and all its inhabitants would perish. Yet, significantly, al-Nawbakhti observes that the Imamis forbade mention of the name of the twelfth and last Imam, the awaited *Mahdi*, who would be chosen by Allah and manifested in his own good time. At the time he wrote, uncertainty among the Shi'ah was at its peak, and the identity of the last Imam had yet to be accepted by Shi'ah consensus.

The period of confusion did not last. Writing later in the fourth/tenth century, al-Mufid's teacher Ibn Babawayhi knew the last Imam to be Muhammad, son of the eleventh Imam, al-Hasan al-'Askari (d. 260/873). Al-Mufid himself added the details that the eleventh Imam had concealed his son's birth owing to the troubled times and the danger he felt might befall the child from the Sunni authorities. The boy was said to have been five years old when his father died. His name and coming were foretold in a Tradition by the Prophet, who said, "If only a single day remained for the world, Allah would lengthen that day so that He could send on it a man from my descendants, whose name is the same as mine. He will fill the world with justice and fairness as it was filled with oppression and tyranny."[21]

Hence, by the process of absorption of some groups and the disappearance or elimination of others, the majority Shi'ah community eventually became identified in history as the Twelver Shi'ah or the Imamites, that is, the followers of the Imams. According to their tradition as well, the twelfth Imam himself decided that no one would be designated his successor. He would remain in concealment, to reappear one day as the *Mahdi* in Mecca, on the day (in an even-numbered year) commemorating al-Husayn's martyrdom, to establish a reign of peace on earth. Ibn Babawayhi, in the earliest account of the Twelver creed, says of the Expected One (*al-muntazar*) that "He it is whom Allah will make victorious over the whole world until from every place the call to prayer will be heard, and all religion will belong entirely to Allah."[22] A further twist to the *Mahdi* doctrine was that the terrestrial paradise would herald the resurrection and the Day of Judgment.

THE IMAMATE

Reverence for the Prophet's immediate family is enjoined upon all Muslims (42:23). Sunnis take this to include 'Ali, Fatimah, and the Prophet's grandsons. For the Shi'ah, on the other hand, the family includes all twelve Imams. With the exception of the last Imam, who is still alive but in hiding or occultation (*ghaybah*), the rest shared a martyr's fate, most by the stealth of poison. A modern scholar has summed up succinctly the religious significance of the Imams for the Shi'ah as follows: "The *imams*, for Shi'i Muslims, may be thought of as a primordial idea in the mind of God which found temporal manifestation in persons occupying a position midway between human and divine beings."[23]

The view itself, however, is not modern but reflects early Shi'ah sources such as their first collection of Traditions compiled by Muhammad Ya'qub ibn Ishaq al-Kulayni (d. 328/939). In one Tradition, for example, the sixth Imam, Ja'far al-Sadiq, interprets the famous Qur'anic Light Verse (24:35) as a reference to the Prophet's family, the phrase *Allah guides to His Light whom He will* meaning that Allah guides to the Imams whom he wills.[24] For the Shi'ah, the Imams were not created, like the rest of humanity, from the dust of the earth but rather from columns of divine light before the world was created. In another Tradition, the Imam Ja'far states that Allah possesses two kinds of knowledge, one known only to himself, and the other which he teaches his angels, his messengers, and his Imams.[25] They are, therefore, the heirs of the prophets, guarantors and transmitters of authentic revelation, and mediators between Allah and his creation. Like the prophets, they possess the power to perform miracles. The Imams were deemed infallible or, perhaps better, protected by Allah from sin and error. Hence their authority in matters spiritual and temporal is absolute. It should be stressed, however, that the Imams do not bring a new message from Allah. They can neither inaugurate a new law nor abolish or modify part or all of the *shari'ah*. Denial of the Imams is regarded as *shirk* by the Shi'ah, the cardinal sin tantamount to the Sunnis' charge against those who associate with or worship other deities than Allah. The sin of Adam and Eve was the sin of envy, for they desired to be *like* the Imams. Mankind's later sin was the *pretension* to be Imams in power and authority, in the way the Caliphs, excluding 'Ali, of course, had acted.

AWAITING THE IMAM'S RETURN

Shi'ah tradition claims that since the death of Adam, Allah, by reason of his grace, has not left the earth without an Imam through whom mankind is guided toward him. In a general sense this refers to all the earlier prophets down to Muhammad and then their successors, the Twelve Imams. This is to be the case until the appearance of the *Mahdi* and the end of terrestrial time. The Imam is a proof (*hujjah*) for his creatures, without which the earth could not survive. Were it otherwise, truth would never be known from falsehood.[26] The Twelve Imams, who are said to possess a complete understanding of the Qur'an, are able to reveal its true meaning to believers. Hence the verse *Surely this Qur'an guides to the way that is straightest* (17:9) is said by Ja'far al-Sadiq to mean that the way is that of the Imams.[27]

A problem which arose in an acute form, therefore, was how the last, the twelfth, Imam could fulfill his functions while in hiding. How could the Shi'ah conduct their day-to-day affairs while Allah's proof remained incommunicado, depriving them of his infallible guidance? Furthermore, despite their actual political passivity, even impotence, the Imams' claim to supreme authority implied that the rule of the Caliphs, Umayyads, and Abbasids alike was illegitimate, inherently unjust, and oppressive. Yet in the physical absence of their own Imam, the Shi'ah seemed doomed to struggle without any legitimate authority of their own, whether spiritual or political. Thus, what was the proper relationship to establish between their own followers and the declared illegitimate rule of the majority Muslim community?

The Shi'ah solution to the first aspect was much the same as that devised in the Sunni community, where the *'ulama'* were held to be the heirs of the Prophet: the Shi'ah religious scholars became the heirs of the Imams. They could not, of course, claim the Imams' essential quality of infallibility. Scholars debated, however, whether they could fulfill certain of the Imam's functions on his behalf or hold them in abeyance until the return of the *Mahdi*. These functions included carrying out the Qur'anic legal punishments (*hudud*), raising the land tax, leading the Friday prayer, and waging war (*jihad*) against their enemies. Traditionally, owing to the Imam's absence, Friday prayer was of less significance for the Shi'ah than the Sunni Muslim. Today, however, its importance has been revived in post-revolutionary Iran.

On questions of theology such as the existence and nature of Allah, his attribute of justice, the necessity of prophecy and the Imamate and matters of eschatology, the Shi'ah eventually adopted a position close to that of the Mu'tazilites.[28] That is, their scholars argued that reason could provide sure and certain knowledge of the fundamentals which revelation then confirmed. One of the most noted Shi'ah theologians, al-Hasan b. Yusuf b. 'Ali b. Mutahhar al-Hilli (d. 726/1326), known as 'Allamah, "the most learned master," has left a brief statement on these matters to which a commentary was appended by a later disciple.[29] 'Allamah al-Hilli was the first Shi'ite to bear the title *Ayatullah* (sign of Allah), a mark of the high regard in which he was held by his fellow Shi'ah scholars. He belonged to the famous Twelver center of learning at Hillah, a town on the Euphrates in Iraq which in the eighth/fourteenth century superseded Baghdad, and Qumm in Iran, as the stronghold of Shi'ah scholarship. Such was his fame that a story is told of his meeting a stranger while traveling to Karbala as a pilgrim who revealed himself to 'Allamah as the Hidden Imam.

Al-Hilli not only emphasized the place of reason in his theology, but also adopted the Mu'tazilite concept of Allah's justice. This stressed the essential distinction between a person's voluntary and involuntary actions and hence one's responsibility for following the commands of Allah and, for the Shi'ah, the way of the Imams. Characteristically, al-Hilli established by rational argument that the Imamate was a kindness from Allah, which act was incumbent upon him. Then, since the Imam was the guardian of the law, he must be also be immune to sin, for in the words of scripture, Allah has said, *My covenant does not embrace evildoers* (2:124).

The scholars' insistence on the exercise of reason was their practical way of replacing the absent Imam's infallible guidance in matters of theology. The search for certain knowledge of the law, on the other hand, resulted finally in the view that the individual effort (*ijtihad*) of a jurist (*mujtahid*) might or might not be successful in uncovering Allah's real intent. However, by the constant renewal of these efforts, an approximation of the truth might be achieved. Absolute certainty in the law must await the return of the Hidden Imam. Until that time, ordinary Shi'ah felt bound to follow the decisions of their *mujtahids*, that is, jurists living among them at any given time. In this manner, the jurists came to exercise powerful authority over the community's daily affairs.

The matter of the relationship between the Shi'ah community and Sunni rulers was treated in part by Sharif al-Murtada (d. 436/1044), who became the leading scholar and head of the Shi'ah after the death of his teacher al-Mufid. His prestige was based not only on his scholarship but also on the fact that he was a descendant of the seventh Imam, Musa al-Kazim. He maintained close relations with the Sunni authorities in Baghdad. Although in theory the Caliph's rule was considered illegitimate and oppressive, al-Murtada faced the very practical question of whether the Shi'ah should work for such a government. His rational (Mu'tazilite) treatment of the traditional doctrine of the Imams spelled out the different options. "Pious men and scholars," he wrote, "have always at various times accepted offices on behalf of unjust rulers . . . The tenure of office is only in appearance on behalf of the unjust ruler. Intrinsically, it is on behalf of the true Imams . . . and the office holder is in reality . . . acting in accordance with their command."[30] Then, employing a characteristic Shi'ah doctrine, he stated that it was permissible, at times even obligatory, to practice precautionary dissimulation (*taqiyah*), that is, conceal one's real beliefs from an unjust ruler in order to protect oneself from harm or to be able to provide benefits for the Shi'ah community as a whole.

During the long occultation of the Hidden Imam, the Shi'ah developed the ethos of a righteous yet oppressed community within the Muslim *ummah*. Their leaders, the *'ulama'*, expounded the themes of suffering and martyrdom which bonded the community to a past governed by their Imams, in preparation for salvation, assured by the re-appearance of their awaited Mahdi. The scholars meanwhile continue to provide an essential ingredient for survival to that end, "a rationalized defense of the moral excellence of an embattled minority."

SHIʿAH–SUNNI PERCEPTIONS

Relations between Shiʿah and Sunni Muslims during the formative periods of each community bore some of the same characteristics as inter-communal relations involving, for example, Muslims and Christians or Jews. With intra-Muslim polemics, the distance between theological pronouncement by one side or the other and day-to-day social realities varied with the political climate of a particular period or place. The Shiʿah enjoyed moments of ascendency during the fourth/tenth and fifth/eleventh centuries when ruling dynasties emerged in Egypt, Syria, Iraq, and Iran, sympathetic to their vision of the past. It was a period during which the ideal of a unified, universal Sunni Caliphate appeared forever unattainable. Even under the impetus of a Sunni resurgence from the fifth/eleventh century, however, scattered concentrations of Shiʿah faithful survived on the strength of their special traditions from the Imams and rituals preserved at both the popular and scholarly levels of the community.

Within Sunni circles, scholars drew their own conclusions concerning what they regarded as Shiʿah "innovations" or accretions to the faith. They stopped short, however, of demanding the total exclusion of the Shiʿah from the community of believers. A well-known contemporary of al-Mufid was the Sunni theologian ʿAbd al-Qahir b. Tahir al-Baghdadi (d. 429/1037). In one of his works he describes the proliferation of factions and groups, present and past, into which the community had divided itself. His book illustrates Muhammad's "self-fulfilling prophecy" that since the Jews were divided into seventy-one factions, the Christians into seventy-two, "my people will be divided into seventy-three," only one of which would be saved from perdition. In al-Baghdadi's view, this was clear reference to the Sunni majority. Nevertheless, he held that in certain respects the Shiʿah belonged to the *ummat al-islam*, while in others they deserved to be denied privileges enjoyed by the Sunni loyalists. The Shiʿah, for example, were entitled to burial in a Muslim graveyard but not to have a prayer said over the deceased; they were not to be prevented from praying in mosques, but any animal slaughtered by a Shiʿah was unlawful food, and finally, a Shiʿah woman who held to her beliefs was not a lawful wife for a Sunni.[31] Twelver jurists responded in their turn. They held that a Shiʿah must not wash the body of a deceased Sunni, except where circumstances caused *taqiyah*, dissimulation, to be invoked. The same applied to a food animal slaughtered by a

Sunni, which could be consumed in order to avoid starvation. A Sunni woman who publicly declared her contempt for the Imams was unlawful as a wife for a Shi'ah man.

During the lifetimes of al-Mufid and al-Baghdadi, a Shi'ah festival was established by sympathetic rulers commemorating 'Ali's designation as the Prophet's successor at Ghadir Khumm. A rival Sunni festival saluting the role of the Caliph Abu Bakr was celebrated not long thereafter. A century later in Cairo, under a Shi'ah regime, festivals celebrating the births of the Prophet, 'Ali, Fatimah, al-Hasan, and al-Husayn were held. All but the Prophet's birthday were later discontinued when political circumstances changed and Sunnis returned to power.

For their part, Shi'ah traditionists, theologians and legal scholars, in the process of elaborating the beliefs and practices of their own community, defined the boundaries between themselves and Sunnis. As we have already noted, they shared with Sunnis the prophetic-revelatory event. However, the Shi'ah add a phrase to the *shahadah*, the Muslims' witness to faith. Following "There is no God but Allah and Muhammad is the Messenger of Allah" it concludes "and 'Ali is the friend (*wali*) of Allah." The focus upon 'Ali (embracing, by extension, the doctrine of the Imamate) is the most distinctive mark of the Shi'ah and their chief difference from all other Muslims.

Other features, specific to Shi'ah belief, may be briefly noted. Early discussions among their scholars raised the question whether the canonical text of the Qur'an preserved intact the original revelation of the Prophet.[32] Some suggested it had been tampered with in a manner which played down the supposed importance of 'Ali and the Imams. Ibn Babawayhi, al-Mufid, and Sharif al-Murtada, however, all accepted the integrity of the Qur'anic text. Shi'ah consensus has subsequently claimed that only the order of some of the *surah*s was changed, not their content; for indeed, to question the integrity of scripture ran the risk of subverting its authority. The Shi'ah believe, on the other hand, that the true interpretation of scripture was transmitted from the Prophet to 'Ali and through him to the succession of Imams. Nevertheless, accusations from Sunni quarters that the Shi'ah are guilty of having fabricated traditions denying the Qur'an's integrity are still heard from time to time, most recently in the years since Khumayni's revolution in Iran.

In most matters of the law, with the exception of the doctrine of leadership, the Imamate, substantial differences between the Shi'ah and Sunni have not emerged historically. This despite the Shi'ah emphasis upon Traditions transmitted by the Imams, whereas Sunni scholars drew upon the much broader pool of the Prophet's Companions as the second source of the law. Where Traditions from the Imams seemed to contradict each other, Shi'ah jurists compared both with accepted Sunni practice and then followed the opposite to it! In the area of family law, however, some significant differences have appeared. The Shi'ah recognize a form of temporary marriage (*mut'ah*) for an agreed period determined in advance. Children born from this union are considered legitimate. The Shi'ah claim that this was approved by the Prophet (on the basis of 4:24); the Caliph 'Umar subsequently abolished it. In Shi'ah inheritance laws, females often enjoy greater advantages than under Sunni law. The Shi'ah also place certain restrictions upon the husband's right to terminate his marriage.

The Sunni world view is, as we have seen, dichotomous. The domain of Islam is opposed to the domain of unbelief, or simply believers versus the rest, who may, of course, freely choose to join the camp of the faithful. The Shi'ah describe themselves as the elect (*al-khassah*), and all others as the commonality (*al-'ammah*). Or, in a more complex three-sided scheme, the Shi'ah world view consists of themselves as true believers; next, Muslims who accept the prophetic-revelatory event but who deny the Imams; and finally, the rest of humankind. Proselytization, therefore, should commence with other Muslims to bring them round to the Shi'ah vision of the faith. How common voluntary "conversion" was in practice from either one side or the other cannot be known. The Shi'ah coexisted with Sunnis in their scattered concentrations across the Muslim *ummah*, until the beginning of the tenth/sixteenth century. Then, in Iran a powerful dynasty emerged which created political structures for the protection and encouragement of the Twelver Shi'ah tradition. For more than two centuries Safavid rulers attracted scholars from other areas, notably Jabal 'Amil in south Lebanon and the Gulf island of Bahrayn, to erect Shi'ah religious culture on firm foundations. These developments produced the most significant expansion of the Shi'ah community since the heady days of al-Mufid and Sharif al-Murtada five centuries earlier. Moreover, the Safavid period saw the Shi'ah *'ulama'*, or mullahs, as they are also known, consolidate their role in this new Shi'ah society which, in retrospect, may be regarded as the beginning of the long gestation of a twentieth-century revolution.

18. Page from a large-format Qur'an, probably from fifteenth-century Persia, showing three verses of *surah* (or chapter) XXIX

19. Modern Turkish calligraphy by Hamid al-Amidi. The text of the opening *surah* of the Qur'an

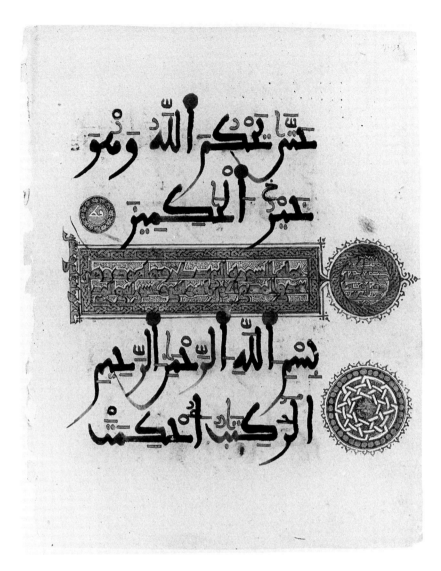

20. Page from a Qur'an probably copied in the thirteenth century in the Muslim
kingdom of Granada, showing the end of *surah* x, and the beginning of *surah* xi

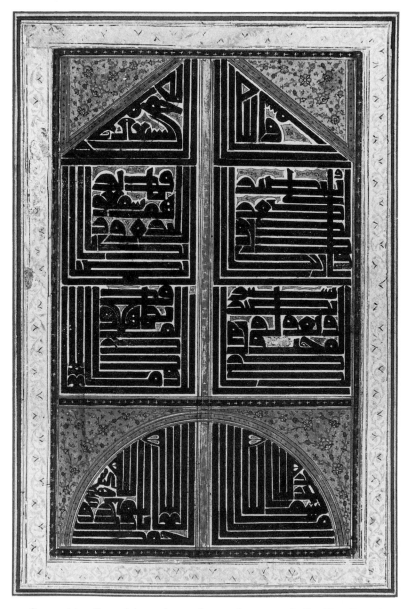

21. Composition from eighteenth- or nineteenth-century India. Heavily stylized Kufic lettering is formed into a shape like a *mihrab*, or prayer niche. The four central panels contain part of *surah* LXVIII of the Qur'an

PART 3

Islam in the modern world

CHAPTER 7

The heartlands and beyond

THE TRAVELER

In the summer of 725/1325 a young man set out for Mecca from his birthplace, Tangiers, in present-day Morocco. The initial aim of the journey (*rihlah*) was to perform the pilgrimage. The traveler who undertook the *rihlah* often combined this religious objective with trade to finance the trip, with scholarly pursuits, or with professional posts such as that of judge or teacher in cities along the way. Rarely have such globe-trotters left accounts of their activities to posterity. In the present instance, however, the young scholar who would become celebrated in world travel literature as Ibn Battutah broke the mold of the traditional *rihlah*, combining his religious obligation with a remarkable thirst for adventure. He fulfilled his pilgrimage duty in the same year and then embarked upon a grand tour which did not bring him back to his native land until a quarter of a century later. He dictated his "description of the world" to a fellow scholar and died in Morocco in either 770/1368 or 779/1377.[1]

Ibn Battutah possibly saw more of the eighth-/fourteenth-century world than any other traveler of his day. From North Africa his journeys took him to Mecca and Medina, thence to the Yemen, Mogadishu, and the trading posts of East Africa, Oman, and the Persian Gulf, across Asia Minor (or Anatolia) and then on through Persia and Afghanistan to Delhi, where he lived for several years. Journeying down the western coast of India, he spent a year and a half in the Maldive Islands, before moving on to Ceylon, Bengal, Sumatra, Java, and finally to China. Before completing the return trip across the Middle East, he took in Granada in al-Andalus and Timbuktu in West Africa.

He was not, of course, the only traveler of his time. Journeys undertaken from a variety of motives created a constant movement of Muslims criss-crossing the *dar al-islam*. Travelers also found their way to tiny pockets of the *ummah* beyond the regions governed and populated by Muslims. In the Muslim quarter of Qanjanfu in China, for example, Ibn Battuta met a fellow Moroccan who had become very prosperous in China and whose brother he was to meet years later in West Africa. Nor was Ibn Battutah a solitary traveler. He journeyed in the company of other scholars, merchants, and pilgrims together with his own attendants. His professional career as a judge (*qadi*) and his family life centered around his travels. He experienced every hazard imaginable, from severe illness, robbery, and capture by brigands on land to shipwreck and plunder by pirates at sea.

IBN BATTUTA'S WORLD

Ibn Battutah's narrative presents Muslim civilization as a mosaic of Muslim societies, united by a deep commitment to the prophetic-revelatory event yet expressing a wide diversity of Muslim experience within local cultures. It is also a picture of change, of gains and losses of territory in the *ummah*. Rarely, however, does Ibn Battutah step into a wholly alien world. Wherever he ventured, he encountered the warmth and welcome of Muslim scholars' homes, Sufis' *khanqah*s and sultans' palaces. As an Arab, he possessed the language of scripture, and as a judge (*qadi*) an intimate knowledge of the religious law. In time, he learned Persian, which served him as well at the Muslim court in Dehli. But he required an interpreter to converse with Turks in Asia Minor, which caused a moment of amusement. Lodging one night with some Sufis, they sent for a theologian who claimed to know Arabic. Ibn Battutah recalls that "He spoke to us in Persian and not understanding us when we spoke Arabic, he excused himself to the brothers saying 'These men speak ancient Arabic and I know only modern Arabic.'"[2] The scholar's attempt to cover his embarrassment nonetheless had the salutary effect of impressing the Sufis, who felt that their visitors must be treated with the greatest respect as they spoke the tongue of the Prophet and his Companions! Even Ibn Battutah's visit to Constantinople, capital of the Christian Byzantine Empire, was eased by a Syrian Jew who acted as interpreter in his audience with the emperor and by an Arabic-speaking Greek assigned to him as a guide.

Anatolia

The journey through Anatolia in 733/1332, which took in his visit to Constantinople, occurred at a period of upheaval and transformation in the region. The Muslim conquests in the first/seventh–eighth century had forced Byzantine emperors to relinquish control over Syria, although for the next four hundred years they contained Muslim attempts to expand into Anatolia. However, in a decisive battle in 464/1071 at Manzikert, north-west of Lake Van in Armenia, forces of central Asian Seljuk Turks overran the Byzantine army. The victory opened up Anatolia to gradual, long-term but permanent Turkish settlement westward which went hand-in-hand with the spread of Islam. A few years earlier, these same warriors, recently converted to Sunni Islam, had seized Baghdad, rescued the Abbasid Caliph from the control of Shi'ah princes and established themselves as defenders and masters of the Caliphate. In addition, Jerusalem and Damascus quickly fell under Seljuk rule. In Anatolia itself, however, Turkish power remained fragmented at first as several rival princedoms competed for territory, allowing Byzantium to retain a foothold.

At the turn of the eighth/fourteenth century, the fame of one Turkish warrior leader, Osman (Turkish form of 'Uthman), began to spread. His defeat of another Byzantine army led to the fall of Bursa, which became Osman's capital, in 726/1326. His followers, who became known as Ottomans, reached the Anatolian coastline with only the narrow waterway of the Dardanelles standing between them and the continent of Europe. This advance coincided with Ibn Battuta's passing through the region. From these modest beginnings there emerged the Ottoman Empire, one of the greatest Muslim powers of all time. Shortly thereafter, the Ottomans secured their presence in Europe with conquests of independent petty Balkan principalities such as the kingdom of Bosnia, the duchy of Herzegovina and later, Bulgaria and Albania. Gradually over the succeeding centuries a convert community of Muslims emerged in these territories under Ottoman suzerainty. The Muslim community of Bosnia-Herzegovina, which survived the demise of the Ottoman Empire following the First World War, today faces a modern version of an ancient political ploy called ethnic cleansing owing to the civil war which has engulfed these parts of the former republic of Yugoslavia.

Constantinople finally fell to the Ottomans in 857/1453, becoming their new imperial capital, Istanbul, as it was known in the vernacular.

It united the Anatolian and European halves of the empire, and at the peak of Ottoman power in the tenth–eleventh/sixteenth–seventeenth centuries, Turkish sultans governed an extensive territory which sprawled from the Dniester River through the Balkans, across Anatolia into Syria and Iraq, down the Arabian peninsula to include the holy cities of Mecca and Medina, and across North Africa from Egypt to Algeria.

Ibn Battutah's observations often have an innocent but nonetheless revealing directness about them. Among the Turks, for example, he noted as remarkable the respect shown to the women, who seemed to him to hold a more dignified position in society than the men and who moreover did not veil their faces. Customs among a people of nomadic origin clearly differed from those of his own long-established urban community in North Africa.

India

During his long sojourn in India, Ibn Battutah witnessed the customs of Muslims there, which also differed from what he had been used to in the older heartlands of the Islamic world. The Muslim invasion of India in the first/eighth century had begun at the same time as the Muslim entry from North Africa into the Iberian peninsula. Expansion and consolidation of a Muslim presence was slow, however, until Delhi became the capital of a Muslim sultanate in 607/1210. The Delhi sultanate was still a leading power in the sub-continent when Ibn Battuta arrived in the Indus valley in 734/1333, some fifty days' march from Delhi and the court of the current ruler, Muhammad b. Tughluq. The country was, of course, inhabited predominantly by Hindus who lived under Muslim rule, signaling the fact that Muslims were, and would always remain, a minority in India as a whole.

Muslim and Hindu lived in mixed communities along the western (Malabar) coast of India, especially in ports where Muslim merchants congregated. Relations were not always peaceful, although Ibn Battuta remarks that in the cosmopolitan port of Hilli there was a Friday mosque "venerated by both Muslims and infidels" which provided travelers and the poor with food from its kitchen. The coastal city of Kawlam further south, ruled by a Hindu, contained a Muslim quarter and a mosque. Ibn Battuta states that Muslims were honored there and that although "The sultan of Kawlam is an infidel called the Tirawari, he respects the Muslims and has severe laws against thieves and profligates," doubtless a matter appreciated by the visiting Maliki judge from Tangiers.[3] While Ibn Battutah refers to Hindus as infidels (as he does Christians), he observes them with a dispassionate eye. Of the Hindu women's ritual of throwing themselves on the funeral pyres of their dead husbands, he merely notes that this could be deemed a commendable if not a compulsory act, as a sign of the widow's fidelity. Hindu yogis, he tells us, were held in high esteem by the Muslim sultan and were frequent company at his court. Later, while visiting the eastern Indian region of Bengal, he set out to meet a renowned Sufi from Tabriz who lived in a mountain cave. He was sought out by Muslim and infidel, alike, and, Ibn Battutah adds, "It was by his labours that the people of these mountains became converted to Islam and that was the reason for his settling among them."[4] This same region was under Muslim rule whose infidel inhabitants, comments Ibn Battutah, were "mulcted of half their crops and pay taxes over and above that."[5] His sense of justice was troubled.

Ibn Battutah's narrative illustrates the point that in the Indian sub-continent, Islam developed along different lines from in the heartlands to the west. Its culture inevitably evolved patterns which were broadly Islamic but whose principal characteristics were Indian. Moreover, unlike other predominantly Muslim regions, including eventually Anatolia, Muslims were never able to Islamize the whole of India. This, despite the later founding of the powerful Muslim Mughal dynasty in the tenth/sixteenth century, which, at its height, embraced almost the entire sub-continent. Although decline set in during the twelfth/eighteenth century, the Mughal Empire survived until it was destroyed by the British after the great Indian Mutiny in 1857 CE.

The Maldive Islands, Sumatra, and China

Ibn Battutah's residence on the Maldive Islands provides a further example of the diversity of practice and perceptions among Muslims within the *ummah*. One feature of the islands which perplexed him was their ruler, a woman, although the real power holder was her husband. In his professional capacity as a judge (*qadi*), he observed of the inhabitants that they were "upright and pious, sound in belief and sincere in thought; their bodies are weak, they are unused to fighting, and their armour is prayer. Once when I ordered a thief's hand to be cut off, a number of those in the room fainted."[6] The punishment for theft as determined in scripture had apparently not been fully assimilated by the Maldivians. The good judge's attempts to impose "proper" norms of modesty in dress were politely but firmly ignored. "Their womenfolk do not cover their heads," he wrote, distressed; "even their queen does so, and they comb their hair and gather it at one side. Most of them wear only an apron from their waists to the ground, the rest of their bodies being uncovered. When I held the qadiship there, I tried to put an end to this practice and ordered them to wear clothes, but I met with no success. No woman was admitted to my presence in a lawsuit unless her body was covered, but apart from that I was unable to effect anything."[7]

After leaving Bengal, Ibn Battutah sailed to the Muslim kingdom of Samudra on the northern tip of the island of Sumatra, part of modern-day Indonesia. From southern India, Muslim traders and missionaries had introduced their faith along the coastal areas of the Malay archipelago, probably during the last decades of the previous (seventh/thirteenth) century. Marco Polo, Ibn Battutah's famous predecessor, had visited Sumatra on his return from China in 692/1292, and he judged that only one of the eight kingdoms on the island had by then converted to Islam. The spread of Islam was sporadic, moving along the trade route during the ninth/fifteenth century from Sumatra to Malacca, and then to northwest Borneo and the southern Philippines and from Java to the Spice Islands, now called the Moluccas. Some 90 percent of Indonesians (and 45 percent of Malaysians) today describe themselves as Muslim and as members of the world-wide *ummah*. Nonetheless, Indonesian Islam differs again from the Muslim cultures of the Middle East, India, and Africa, owing to the influences upon it of the pre-Islamic Indonesian traditions and folkways strongly influenced by Hinduism and Buddhism.

China greatly impressed Ibn Battutah. It was, he said, the safest and best-regulated country for a traveler. Every city had a quarter where Muslim merchants and their families lived by themselves, honored and respected. These quarters would have their own Friday mosque, a hospice for travelers, and a bazaar. "They have also a *qadi* and a *shaykh*, for in every one of the cities of China there must always be a Shaykh al-Islam, who acts as intermediary between the government and the Muslim community, and a *qadi* to decide legal cases between them."[8] However, in contrast to his experiences in India and Sumatra, Ibn Battuta expresses a more conscious awareness of traveling amidst an alien people and civilization. "The land of China," he writes, "in spite of all that is agreeable in it, did not attract me. On the contrary I was sorely grieved that heathendom had so strong a hold over it. Whenever I went out of my house I used to see any number of revolting things, and that distressed me so much that I used to keep indoors and only go out in case of necessity."[9] Arab and Persian merchants had settled in the port cities of southeast China during the late Tang dynasty (618–907 CE). They married Chinese women and gradually adapted to Chinese cultural patterns except, of course, where religious taboos were an obstacle, such as the prohibition of the consumption of pork. These were the ancestors of today's Hui people, who, together with nearly a dozen other ethnic groups, comprise the Muslim minority of China, just over 2 percent of the total population.

Return to the West

Ibn Battutah saw his native Tangiers again in 750/1349 when he visited the tomb of his mother. From there he crossed the Straits to Gibraltar and into al-Andalus. He was moved by the spirit of *jihad* since the Christian king, Alphonso XI, had recently died in his attempt to recapture Gibraltar from Muslim control. The kingdom of Granada was the last remaining Muslim state in the Iberian peninsula and survived until its fall to the Catholic monarchs, Ferdinand and Isabella, in 1492 CE, an event which ultimately led to the expulsion of Muslims from the entire peninsula. Ibn Battuta did not himself engage in battle against Christian forces, but rather seems to have contributed to the *jihad* by helping to raise money for the ransom of Muslim prisoners. In Granada Ibn Battuta met a number of distinguished scholars including a company of Sufis from Anatolia, Iran, and as far away as India.

Ibn Battutah's final journey took him to the West African kingdom of Mali in the Niger River valley. Islam had penetrated from the north into the savannah belt in the fifth/eleventh century, initially through foreign Muslim residents, traders, and itinerant preachers who had settled there. In Ibn Battuta's time, greater local support for Islam had been won and some African states, like Mali, had Muslim rulers. Nonetheless, Islamic values necessarily coexisted with local pagan customs. Monarchs upheld the traditional view of divine kingship and subjects continued to prostrate themselves in the king's presence. On Muslim festivals, both the prayer leader and pagan poets addressed the king. Ibn Battutah reports, however, that the main mosque in the capital was overflowing for the Friday communal prayers and young people were keen to memorize the Qur'an, even in a language they did not understand. From Mali Islam spread to Hausa land, where the rulers of trade centers like Kano and Katsina had recently converted in the decades before Ibn Battuta's arrival in the Niger valley.

A surprise awaited him akin to his encounter with the Muslims of the Maldive Islands. In the town of Iwalatan, he remarks upon the great beauty of the women, who are shown more honor than the men.

The state of affairs amongst these people is indeed extraordinary. Their men show no signs of jealousy whatever; no one claims descent from his father, but on the contrary from his mother's brother. A person's heirs are his sister's sons, not his own sons. This is a thing I have seen nowhere in the world except among the Indians of Malabar. But those are heathens; *these* people are Muslims, punctilious in observing the hours of prayer, studying books of law, and memorizing the Qur'an. Yet their women show no bashfulness before men and do not veil themselves, though they are assiduous in attending the prayers.[10]

A further shock greeted him. Women and men alike had "friends" and "companions" from outside their own immediate families. A wife, indeed, might entertain a male "companion" in her house during her husband's absence. Even the local *qadi*, without any apparent sense of shame, comments Ibn Battutah, was entertaining a beautiful young lady in his house when he arrived on a visit!

UNIT IN DIVERSITY

From west to east and back again, Ibn Battutah's travelogue offers a portrait of the eighth-/fourteenth-century *ummah* as he perceived it throughout its vast geographical extent in richly diverse locales. He appears in his own narrative, not only as an observer keenly engaged in the world about him, but also as a fixed point of reference around which his world revolved. He traveled as a *qadi*, representative of the normative values of the Maliki school of Sunni Islam. As a traveler he also observed, far from his birthplace in North Africa, the customs of other Muslims, pious and devout by his own testimony, who lived according to customs of which the law, as he understood it, disapproved.

The contrasts at times shocked his sensibilities. However, with the same spirit he showed to non-Muslims, whom he nevertheless referred to without rancor as heathens, he refrained from adopting a strident tone of condemnation toward the quite different manners of Muslim behavior, or their only partially Islamized customs. Their devotion to scripture and to prayer and pious behavior toward others kept these men and women firmly within the world-wide *ummah* as he experienced it. He felt a sense of belonging wherever he met Muslims, an intangible bond of unity amidst the many and varied cultures in which he encountered them.

Ibn Battutah experienced the *ummah* in ebb and flow. He witnessed both the declining Muslim fortunes in al-Andalus and the expansion of Turkish power in Anatolia on the threshold of continental Europe. In Iran and Iraq he saw cities and towns still struggling to recover from the ravages wrought by the invasions of pagan Mongol tribesmen led by Genghis Khan (d. 625/1227) and his descendants from central Asia a century earlier. The Mongol conquest had effectively ended the long waning fortunes of the Abbasid Caliphate and those of its once proud and flourishing capital, Baghdad. The westward roll of these waves of warring tribesmen was finally checked by a decisive military victory of the Egyptian Mamluks (whose dynasty lasted from 648/1250 to 922/1517) over the invaders at Ayn Jalut in Syria in 659/1260. Mongol successor states were established in the conquered territories under rulers who had adopted Islam. Ibn Battuta passed through the lands of one successor state, the Il-Khanids, at the moment it was passing into the pages of history.

On the other hand, a Muslim presence continued slowly but steadily to spread beyond the limits that Ibn Battutah knew in his own day: in India, the Malay archipelago, Sumatra, Java, and the Indo-Chinese coast; in areas of Central Europe embracing large parts of the Don, Volga, and Ural River basins; in Asia, north and east of the Syr-Darya River as far as the province of Kansu in China and southwest to the province of Yunnan; and across sub-Saharan Africa. Sultans and soldiers, merchants and Sufis were the most active agents of this unfolding process of conversion and control. The spread of the faith and Muslim rule often went together, especially in certain peripheral regions adjacent to other major cultural blocs. Arabic remained the universal language of ritual, while along with Arabic, Persian, and Turkish, other languages such as Malay and Urdu would become modes of expression of high Muslim culture.

Islamic lore from the older Middle Eastern heartlands (which had itself assimilated elements from previous Middle Eastern cultures) spread unevenly into areas newly opened to the trade and missionary ventures of Ibn Battutah's day and later. Islam had to compete vigorously with local customs wherever it encountered them. Even where the process of conversion was well advanced in these local communities newly absorbed into the *ummah*, they were not mere replicas of the original heartlands. This much Ibn Battutah had seen for himself. The *qadis* could not apply the minutiae of the law's social provisions everywhere the same way; and the Sufis of this era, perhaps the most prolific preachers of the faith among the lower and rural orders of society, often succeeded where the jurist could not, by investing local practices with Islamic credentials. Islamic sanctions, therefore, intermingled with the older sanctions of local or tribal custom.

There was, nevertheless, a shared awareness of being Muslim throughout the *ummah*, a feeling engendered in part by shared rituals of worship, especially prayer and fasting, but reinforced, too, by institutions discussed in previous chapters, such as the ritual pilgrimage to Mecca and travel for the purposes of trade and commerce, learning and teaching. At the core of this shared sense of belonging which cut across ethnic, racial, and even linguistic barriers was the message of the Book, Allah's immutable will and command to humankind. The Book expressed, too, the Prophet's own powerful consciousness of the One Creator, Sustainer, and Judge before whom each person was individually and equally responsible for his or her salvation. No matter that the Book was written in Arabic, a language to which many recent converts had no direct access. Muslims who knew the Book (or at least the essence of its message) taught it to others. The Qur'an was the universal basis upon which the Islamic experience was founded, its message stretching across geographical and cultural divides.

EMPIRES OF THE SULTANS

Ibn Battutah was unaware that he was witnessing the commencement of a new Islamic world order. His travels had taken him through territories where only the faintest stirrings were evident of the rise of three future major imperial powers. One would eventually dominate the western Islamic lands, another much of the region of the eastern *ummah*. As has already been noted these were, respectively, the Ottoman Empire centered upon its capital Istanbul and the Mughal

Empire in India. The third power to rival these two was the Shi'ite dynasty of the Safavids, which sprang up between them in Iran. The heyday of these imperial giants belonged to the tenth/sixteenth and eleventh/seventeenth centuries, during which period Muslim political, economic, and religious life was dominated by and governed from the courts of their sultans.

Conflict between them, whether intermittent or prolonged, was unavoidable. This was especially so as the Ottomans represented the defense of Sunni Muslim interests and the Safavids those of the Shi'ah. Ottoman sultans saw themselves as inheritors of the role of the Abbasid Caliphs, upholders of the *shari'ah*, protectors of the Meccan pilgrimage and guardians of the Muslim holy places. Safavid rule differed. It emerged from the combination of followers of a Sunni Sufi brotherhood and militant Shi'ah Turkoman tribesmen of eastern Anatolia, Armenia, and northern Syria. The promulgation of Shi'ah doctrine as the official expression of Islam necessitated its imposition upon a population that was still overwhelmingly Sunni. The dynasty's founder, Shah Isma'il (d. 930/1524), even proclaimed himself a descendant of the twelfth Imam and a *Mahdi*. Shi'ism did nonetheless act as a unifying force within Safavid domains against both the Ottomans and the Mughals by skillfully tapping into a latent Iranian "national" sentiment. Moreover, once Shi'ism was firmly established, the Safavid regime became a center of attraction for small, isolated Shi'ah communities elsewhere, as in southern Lebanon and the Persian Gulf. Lesser Shi'ah dynasties in India also maintained contact with the Safavid power. The Mughal sultans for their part were preoccupied with yet another problem, that of having to govern a continent in which the faith of the Muslim ruling community was engulfed by the majority Hindu culture.

Despite differences in politico-religious environment and the policies of individual rulers, the three imperial powers shared much in common. The ruling families were all Turkic in ethnic origin and tongue, while the language of diplomacy used between them was Persian. Their empires have been called the "Gunpowder Empires" since they (like their European contemporaries) put gunpowder technology to political and military ends. Rule was based upon a combination of military strength, a highly centralized bureaucracy geared to the efficient gathering of taxes from the land, trade and commerce, and religious legitimacy. A ruling establishment of the three components, the military, bureaucrats, and the *'ulama'*, was thus both maintained in support of the state and heavily patronized by it. In theory each sultan was subject to the *shariʿah*. In practice they were independent monarchs. However, despite dynastic control of religious affairs, it was the religious scholars of the establishment who gave to society its sense of political-religious identity, or the Sufis who provided a similar sense of belonging for the individual. The sultans appointed a chief religious official to ensure the proper functioning of the Islamic educational and legal systems, who also acted as the spokesman for the *ʿulama*'. He supervised the disbursement of income from religious endowments for the building and maintenance of mosques, schools, colleges (*madrasahs*), hospitals, and caravanserais for the use of travelers, scholars, and traders.

By the twelfth/eighteenth century, the fortunes of each empire were running swiftly in reverse. Political decline was the backdrop against which calls were raised for religious revival or a transformation in the relationship between the ruling establishment and religious authority. In the following pages, little more than a brief sketch is possible of the fates of these empires from their heights in the tenth/sixteenth and early eleventh/seventeenth centuries to the beginning of the modern period in the thirteenth/nineteenth century, noting the distinctive features of religious policy within the ruling establishment of each imperial dynasty. These heights are measured by the reigns of three sultans of extraordinary ability, each of which spanned more than four decades. Each reign provides a kind of dynastic snapshot illustrating the point from which these, the most outstanding Muslim societies of their day, moved toward the modern era. The sultans in question are the Ottoman Sulayman, surnamed the Magnificent (rg. 927–974/1520–1566), the Mughal Akbar, whose very name was a title meaning the Greatest (rg. 964–1013/1556–1605), and the Safavid Shah ʿAbbas, surnamed the Great (rg. 985–1038/1587–1629).

The Ottomans

Sulayman the Magnificent belonged to the longest enduring dynasty in Islamic history, which survived, in an increasingly weakened and diminished state, until 1923CE, when the republic of Turkey was established out of its imperial remains. As Sulayman ascended the throne, the Mamluk dynasty of Syria and Egypt had just succumbed to Turkish military power; Mecca and Medina acknowledged Ottoman suzerainty at the same time. The addition of these large territories to Ottoman domains left Sulayman free to concentrate on expanding Ottoman presence in Europe. Major cities like Belgrade and Budapest fell while the first siege of Vienna was attempted in 936/1529. Although unsuccessful, Ottoman penetration into the very heart of Christian Europe caused shudders of fear to ripple through the courts of its monarchs. Next, Sulayman turned to his Safavid enemies in Iran, and further successful campaigns lifted from Shi'ah control the old heartlands of the Abbasid Caliphate, including Baghdad, as far as the Persian Gulf. His supremacy in Sunni Islam was unchallenged.

Sulayman the military leader was also a gifted administrator, known to his own people as the Law Giver (*Kanuni*). He established a well-regulated centralized system of justice to meet the needs of his highly cosmopolitan empire, where the lives and property of all were protected regardless of religion. Two institutions, whose antecedents dated to the early generations of the *ummah*, were distinctive of Ottoman rule. The first was the millet system, a variation of the institution of the *dhimmi* or protected non-Muslim. A millet was an autonomous confessional community governed by its own religious leader to deal with its internal affairs such as religion, education, justice, and social security. There was a millet for the Greek Orthodox subjects of the sultan whose head was the patriarch of Istanbul; one for the Jews, with the grand rabbi of Istanbul as its head, and the Armenian millet, also with a patriarch as its head.

The second institution was state law or *kanun*, also known as the customary law of the sultan. Ottoman law combined traditions of central Asian Turkish origin, pre-Islamic imperial Persia, and, of course, the Islamic law of the *shari'ah*. The *shari'ah*, as we have seen previously, dealt comprehensively with personal law and community life but had little to say on state organization and administration. The *shari'ah* did, however, recognize the right of the ruler to legislate in matters affecting the public interest but which were not treated by the religious law. The Abbasids, for example, had issued financial regulations which were independent of the *shari'ah*.

The scale and scope of state law grew in the practice of all Muslim states established during the post-Mongol period, that is, after the mid seventh/thirteenth century. As the Ottoman domains increased in size, the imperial administration required to run affairs smoothly became more complex. At first Ottoman state law touched upon the areas of military, administrative, financial, and penal law. Sulayman,

however, appointed as chief jurisconsult (*shaykh al-islam*) a legal
expert, Abu al-Su'ud, who for nearly thirty years offered legal
decisions (*fatwas*) on a wide range of questions such as property law
which until then had been the sole province of the *shari'ah*. He was
always careful that his decisions did not conflict with the religious
law. He expanded state law by legalizing a sultan's *kanun* in this
fashion, issuing a *fatwa* declaring its compatibility with the principles
of the *shari'ah*. '*Ulama*' of the ruling establishment could, in theory,
challenge a *kanun* if they felt conflict did exist, but so long as the
sultan's authority remained supreme this was seldom done, since their
positions were dependent upon his pleasure.

Throughout the empire, a judge's (*qadi*) court in every local district
handled the affairs of the Muslim majority. A government appointee,
the *qadi* performed judicial and administrative functions applying
both the religious and *kanun* law. Like his predecessors, he had
recourse to the advice of experts in jurisprudence who would issue
judgments (*fatwas*) on legal questions put to them. These experts
(*muftis*) were appointed by the chief jurisconsult in Istanbul. The
Hanafi school of law was the one officially acknowledged by the
Ottoman government, but in provinces where another school was
customary, like the Shafi'i school in Egypt, Shafi'i *muftis* were
appointed there as well. During the long decline of Ottoman central
authority, the *qadi* in many places became virtually responsible for
the running of local government.

In 1095/1683, the second Ottoman siege of Vienna failed. It
marked the end of the Ottoman threat in Europe, and in subsequent
campaigns the once-vaunted Turkish army collapsed. Against the
attempts of a number of reforming prime ministers to inject new
vitality into imperial governmental structures, local and provincial
notables strove to exert a greater control over the affairs of their own
districts. Among the '*ulama*' of the ruling establishment as well, the
former standards of appointment to the post of *shaykh al-islam* based
on merit, established by Sulayman, had given way to widespread
nepotism. In addition, conflicts within the establishment between
strict upholders of the *shari'ah* and those who supported the greater
validity of *kanun* law reflected not only the decline in the sultan's
authority and the decentralization of political control but also a
struggle among the '*ulama*', bureaucrats, and the military for dominance
of, or at least greater influence within, the ruling institution.

In the provinces, beyond the struggles which preoccupied the ruling establishment in Istanbul, the *'ulama'* not associated with the state-sponsored hierarchy (like the *qadis* and the *muftis*) were more closely concerned with local issues and developments in the way they always had been. These included the many hundreds of individuals involved in the running of mosques, the prayer leader (*imam*), the *mu'adhdhin* who called the faithful to prayer, and the preacher (*khatib*) at the Friday prayer, as well as Qur'an reciters, persons in charge of the maintenance of cemeteries and others who offered prayers for the dead. Also included were independent *muftis* who were recognized in their local communities as men of learning and probity whose advice could be sought on a myriad of daily problems.

Other activities also continued unbroken from previous ages throughout the period of Ottoman decline in the eleventh/seventeenth and twelvth/eighteenth centuries. Traveling scholars of great or small reputation still formed an international network of contacts which paid scant attention to imperial or lesser political frontiers. One specific object of this cosmopolitan enterprise was the study of *hadith*, the Traditions of the Prophet. This activity may have increased in intensity as a means of alleviating the anxiety caused by the contemporary climate of turmoil, providing a positive basis for a renewed spirit of social and moral reconstruction.

Another aspect of continued inter-regional contact was the spread of certain reforming Sufi brotherhoods. In particular, the influence of a rejuvenated Naqshbandiyyah spread westward from India to Damascus and Mecca bringing with it an attitude of stricter adherence to the law and the prophetic Traditions coupled with a rejection of the more colorful excesses of brotherhoods which had attracted widespread popular following. Moreover, wherever they went, the Naqshbandiyyah actively attempted to influence members of the ruling establishment to adopt their outlook in the belief that if the practices of government were reformed the rest of society would follow suit.

In these several ways, *'ulama'*, especially those outside the official circles of government, kept abreast of developments in all parts of the *ummah*. Their cosmospolitan outlook was a factor in stimulating the call for reconstruction and revival which was to spread in the twelfth/eighteenth century.

The Mughals

Akbar, like his Ottoman counterpart Sulayman, was a soldier-administrator of great skill. The real founder of the Mughal dynasty, he was a Muslim descendant of the two famous pagan conquerors Ghengis Khan and Tamerlane. His military campaigns and diplomacy considerably extended Muslim control over large areas of the sub-continent. Like Sulayman's, his domains were characterized by a religious-cultural pluralism, a situation made more urgent, moreover, by the relatively rapid expansion of their respective empires under their leadership. Consolidation of conquest required in each case, therefore, a tolerant openness to subjects of every religious community. Akbar's policies aimed at the creation of a centralized state together with the establishment of social harmony between Muslims and the Hindu majority. His approach differed, however, from the Ottoman solution to pluralism in the millet system.

Akbar was an illiterate but deeply religious person. For many years he regularly visited Ajmer and the tomb of Mu'in al-Din Chishti, founder of the brotherhood of that name. He also visited the retreat of a Chisti holy man, Salim, who foretold the birth of his son the following year. The son, called Salim after the holy man, became Akbar's successor with the regnal title of Jahangir. It was to honor this "friend of Allah" (*wali Allah*) that Akbar constructed his new walled capital at Fathpur Sikri and where, within the precinct of the great mosque, the tomb of Salim Chisti was built. Within the same capital complex was the House of Worship (*ibadat khana* or *diwan-i khass*). Here Chisti religious exercises were performed and, later, Akbar initiated debates on a rationalist approach to religion and on a comparative investigation of religions in general. Muslims of differing religious standpoints, Hindus, Christians, Jains, Zoroastrians, and Jews, took part in these discussions. Akbar was influenced by Ibn al-'Arabi's mystical-philosophical doctrine of the Perfect Man. His disciple and biographer, Abu al-Fadl of Agra (d. 1011/1602), presents him as such, and as the axis (*qutb*) around whom all the world revolves, the sole spiritual guide of his own time. Ibn al-'Arabi's ideas had provided the essential meeting ground for Muslims and Hindus and had stimulated a mushroom growth of sects based on a pantheistic approach to religion.

Akbar's attitude in the prevailing climate gave rise to unease in certain quarters of the *'ulama'* that he was claiming for himself near prophetic status, or worse, identity with the divinity. On the other hand, as the end of the first Muslim millennium (1000/1591) was approaching, some scholars, searching for the traditional renewer (*mujaddid*) of faith toward the end of each century, suggested that Akbar could be the renewer of the second Muslim millennium, or lord of the age. Then Akbar issued his "infallibility decree," in which it was declared that the just ruler (meaning himself) had the authority to decide between conflicting interpretations of jurists in the application of the *shariʿah*, thus effectively removing this privilege from the *ʿulamaʾ*. Next, in 989/1581 Akbar proclaimed his eclectic "divine way" (*din-i illahi*), which asserted reason as the method of religion and emphasized the truth to be found in all faiths. Other measures he took were allowing his Hindu wives to practice their faith; abolishing the poll-tax (*jizyah*) on all non-Muslims; and abolishing the pilgrimage tax on Hindus and the obligatory *zakat* on Muslims, although Muslims could continue to offer alms to the poor and needy directly and voluntarily. Hindus were also to be found in the financial administration of government and in the military, cooperating with Muslims in the effective management of the empire.

Akbar's "divine way" has been described by a modern Muslim scholar as "the emperor's spiritual sport."[11] Initiates numbered a mere eighteen, only one of whom was Hindu, and Akbar's personal insights on religion were only shared with them inside the confines of the palace. On the other hand, the same commentator describes Akbar's understanding of true Islam as "tolerance and understanding and an extension of human rights and privileges reserved in earlier Indo-Muslim political philosophy for Muslims alone, to all non-Muslims, including the rights of conversion and reconversion, promulgation of laws of marriage and laws against abduction, freedom of worship and construction of the houses of worship."[12] Whether or not Akbar's personal religious views might have influenced a wider audience, the danger to Islam, as opponents saw it, was eventual absorption by Hindu culture.

Some of Akbar's Muslim contemporaries viewed him as an apostate. This was not, however, a term used by one of the most outstanding and severe of his critics, Ahmad Sirhindi (d. 1034/1624). Much of what Akbar advocated had precedents in the practice of Muslim rulers elsewhere, including the adoption of moral principles not insisted upon by the *shariʿah* but, equally, not contrary to it. Some of his reforms could certainly have been attacked as innovations

(s. *bidʿah*), but, as in the case of similar accusations in the earlier history of Islam, a declared innovation at one time did not inevitably make it an innovation for all time. Sirhindi condemned Akbar's concessions to Hindus as innovations. He argued that although innovations may have been tolerated in the glory days of Islam, they could not in the present age of decline. The inspiration for his attack on the fusion of ideas of different religions was drawn from scripture, which stated *to you your religion and for me my religion* (109:6).

Sirhindi was a follower of the Naqshbandiyyah brotherhood, which, from its central Asian origins in Bukhara of the eighth/fourteenth century, had reached India by the close of the tenth/sixteenth century. From the beginning, Islam in India had been propagated mainly by Sufis, who enjoyed success among both Hindu and Buddhist populations, but especially among lower-caste Hindus, drawn to egalitarian Islamic values. Sirhindi recognized that Akbar's spiritual attitude lay within Sufism as it had developed in the Indian context. But he attacked the Sufi interpretation of Ibn al-'Arabi's theosophical system, which claimed that the height of the mystical experience was union, or absolute nearness or identity of the Sufi seeker with Allah. He confronted the tension between the perennial mystical aspiration for the immanence of Allah and the scholars' assertion of his transcendence by steering a middle course which emphasized the provisions of the *shariʿah*. He applied to the Indian situation the maxim of his own teacher Baqi bi'Llah (d. 1012/1603) that "not mystic emotions but adherence to the *shariʿah* should be the ideal." Moreover, he insisted that the true goal of the mystical experience affirmed the ultimate ontological gap between the nature of Allah and his creatures. In other words, the experience of oneness was the phenomenological unity of vision (*wahdat al-shuhud*), not Ibn al-'Arabi's ontological unity of being (*wahdat al-wujud*). Sirhindi's fear at bottom was that Indian Sufism in its pantheistic or monist guises, which had developed much in common with Hindu esoteric experience and the popular reverence of holy men, was causing the disintegration of the monotheistic ideals of Islam in India. Sirhindi's call was for a more particularist, communalist interpretation of the Islamic mission. How that could be fulfilled in a situation of declining Muslim political power in India was a dilemma Indian Muslims never satisfactorily resolved. The renewed vigor which Sirhindi injected into the Naqshbaniyyah was in any case transplanted by the brotherhood into the Ottoman territories over the next century.

Akbar's syncretic policies were pursued by his immediate successors, Jahangir (d. 1037/1627) and Shah Jahan (d. 1069/1658). By the end of the century, however, the Emperor Aurangzeb (d. 1119/1707) had broken with the empire's eclectic heritage. At the same time, the empire's resources were approaching the point of exhaustion, and Muslim imperial power was being challenged by a number of rebel Hindu and Sikh revolts. By the turn of the twelfth/eighteenth century, the declining Muslim Empire in India was, like the Ottoman, awaiting a summons to religious renewal.

The Safavids

The Safavids were the shortest lived of the three dynastic empires. The last of the line, Shah Sultan Husayn, was overthrown by invading Afghan forces in 1134/1722, less than a century after the death of 'Abbas. 'Abbas's hold over power, however, was absolute. He shared with his Ottoman and Mughal counterparts a passion for public works. It is said that at his death, in his capital Isfahan alone, there were some 160 mosques, 50 colleges, 1,800 caravanserais, and nearly 300 baths. By 'Abbas's time, some of the more extreme claims of the founder Isma'il had been muted. The Safavids, nonetheless, continued to project themselves as the sole legitimate representatives and agents of the Hidden Imam, giving them a religious aura which no subsequent ruler in Iran would possess, including the late Muhammad Reza Shah Pahlavi. During the reign of Abbas's predecessor, Shah Tahmasp (d. 984/1576), Twelver Shi'ah works were translated from Arabic into Persian to make them more widely accessible. Shi'ah scholars from abroad were imported into the Safavid court to help create an indigenous cadre of scholars to spread Shi'ah ideas among the populace. One of these scholars, 'Ali al-Karaki (d. 940/1534), from Jabal 'Amil in southern Lebanon, was influential enough to become Shah Tahmasp's deputy, which permitted him to manage the expenditure of taxes raised on behalf of the Hidden Imam. Shah 'Abbas, however, replaced the scholar's authority with his own, although he supported the Shi'ah by creating a religious endowment (*waqf*) for the benefit of the twelve Imams and making bequests to religious institutions from his private treasury.

One consequence of the early Safavids' imposition of Shi'ah doctrines from above was that Twelver Shi'ah mullahs, as they were known, suddenly acquired a status in Iranian society they had not previously enjoyed. The mullahs were patronized by the state as the chief agents of the transformation of Iran into a Shi'ah society. So long as the emperors, like 'Abbas, retained absolute control of the reins of state, the mullahs accepted, indeed supported, their claims to be descended from the Imams. The state and the mullahs, therefore, served each other's needs. The mullahs performed much the same roles as the *'ulama'* in Sunni Ottoman and Mughal societies, as prayer leaders, legal experts, judges, and so on. However, state patronage seems to have benefited the mullahs economically as well as politically, in a manner which placed them at an advantage over their Sunni counterparts. That is, in addition to receiving salaries for their official and religious duties, the mullahs became administrators of the income from enormous pious endowments, and their control over certain religious taxes was endorsed. By the end of the Safavid period, the mullahs were supported by the considerable wealth accumulated from these sources. Another consequence of 'Abbas's rule was that Sufi brotherhoods were condemned as heretical and they all but disappeared from Iran. Visiting Sufi tombs and belief in the performance of miracles by the "friends of Allah" (*wali Allah*) were regarded as demeaning the dignity and authority of the Imams. By the late twelfth/eighteenth century this trend had been reversed somewhat with the return from India of the Shi'ah Ni'matullahi brotherhood to Iran.

As the power of the Safavids weakened during the eleventh/ seventeenth century, some leading mullahs, known as *mujtahid*s, began to question the emperors' legitimacy to rule. Twelver Shi'ah theorists who had developed their doctrines and legal theory by the fifth/eleventh century had done so without the luxury of protection from any government. This had also allowed them to admit only the Imams as legitimate rulers, thereby in theory denying the legitimacy of any other ruler. The notion debated in Safavid times was whether the leading *mujtahid* of the day could become the Hidden Imam's representative and therefore the highest spiritual authority without, of course, possessing the Imams' infallibility. While the idea directly challenged the Safavids' own pretensions, it was not actively pursued. It did, however, eventually pave the way for the *mujtahid*s' opposition to all secular power, even to a government which professed Shi'ah loyalty. Ultimately it led to the twentieth-century claim by the late Ayatullah Khumayni that the *mujtahid*s could rule directly.

Following the Safavid collapse in the first quarter of the twelfth/

eighteenth century, events led to a period of disorder, the rise of powerful tribal leaders, and further economic decline. A curious interlude ensued. Nadir Shah, a member of the Turkoman Afshar tribe which had originally supported the Safavids, emerged from the confusion to become *de facto* ruler in 1142/1729. His campaigns against both Ottomans and Mughals were economically ruinous for the country, and he was assassinated in 1160/1747. For political reasons he attempted to integrate a radically "reformed" 'Shi'ism into mainstream Sunni Islam and thereby claim leadership of the Islamic world for himself. Although he was not a Sunni, he brought an end to the Shi'ah practice of publicly cursing the first three Caliphs, Abu Bakr, 'Umar, and 'Uthman, in the call to prayer and the Friday sermon. More dramatically, however, he sought to have Shi'ism recognized by all as the fifth Ja'fari *madhhab*, named after the Imam Ja'far al-Sadiq, alongside the four Sunni legal schools of the Hanafis, Hanbalis, Shafi'is, and Malikis. The attempt failed. Another four decades of political disunity and turmoil followed Nadir Shah's death. It was not until 1794 that the Qajars succeeded in establishing a dynasty and they ruled until 1925.

The reigns of the great sultans marked a peak not only of medieval Muslim political power but also of Islamic cultural florescence. Visible to a modern-day traveler to Turkey, Iran, or India are monuments which have survived as proof of the former splendor of their one-time imperial capitals. Among such monuments, which include colleges of learning (*madrasah*s), mausoleums, hospitals, Sufi *khanqah*s, royal palaces, and gardens, there are, of course, the mosques. The early formulation and development of religious doctrine, the law, and mysticism which have occupied our attention in the previous chapters came into being chiefly within the urban ambience of the mosque, the most familiar and recognizable edifice associated with Islam. Later, the *madrasah* became the center of intellectual nourishment, while in the *khanqah* the spiritual fervor of daily life was preserved. The mosque, nonetheless, remained the focal point of communal worship (and other activities) which formed a link in a universal chain binding Muslims everywhere together as witnesses to the message and the Messenger. Fortunately, mosques of the early Islamic centuries survive to the present, such as the Dome of the Rock in Jerusalem and the great mosques of Samarra in Iraq, Qayrawan in Tunisia, and Cordoba in Spain. Countless more, however, have succumbed to the vicissitudes of time. On the other hand, it is the case that some of the greatest surviving examples of mosque architecture belong to the reigns of Sulayman, Akbar, and Abbas. A mere visual impression is insufficient for an appreciation of the significance of the structure and design of the great mosques of this or indeed any other period. It is appropriate, therefore, to pause here and reflect upon the origin and development of the mosque and its spiritual significance in Islamic culture; examples of Ottoman, Safavid, and Moghul construction will be noted. Mosque architecture presents a rich variety of motifs, materials, and styles differentiated from one period and place to another. At the same time the mosque has embodied and preserved a fundamental unity of purpose across the *ummah* and beyond, wherever Muslims were to be found. The diverse cultures Ibn Battutah encountered throughout his travels were, in this respect, made familar to him by a unity of artistic and spiritual purpose of the mosques he worshiped in.

THE MOSQUE: STRUCTURE AND COMMUNAL FUNCTION

The word "mosque" in Arabic is *masjid* (plural, *masajid*), meaning a place of prostration. It is where the faithful perform their devotions, the five daily prayers, a ritual involving kneeling and touching the forehead upon the ground in humble prostration before Allah. In Islam this place of prostration need not be a sanctuary set apart for such worship. It could be any place where humility before Allah is expressed in prayer. The Prophet is recalled in a Tradition saying that "The earth is a *masjid* for you, so pray wherever you are at the time of prayer."[13] The person in an act of private devotion at home upon a prayer mat or the traveler kneeling in prayer in the desert sand enters, as it were, a *masjid*.

The genesis of the mosque, tradition reveals, is to be found in the house erected by the Prophet in Medina immediately after his safe arrival from Mecca. The structure was completed in the first months of the new Islamic era marked by the *hijrah* (1/622). It was a large enclosure, the mud brick walls running more than fifty meters along each side, with a open portico at one end constructed from a double row of palm-trunk columns and roofed with palm leaves and mud. A smaller roofed structure occupied a portion of the wall opposite the portico, near the main entrance, said to be for the protection of impoverished members of the young community. A number of huts for Muhammad and his family were attached to the outside of one wall, each with its entrance into the expansive courtyard. Animals, too, were allowed into the enclosure. The primitive simplicity of this structure made it something of an all-purpose community center where, together with meetings for general instruction in the faith and discussions of a political or military nature, prayer took place.

The major mosques of cities and towns in time became commonly known as *jami'* or congregational mosques, distinguishing them from the smaller neighborhood *masjid*, or the mosque which was an adjunct to a tomb. The *jami'* mosques retained the enclosure (after the fashion of the Prophet's house) with an open courtyard (*sahn*) and covered sanctuary for prayer divided by rows of columns. The courtyard usually contained a large water basin at which the necessary ablutions were made before prayer. As the faithful kneel in prayer toward the Ka'bah in Mecca, the back or *qiblah* wall of the mosque was oriented in that direction. On the interior of the *qiblah* wall there is an arched concave niche, the *mihrab*, which is often very finely decorated. The importance of the *mihrab* was often heightened by the construction of a dome in front of it. The *imam* or prayer leader (not to be confused with the Shi'ah spiritual leader) leads the congregational prayer from in front of this niche. Beside the *mihrab* to the right is the *minbar*, a pulpit-like structure of wood or stone with a flight of steps from the top of which the sermon (*khutbah*) is delivered at the Friday noontime congregational prayer. Traditionally, the sermon had a political touch inasmuch as it mentioned the name of the current ruler, thereby publicly acknowledging the community's allegiance to him. At times, the ruler's enemies were cursed from the *minbar*. Today, sermons not infrequently can be couched in veiled or coded messages of political criticism of a government's policies if they are perceived as damaging to the public interest.

The Friday congregational prayer meetings were reminiscent of the communal spirit of the Prophet's dwelling. It was Muhammad himself, moreover, who asserted that praying in the company of others was twenty-five times more meritorious than individual prayer at home. Other activites than worship were carried out in the mosque. We have previously noted its function as a center of learning, especially in the Qur'anic sciences and the law; jurists delivered their legal decisions within its precincts. Students and devout ascetics also lived in mosques for lengthy periods. In some places, the mosque kitchen provided food for these pious souls as well as for the poor and needy. At an early period, before the rise of imperial bureaucracies, the mosque had served, too, for the conduct of government business. In short, the mosque at times became the focal point of many popular activities which, even if officially frowned upon, never diminished its central religious importance in community life. The English scholar E. W. Lane, who lived for several years in mid-nineteenth-century Cairo, observed that "In many of the larger mosques, particularly in the afternoon, persons are seen lounging, chatting, eating, sleeping, and sometimes spinning or sewing, or engaged in some other simple craft; but, nothwithstanding such practices, which are contrary to the precepts of their prophet, the Muslims very highly respect their mosques."[14]

Finally, the *jami'* mosque's most familiar feature to the outside observer is the minaret (from the Arabic *minarah*). This is a high tower, generally attached to the mosque itself, from which the faithful are summoned to their daily prayers. The very earliest mosques, however, were without a minaret, a style traditionally found also in Indonesia and China and, occasionally, elsewhere, as in pre-Mughal India; Turkish mosques, on the other hand, often have more than one. The size and shape of the minaret varies considerably: square, spiral, cylindrical, and composite types are known.

The mosque: imperial styles

The basic Arab-style enclosed courtyard-sanctuary mosque was the predominant type from Syria westward across North Africa and into the Iberian peninsula. Elsewhere, modifications on this pattern were made while, in addition, the particular style of one region was often transferred to another. In Anatolia, for example, the courtyard was dispensed with, probably in response to the bitterly cold winters of the region, the minaret usually being placed outside the mosque. The totally covered sanctuary remained a chief characteristic of Turkish mosque architecture where the role of the dome was developed to the highest perfection as the device for covering the entire internal space. The result produces a startling contrast with the earlier sanctuary type. For example, the interior of the mosque at Cordoba, begun in 137/784, and enlarged over the next two centuries, appears as an endless forest of graceful, arcaded columns. In contrast is the Sulaymaniyeh mosque (963/1556) in Istanbul, named after the sultan Sulayman, and which is the masterpiece of the famous Ottoman architect Sinan (d. 996/1588). In the total absence of columns, its richly decorated domic interior suggests the infinite space of the heavens. Sinan surpassed all his previous work in the Selimye mosque at Edirne (982/1574), which possesses the largest of all Ottoman central domes (at 31 meters in diameter) and the tallest quartet of minarets (at 71 meters in height).

The tradition of mosque building in Iran at first followed the Arab style. It then evolved its own distinctive character by adding to the traditional columned hall a large domed chamber marking the direction of the *qiblah* wall, and to each side of the courtyard enclosure a vaulted open hall with a rectangular arched façade called an *iwan*. The great mosque at Yazd is one example, built in the period of Ibn Battuta's travels. Another, constructed during the reign of Shah 'Abbas, is the Masjid-i Shah (1021–1040/1612–1630) in his capital, Isfahan. The use of tilework on the entrance portals, the *iwans*, domes, and minarets of the Iranian mosque sets off its brilliant blue or turquoise exterior from the sombre grey of its Ottoman contemporary.

In India, little remains of Islamic buildings at the time of the conquest in the second/eighth century. From the sixth/twelfth century, however, the mosques of the sub-continent can be said to contrast less with mosque styles elsewhere than with the Hindu temple architecture in its very midst of which the Muslim mosque was the direct antithesis. The interior gloom of the temple, its idols, figure representations, and the belief system they implied were anathema to the Muslims' manner of worshiping the One, Unique deity. As the real founder of the Mughal Empire, Akbar embarked upon an ambitious building program. He completed the construction of a new capital in 980/1574 at Fathpur Sikri, some twenty miles from Agra. The *jami'* mosque which, like the rest of the city, was built of red sandstone, is a synthesis of several Muslim styles characteristic of Mughal architecture as a whole. The giant courtyard plan, however, broadly reflects the Arab prototype.

The great mosques mentioned here are imperial monuments built by sultans for the congregational worship of the faithful on Friday. They are dwarfed, in number only, by the thousands of small and modest mosques built and maintained from the income of religious endowments established by private individuals for daily prayer in a town or city quarter. The common motive behind mosque construction may be traced to a Tradition of the Prophet that "Anyone who builds a mosque for Allah, He will build a house for him in paradise."[15]

The essential point expressed here is that the mosque is the primary place where the faithful, either as individuals or as a community, continually remember Allah in their worship. This constant purpose, the remembrance of Allah, is reflected in the mosque's ornamentation, which provides the basic aesthetic unity of mosques everywhere, whatever the regional architectural style.

The mosque and the Infinite

Allah must be remembered, but he cannot be represented by any image or symbol. He is completely other than human and other than nature. His creation, man and nature, is mutable, perishable. Allah is immutable, infinite. The way of aesthetically expressing the infinite is to provide a stimulus which leads the believer to an intuition of the divine presence. The stimulus in the art of the mosque is an abstract pattern with neither beginning nor end, conveying the impression of infinity. The pattern, called the arabesque, is in its broadest sense a complex and stylized design of intertwined figures, geometric, floral, or calligraphic. The pattern has no central focus but rather is composed of numerous parts combined to make up a larger design. And these larger combinations may themselves be connected to other entities in an even more complex arrangement. The pattern is not static but moves from one module to another. The observer, therefore, by means of the imagination will extend the evolving, repeating pattern beyond the edge of a panel on a wall, beyond the curvature of a dome or vault, or beyond a row of arched columns.[16] The aesthetic effect upon the faithful at prayer in the mosque is a resonance of the scriptural passage that wherever one turns, one is in the presence of Allah.

Contact with the divine presence is reinforced by the employment of calligraphic art in the mosque. Calligraphy is the most characteristic and highly developed of Islamic arts, influenced by practical developments necessary for the reproduction of the Qur'an, the word of Allah. Calligraphy appears on both religious and secular objects such as coins, utensils, ceramics, textiles, and gravestones. During the first centuries the script most commonly used for making copies of the Qur'an was called Kufic, named after the early Islamic city of Kufa in Iraq. It was square and angular in form, unlike the more cursive and rounded scripts which became dominant later. The Kufic script, in its plain or floriated and plaited variants, was well suited to the skills of stone carvers and tile makers to reproduce passages from the Qur'an which appear as ornamentation on mosque walls and domes. An excellent early example of this use is to be found in the Dome of the Rock in Jerusalem. A Muslim scholar has expressed the fundamental relation between this art and the divine as follows: "If Islamic art can serve as support for remembrance of the One, it is because, although made by men, it derives from a supra-individual inspiration and a *hikmah* (wisdom) from Him."[17] Contact in the mosque with the divine presence, therefore, is contact with the divine will.

If the Qur'an is viewed as the universal basis of Islamic experience, the mosque is the place of universal public witness to that experience. From Mali in west Africa to Mindanao in the southern Philippines, mosques everywhere are oriented toward Mecca, spiritual center of the *ummah*, birthplace of the Prophet Muhammad, and host to the cosmopolitan annual pilgrimage. From any mosque within the *ummah* proper and beyond, the Muslim is aware of being part of a divinely centered and guided community. There is a consciousness, too, of the moral and ethical demands of revelation as the worshiper's eye catches their patterned presence in panels carved or painted with Allah's word.

ZENITH AND DECLINE OF EMPIRE

Following the reigns of the sultans Sulayman, Akbar, and 'Abbas, decline in the fortunes of their respective dynasties was steady, although the rate varied in each case and final collapse came at different times. Political weakness, measured by military defeat from without or increasingly militant opposition to the sultans' autocratic rule from within, brought with it the perception that the official representatives of religion had become tainted by the patronage of their imperial masters.

This was but one aspect of the growing corruption of the state. By the twelfth/eighteenth century, it was evident to many that not only the political but the moral fabric of society as a whole was being torn asunder. According to a medical dictum familiar to Muslims of the time, when a disease afflicted the soul, the body soon withered away. When the analogy was applied to society it was said that "the king is the soul and the people the body. If the king goes astray the people will follow suit." Religious diagnosticians were not slow to point out that the disease of state had already spread to society proper, the main symptom being the spiritual decay of the Sufi brotherhoods. The brotherhoods had once been in the vanguard of bringing converts to the faith in the eastern and western reaches of the *ummah*, but their latitudinarian tendencies, prone at times to drift into antinomianism, were now judged to have compromised too much with similar local tendencies and indigenous customs everywhere. True faith had been weakened, and a cure was required as a matter of urgency.

PRE-MODERN MOVEMENTS OF RENEWAL: THE EIGHTEENTH CENTURY

Imperial poltical decline and the reorientation of certain Sufi brotherhoods are two factors which affected the religious climate of the tenth/sixteenth and eleventh/seventeenth centuries. A third factor was added in the twelfth/eighteenth century, namely the emergence of movements of religious renewal. However, owing to the particular relationship between the Safavid state and the religious scholars, Shi'ah experience in Iran during the twelfth/eighteenth century differed significantly from Sunni experience in the lands of the Ottomans and Mughals.

Iran

The Shahs of the Qajar dynasty ruled Iran without the legitimacy of their Safavid predecessors, who had so skillfully fused Shi'ism with Iranian "national" consciousness. Their claim to be descended from the seventh Imam had also been acknowledged but was then quietly buried along with the last of the line. During the twelfth/eighteenth century and throughout the long interregnum between the Safavid and Qajar dynasties, Shi'ah religious leaders vigorously defended their financial independence against all transient rulers and managed to emancipate their community from any essential link with the institution of the monarchy.

This success resulted in part from developments within the ranks of the relgious elite themselves. Two major currents of Shi'ah thought were represented by the parties of the Akhbaris and the Usulis.[18] The former dominated the Shi'ah centers of learning in Iraq, Najaf, and Karbala, then under Ottoman control. From the relative safety of these shrine cities, the Akhbaris vilified their Usuli opponents across the border in Iran. The conflict between them centered upon the exercise by the *mujtahid* of fresh, interpretive, independent judgment on all matters of religious practice and the nature of religious authority in the absence of the Imam.

Allowing for differing shades of opinion among the Akhbaris and attempts to bridge the gap between the two sides, the Akhbaris held that the only legitimate sources of legal knowledge are the Qur'an and the Traditions of the Prophet and the Imams. Since the community must continue to submit to the Imams' guidance, however remote in time that was, Traditions were the best guide to their true intentions. As to the other sources of law, allowed for in Sunni legal thought, the Akhbaris dismissed *ijma'* as irrelevant and *qiyas* as Satan's tool. Implicit in their position was the view that the Imams had dealt with all major questions in their Traditions which might in future arise. On the other hand, Usulis claimed for the *mujtahids* a key role in the interpretation of law and doctrine in order to deal with changing socio-historical conditions. As an expert in the Traditions as well as other branches of knowledge, the *mujtahid* was distinguished by the independent use of reason applied to the sources. The *mujtahid* claimed to achieve only probable knowledge of the Imams' intentions, in contrast with the Akhbari, who claimed a near, albeit not absolute, degree of certainty as to the detail of the Imams' teachings. Since *mujtahids'* decisions were fallible, differences of opinion were allowed and decisions could be reversed. More importantly, the Usulis rejected the Akhbari principle of *taqlid al-mayyit*, that is, adhering solely to the views of deceased religious leaders. Instead, Usulis insisted that all believers must choose and follow a living *mujtahid* and abide strictly by his decisions, a doctrine which had several important implications. One was that every new generation required its own *mujtahids* to interpret the law; second, it gave the *mujtahids* authority in the community beyond anything Sunni *'ulama'* could claim for themselves, and third, it gave their judgments a status above even the decrees of state.

Victory of the Usulis over the Akhbaris by the end of the century led to the idea of a collective leadership of *mujtahids* and the development of a hierarchy within the religious class. The head of the hierarchy was selected and acknowledged by the leading, qualified *mujtahids* from among themselves. Each in theory was a source for imitation (*marja' al-taqlid*) by others, who were bound to accept the *mujtahid*'s judgment without question. In effect, the *mujtahids* had appropriated the prerogatives of the Hidden Imam, and the basis of their authority was now independent of state patronage as it had not been under the Safavids. As a social group, one closely allied to the small landholding class and the bazaar merchants, they were established as a formidable force against the secular power of the court.

The holy cities: Mecca and Medina

The holy cities of Mecca and Medina (*al-Haramayn*) had been the first objective of Ibn Battutah's great globe-trotting adventure. As the primary goal of the Muslim pilgrim and as the compass point toward which the Muslim prays, Mecca has remained through the ages the spiritual center of the *ummah*. In the twelfth/eighteenth century the cities were under the protection of the Ottoman sultan, who was also responsible for the safety of the caravans heading from Damascus for the annual pilgrimage. Mecca itself was run by local families known as the *shurafa'* (s. *sharif*) claiming descent from the Prophet. Together, Mecca and Medina were also major cosmopolitan centers where scholars from every corner of the *ummah* came to live, often for lengthy periods, to engage in the study of the religious sciences, to teach, and to exchange ideas before returning to their native lands.

The interaction between resident and visiting scholars did not create a distinctive *Haramayn* school of thought so much as a dynamic sounding board for the contemporary concerns of Muslims everywhere. Questions about the decline of Muslim states and of spiritual decadence were too large and pressing to have been avoided in daily discussion. In this manner, the *Haramayn* had connections with most currents of religious thought and developments throughout the century. One example is the famous Sufi 'Abd al-Ra'uf al-Sinkili (d. ca. 1105/1693), who traveled from Sumatra to the *Haramayn*, where he resided and studied for nearly twenty years. Upon his return to the kingdom of Acheh, the ruler commissioned a legal work from him which he wrote in the local Pasai-Malay language. Al-Sinkili belonged to the contemporary climate of reorientation in Sufi thought, away from the influence of Ibn al-'Arabi toward the position advocated by Ahmad Sirhindi. Shi'ah scholars also found a scholarly refuge in the *Haramayn*. Muhammad Amin al-Astarabadi, the Akhbari scholar, wrote his most famous treatise in Mecca, where he died in 1036/1627. In another way the *Haramayn* was a microcosm of the *ummah*. Shi'ah scholars in Mecca on one occasion appealed to their colleagues in Isfahan to end the public cursing of the first three Caliphs since Sunnis were retaliating against them!

More intriguing for developments in the twelfth/eighteenth century is the presence in the *Haramayn* of two contemporaries who, if they did not know or meet each other, very likely studied under some of the same teachers. The one was the Indian Shah Wali Allah (1113–1176/ 1702–1762) of Delhi, the other Muhammad ibn 'Abd al-Wahhab (1114–1206/1703–1792), born in the Najd in Arabia.

Shah Wali Allah al-Dihlawi

Shah Wali Allah studied the Qur'an and Traditions under the guidance of his father, who also initiated him into the Naqshbandi brotherhood. From this upbringing, Wali Allah was imbued with the brotherhood's ethos of individual contemplation and social activism. He addressed himself to the problems raised by Sirhindi's approach to the mystical philosophy of Ibn al-'Arabi, and to the related question of the Muslims' waning political and spiritual strength, while confronting the contemporary climate of militant Hindu religious revival. Upon his return from Mecca and Medina, where he had intensively studied the Traditions of the Prophet, he was fully aware of the disunity of the Indian Muslim community: between Sunni and Shi'ah; between scholars of the law and Tradition; and between these scholars and the Sufis. It was these splits that he devoted his life to resolving and reconciling.[19]

His proposed compromise between the Sufi ideas of Ibn al-'Arabi and Sirhindi was that their views were essentially the same, being no more than the difference between two metaphors of the one experiential reality. While this may have opened the way in the end for the return of pantheistic ideas into the spiritual life, Shah Wali Allah's primary concern was to heal the festering wounds of his own community. On the level of customs, he objected to the Hindu prohibition of widows remarrying, a practice which had crept into the Muslim community. Other practices which he criticized were excessive amounts for a dowry in marriage contracts; extravagant expense on celebrations beyond the two fixed by the Prophet for marriage and birth of a child; and frequent ceremonies of mourning for the deceased.[20]

Shah Wali Allah accommodated the Sufi insistence on the inner reform of the individual. Nonetheless, a revitalized faith capable of meeting new problems in a new age was one based upon a process of reinterpretation in the light of reason to produce solutions suited to the requirements of a given community. The major instrument of this rejuvenation was a renewed emphasis on *ijtihad*. As we have seen, the Shi'ah Usulis advocated against their opponents, the Akhbaris, the crucial importance of this same tool applied to the teachings of the Imams. For Shah Wali Allah, of course, *ijtihad* applied to the teachings of the four Sunni schools of law, whose founders had become revered as the great pioneering *mujtahid*s of the early community. Wali Allah rejected strict adherence to any one school as though its founder were infallible and he denounced the current fanatic rivalry between the schools, each declaring the validity of its teachings alone. A Sunni follower of Malik, he argued, might equally defer to the authority of Abu Hanifah on certain points of the law. No jurist's judgment, in other words, could replace a careful reassessment of the only two infallible sources of religious law, the Qur'an and the prophetic Traditions. Direct reference to the sources and the elimination of all intermediate authority necessarily meant reinterpretation of those sources. Hence, blind imitation (*taqlid*) of a school, or of a single jurist, was vigorously denounced. This underlined the fundamental egalitarian notion in Sunni thought that the only acknowledged hierarchy in society was one based on piety and learning; any Muslim could, by arduous endeavor, learn the principles of the law and become a *mujtahid*.

Shah Wali Allah hoped that the new spirit of *ijtihad* would liberate Islamic religious thought from the narrow, bitter controversies of the present and recent past and restore Muslim solidarity and power in the sub-continent to its former glory. A further contribution to his mission of renewal was his translation of the Qur'an into Persian, while his sons translated it into Urdu. By bringing scripture directly within the reach of all literate Muslims, Wali Allah provided a means for them to bypass scholars whom he considered hide bound to their own schools. Finally, he founded a school where the study of the Qur'an and *hadith* was popularized so as to rekindle a desire in Muslims to examine the sources of the law afresh for themselves. Muslim power did not recover in India, although Wali Allah's influence upon later generations of Indian Muslim thinkers and his impact upon Sunni communities elsewhere were considerable.

In any event, despite Shah Wali Allah's best efforts, *'ulama'*-led attempts at renewal in the twelfth- /eighteenth-century contexts of Sunni India or the Ottoman Empire were less likely to lead to a "take-off" stage than a mullah-led revival in Shi'ah Iran. Sunni *mujtahid*s, as individual scholars of different schools, lacked the degree of cohesion of the Shi'ah *mujtahids*, who could act collectively as a counterweight to weak political government, which they regarded as essentially illegitimate. Sunni *'ulama'* tended to serve as mediators between the people and government, rather than as a countervailing force to the latter. The *'ulama'* of the imperial ruling establishments especially believed that however "un-Islamic" a government's general conduct of policy might be regarded, disowning its legitimacy invited the greater threat of internal discord and turmoil. The task of Sunni *'ulama'*, as spokesmen for the community, was to urge the restoration of good (i.e. Islamic) government. The task of the Shi'ah mullahs was to challenge alleged illegitimate rule and replace it with government led by themselves as representatives of the absent Imam.

There was another alternative. *'Ulama'* living in the peripheral regions of empire, removed from the immediate clutches of government, could raise the call for a renewal or restoration of Islamic society by organizing militant movements against the social and moral degradation they perceived around them. Some succeeded, for shorter or longer periods, to make an impact upon the local contemporary religious-political scene. One movement in particular gained widespread fame.

Muhammad Ibn 'Abd al-Wahhab

Circumstances in central Arabia differed from those of Wali Allah's India. Beyond the immediate environs of Mecca and Medina, Arabia was a provincial backwater of the Ottoman Empire. Unlike India, Islam in Arabia did not face a threat from a sophisticated religious culture like Hinduism. The challenge instead, as Ibn Abd al-Wahhab perceived it, came from a lapse into a state of near paganism. Veneration of trees and stone were purely pagan practices, worship and sacrifice at Sufi tombs a perversion of the belief in the oneness (*tawhid*) of the transcendent Allah. Arabia slumbered in the sinful ignorance of pre-Islamic times (*jahiliyyah*).

Ibn 'Abd al-Wahhab was tutored first by his father, a Hanbali judge and teacher in their home town. The young man proceeded to Mecca and Medina, where he studied under another scholar who likely introduced him to the works of Ibn Taymiyyah, the eighth-/ fourteenth-century Hanbali theologian and jurist. Ibn Taymiyyah's thought emphasized the individual and the community but laid greater stress on the social virtues of solidarity and justice than on individual virtues. He condemned Sufi deviations from the doctrines, rituals, and morals of the straight path; but he did not condemn Sufism absolutely. Indeed, he held that the law of the jurist, the rationality of the theologian, and the intuition of the mystic were parts of a harmonious whole which required integration, not emphasis upon one to the exclusion of the others. The pristine core of faith was the Qur'an and the Traditions. Hence in theory an informed, independent analysis (*ijtihad*) of the sources was essential. This allowed one to follow in the steps of the Prophet and his Companions, as it were, rather than stumble blindly along the path of the schools of law.

Ibn Taymiyyah's views, focusing upon the socio-moral reconstruction of Muslim society, informed much of the spirit of renewal in the twelfth/eighteenth century. This was the heart of Ibn 'Abd al-Wahhab's summons to Muslims. His affirmation of the oneness of Allah developed into a radical, uncompromising mission against the moral degradation of society brought about by the un-Islamic accretions and superstitions in the beliefs and practices of his day. However, unlike Ibn Taymiyyah and his own contemporary Shah Wali Allah, Ibn 'Abd al-Wahhab rejected Sufism out of hand. Ironically, in practice he turned the exercise of *ijtihad* into an almost literal imitation (*taqlid*) of the customs of the Prophet and his Companions as preserved in the scholarly legacy of the first two or three Islamic centuries. In a letter to a bedouin chief in Syria, he expressed this view on following the Traditions of the Prophet: "you have the books; consult them, and take nothing from what I say; but when you learn from your books what the Prophet said, follow it, even if most people go against it."[21]

Ibn 'Abd al-Wahhab's puritanical teachings landed him in trouble with opponents in his home town, which he was obliged to abandon. He denounced all who did not heed his message as unbelievers (*kuffar*), an attitude reminiscent of the Kharijite *jihad* movements of Islam's early days. A local chieftain, Muhammad ibn Sa'ud (d. /1765) of Dar'iyyah, responded to the preacher's call, and the two joined forces to found a militant Islamic polity which enjoyed rapid success in the Najd region of Arabia. Later Sa'udi-Wahabbi campaigns included the destruction of the Shi'ah shrine cities in southern Iraq and the capture of Mecca in 1803 CE. This latter success alarmed the Ottoman government, which despatched an army to crush the movement. The decisive defeat of their bedouin troops in 1818 brought to an end the first Sa'udi-Wahhabi venture, the forerunner of the twentieth-century successor state of Saudi Arabia.

Other attempts at renewal erupted in many parts of the Islamic world during the twelfth/eighteenth and through the thirteenth/nineteenth century. Only the main ones can be mentioned. One, influenced by Shah Wali Allah, was the *Mujahidin* movement of Ahmad Barelwi, a disciple of Wali Allah's son 'Abdul 'Aziz and of Shah Isma'il, a grandson of Wali Allah. Both Barelwi and Shah Isma'il died in their *jihad* against the Sikhs in northern India in 1831. The Fara'idi movement founded by Shari'at Allah (d. 1840) and continued by his son Wudud Miyan (d. 1860) arose among the peasantry of Bengal. In Sumatra between 1803 and 1837, a group of scholars formed a movement to reform local religious practices. Northern Nigeria was the setting of another movement led by 'Uthman Dan Fodio (d. 1817), who established the Caliphate of Sokoto, which survived until 1903. Dan Fodio's *jihad* movement acted as a stimulus for another in Guinea, Mali, and Senegal led by Hajji 'Umar Tal (d. 1865). A Sufi brotherhood, the Sanusiyyah, was founded by Muhammad b. 'Ali al-Sanusi (d. 1859) in the Cyrenaica district of the autonomous Ottoman province of Libya. In the Sudan, Muhammad Ahmad b. 'Abdallah (d. 1885) proclaimed himself the *Mahdi*, sent by Allah to restore justice on earth. Muhammad 'Abdallah Hasan (d. 1920), leader of the Salihiyyah brotherhood, conducted a campaign of renewal along the coastal areas of Somalia. Finally, even in distant China, Muslim movements in the provinces of Yunnan and Kansu broke into open rebellion between 1855 and 1873 against the waning power of the Chinese emperor; Muslims there were concerned with the heavy concessions made over the centuries to Chinese traditions which had diluted the distinctive nature of Muslim belief.

Movements spread over so long a period and occurring in such different socio-political circumstances and cultural locales could not be entirely identical in their doctrines and organization. They were a response, nevertheless, to the increasingly widespread experience among Muslims that their societies and shared Islamic values had been deeply infiltrated by un-Islamic norms. Implicit in these movements was, on the one hand, a critique of the interpretation of Islam by scholars of the religious establishments. On the other hand, the early success of Sufism in Africa and India owing to an openness to other cultures was now criticized for its superstitions and excesses in ritual. What most concerned the leaders of these movements was that current realities failed to match an idealized socio-political and spiritual model of the past. Modern commentators differ concerning whether they wanted literally to reestablish the Prophet's community or simply to apply the Qur'an and *sunnah* more strictly to contemporary conditions. All these efforts at renewal did, however, share a common characteristic: an emphasis upon the moral reconstruction of contemporary society based upon active, even militant, missions aimed at restoring a world infused with the spirit of the Qur'an and *sunnah* of the Prophet, for which purpose a reexamination of those sources by *ijtihad* was universally proposed.

The concepts of renewal (*tajdid*) and *ijtihad* were closely related, based upon a Tradition that Allah would send to his community at the turn of each century someone to restore or renew its religion. Individual scholars through the centuries had been identified as (or claimed for themselves the role of) renewers (s. *mujaddid*) of the faith; such claims were largely regional in character and often met with contemporary disagreement. Past renewers included al-Shafi'i for the second century, al-Ash'ari for the third, and al-Ghazali for the fifth. What is striking about the twelfth/eighteenth and thirteenth/nineteenth centuries is the almost universal awareness of the need for restoration of the *ummah* expressed by these numerous discrete renewal movements. The *ummah* had apparently reached a crisis of unprecedented scale. Nor was the turn of the century any more a point of disequilibrium. The crisis was as prolonged as it was widespread. A Tradition, reported in all the major collections, describes the best generation of Muslims as that of the Prophet, then the one following, and then the one after that, and so on. In another Tradition, the Prophet predicted that after the generations of his Companions and Successors, the community would be invaded by untruth. Corruption and decline had been foretold. It was time to renew the spirit of the best of all generations. But was it too late?

CHAPTER 8

Issues in contemporary Islam

A MOROCCAN IN PARIS

On Saturday, 17 January 1846, an official party of Moroccans stood solemnly on the Champs-de-Mars in Paris. They were reviewing a display of the French military forces put on by King Louis-Philippe to honor a special mission of the Moroccan ambassador. A member of the party was Muhammad al-Saffar. Born in Tetuan, he was educated there and in the highly respected university-mosque of Qarawiyin in Fez, where he acquired the traditional knowledge of a Muslim scholar. He returned to Tetuan to work as a notary in the law court and to teach Traditions and jurisprudence in the city's main mosque. Owing to his abilities and character, he was later appointed to the service of the governor of Tetuan. The sultan of Morocco chose this governor, 'Abd al-Qadir Ash'ath, as his ambassador extraordinary to France, and Muhammad al-Saffar joined his entourage as the one in charge of religious matters, conducting prayers and reading from the Qur'an. His self-appointed task was to write an account of their travels to France, which, including the sea voyage to and from Marseilles, lasted eighty-five days.[1]

The spectacle of the French cavalry, artillery, and infantry parading past in splendid order stunned the Moroccan visitors. Muhammad al-Saffar was moved to make this general observation on the event in his account:

In comparison with the weakness of Islam, the dissipation of its strength, and the disrupted condition of its people, how confident they are, how impressive their state of readiness, how competent they are in matters of state, how firm their laws, how capable in war and successful in vanquishing their enemies – not because of their courage, bravery, or religious zeal, but because of their marvellous organization, their uncanny mastery over affairs and their strict adherence to the law . . . If you could see their conduct and their laws [at work], you would be profoundly impressed with them, despite their infidelity (*kufruhum*) and the extinction of the light of religion from their hearts . . . May Allah return to Islam its strength and renew His support for [our] faith with the help of the Prophet.[2]

Above all, Muhammad al-Saffar was struck by the purposeful organization and prudent planning he witnessed everywhere in France, but especially in Paris. Organization was on a scale and of a style he had not previously experienced. It was new, modern and resulted, he observed, from an attitude of the French, who

are not content with knowing things by tradition, but study the roots of a matter [before] drawing conclusions. Only then do they decide whether to accept or reject it . . . If a craftsman does something [new], his prestige and reputation are increased. Then the state rewards him, praises him and makes much of him. In that way the desire for progress is cultivated among them . . . Whatever they hear, see, invent or learn from others they record in registers and keep forever.[3]

Among the innovations created by this progressive attitude, he was enchanted by the railway train, the newspaper, billboard advertisements, the theatre, book printing and lithographing, and the telegraph, a device which, he said, "completely staggers the senses." He describes it as "a force that carries news from one place to another in an instant with complete clarity and accuracy, even if the two places are far apart, because it is done with writing."[4]

As a scholar (*'alim*) himself, Muhammad al-Saffar reflected upon how even the traditional Christian approach to knowledge in Europe had been displaced by new attitudes to learning. "A learned man (*'alim*) there," he says,

is someone who is able to invent new and useful [ideas] and demonstrate their fine points by presenting sound proofs to those who doubt or oppose his findings. The name *'alim* for them is not limited to someone who has studied the sources of the religion of the Christians and its various branches – they are called priests – for knowing that is rather undistinguished [in their view] as compared with knowing the other logical and precise sciences.[5]

Despite his acknowledgment of the advantages of the new learning, the displacement for him also signaled a spiritual loss.

The goal of modern French education and planning was not lost upon the perceptive visitor: it was the scientific organization of production for the creation of wealth. He was bemused to learn that commerce was a science the French taught and even wrote books about! There was, he thought, a darker side to these activities. Commerce went beyond mere buying and selling, for they had something else called a "bank". Like most of their business dealings, this institution depended heavily upon "usury," lending money at a known rate of interest, a practice deemed sinful by Muslim scholars.

Notwithstanding his admiration for many aspects of French life, his understanding of their business practices led Muhammad al-Saffar to conclude in general terms that although they "know well what is apparent in the life of this world, [they] are completely ignorant about the hereafter."[6] France was a well-ordered, dynamic society, but it was driven by the demands of commerce rather than guided by the norms of religion. With considerable relief, Muhammad al-Saffar journeyed back to his own, familiar world, where the daily routine was measured by the ritual of prayer rather than by the ticking of a banker's clock. He spent the remainder of his days as a respected adviser and minister to the Moroccan sultans, but he left no further record of his thoughts on the profound and rapid changes the Muslim world was undergoing.

THE NEW EUROPE AND THE OLD WORLD

As we have seen in the previous chapter, widespread movements of renewal in the eighteenth century reflected Muslims' awareness of their weakening political structures and spiritual degeneration. Criticism of the deteriorating state of affairs gradually spread across the breadth of the community and continued, with undiminished momentum, throughout the nineteenth century. The impetus for renewal and reinterpretation by means of *ijtihad* was not at this time to find fresh solutions to contemporary circumstances. Rather it was to rediscover forgotten signposts from the past.

The nineteenth century, however, sharpened the crisis in a critical way. Conditions throughout the Muslim world were changing so rapidly that new answers were urgently required based both upon creative conservation of Muslim culture and adaptation to dramatic new realities. Gone was the old, confident perception of the "Islamic world" as a bulwark or vanguard against the "infidel world" which Ibn Battutah had experienced. What Muhammad al-Saffar witnessed, on the other hand, was the rise of a successful, secularizing world which was beginning its remorseless expansion against the shrinking frontiers of the *dar al-Islam*.

In a revealing aside to his description of the military parade, Muhammad al-Saffar was aware of the changing times. Ostensibly, the French king had staged the ceremony as a mark of his high esteem for the Moroccan visitors. The Moroccans themselves, however, sensed it to be "more a gesture of spiteful mockery."[7] Military and economic might were signs of the new France, born of the Revolution of 1798 and come of age in the Napoleonic era. Its competition with other European nations intensified, not in Europe alone, but also for influence abroad in Africa and Asia. France under Bonaparte had already exercised its military strength in a major campaign against a Muslim territory, although the invasion of Egypt and Palestine in 1798 was short-lived as British and Ottoman forces defeated the French in 1801. The campaign nonetheless exposed the extent of the decay and weakness of Muslim institutions. Al-Saffar could not have been unaware of the continuing French military threat, for in 1830, their forces invaded and occupied Morocco's neighbor, Algiers. By stages, the occupation was extended to the Algerian interior. Then, in 1844, the French government bombarded the Moroccan port of Tangiers, forcing the Moroccan sultan to withdraw his support from 'Abd al-Qadir, the leader of the Algerian resistance. The Moroccan visit to Paris had been planned to overcome this crisis diplomatically. The visitors, however, were left in no doubt as to the veiled political threat in the king's display of his nation's military machine. By the time of al-Saffar's death in 1881, French domination in North Africa had extended to Tunisia, and in 1912 Morocco also succumbed to the same fate.

Almost everywhere throughout the nineteenth century the Muslim world failed to check the inexorable expansion of European economic and military power, which brought in its wake the challenge of new relationships and ideas. In the military sphere, the European challenge also raised the specter of a modern Crusading era as Muslim lands were occupied once again by Christian armies. The crusading spirit was plain enough when the French transformed the Great Mosque in Algiers into a cathedral and the newly appointed archbishop pronounced the church's mission to convert the Arabs from their "barbaric faith." In India, a British official declared it part of the divine plan to spread the Christian faith in its purest apostolic form among the heathen. European missionaries who followed their nation's flag to distant lands were a mixed blessing in the Muslim world. They provided access to the new learning of Europe in their foreign language schools, yet at the same time attempted to win converts to Christianity. The "civilizing mission," as the French termed European overseas expansion, in which the churches played an active part, was experienced by many Muslims as a potential threat to their identity and faith. Less defensive *'ulama'* saw the missionaries' activities as a splendid example of zeal in the service of faith, an example they urged, from which Muslims themselves could learn.

In the economic sphere, a shift in relationships between Europe and the Muslim world was slower, more subtle, and apparently less threatening. In the long run, however, it was as important as military conquest and political domination. A good example is the ubiquitous custom of drinking coffee.[8] Coffee was first introduced into Europe from southern Arabia in the sixteenth century and for more than a hundred years remained an important export item; sugar, the standard accompaniment to coffee, was imported into Europe from Egypt and North Africa. By the end of the eighteenth century the pattern of trade was largely reversed: cheaper coffee was being exported to the Middle East from French and English colonial possessions in the West Indies and from Dutch plantations in Java; cheaper sugar, also from the West Indies, found its way into Middle Eastern markets at the same time. To complete the scene of change, waiters in the coffee shops of Cairo, Damascus, or Marrakesh now wore garments made from imported cloth manufactured in England from raw Middle Eastern cotton. Until then, the same garments would have been made from home-spun Egyptian or Syrian cloth. Muslim countries of the Middle East and south Asia were gradually being drawn more tightly into the economic orbit of an industrializing Europe searching for raw materials and new markets for its products.

Britain, France's chief European rival and the world's leading industrial power, was not idle in the race to extend its commercial and political influence abroad. By the end of the nineteenth century, British foreign policy led to direct intervention in and control of vast territories inhabited wholly or by significantly large populations of Muslims in West and East Africa, Egypt and the Sudan, Aden and the Trucial States of the Arab/Persian Gulf, India, and north Borneo and Malaya in southeast Asia. Anglo-French rivalry was extended in the immediate aftermath of the First World War to the two countries dividing the remnants of the now defunct Ottoman Empire between them. The League of Nations (forerunner of the United Nations), founded and dominated by the Western nations which had emerged victorious from the war against Germany and its Ottoman ally, granted France a mandate over Syria and Lebanon, while Palestine and Iraq were mandated to Britain.

Although Britain and France were the major beneficiaries of this global politico-economic carve-up, especially as it affected Muslim areas, other Europeans, for example the Dutch, Belgians, Germans, Italians, Spanish, and Portuguese were actively involved as well. By the beginning of the twentieth century, the only significant Muslim territories to have escaped direct European political domination were Turkey (the core of the old Ottoman Empire), Iran, Afghanistan, the Yemen, and the holy cities of Mecca and Medina in Arabia.

Could the Islamic world be revitalized by the principles of the *shari'ah* alone, or was it essential to borrow from the ideas and practices of a modern, secular Europe? Indeed, did the cultural norms of these two worlds fundamentally contradict each other? Or, were they in some way complementary? These were questions addressed by many Muslims in the nineteenth century who had begun to think in terms not simply of renewal, but rather of complete reform.

THE OPEN DOOR TO REFORM

Until the 1870s, Muslim views of the new Europe were on the whole positive. Since the mid eighteenth century Muslim observers of Europe had been concerned with European methods of government and with the art and science of war. Ottoman and Mughal mandarins, for example, urged the acquisition of the new military sciences and techniques in order to restore the power of their respective regimes. In the nineteenth century, Muslim curiosity about Europe broadened to include issues affecting the interests of social classes other than those of the rulers alone. Muslim travelers who left accounts of their experiences selected aspects of European culture not simply for their novelty. They tended to emphasize those aspects which contrasted most sharply with what they believed were the causes of weakness in their own societies.

One traveler who had preceded Muhammad al-Saffar to France was the Egyptian Rifa'ah al-Tahtawi (d. 1873).[9] He came from a family of religious scholars and was himself a graduate of the al-Azhar university-mosque in Cairo. At the time, the al-Azhar was the leading rival in the Sunni world to the teaching institutions in Mecca and Medina. Egypt's autocratic ruler, Muhammad 'Ali (d. 1849), had placed al-Tahtawi in charge of religious affairs for a students' mission to France. The students were to study language and a broad range of sciences. These skills would then be used to translate modern European works into Arabic and Turkish for the benefit of educating officers of Muhammad 'Ali's new army. Al-Tahtawi lived in Paris from 1826 to 1831. He learned French, read widely, and translated much of what he read for his own private or future official use. Once back in Egypt, he was made head of Muhammad 'Ali's School of Languages, and later he became director of its affiliated bureau of translation. His own translations included volumes on military science, history, and geography, while he supervised the translation of numerous more technical and non-technical texts. His total output also included several important original works, among them a travel account which first appeared in 1834 and was reprinted in 1848. It was widely read outside Egypt – Muhammad al-Saffar had relied upon al-Tahtawi at several points in his own narrative.

Although an admirer of Muhammad 'Ali's efforts to reform Egypt's economy, army, and government, al-Tahtawi was not uncritical of his and other contemporary Muslim regimes. The French political system which he frankly admired, based upon a constitution, the protection of individual freedoms, and the exercise of justice, contrasted so sharply with the current practice of his own government that criticism did not need to be made more explicit. Nevertheless, al-Tahtawi, like Muhammad al-Saffar, was deeply committed to the values of his own culture. He noted that the French statutes were not derived from divine books and therefore totally differed from the *shari'ah*. On the French Constitution, which he translated and annotated for a learned Arabic readership, he wrote that

> though most of what is in it is not to be found in the Book of God nor in the Tradition of the Prophet (Peace Be Unto Him) . . . you will understand how their *reason* led them to recognize that Justice and Equity are prerequisites for the welfare and well-being of states and peoples; and how the rulers and the ruled followed these laws, which permitted their countries to prosper, their knowledge to increase, their domains to expand and their hearts to be at rest.[10]

For the French, he commented, national welfare and human progress had taken the place of religion, and reason alone was their new deity.

It was evident to al-Tahtawi that there was an incompatibility, if not a total contradiction, between Muslim and French cultures. Moreover, he expressed his unease that unless a Muslim's faith were firm and steadfast, he could be seduced by the material advances Europe displayed. For al-Tahtawi, the greater purpose of Islamic society was to fulfill the will of Allah and thereby secure salvation in the hereafter *as well as* to achieve a state of well-being for all its citizens in this life. The *shari'ah*, therefore, could, and needed to be, reinterpreted to meet the demands of modern times. He encouraged Muslim jurists to employ more widely the accepted principle of *takhayyur*, that is, seeking solutions to specific questions outside the teachings of their own particular school of law. Thus, for example, a Hanafi might choose to comb through Maliki law for an interpretation of a case more in tune with his times.

Khayr al-Din (d. 1889), an Ottoman soldier, statesman, and traveler who in 1867 published a long account of his several journeys to Europe between 1850 and 1865, agreed with this and much else of what al-Tahtawi had written in the previous generation. However, he played down the gap between European and Muslim cultures. Muslims, he asserted, must not persist "in closing their eyes to what is praiseworthy and *in conformity with our own religious law* in the practice of adherents of other religions, simply because they have the idea engraved on their minds that all acts and institutions of those who are not Muslims should be avoided."[11] Christianity (in the sense of its revelation), he argued, was not the cause of Europe's present worldly progress. Therefore borrowing from Europe held no danger for the Muslim faithful. Indeed, borrowing European institutions like constitutionalism, justice, and sound government, for example, was simply adopting what Islamic society had itself once possessed in the past and had since lost. Borrowing would thus fulfill the original spirit and purpose of the *shari'ah*. Al-Tahtawi, Khayr al-Din, and other commentators on Europe of their day defended modern civilization, but in terms of traditional Islam. The adoption of beneficial aspects of European culture should only be accomplished within the framework of the *shari'ah*, which, for them, provided the basis of Islam's unquestioned religio-moral superiority over Europe.

One area of improvement in Muslim society which both al-Tahtawi and Khayr al-Din vigorously advocated was change in the training of the *'ulama'*. Traditionally, they had been advisers to government, and rulers should once again respect and honor them. At the same time, in order to reinterpret the law to meet the new age, the *'ulama'* had to understand what the modern world was about and how it worked. They should, therefore, also study the modern sciences. In addition, lay specialists in these fields, such as engineers and doctors, must have the same standing as the *'ulama'* in order that government may benefit also from their expertise. This was a significant departure from the traditional concept of knowledge and the *'ulama'*'s role, and it also accounted for the recent emergence of a small but growing cadre of lay specialists in Muslim society. No longer should the *'ulama'* be the sole guardians of a fixed tradition, mastering what was already known and transmitting this body of knowledge to their disciples. Knowledge was, on the contrary, cumulative, and the point of departure for the modern scholar (*'alim*) was in the way he could add to or modify current understanding on the basis of his own and others' investigations.

Finally, it was perceived that a just society was impossible without the active participation of a politically educated citizenry conscious of its freedoms and responsibilities. Muslim observers were impressed with the number and variety of voluntary and non-governmental organizations which contributed to the welfare of European society as a whole. These included hospitals and charities, and cultural associations such as museums and libraries; similar institutions in Muslim societies were in total disorder and decline. In other words, European society appeared to these observers as an organic unity in which government and the people mutually supported each other, another ingredient lacking in their own societies.

Muslims' views such as those sketched above and the contrast they depicted between Europe and their own contemporary societies were more widespread in the decades following the first publication of al-Tahtawi's popular travel account. By the 1870s, the appearance of the first newspapers, admittedly not the organs of mass circulation of a later period, assisted in disseminating more knowledge of Europe conveyed by writers acquainted with its literature and conversant with its ideas and progess. It remained true that at this point in the encounter, Muslims continued to view Europeans as Christian and that the profoundly secular nature of change in European societies was as yet not fully grasped or appreciated. Christians, it was held, had simply lost the fervor for their faith and were beguiled by the blandishments of material success.

For Muslims still committed to their faith and tradition, reform was a matter of urgency in all the spheres of daily life. The half-century from the 1880s to the 1930s marked the period of the most significant Muslim attempts at reform. During the same period, however, the dramatic transformation of much of the community under the forces of global European imperialism made the success of these efforts at reform (*islah*) highly problematic. Moreover, owing to the direct experience of European power and domination over much of the Islamic world, the once widespread, positive views of the West became mixed with expressions of criticism.

THE STRUGGLE FOR REFORM

Two events in distant, separate parts of the *ummah* will help illustrate the political background against which reformists developed their thought down to the turn of the present century. In 1882 the British occupied Egypt, which was nominally still a province of the Ottoman Empire but was under the autonomous khedival rule of a descendant of Muhammad 'Ali. British control effectively came to an end seventy years later, when the Egyptians achieved their independence in 1952. In India, the long-standing British presence represented by the powerful East India Company was converted into absolute political dominion of the sub-continent following the crushing of the Indian Mutiny against the British in 1857. Ninety years later, in 1947, two nations, India and Pakistan, emerged from this turbulent imperial heritage. The occupation of India and Egypt were not isolated events but part of the competitive process of European imperial expansion in general. In terms of British global design alone, Egypt and India were significantly linked to one another. Control of Egypt gave Britain command of the recently completed Suez Canal, which provided easy access from the Mediterranean Sea to the Red Sea and eastward to India, the "jewel in the crown" of British overseas possessions. Egypt and India were also important in this period for another reason. Together they produced two of the most outstanding figures of the modern Muslim reform movement. These were the Egyptian Muhammad 'Abduh (d. 1905) and the Indian Sayyid Ahmad Khan (d. 1898). Theirs were not the only voices of reform, but they were the most influential figures, in terms both of their disciples and of those who took their positions as a point of departure for different, more critical standpoints.

In the experience of al-Tahtawi and Muhammad al-Saffar, representative of many religious scholars of their generation, the modern idea of the "nation-state" was a foreign concept. Indeed, it was of European origin. Each man, naturally, had a strong sense of attachment to his family and to the town in which he was born. Both felt a loyalty to the rulers of their respective regimes, working as they did for the khedives of Egypt and the sultans of Morocco. Beyond this, however, their consciousness of belonging was to the universal community of Muslims, the *ummah*. This was the world through which Ibn Battutah had once journeyed with a sense of familiarity, acceptance, and belonging wherever he went, despite the differences in local cultures.

In the late nineteenth and early twentieth centuries, that feeling of universal fellowship still survived, but it was under serious threat. In the process of carving up the globe in their own interests, European imperialists were at the same time laying down the future boundaries of dozens of independent nation-states which, territorially, had never existed before. The experience of European control coupled with the struggle for independence resulted in the creation of Muslim nation-states which, in terms of providing a group identity, became an alternative to the universal *ummah*. As a focus of loyalty the *ummah* at times competed with and at other times complemented the idea of the nation-state. Some Muslims attempted to keep alive the idea of the universal *ummah* by supporting pan-Islamic political sentiment or the idea of an Ottoman Caliphate as the primary symbol of loyalty. These efforts were all short-lived and came to nothing. For others, who opted for a primary loyalty to the nation-state, there remained the question whether the state apparatus would be fashioned after Islamic or Western secular norms. Some Muslims painted their nationalist banners with religious symbols and slogans in the struggle for independence from European rule. Still others adopted the European model of secularism and called for religion to be relegated to the individual's conscience, without importance to the public life of the nation. The best example of this latter course was the republic of Turkey, whose founder and first president, the charismatic Kemal Ataturk, abolished the Caliphate in 1924, replaced the *shari'ah* in its entirety with European laws, proscribed the Sufi brotherhoods, and closed down religious schools.

In the radically new climate of change, Muslim reformers, while aware of and sympathetic to developments in parts of the *ummah* other than their own, responded in the first instance to the realities confronting their own immediate communities. It is for this reason, too, that reformers everywhere, while acknowledging that their societies required both material and moral rejuvenation, expressed a primary concern for social and political rather than purely spiritual matters.

Sir Sayyid Ahmad Khan

Sayyid Ahmad Khan began his working life as a magistrate in the employ of the powerful British East India Company in Delhi, where he was born in 1817. He had already published several short pieces on religious matters when the Hindu-Muslim Mutiny of 1857 erupted. Since the British held the Muslims chiefly responsible for the uprising, Ahmad Khan devoted himself to achieving mutual reconciliation with India's masters, whom he had, in any case, long admired. He founded for this purpose a quarterly journal, *On the Loyal Muhammadans of India*, published in Urdu and English. This was forced to close for want of funds after only three issues.[12] His activities continued to be mainly literary and educational. In 1869–1870 he journeyed to England and France and subsequently wrote a travelogue of his impressions. He adopted a Victorian style of living, a move he urged upon the Muslim readers of another Urdu journal he founded and to which he contributed significantly. At Aligarh (in the former United Provinces of India) he established a school which later (1878) became the Muhammadan Anglo-Oriental College, consciously modeled on Cambridge University in England. Many of the staff were British and from other European nations, some students were Hindu, and the language of instruction was English, except in the subject of religion. Raised to university status in 1920, it produced many of the Muslims educated in modern learning up to the partition of India and the creation of Pakistan in 1947. Sayyid Ahmad Khan also found time to set up a society for the translation of European works on physical sciences into Urdu, while his own major publications included a partial commentary on the Bible, a collection of essays on the life of the Prophet, and a commentary on the Qur'an. In 1888 his life's work was rewarded with a knighthood from the British government.

Sayyid Ahmad Khan was the most radical Muslim reformer of his generation, whether in India or abroad. Circumstances required radical action. Muslims had lost their dominant position in India and were thoroughly demoralized. Moreover, they faced a British imperial administration which tended to favor the Hindu majority. And worse, Muslims had no effective religious leadership to help them adjust to and cope with the demands of modernity and the West. Sayyid Ahmad Khan, with the assistance of a few like-minded colleagues, attempted to fill the void.

His work in the field of education was the practical side of a long and distinguished career. It also reflected both the difficulties and dangers inherent in the reform process which other reformers would also experience. Aligarh's students, for example, were trained in the British curriculum of the liberal arts and sciences mainly for service in the Anglo-Indian government. Their compulsory religious education, however, was conducted in the traditional manner owing in part to the '*ulama*''s stiff resistance to the founder's own religious ideas. As a result, graduates emerged who had been exposed to two quite unrelated and unintegrated educational traditions. The superficially westernized products of this institution led critics to label them as "Western-struck" (*gharb zadah*). One commentator has observed that as for Sayyid Ahmad Khan's dream "to refertilize Islamic thought and create a new science of theology vibrant with a new and potential Islamic message, Aligarh was doomed to failure from the very start."[13] Aligarh did, however, contribute to the creation of a young leadership which stood for the political separatism of Muslims in India and which was opposed to the increasingly assertive, Hindu-dominated, Indian National Congress founded in 1885.

Sayyid Ahmad Khan's intellectual labors may in any case be examined independently of the success or otherwise of the Aligarh experiment. His "new science of theology" drew inspiration from the work of Shah Wali Allah but was cast in a more rationalist mold. His thought was more radical even than that of the early Mu'tazilites from whom he also derived support. In a lecture on Islam, he asserted the need for "a modern theology [*'ilm al-kalam*] by which we either render futile the tenets of the modern sciences or [show them to be] doubtful, or bring them into harmony with the doctrines of Islam."[14] He argued that the disaffection with religion caused by its competition with the methods and discoveries of science was not a fault inherent in the religion, but a result of the errors of interpretation and understanding with which '*ulama*' had encrusted it over the centuries. Employing his own methods of Qur'anic exegesis, Sayyid Ahmad Khan claimed that he would demonstrate the truth of Islam by the single criterion of whether it was "in correspondence with the natural disposition of man, or with nature. If yes, then . . . such correspondence is a clear sign that this religion has been sent by that person which has created man."[15]

His argument postulated that the universe and the laws of nature by which it is governed were created. Their creator was Allah. Allah also created laws of revelation, his commands and prohibitions, as a necessary guide for the societies in which mankind must live. These laws were intuited by certain gifted individuals who, from time to time, have appeared in history as prophets. Muhammad was one such prophet. The laws contained in the Qur'an for the benefit of human society corresponded to the divinely ordained laws of nature for the governance of the universe. Through a prophet's natural, yet highly developed instinct, the principles of divine law are intuited and revealed to mankind, just as the laws of nature are uncovered through the rational process of scientific investigation. Hence, there is no contradiction between the word of Allah and his work: revelation and the laws of nature are identical, and Islam is entirely compatible with modern scientific thought.

One corollary of this argument was that miracles mentioned in the Qur'an had to be interpreted metaphorically. As the laws of nature are immutable, they cannot be interrupted or reversed, so the supernatural was excluded from consideration. He did not, however, deny the miraculous nature of Muhammad's prophetic role which, he insisted, was in harmony with reason. One miracle, attributed to the Prophet in the *hadith*, was his night journey to Jerusalem from Mecca and his ascension to heaven and into the divine presence; this tradition Sayyid Ahmad Khan reinterpreted as neither a physical nor a spiritual experience, but simply a dream. His approach to the entire corpus of prophetic Tradition, including the works of the great collectors al-Bukhari and Muslim, was undertaken in an equally rational spirit. With some exceptions, he regarded this second source of the law as containing material contrary to reason and the Prophet's dignity. Traditions, he argued, had been manufactured by Muslims of the early centuries from a variety of motives, pious and political. These should be rejected. The few genuine examples which were in line with Qur'anic injunctions must, of course, be preserved.

The Indian reformer's ideas provoked deep resentment among the more conservative *'ulama'* of his community. They rejected his assault upon the Traditions and his rationalization of the Qur'an. Both of these seemed seriously to limit the scope and application of the *shari'ah*, since in Sayyid Ahmad Khan's view, society's moral and legal code must be based on natural law. He had been influenced by the writings of the Scottish political economist Adam Smith. Employing Smith's law of supply and demand, he argued that as the traditional disciplines of *hadith* and jurisprudence (*fiqh*) had lost their validity, they were bound to be replaced by science and modern education. Certainly, too, his suspicion of pan-Islamic sentiment and his continued loyalty to the British presence in India at a time when Hindus were beginning to press for independence would have further helped undermine his authority. There is no doubt, however, that he established the agenda for the reform of Islamic thought and set its course into uncharted waters. His rational exegesis of scripture and his critical questioning of the authenticity of the Traditions were conducted in a liberal spirit of *ijtihad* which he insisted every Muslim was entitled to exercise, since it was not the prerogative of the *'ulama'* only. His goal was to remain true to the immutable principles of Islamic teachings as embodied in the Qur'an and which were in harmony with reason, while recognizing that the norms and practices governing society inevitably change from one period to another. The Aligarh movement which Sayyid Ahmad Khan initiated could not be ignored either by contemporaries or successors, whether among modernist supporters or conservative opponents. However, with its limited organizational base and its highly speculative theology, the Aligarh movement necessarily only touched the interests of the upper- and upper- middle-class urban Muslim. The religious concerns of the vast majority of the community remained in the care of the traditional religious leadership.

Muhammad 'Abduh

Muhammad 'Abduh's life and thought[16] ran a different course from that of his older, aristocratic contemporary, Sayyid Ahmad Khan. Born in a village in the Egyptian delta, 'Abduh received his early instruction in a mosque in Tanta and then completed his education at the al-Azhar mosque-university in Cairo between the years 1869 and 1877. He taught first at the al-Azhar and then in a newly established college for the training of judges and teachers in government schools.

During his al-Azhar student days he came into contact with the nomadic, firebrand teacher and orator Jamal al-Din al-Afghani (d. 1897).[17] Al-Afghani preached a theme common to all the reformers, that Muslims could restore the vitality of their societies by reclaiming from the West the rational sciences, including philosophy, which the West had largely borrowed from Muslim culture while it still encouraged a spirit of inquiry. Therefore, in learning science and technology afresh from the West, Muslims would be recovering their own past achievements and fulfilling the injunctions of the Qur'an to explore all manner of knowledge within Allah's creation. Like al-Tahtawi before him, he urged that Muslims seek good fortune in two worlds, the here-and-now and the hereafter. And he used the Qur'anic verse *Allah changes not what is in a people until they change what is in themselves* (13:11) almost as the motto of the reform movement. At the same time, he was an active campaigner against European imperialism and stressed the need for Muslims to assert their identity and solidarity. For this reason, he charged Sayyid Ahmad Khan with betrayal and selling out to the British, who were, he said, delighted with his doctrines "as a means to their goal of obliterating the Islamic religion in the Indian territory."[18]

Al-Afghani's influence and the political crisis in Egypt during the early 1880s caused 'Abduh to side with opposition groups against the autocracy of the ruling khedive and his British and French supporters. When Britain occupied Egypt in 1882, 'Abduh was arrested, imprisoned, and finally exiled. He spent time in Paris with al-Afghani publishing a reformist journal, then in Beirut teaching, and he was finally allowed to return to Egypt in 1888. By now he had accepted the political and military realities of the British occupation. Until his death in 1905, he held several important positions including that of chief *mufti* of Egypt, which involved him directly in reforms of the law, the courts, and the al-Azhar.

In his writings and official capacity, 'Abduh addressed the problems of the inner decay of his society and the need for reform. Like Sayyid Ahmad Khan, he thought in terms of a "national" community of Muslims, with the difference that in India, Muslims were a potentially threatened minority, whereas in Egypt they were not. They each confronted essentially the same question: Was it possible to live in the modern world and remain a Muslim? In some ways their answers were similar too. Islam for both was the religion of reason and of human nature. In the acquisition of religious knowledge, 'Abduh urged "a return to its first sources, and to weigh them in the scales of human reason ... and to prove that, seen in this light, religion must be counted a friend of science."[19]

On the other hand, Muhammad ʿAbduh, owing to his background, education, and the particular circumstances of Egypt itself, was perhaps more sensitive than Sayyid Ahmad Khan to the practical problems and dangers involved in creating a dualist society, that is, one based partly on values derived from revelation and partly on reason and the spirit of mundane utility. The danger was especially evident in the fields of the law and education. Under British rule, India and Egypt experienced the importation of many aspects of English criminal and civil law which left only the area of the *shariʿah* dealing with family law (marriage, divorce, inheritance) relatively untouched. This point will be dealt with in more detail below.

In education, the private initiative of the Aligarh experiment in India had demonstrated the weaknesses of producing graduates who fully belonged neither to the indigenous nor to the foreign ruling culture. Egypt faced the problem in a somewhat different way. A dual education system had already been partially created during the rule of Muhammad ʿAli, who needed trained personnel for his new bureaucracy and army. Under British rule, the first Consul-General was the autocratic Lord Cromer, who believed that Islam was the antithesis of reason and therefore utterly incapable of reform. During his long rule (1883–1907) the Egyptian government gave scant support to the development of a reformed, modern, state primary or secondary education. By 1902, fewer than a hundred students a year graduated from the three state schools.[20] Moreover, only the well-off could afford to pay the tuition fee demanded; poor families continued to send their children to Qurʾanic schools which, for the brightest, opened the way to a traditional higher education in the al-Azhar. Cromer himself actively discouraged the establishment of a modern university because, from his previous experience in India, he believed it only manufactured malcontents and agitators for the nationalist cause.

In his professional roles, ʿAbduh was caught between the counter-progressive educational policies of the colonial authorities and the stubborn resistance of the *ʿulamaʾ* to changes which he himself proposed to the running of the al-Azhar. He had wanted not only to introduce modern learning into its traditional curriculum but also to revive certain Islamic classics, including works by rationalist Muʿtazilite theologians, which had long been ignored for their supposed heretical teachings. His hope of training a new cadre of *ʿulamaʾ* to guard and interpret a reformed faith ended in frustration and disappointment.

In disgust at the *'ulama'*'s delaying tactics, 'Abduh supported the idea of a modern institution of higher education, which was at last realized by the founding of Cairo University in 1914, seven years after Cromer's replacement as Consul-General. 'Abduh's purpose remained constant. He sought to bridge the gap within his society between the old and the new, yet to link such change to the principles of the faith. As a reformer, however, he confronted obstacles to his efforts erected by both colonial officialdom and the religious establishment.

'Abduh and the Salafiyyah

'Abduh's call for a return to the sources was the hallmark of all reformist thought, although he was more cautious in his approach than Sayyid Ahmad Khan. The sources referred to were three: the Qur'an, the *sunnah* of the Prophet, and the flexible but vague notion of the "pious forefathers" (*al-salaf al-salih*). This last concept gave to the reform movement inspired by 'Abduh and his disciples the name of the Salafiyyah, whose influence was acknowledged by other reformers such as 'Abd al-Hamid Ibn Badis (d. 1940) in colonial French Algeria and the Muhammadiyyah movement (and later the Masjumi party) in Dutch-dominated Indonesia.

One of 'Abduh's most important works was the small volume entitled *The Theology of Unity*.[21] In the prologue, he set out his overall theme that

Muslims are of one mind in the conviction that there are many things in religion which can only be believed by the way of reason, such as the knowledge of [Allah's] existence, of His power to send messengers, of His knowledge of the content of their inspiration, of His will to give them particular messages, and, with these, many consequent points relating to the comprehension and evidence of prophetic mission. So Muslims are of one mind that *though there may be in religion that which transcends the understanding, there is nothing which reason finds impossible.*[22]

The prophetic-revelatory event, as outlined in the first chapter above, was viewed by 'Abduh as susceptible to rational demonstration and was not merely the consequence of acceptance by "blind faith." Of the Qur'an he asked rhetorically, "Is not the appearance of such a book, from the lips of an illiterate man [the Prophet], the greatest miracle and clearest evidence that it is not of human origin?"[23] Scripture and prophecy mutually confirmed one another.

Concerning the discipline of Qur'anic exegesis, reformists like

'Abduh held that although there were certain scriptural verses whose mystery could not be penetrated (such as the true nature of the divine attributes and the afterlife), it was possible to read and meditate upon the contents of the Qur'an with the same clarity as the very first generations of Muslims. The modern reader could thus derive the same essential moral and inspirational content from the Book as the first Muslims had done, before theological and legal rivalries injected the poison of factionalism into the community.

For 'Abduh, as with other reformers including Sayid Ahmad Khan, the *sunnah* was regarded as an explanatory instrument making scripture explicit. This seems to have meant for 'Abduh that he did not accept the *sunnah* as the second source of the law (*fiqh*) as a whole, but simply for the dogmas of faith and of the forms of worship;[24] he regarded only a small portion of the *hadith* as authentic, although he conceded that many of the later fabrications might nevertheless have genuinely captured the spirit of the Prophet. In other words, the Qur'an and the authentic *sunnah* laid down specific rules about worship (*'ibadat*) and covered other important matters of dogma such as belief in the previous prophets sent by Allah and the afterlife. With regard to social relations (*mu'amalat*), however, only general principles were dealt with in these sources, leaving the way open to the individual to apply human judgment (*ijtihad*) as the circumstances of society changed. Owing to their limited acceptance of the *sunnah*, the Salafiyyah argued that Islam could be reduced to the Qur'an. At the same time, however, they insisted on the social, political and ethical, that is, the broad cultural dimensions of Islam for which the entire *sunnah* and the example of the "pious forefathers" provided valuable, if not strictly canonical, guidance. Reformers consciously sought to avoid the danger of appearing to reduce Islam solely to a set of rituals and a few metaphysical beliefs.

The two sources, the Qur'an and the *sunnah*, were linked to a third. The "pious forefathers" were those Muslims of the early community who in some cases may have known the Prophet, or else some of his Companions or even their Successors and their Successors after them. The concept was elastic. Some reformers intended by the term *al-salaf al-salih* the first three generations of Muslims; for others, it covered the period down to the middle of the third/ninth century. It meant to convey, however, those who had lived by and had faithfully transmitted the spiritual inheritance of the Prophet. More important in 'Abduh's thought is his certainty as to the grave effects upon the community when the influence of their guidance and piety had vanished. At that point, he wrote,

there supervened the various successive insurrections aimed at the civil power, in which it was the obscurantists who got the upper hand, destroying the remaining traces of the rational temper which had its source in the Islamic faith . . . As a consequence a complete intellectual confusion beset the Muslims under their ignorant rulers. Ideas which had not found any place in science [religious knowledge] found sponsors who asserted things Islam had never before tolerated. Fostered by the general educational poverty, they gained ground, aided too by *the remoteness of men from the pristine sources of the faith* . . . There can be no doubt that the consequences befalling the masses in their beliefs and principles, from this prolonged disaster with its widespread confusion, were grievous and heavy.[25]

A combination of obscurantists, ignorant rulers, and remoteness from the "pious forefathers" had, in 'Abduh's view, brought about the current lamentable state of affairs with which the reformers had to contend. Other figures, too, were held in high esteem by reformers, although they did not belong to the generations of the "pious forefathers." Scholars like al-Ghazali (d. 505/1111) and Ibn Taymiyyah (d. 728/1328) were regarded as independent-minded and free of the narrow obscurantism which characterized much of the religious scholarship of their own days.

Salafiyyah reformers summoned Muslims to walk the pathways of the modern world while following in the simple and true footsteps of their virtuous predecessors. The moral renewal which their program entailed was, on the one hand, a fight against servile adherence (*taqlid*), in particular to the authority of the four schools of law. This, according to 'Abduh, was to emulate faithfully the Prophet, who, in his preaching, "took up the cudgels against the slaves of habit and the traditionalists, calling on them to liberate themselves from their bondage and throw off the chains withholding them from action and hope."[26] On the other hand, the reformers sought to rescue their societies from a numbing sense of alienation from the modern world and to instill in the individual a commitment to the authentic moral and cultural tradition of the community mirrored by and preserved in the example of its early generations.

The modern world for these reformers implicitly meant their own community's particular experience of the multiple impact, political, economic, intellectual, and moral, of imperialism. Whatever benefits foreign rulers bequeathed to their dominions (and in Egypt, for example, these were chiefly financial reform and improvement of the economy), their control was absolute, even despotic. This failed to solve the fundamental problem of an absence of a moral relationship between the rulers and the ruled. Imperialism, good or bad, was always a relationship between power and powerlessness; when the power was foreign in every possible manner, the sense of impotence among the ruled was the more degrading. Muslims who visited the capitals of Europe during the height of the imperialist era were struck by the double standards observed by these centers of modern civilization: liberty and freedom enjoyed by citizens of the colonial powers at home and abroad, and the negation of these same principles for the peoples they ruled.

For all that, reformers had gone as far as they could in confronting both the colonial challenge and the problems of rejuvenating their own societies. The reactions to the reformers' programs among their own disciples and other groups of the *'ulama'* were predictably varied. The Syrian-born Rashid Rida became a close associate of 'Abduh's, and together they published the journal *al-Manar*, the major vehicle of their reformist ideas which Rida continued until his death in 1935. In India, the philosopher-poet Muhammad Iqbal (d. 1938) carried on the reform tradition of Sayyid Ahmad Khan. In particular, he shared his predecessor's anxiety over the problem of a genuine and lasting Muslim–Hindu harmony, and finally concluded that Muslim identity could only be preserved within a separate region or state.

Other writers adopted a purely apologetic stance, the ground having been prepared for them unwittingly by arguments of the reform leaders, Muhammad 'Abduh and Sayyid Ahmad Khan. For the apologist, Islam was declared to be in complete conformity with modern civilization. Islam simply became dissolved in modern thought. This was a reversal of 'Abduh's assertion that true civilization was in conformity with Islam. However, both Muslim reformers and apologists employed certain traditional concepts of Islamic thought identifying them with dominant ideas of modern Europe: for example, *shura*, the practice of consultation between the ruler and his advisers, became parliamentary democracy; *ijma'*, the consensus among legal scholars, became public opinion; and *bay'ah*, the act of allegiance paid to a new Caliph by society's leading notables, became synonymous with the right of universal suffrage, and so on.

At the other end of the spectrum, certain writers unequivocally established a total separation between the norms of religion and those governing society. An occasional voice was heard, too, insisting upon the moral as well as the material superiority of Europe over contemporary Islamic culture. It was a hint as to how far thought, albeit a minority view, had moved in the few decades since the European travels of al-Tahtawi and Muhammad al-Saffar.

For many conservative *'ulama'*, however, the reformers indulged in blatant innovation (*bid'ah*) and were bent upon causing anarchy in the community by making too many concessions to modern Western thought and institutions. Their reaction was based upon a proud desire to protect a rich tradition, more than a thousand years old, which they regarded as divine and complete. The depth of suspicion and misunderstanding between the conservatives and their reformer adversaries was profound. Reformers, in their search for freedom from a slavish imitation (*taqlid*) of a corrupted past, accused their opponents of being out of touch with the modern world. The conservative *'ulama'* responded defensively and viewed *taqlid* as a religious obligation in defence of a divine and immutable tradition.

The issues which reform thinkers raised concerning the challenge of modern conditions to religious thought made them vulnerable to the charge that their exercise of *ijtihad* was tantamount to irresponsible, libertine free-thinking, the effect of which was to banish the will of Allah from virtually every aspect of daily life except ritual. In their approach, reformers assumed a much sharper distinction between the *shari'ah* and *fiqh* than had the classical jurists. That is to say, the classical jurists had understood the *shari'ah* as Allah's unchanging will, comprehensive and embracing the whole sweep of the law. *Fiqh* for them was the understanding of the rules by which the law was derived from the sacred sources, the Qur'an and the *sunnah* of the Prophet, and included in particular the details of its application. The body of law (*fiqh*) thus derived by scholars of the great classical schools was also regarded as sacrosanct. Reformers, however, saw the *shari'ah* as embracing only the categorical injuctions of the Qur'an and the much smaller but authentic body of *sunnah*, both of course being eternally valid, while *fiqh* was the human understanding of the sacred sources in time and place, which was therefore legitimately subject to change.

The gulf between the views of conservative and reformer was always going to be difficult to bridge. The conservative would not concede that the law could be shaped by society; rather, the law was a blueprint to which society must conform. 'Abduh had acknowledged that future generations would seek to reinterpret the law (*fiqh*) by the exercise of *ijtihad* in the light of ever-changing circumstances in society. He also recognized, as al-Tahtawi had before him, that the notion of a learned person (*'alim*) must be extended to include more than one trained only in the traditional religious sciences. Modern knowledge, beyond the competence of most *'ulama'*, was essential to meet the needs of modern times. This raised a second point of friction with the conservatives who held that the *'ulama'* alone possessed the expertise required to exercise *ijtihad*.

REFORMERS AND THE IMPERIALIST LEGACY

In the period leading to the achievement of independence from European imperial rule, which was completed by the beginning of the 1960s, secularist Muslims were often guilty of an uncritical admiration of the West. Conservatives for their part tended on the whole to dismiss the West as irrelevant to the needs and aims of Muslim society.

Reformers, on the other hand, had tried to find a thread of continuity between the Islamic past and the modern present. The weakness of their movement lay chiefly in its intellectual character. It remained without adequate institutional support to foster and develop reforms and to train personnel for future leadership roles in society. In this respect, secularists had won the day. In no instance did a nation of Muslims, newly independent from European rule, produce a religiously oriented group or party to form the government. This may be explained in part by the unresolved divisions between the conservative and reform tendencies which prevented any united Islamic front from developing. It proved no easier to build firm alliances between *Islamic* and secularist nationalist groups. The norm was for the governments of independent Muslim nations to be drawn from the secularist elite which had, as in Egypt, come to prominence during the era of European rule, largely encouraged by imperialist policies. In this manner, European governments were able to maintain their important political and hence commercial links with former dominions. The exceptions were countries which had not experienced direct European domination and opted for quite different directions. The republic of Turkey, for example, followed the secularist path, while the kingdom of Saudi Arabia remained firmly within its Wahhabi tradition. Reformers were nevertheless successful in raising Muslim consciousness to the need for social-welfare strategies and modern education systems based upon Islamic social and moral values.

Elsewhere, the withdrawal of Europe from colonial rule was accompanied by or resulted in tragic conflict. A few examples will illustrate this point. Algeria was one of the latest countries to achieve its independence, in 1962. This brought to an end 132 years of French control and colonization, but only after a bloody eight year liberation struggle to break French resistance and repression. Algeria's economy had been totally absorbed into that of mainland France and its Arab culture largely destroyed by the French. Recovery from this enforced assimilation meant that the search for a new, modern identity had to recommence. That search continues to this day amid increasing economic and social turmoil and confrontation between radical Islamic groups and the Algerian government.

The unity of the British raj in the Indian sub-continent dissolved in 1947, when the rival nations of Pakistan and India were founded. Millions died and were displaced in the widespread communal violence. A massive, panic-riven exchange of populations took place, as Muslim and Hindu alike sought safe haven among a majority of their own kind. Many Muslims, conservative and reform, had rejected moves toward the creation of a separate Muslim state, advocated by the Muslim League (founded in 1906) from 1940 onward. Abu al-Kalam Azad (d. 1958) had come into contact with Salafiyyah reform ideas while traveling and studying in Arab lands. This influence led him to denounce a separatist nationalism based on Islam. Indeed, he claimed to have found a precedent in the Prophet's career for his cooperation with the Indian National Congress and for a program of integrated Hindu–Muslim nationalism. The community established by the Prophet in Medina from 622 until his death a decade later had contained both Muslim and non-Muslim. Moreover, argued Azad, the essential faith of all religions is the same, whereas each religious community is guided by a divine law particular to itself. Conservative Muslims, including the leading teachers of the Deoband Theological Seminary and other *'ulama'*, supported Azad's move toward a pluralist religious coexistence in India. The majority of Muslims, however, rejected the political direction of his thought and opted for separation, following the lead of the Muslim League inspired in part by the reformist thought of Sayyid Ahmad Khan but also by his more activist disciple Muhammad Iqbal. Iqbal had become convinced that Muslims could not secure adequate guarantees of protection for their community within a larger Indian nation, and in 1930 he addressed the Muslim League proposing the creation of a separate state. Supporters of the idea were primarily concerned with protecting the Muslim minority in India rather than in working out how an independent *Muslim* state should be defined politically. The irony of the situation was that the leader of the Muslim League and first president of Pakistan was a Western-trained lawyer, Muhammad 'Ali Jinnah (d. 1948), from the minority Indian Shi'ah community. The critics' fear was that the new state of Pakistan would be completely secular rather than religious in orientation. In the years following Pakistan's independence, the quest for an identity to match its *raison d'être* has not yet ended.

Finally, the withdrawal of Britain and France from their respective mandates in Palestine and Lebanon resulted in the immediate eruption of violence in the former and partially contributed to future violence in the latter. With its acquisition of the mandate over Palestine (1922), the British government had committed itself to a policy of colonization by a *third* party. Zionist leaders of the Jewish nationalist movement had sought and won British support for their plan to establish a Jewish National Home in Palestine. Palestinian leaders understood British policy to mean the gradual transformation of their land into a Jewish state. This would be accomplished through controlled, but theoretically unlimited, Jewish immigration and acquisition of land for Jewish settlement. Democratic institutions would not be contemplated for Palestinians until Jews constituted a majority of the population. In 1922 this meant that the 90 percent Muslim and Christian Palestinian majority (the remaining 10 percent of the Palestinian community was Jewish) would become a future minority under alien Jewish state institutions. Palestinians were never consulted on the conception or formulation of the policy. Nor were they ever provided a legal channel by which to challenge or block the details of its implementation. Violence was the inevitable outcome. A prolonged uprising between 1936 and 1939 was brutally crushed by British force and Palestinians were left with neither the leadership nor the means to carry on the struggle. The rapidly swollen Jewish community, on the other hand, maintained the advantages of British protection while developing its own military capacity with which to face future events. In 1947, an American led campaign succeeded in securing the United Nations' agreement upon the partition of Palestine into Jewish and Palestinian states. The Jewish leadership declared the establishment of the state of Israel (1948) in its portion of Palestine. During the ensuing war it acquired a considerable area in the Palestinian portion as well. In the process, Palestinians were driven from their villages and towns into neighboring countries to make way for further Jewish settlement. The Palestine refugee problem was thereby created, and despite the recent peace accords between the Palestine Liberation Organization and Israel, this major political problem still awaits a final solution.

One consequence of the 1948 war was the sudden influx into Lebanon of many thousands of Palestinian refugees, which overnight swelled the population of the tiny country by 10 percent. Lebanon had officially become independent two years previously. By the terms of the National Pact (1943), negotiated between the French and Lebanon's political leadership, parliament would be composed of members representing the various confessional communities, Christian and Muslim, according to the size of each determined by a census undertaken by the French in 1932. The census was later widely suspected of exaggerating the size of France's allies among the Christian community. The proportion of parliamentary membership was fixed at six Christians to five Muslims; the head of state would always be a Maronite Christian, the Prime Minister, a Sunni Muslim and the speaker of the parliament, a Shi'ah Muslim. The Pact did not take into account future demographic changes in the population. Nor could it foresee the impact of the 1948 war in Palestine. The wave of Palestinian refugees was generously accepted by Lebanon on humanitarian grounds, but a swift political solution to their presence was problematic. In the first place, the Palestinians themselves sought a return to their homes after the end to hostilities, a prospect consistently denied them by successive Israeli governments. From the Lebanese viewpoint, the Palestinians could not be absorbed as citizens (as they were overwhelmingly Muslim) without upsetting the delicate political balance between the confessional communities. The Palestinian presence, however, was a ticking timebomb waiting to explode so long as an overall solution to the Palestinian–Israeli problem was not found. The timebomb did explode in 1975, with the beginning of a prolonged Lebanese civil war which lasted for sixteen years. Israel contributed to the conflict by its support of the Christian Maronite community and then by its invasions of Lebanon in 1978 and the even more devastating rampage in 1982.

Of the political crises just mentioned, the Palestinian problem resonated in a particular way for Muslims of all persuasions far beyond the sanctuaries of Jerusalem, a city deemed holy by all three of the monotheistic faiths. According to tradition, Jerusalem was the Prophet's destination in his night journey from Mecca accompanied by the angel Gabriel, and from where he had ascended into heaven and the presence of Allah. The more politically committed Muslim, however, saw the creation of the state of Israel as an enduring reminder of the injustices of the imperialist era, and a symbol, too, of the continuing weakness of contemporary Muslim societies.

REFORMERS AND FAMILY LAW

Reformist ideas on changes affecting the religious law helped create a climate of opinion in which governments could deal with the specific fields of marriage, divorce, and inheritance. As we have seen in the chapter on the *shari'ah*, these subjects reflected Muslims' central concern with the family, the bedrock of society.[27] This was the one area of the *shari'ah* which had been least affected by the widespread adoption of European civil and criminal codes of law during the latter half of the nineteenth century.

Egypt and India again led the way in the 1920s and 1930s, and the influence of family-law reforms there spread to other Muslim countries. 'Abduh had argued that the Qur'an permitted polygyny only as a means of providing legal protection for widows and orphans in the prevailing conditions of the Prophet's day. Combining a reading of two separate verses, he stressed that the true intent of scripture was in fact monogamy, since in practice it would prove impossible to fulfill the necessary condition (4:129) of polygyny, namely the equal and impartial treatment of each wife (4:3). Abduh's disciple, Qasim Amin, went further. He attacked the practices of arranged marriages and the husband's unlimited right of divorce as later social customs which had become embedded in religion. They must therefore change in accordance with changing times. He applied to the Qur'an and *hadith* the principle that in the absence of a clear text on these matters, or with a text susceptible to alternative meanings, consideration of a woman's welfare should be paramount.

Reforms of the *shari'ah* courts in Egypt had begun in 1897. By 1920 child marriages had become greatly restricted while women were permitted more clearly defined grounds for divorce than they had previously enjoyed. These included maltreatment, desertion and the husband's failure to provide maintenance. Following the legal principle of selection (*takhayyur*), the measures were introduced from the more liberal Maliki school of law to replace the stricter provisions of the dominant Hanafi school in Egypt. In these reforms, apart from the principle of selection, a legal device known as "patching up" (*talfiq*) was also employed. This was a combination of the views or particular elements from the views of different schools or of individual jurists, which could include borrowing from Shi'ah legal practice.

In addition, the husband's almost unlimited right to initiate a divorce was restricted. This meant, in particular, an effective end to the use of the irrevocable triple divorce formula (*talaq al-bid'ah*) which jurists had traditionally regarded as an innovation but nevertheless supported as valid. Unsuccessful, however, was the attempt to borrow a practice recognized in the Hanbali school. This would have provided that a woman could stipulate in her marriage contract that her husband was prohibited from taking a second wife. The move caused great controversy and was dropped, although it found its way later, in the 1950s, into family law reforms passed by governments in recently independent Syria and Jordan. The most radical move against polygyny in the new secularizing states was the outright abolition of the practice in 1957 by Tunisia, which based its law, too, on 'Abduh's reasoning. Although a significant start had been made in Egypt, further major reforms had to await the period following its own independence after 1952.

In India, a scholar of the conservative Deoband Theological Seminary, Mumtaz 'Ali, had come under the influence of Sayyid Ahmad Khan and henceforth became a champion of women's education and rights. He refuted the traditional arguments upholding man's superiority over woman, stating they were based upon patriarchal custom and a willful misreading of scripture. Women's evident difference from men implied neither biological nor mental inferiority. In terms similar to those of 'Abduh and Amin, 'Ali denounced polygyny, arranged and child marriages, and purdah, a woman's seclusion in the home. The British presence in India had led to interference in Indian legal affairs as early as 1772, but it was not until 1862 that Islamic law and legal practice were substantially modified by English codes and procedures, resulting in what became known as Anglo-Muhammadan law. Then much later, in 1929 and 1939, reforms in the areas of marriage and divorce were tackled, limiting child unions and granting women rights of divorce similar to, but possibly less far-reaching than, those passed earlier in Egypt. As in Egypt, however, Muslims in India were able to push ahead with further reforms only in the post-independence period.

The reforms in family law during the 1920s and 1930s were executed by regimes seeking to govern ostensibly by Western programs and methods. They were influenced by the ideas of the Salafiyyah reformers but they acted also in the context of continued European presence and political control. In the 1930s and more especially in the 1940s and 1950s, another trend of religious thought emerged opposed to much of what the reformers stood for as well as the model of Western civilization which challenged Islam on its own soil. In the following section, this trend will be examined in the development of the two movements which proposed a radical reponse to the crisis of Islam and modernity. These are the Muslim Brothers (*al-Ikhwan al-Muslimun*), which originated in Egypt, and the Islamic Association (*Jama'at-i Islami*), which was founded in pre-partition India but continued its activities on the Pakistani political scene.

THE RADICAL REJOINDER

Each of these movements has now survived more than half a century. For periods of short or long duration, governments which have found their challenge intolerable have proscribed their public activities. Nevertheless, each claims support in many countries. These movements and their more recent extremist offshoots have been labeled "fundamentalist" by journalists and academics alike. The term only became popular, however, after the Iranian revolution of 1979. Thereafter, Muslim groups expressing views judged to be anti-Western or anti-modern were lumped together as "fundamentalist." The label is borrowed from the twentieth-century American Protestants who emphasize, among other matters, that a literal reading of the Bible is fundamental to Christian teaching. The almost indiscriminate application of the term to movements in the Islamic world, usually in a derogatory sense implying a fanatic dedicated to political violence, has left it debased and with little meaning.[28] Too often, from a secular, liberal perspective, "fundamentalist" is simply a code word to distinguish "us" (the good guys) from "them" (the bad guys). It is, therefore, preferable to place these movements within the tradition of renewal and reform which has already been examined above. Features common to this tradition are a call for a return to the principles embedded in the Qur'an and the prophetic *sunnah*, an insistence on the independent interpretation of these sources, and the claim that they offer the only authentic expression of the Islamic experience.[29] These movements may be called radical in the sense that they oppose both the political passivity of the conservative *'ulama'* and their collaboration with established secularizing governments, as well as the excessive concessions they believe modernist reformers have made to Western thought and practice. On the other hand, it should be noted that despite their common characteristics there are significant differences between the Muslim Brothers and the Islamic Association, and indeed between them and other so-called "fundamentalist," or better, radical groups such as those operating in Algeria and in Israeli-occupied Gaza. The following discussion will focus on their views of the Islamic state, which is a central concern to them all.

The society of Muslim Brothers was founded by Hasan al-Banna in 1928, when he was just twenty-two years of age. His education consisted of an early mosque education, influenced by his father – a teacher and author of religious works – coupled with a long and close association with Sufism. He completed his studies at a college of higher modern learning in Cairo. His first post as a teacher of Arabic was in the Suez Canal town of Isma'iliyyah, where the Muslim Brothers were first organized. He remained in teaching for another twenty years, but his chief thought and energies were devoted to the society he founded. His life was cut short violently, probably by a government agent, in 1949.[30]

The movement matured in the years between the two World Wars during a period of prolonged internal political and economic turmoil and of external threat in the form of the conflict between Palestinians and Zionists, who pressed ahead with their goal of establishing a Jewish state sponsored and supported by British mandate policy. Al-Banna's analysis of Egypt's current problems touched upon three areas. First, he charged the *'ulama'* of al-Azhar, as leading spokesmen of Sunni Islam, with failure to provide genuine spiritual guidance for Muslims and with neglect in resisting the penetration of foreign values, factors which had contributed to the moral decay and increasing fragmentation of Egyptian society. Second, the Egyptian political scene was riven by factions each pursuing its own narrow self-interest, which further exacerbated national disunity and perpetuated social injustice and the oppression and exploitation of the masses. Worse, the whole political establishment was corrupt. Political leaders were only nominally Muslim, and in reality they served the interests of the foreign, imperial power. Britain had retained effective control of the country even after granting Egypt qualified "independence" in 1923. The importation of Western models of government, laws, and education which were alien to Islamic norms had created a growing gulf between the values of the ruling class and those of the Egyptian people. Finally, on the subject of the West, which included both the capitalist and communist worlds, al-Banna's attitude was mixed as he saw positive and negative elements in each. The common denominator of the two systems, however, was a degenerating materialism. Imperialism of whatever color (British, French, American, or Russian) was viewed as a direct crusading threat of Western civilization against Muslim civilization. The threat was not merely physical but spiritual too. As al-Banna was fond of saying, "Eject imperialism from your souls, and it will leave your lands."[31]

The Islamic Association was founded in Lahore in 1941, during the last years of British rule in India. Its founder, Abu A'la Mawdudi (d. 1979), would have shared his Egyptian contemporary's disgust with imperialism. But Mawdudi's overriding concern was the continued, secure existence of the Muslim community in the sub-continent, with its overwhelming Hindu population. Mawdudi came from a deeply religious background which, like al-Banna's, included close contact with Sufism as his father was descended from the line of "friends of Allah" (*awliya'*) of the Chishtiyyah brotherhood. Unlike al-Banna, however, he received little formal education of a modern kind but was, like the Egyptian, gifted with an inquiring, independent mind. He spent the first years of his professional life as a newspaper journalist and editor, which disciplined him as a writer and gave him an outlet to express his views on a vast range of subjects of concern to Muslims. He later assumed responsibility for the journal *Tarjuman al-Qur'an*. This became the main vehicle in his campaign to persuade the Indian Muslim leadership to rescue their community from the danger implicit in the program of the Hindu-dominated Indian National Congress. This stressed the unity of India as a nation and the necessity for a future independent government to be democratic and secular. Mawdudi, however, insisted that Islam was the antithesis of nationalism and that Muslims were bound together solely by their commitment to the will of Allah rather than by any other bond of association like language or race. Freedom from foreign rule was desirable, but for Muslims that would only result in exchanging one master, the British, for another, the Hindu. Mawdudi argued further that a secular state was equally a danger to Muslims since Islam in its very essence meant a religious-based polity. The separation of religion from politics, characteristic of the Western secular state, was inconceivable in Islam. Mawdudi originally opposed the idea of Pakistan as a homeland for Muslims, advocated by the Muslim League under Muhammad 'Ali Jinnah. He correctly assessed the proposition as simply a secularist Muslim version of nationalism which held the same dangers for the spiritual welfare of the community as did any other nationalist ideology.

Mawdudi's understanding of the Western nation-state coincided with al-Banna's, and they shared a vision of the remedy, namely an Islamic state. Since their movements immediately confronted different problems, in practice they were distinct. Mawdudi's Islamic Association was elitist, its purpose being to train a cadre of leaders, a righteous party, as he called it, capable of rebuilding Muslim society in India from the top down. When in 1947 the partition of India was a *fait accompli*, Mawdudi was forced to move to Pakistan. There he resumed his campaign in the political arena to have the constitution of the fledgling state based solidly upon Islamic principles. In Egypt at about the same time, al-Banna had also proposed a theoretical blueprint for the new Islamic order, but had initiated in addition a program of reform and action which was far more populist than Mawdudi's. Until it was dissolved in 1954, al-Banna's society engaged in a number of commercial and small industrial enterprises which helped establish its reputation as "the spokesman for the needs and expectations of the vast and inarticulate body of Egyptian labour."[32] The society's broad social-welfare program included the provision of alternative institutions to those of the government in the fields of education, public health, and social services, all of which reached both rural and urban populations. Apart from meeting people's needs neglected through the Egyptian government's incompetence or indifference, the society's aim was to set an example to others of true Islamic morality.

The solution proposed by both al-Banna and Mawdudi to correct Muslims' debilitated condition was the creation of an Islamic order or state. The intent was not to retreat to the society of seventh-century Arabia but rather to return to pure Islamic principles as they saw them. They argued that in the Prophet's time and immediately after there had existed a social order in conformity with the will and command of Allah. That model should once again be the inspiration for a Muslim renaissance in the twentieth century. The model, moreover, was explicitly not that of post-Enlightenment Western civilization. Al-Banna had on one occasion candidly stated that in the teachings of Islam, there is no "rendering to Caesar that which is Caesar's and to God that which is God's. Rather . . . Caesar and what belongs to Caesar is for God Almighty alone."[33]

THE ISLAMIC STATE

The general theory of an Islamic state begins with a consideration of the *shari'ah* and its validity for modern times.[34] The creator laid down laws governing the natural universe. He also prescribed a law for human conduct in the *shari'ah*. Unlike the natural order, which cannot but follow its predetermined laws, mankind has the freedom to rebel and follow its own "man-made" laws. This is, however, a form of unbelief (*shirk*). Non-submission to the will of Allah is not only an act of ingratitude (*kufr*) for divine mercies, but also a choice for evil and misery in this world and punishment in the next. The centrality of the *shari'ah* for radical thinkers is the hallmark of an authentic Islamic system and the feature distinguishing the uniqueness of that system over against any other civilized order. In Mawdudi's words, "The Shari'ah is a complete scheme of life and an all-embracing social order where nothing is superfluous and nothing lacking."[35] The umbrella-like nature of the law covered every aspect of human existence. It did not deal only with the believer's relationship to Allah, but with the proper relationship among believers as well as between the Muslim community and others. Specifically, it implied the opposite to the secular notion of a division between religion and the state. Secularism, in the Muslim view, destroys the transcendence of all moral values. Even one of Mawdudi's most vigorous critics, Fazlur Rahman, described Muslim scripture as an expression of "deep God consciousness [that] is creatively and organically related to the founding of an ethical sociopolitical order in the world, since, in the view of the Qur'an, those who forget God eventually forget themselves (59:19) and their individual and corporate personalities disintegrate."[36]

From the basic principle of Allah's sovereignty over all, the problem then arose. What role does the *sunnah* play in determining the content of the divine will? Both Mawdudi and theorists among the Muslim Brothers appear to have adopted the position of the modern reformers, that is, that blind acceptance of the *hadith* corpus and slavish imitation of the tradition of the jurists would not meet the needs of Muslims. In other words, *ijtihad* was stressed over *taqlid*, and so the *shari'ah* was both adaptable and relevant to modern times.[37]

The state over which Allah was sovereign was not, however, a theocracy, in the Christian understanding of term. On the basis of the Qur'anic principle (24:55) that Allah appointed humankind as his vicegerents to rule on earth, the human governor was himself answerable to Allah on the one hand and to his entire community on the other. The governor who must act according to the dictates of the *shari'ah* can only rule with the consent of the community. He may be removed from office for failing to sustain confidence in his rule. This introduced the other major principle of the Islamic state, that of consultation (*shura*, 42:38), which guaranteed human control of community affairs, but within the bounds of the *shari'ah*. Consultation applies to the choice of the head of state as well as to all the decisions executed by the state. The precise network of consultation is, of course, not spelled out in the *shari'ah*, the appropriate institutions being dependent upon conditions at the time and place they are required. The consultative body is envisaged as acting as the people's representative. Al-Banna called the relationship between the ruler and the ruled a "social contract," and Mawdudi described the Islamic polity as a "theo-democracy." What is clear is that neither envisaged the consultative body to lie exclusively in the hands of the traditional *'ulama'*. The Islamic state, therefore, rested upon Allah's sovereignty and the governorship by man. Although human legislation is not excluded, the religious law simply guides it along the right path. Governorship by man was meant literally. The ruler of an Islamic state must be male, Muslim, knowledgeable in the law and, more importantly, possess the qualities of justice, virtue, and piety. He need not, as in the classical formulation, be a member of the Prophet's tribe of Quraysh.

These ideas of the Islamic state were advanced by radicals in the 1930s and 1940s as the global cure to Muslim problems in the modern world. The Muslim Brothers in this period claimed not to be just another factional party on the Egyptian political scene but a movement addressing all Egyptians (if not immediately all Muslims). Mawdudi's Islamic Association only entered the political arena in the upheaval of post-partition India and the creation of Pakistan. The leaders of the secularizing regimes of independent Pakistan (after 1947) and Egypt (after 1952) viewed the radicals as a direct threat to their own nationalist programs for development and modernization. The Muslim Brothers were banned in 1954 and driven underground during the long presidency of Gamal Abd al-Nasser (d. 1970). One of their leading intellectuals, Sayyid Qutb, was executed in 1966. They enjoyed a public revival under Abd al-Nasser's successor Anwar Sadat (d. 1981). His successor, President Mubarak, banned them once again but allowed their restricted political participation within the activities of other legal opposition parties. Mawdudi's Association over the years has faced less official harassment than the Muslim Brothers, but Mawdudi did experience brief spells in prison and faced the death sentence at one point, a decision which was later commuted.

A third radical organization may be mentioned here. The Islamic Liberation Party differed from the Islamic Association and the Muslim Brothers in the sense that, from its inception in Jerusalem in 1952, it openly declared itself a political party. It resembled them, on the other hand, through its party ideology of Islam and its declared goal of the establishment of an Islamic state. But it also went much further by calling for the restoration of the Caliphate as an institution unifying the whole Islamic world. The founder was Taqi al-Din al-Nabahani (d. 1977), a Palestinian intellectual and graduate of the al-Azhar in Cairo, who began his professional life as a school-teacher and judge in northern Palestine prior to the creation of the state of Israel. The overall model for the party's activities is drawn from al-Nabahani's understanding of the stages of the Prophet's life in Mecca and Medina; the details of its organization, however, are drawn from the modern experience of communist or other revolutionary parties in Europe. Al-Nabahani's denunciation of all residual forms of Western imperialism, economic, political, and cultural, as a plot to penetrate and destabilize the Islamic world and his condemnation of the Western materialist spirit are echoed in the writings of other groups as well. A distinctive feature of his own thought is the attention he has given to a detailed exposition of the nature of the Islamic state, its institutions and constitution, matters which other groups have always preferred to describe in vague and general terms. The Party claims representation throughout the Arab world as well as Turkey, Pakistan, Malaysia, and Indonesia, and even parts of Europe. It cannot operate freely and legally in many places owing to its open opposition to all presently established regimes in the Muslim world. As with other radical groups a significant proportion of the Party's membership seems to be drawn from high-school and university students and graduates in many of the modern professions such as medicine and engineering. One weakness of the Party's organization is its intellectualist stance and its non-involvement in social, medical, and educational projects. Hence, although its founder was himself Palestinian, the Party has not had the same success among Palestinians that the Muslim Brothers have had during the years of the *intifadah* in the Israeli-occupied areas of Gaza and the West Bank.[38]

The claim of the radical groups to possess the solution to Muslims' contemporary problems has been dismissed by secular critics as hopelessly utopian. Hamid Enayat put it this way. "The hope, or conviction, that rulers can be kept out of mischief by adhering to a certain set of doctrines, or leading an ascetic way of life, is as old as the notion of Utopia in human history. It is a noble idea, but one which has so far rarely worked in practice."[39] The judgment is valid if the radical blueprint of the Islamic state is assumed to be thoroughly utopian in nature. On the other hand, if the radical groups' proposals envisage adequate institutional checks on the power and behavior of the ruler by means of a consultative body responsible to the community, there is a possibility that a "theo-democracy" could function in practice. The radicals' ideology appears attractive because it addresses people's real or perceived sense of deprivation and/or humiliation. A theme which runs through all the radicals' programs is the demand for social and economic justice in their societies as a corollary to freedom from political oppression. Nonetheless, it is also possible that once in power radicals would prove as incapable of achieving these goals as the existing secular leaders have been to the present. Radicals insist that they seek both an authentic Muslim identity and modernization, rather than simply the latter for its own sake in the manner of the secularists. Their critics retort that the radicals are concerned with the question of identity at the expense of modernization.

By the 1970s, the assumption by Western social scientists that secularization was a universal and irreversible process was being exposed as a profound misconception. According to the argument, as an essential feature of modern society, secularism necessarily meant that religion would no longer play an important part in the political and cultural life of a society. The proposition, which may still be valid for Western Christian societies, is clearly of less relevance to peoples experiencing the forces of rapid modernization but adhering to a different religious tradition. This, of course, was more or less what radical Muslim groups had been arguing for some time, albeit from a very different intellectual perspective.

The radical Muslim diagnosis of the ills of their own societies has been aided by the fact that social theories of development and the actual performance of modernization experiments based on Western models have been tried in their own societies and found wanting; democratic liberalism of the late imperialist period gave way in the 1960s to doctrines of socialism which, by the end of the 1970s, had failed as dismally as their predecessors. The point was reached when the political capital of the secular, modernizing Muslim leaders began to run out and some started to play "the Islamic card." Some leaders, more or less cynically, introduced bits and pieces of the *shari'ah* as a public gesture of "Islamization" of their regimes. This often went along with attempts to transform their public image into that of devout, practicing Muslims. For Ja'far al-Numayri, Anwar Sadat, and Zia al-Haqq, former presidents respectively of the Sudan, Egypt, and Pakistan, such attempts were of no avail. The first was overthrown, the second was assassinated, and the third died mysteriously in an aeroplane crash. By the late 1980s and early 1990s, the Muslim perception, radical and conservative, of "the failure of the West"[40] in its broadest geographical sense was underlined by the collapse of communism in Eastern Europe and by economic stagnation, rising unemployment figures, and drug-related crime and violence in the cities of Euro-American societies.

Nonetheless, more than any other recent event in the Islamic world, that which captured world attention was the descent of an elderly, bearded, black-robed and turbaned religious figure from an aeroplane in Tehran airport in February 1979.

The case of Iran

The fall of the late Shah Muhammad Reza's Pahlavi dynasty in 1979 and the creation of the Islamic republic of Iran run by religious dignitaries caught most observers totally off-guard. The first reaction was that the West had lost a friend in the Shah, who, for years, had successfully projected himself as the architect of his country's modernization and as the leader of a stable, oil-rich state. The second tremor to run through the corridors of power and the editorial offices of the Western press was that a leading Shi'ah religious figure, possessing an inexplicable charismatic attraction and mass following, was now head of the Iranian state. It must be added that most secular-minded Muslim politicians and journalists shared the view of their Western counterparts that the political stage was not the legitimate place for religious leaders like Ayatullah Khumayni and company to act out their fantastic and narrow visions of a new social order.

In the discussion of the Shi'ah in Chapter 6, we learned that one of the community's central beliefs was that the twelfth and last of the line of Imams was in protective concealment and would return at the end of time as a prelude to the last judgment. Meanwhile, a practical question was raised. In the absence of the Imam, who could fulfill his functions and guide the community until his return? Under the rule of the Safavid Shahs who transformed Iran into a Shi'ah polity, the issue was left unsettled. For most of the time the Shah and the *'ulama'* served each other's interests. The *'ulama'* did, however, debate the idea that the leading religious scholar among their ranks could be acknowledged as the Imam's representative on earth. If pursued to its logical conclusion, this notion would imply a challenge to the legitimacy of any secular power which claimed the right to govern Iran. Although the issue was not pursued during the Qajar period (1794–1925), the Shahs of this dynasty could not claim legitimacy, as the Safavids had done, on the basis of their descent from the Imams. Consequently, the *'ulama'* began successfully to assert a greater role in society, gradually appropriating some of the Imam's prerogatives without, of course, claiming his essential quality of infallibility. They retained in any case the exclusive authority for the supervision and application of the law. Ordinary Shi'ah faithful were bound to follow the guidance of the jurists who lived among them and could answer their needs. The *'ulama'*'s social position in the community was strengthened by their control over financial resources drawn from religious endowments, special taxes, and donations from the faithful. In the latter half of the nineteenth century, during the long reign of the Qajar Shah, Nasir al-Din (1848–1896), the spiritual and material bases of the *'ulama'*'s authority were fused by the creation of the position of supreme head of the *mujtahids* called the "Source of Imitation" (Arabic: *marja' al-taqlid*). He was regarded as the highest living religious authority, whose decisions were deemed worthy of acceptance by all Shiʻah. It was in this period as well that relations between the *ʻulama'* and the ruling dynasty deteriorated.

Qajar authority, never as dominant as that of the Safavids, was in full decline when, in 1890, the country erupted in political crisis. The last years of Nasir al-Din's rule were marked by corruption and financial chaos on the one hand and, on the other, the increasing pressure from Iran's northern neighbor, Russia, and from the growing influence of the world's major imperial sea power, Britain. The Shah's granting of a monopoly concession over the production, sale, and export of tobacco to a British businessman in March 1890 sparked the first mass movement of protest in Iran's history led by the *marjaʻ al-taqlid* and the *ʻulama'* against internal corruption and what was seen as a threat to Islam from outside forces. The concession was canceled in 1892. Another more important and widespread movement of discontent broke out in 1905–1906, involving both liberal nationalist and religious opposition elements to the Shah's government. The Shah finally capitulated to their demands and issued an imperial decree to establish a National Consultative Assembly which would draw up a Constitution. Both measures were intended to reform the state and limit the despotic powers of the monarch. The influence of the *ʻulama'* on the Constitution is evident in its appendix. They underlined their sole claim to represent the Hidden Imam by the device of a committee of five *mujtahid*s who would oversee all parliamentary decisions and laws to ensure that they were compatible with the *shariʻah*. The experiment in Constitutional monarchy ended in 1911, and with the growing influence of Russia and Britain, Qajar control of the country disintegrated completely. Following a coup backed by the Cossack Brigades under one Colonel Reza Khan in 1921, the parliament in Tehran declared an end to the Qajar dynasty and replaced it with Reza Khan as Shah in 1925.

Throughout his reign Reza Shah (1925–1941), following the example set by Kemal Ataturk in Turkey, set about reforming Iran on the European model. The Shah, however, ignored its democratic principles and ruled in the absolute manner of the Shahs of the past. He also systematically undermined the *ʻulama'* influence by replacing their jurisdiction of the law and control over education with secular European-style institutions. Resistance from the *ʻulama'* was sporadic, disunited, and ineffectual. The best-known religious figures of the period adopted a traditional attitude, abstained from politics, and dismissed all secular affairs as the work of the devil. The Shah's reign was brought to an end by the wartime policies of Britain and Russia. Their military occupation of Iran forced the Shah's abdication in favor of his young son, Muhammad Reza.

Over the next decade the *'ulama'* were able to regain some of their lost privileges from the inexperienced and weak Shah. On the other hand, they abstained from meddling in politics, even during the heady days of 1951, when the popular Prime Minister, Muhammad Musaddiq, removed the Iranian oil industry from foreign ownership by nationalization. Musaddiq's removal by a CIA-backed coup in 1953 was not unwelcome news to the *'ulama'*, who found his modernization policy unpalatable. A turning point in relations between the court and the *'ulama'* came in 1960, when the highly respected *marja' al-taqlid*, Ayatullah Husayn b. 'Ali al-Tabataba'i, publicly opposed the Shah's land-reform proposals among other measures, including his support for Israel, who were training his feared internal security service, SAVAK. The move was unusual, for the Ayatullah had previously abstained from political involvement and had urged the other *'ulama'* to do likewise. Al-Tabataba'i died the following year, leaving the *'ulama'* without an acknowledged leader at a time when the Shah resorted to ever more severe methods of suppressing all opposition to his authority. Intense discussion began among the *'ulama'* as to the future shape of their organization. An important concern was reform in the sources of the *'ulama'*'s income in order to make them independent of both the state and the voluntary donations of the faithful. The Shah rejected all proposals which would make the *'ulama'* independent of state control. From then on, a group of radical *mujtahids* began to organize opposition to the regime.

Their leader was the relatively unknown figure Ayatullah Ruhallah Khumayni. Now in his late fifties, Khumayni had been associated first with the circle of Ayatullah 'Abd al-Karim Yazdi Ha'iri (d. 1937), the *marja' al-taqlid* who, in the 1920s, reestablished the city of Qumm as the foremost place of learning for the Shi'ah and then as an assistant to his successor, the above-mentioned Tabataba'i. In these early years Khumayni was already a bitter critic of the monarchy, although he followed Tabataba'i in the 1950s by withdrawing from direct participation in the political arena.

At the beginning of 1963 tension heightened. The Shah launched a continuation of his reform program which became known as the White Revolution. Khumayni and his followers staged massive demonstrations against the new measures which were again brutally dealt with by the Shah's forces; Khumayni himself was arrested and then deported in 1964. He spent the next fifteen years in exile in Iraq, conducting his campaign against the Shah's autocratic rule, his ties with the United States, and his disregard of Islamic morals, which, he stated repeatedly, encouraged the spread of imperialist culture and polluted the youth of the entire country. Khumayni's ideas at this time reflected the thought world of radical thinkers elsewhere like Mawdudi and the chief theoretician of the Muslim Brothers, Sayyid Qutb.[41] Although the *'ulama'* had direct access to his works in Arabic, they were translated into Persian and thereby reached a much wider audience. A major appeal of these Sunni writings was the dark contrast painted between the Islamic and the secular state, or between the rule of Allah and the rule of idolators.

Following Khumayni's removal from Iran, the Shah conducted a fierce attack over the next decade against religious institutions and attempted to destroy or replace Islamic symbols with fictitious ones from the pre-Islamic imperial Persian past. Khumayni and his supporters within the country countered by delving into the rich store of Shi'ah symbolism of struggle, sacrifice, and martyrdom in the face of tyranny. The Shah was cast as the evil Yazid, slayer of Imam Husayn, and in the popular imagination, Khumayni became the awaited last Imam. The contest was not, however, confined solely to religious symbols. In 1972, the government inexplicably decided to replace the production of traditional fresh-baked bread with the tasteless machine-made American-style loaf. Resistance from bakers and consumers alike was fierce, but thousands of bakers nevertheless lost their jobs. Proposals like this made it easier for opposition circles to ridicule every move of so-called reform and modernization as a threat to authentic Iranian culture.

During his exile, Khumayni turned his mind seriously to the exposition of an Islamic government to stand as an alternative to the Shah's. In 1970 he published his innovative theory of the *wilayat al-faqih*, the mandate of the jurisconsult.[42] In this he expanded upon eighteenth-century Shi'ah arguments concerning the religious authority of the *mujtahids*. He established a case for qualified *'ulama'*, as the authoritative interpreters of the sacred law in the absence of the Hidden Imam, to assume the right to rule. The theory was in place: only the opportunity to put it into practice was required. The moment was, indeed, fast approaching, for the end of the 1970s marked the beginning of the fifteenth Islamic century, the moment in traditional Islamic thought for the appearance of a great figure of renewal (*mujaddid*). Against the background of growing popular fury toward the Shah's regime, religious symbols were a potent means of mass mobilization. In December 1978, the commemoration of the martyrdom of Imam Husayn was the occasion for massive public demonstrations against the Shah, who finally departed Iran, a sick and broken man, four weeks later.

Amidst the very complex factors at work in bringing Khumayni and the *'ulama'* to power in Iran, two images stand out. One is of Khumayni himself, whose person attracted and momentarily united opposition groups of very different colors and interests. The configuration of this persona, one observer has written, "stresses stoicism and determination in a tragic world where injustice and corruption all too often prevail. It is a continuation of the emotional configuration of the Karbala story, which forms the central symbolic core of popular religion in Iran."[43] The other image is that of the Iranian state, once thought to be possibly the most powerful in the Middle East. Of its paralysis and collapse, another observer has said, "The mammoth edifice of the state became hollow as a result of the complete withdrawal of moral commitment to its preservation."[44] The same author concludes that the radicals' revolutionary ideology was a powerful response to the search for authenticity. "Rather than creating a new substitute for religion, as did the Communists and the Nazis, the Islamic militants have fortified an already vigorous religion with the ideological armour necessary for battle in the arena of mass politics. In doing so they have made their distinct contribution to world history."[45]

This is not the place to speculate on whether the Iranian revolution will endure in the long run. Shortly after Khumayni was installed, Iran faced a prolonged and damaging war with Iraq. The war helped to rally Iranian national sentiment behind the new regime against internal opposition which was outmanoeuvred and finally ruthlessly eliminated as well as against the Iraqi aggressor, Saddam Husayn. The conflict left Khumayni's successors and the country to cope with mounting economic problems which will not be solved in the near future. Nor is this the place to speculate on whether the Iranian experiment can be replicated in other non-Shi'ah environments of the Islamic world. Political repression and deteriorating economic conditions could fuel support for radical movements flying Islam as their banner. Whether they have the organization, the will, and the public support to challenge successfully the power of the state only time will tell. One final question which can be examined in the radical Muslim theory of society is the role and status of women, which represents another challenge to the modern secular model.

WOMEN, THE FAMILY, AND THE ISLAMIC STATE

Earlier in this chapter reforms in Muslim family law were discussed as they affected the areas of marriage and divorce. These were introduced during the last stage of direct European control in the Islamic world, a period when Muslim reformers proposed ways and means of adapting the *shari'ah* to modern conditions and when secular modernist leaders were endeavoring to remodel their societies along the lines of the Western pattern. In the next stage of independent states, some governments passed more reforms with the intent of further improving women's position. Specific reforms dealt with the restriction or abolition of polygyny, registration of marriages, and the minimum age for intending couples, restriction of the privileged right of the husband to divorce, and problems of custody and maintenance of children of divorced parents. Change at the best of times is an uneven and bumpy road. As a result, the application of Muslim family law today varies enormously throughout the Islamic world. Turkey, for example, abolished the *shari'ah* and replaced the religious courts and family law with secular European equivalents. Saudi Arabia, on the other hand, has retained both the religious courts and the law. Pakistan, ostensibly created as an Islamic state, has until now gone some way along the secular path, away from strictly traditional religious norms.[46]

The family and women's role in it have not only been affected in recent decades by changes in laws of personal status. Broader structural changes affecting all Muslim societies have played a major part. Industrialization, technological development, and rapid urbanization in societies which until recently were, and in many places still are, rural and agriculturally based are but a few of the interrelated variables in the disruptive transformation all Third World countries have experienced since the end of the Second World War. Modernization, however, is a double-edged sword. Development schemes can produce unforeseen and contradictory results, affecting women's position for good and ill. State-introduced health programs, for example, lowered the rates of maternal and infant mortality and extended life expectancy. These trends, however, contributed to marked population growth, which increased the burden of childrearing, notably among women of the poorer rural or urban classes, where the use of contraception is badly understood or deemed socially unacceptable. State-promoted mass-education programs have addressed the problem of widespread illiteracy among both men and women; women, however, have yet to benefit from a basic education to the same degree as men. Education among a minority of females from the more privileged classes has presented them with a greater range of alternatives in their lives and an altered perception of their roles. Particularly in urban areas, women tend to seek higher levels of education; they therefore marry at a later age and have fewer children; they may also seek employment outside the home giving them a degree of financial independence and hence greater freedom, ultimately, in making decisions in the home.

Over time, changes in society positively affecting the position of women have slowly begun to undermine the structures of classical patriarchal society. Historically, a belt of classical patriarchal societies extended from North Africa through the Middle East to India and China, thus embracing the religious cultures of Hinduism, Confucianism, and Islam. In these societies descent, property, and residence are governed through the male line, which has resulted in various traditional systems of control and subordination of women. This is most evident in urban settings, where women were secluded in the private sphere of the home whereas men dominated the public sphere of the market and government. In rural and nomadic settings, the separation of the private and public domains was less important, although male control of women was exercised in other ways. In the post-independence era of Muslim states, as women have become more visible by their participation in most facets of the public life of cities, the traditional mechanisms of male domination can be assumed to be endangered by the pressures of change in modern society.

It is nonetheless true that elsewhere patriarchal structures and values have been modernized in "neopatriarchal" forms, and male domination of the family and state remains firmly entrenched.[47] The neopatriarchal state, using Islam as an ideology, has reintroduced restrictions by enforcing aspects of Muslim family law. Such measures have already taken place in the 1970s and 1980s, for example in the Sudan, Algeria, and Egypt. These moves to "Islamize" family law have been partly in response to pressure and criticism from conservative and radical quarters, and partly out of a search for renewed legitimacy by the regimes concerned.

From the experience of transformation of Muslim societies in the modern world, an apparently contradictory phenomenon can be detected where women's strategies for coping with change are concerned. On the one hand there are secular, liberal feminists who consistently support greater opportunities for women. They reject the call of radical groups to mold society according to the norms of the *shari'ah*. Religious laws, they argue, run against the spirit and the letter of the United Nations Convention, which supports the elimination of discrimination against women in whatever form it may take. For them, polygyny, seclusion in the home, the husband's privileged right of divorce, and so on are all examples of discrimination to be done away with for good.

On the other hand, women play an important role in the same radical Muslim movements which secular feminists condemn. For these groups and their female activists, the question of women's rights is irrelevant, for Islam established such rights centuries before they were achieved in Western societies. Women have rights equal to those of men, and, although the details vary from one group to another, the basis of the argument lies in the traditional interpretation of scripture, *Men are in charge of women, because Allah has endowed the one with more, and because they spend of their property for their support. Therefore the righteous women are the obedient, guarding in secret that which Allah has guarded* (4:34). According to many, women have the right to education, to religious instruction, to honor and respect, to the vote, and to employment. There are, however, restrictions sanctioned by the religious law for the welfare and stability of society as a whole. A woman can be neither a political leader nor a judge; she must only appear in public modestly dressed, and her natural and sacred task is to keep the household smoothly functioning and to raise and instruct her children to be good Muslims. Men, for their part, must shoulder the burden of providing for the family in material ways. Liberation for a woman does not mean being like a male, or taking up male tasks, but rather being herself and fulfilling the destiny Allah created for her.

To the Muslim "feminist," the secular "feminist" has betrayed her culture and religion and sold out to an alien West; the secularized woman represents a threat to the stability of the traditional order within the family. From the Muslim feminist perspective, therefore, far from being inferior to men, women are equal but different, physiologically and psychologically. Men and women thus perform different but necessarily complementary roles. Radicals, however, do justify certain inequalities such as polygny on dubious scriptural grounds (as Muslim reformers had already recognized), whereas in fact such a practice properly belongs to the value system of the classical patriarchies as a means of controlling women. The radical Muslim feminist accepts patriarchal norms as genuinely religious because of the sense of honor and security she derives from her role within the family. She shares with the majority of women in her own society what is seen as a long-term benefit of her early subordination to the control of a father or brother. A concise description of a woman's place in this context is given by Kandiyoti, who says,

The cyclical nature of women's power and their anticipation of inheriting the authority of senior women encourages a thorough internalization of this form of patriarchy by the women themselves. Subordination to men is offset by the control older women have over younger women. Women have access to the only type of labour power they can control, and to old-age security, however, through their married sons. Since sons are a woman's most critical resource, ensuring their lifelong loyalty is an enduring preoccupation.[48]

Confronted with the threat of Western institutions and values and the unpredictable consequences of secular change, the radical opts to counter uncertainty by seeking security in the familiar, made the more valuable when it is believed to be sanctioned by a sacred source.

Another strategy of contemporary women is to work for change within Islam by engaging in the reinterpretation of the Qur'an and prophetic *sunnah*, or by creating an Islamic women's history. Theirs is an exercise in demystification of the Islamic tradition to rescue it from the exclusively male enterprise it has been over the centuries. This strategy utterly rejects the misogynous notions about women such as those expressed by the popular Egyptian writer 'Abbas Mahmud al-'Aqqad, who, in *Woman in the Qur'an* (1959), said, "Men are the sole source of every accepted definition of good conduct whether for men or women. Woman has never been a true source of anything to do with ethics or good character even though she brings up the children. The guidelines are provided by the male."[49] Even a true radical Muslim feminist would reject such a crude estimate of her worth. The best-known champion of this approach is possibly the Moroccan sociologist Fatima Mernissi, who, in her study *Women and Islam*,

observed that when completing the work she had come to understand
that

if women's rights are a problem for some modern Muslim men, it is neither
because of the Koran nor the Prophet, nor the Islamic tradition, but simply
because those rights conflict with the interests of a male elite. The elite
faction is trying to convince us that their egoistic, highly subjective and
mediocre view of culture and society has a sacred basis . . . Islam was not sent
from heaven to foster egoism and mediocrity.[50]

Taken together, the female secular, radical, and scholarly groups
(and, indeed, their male counterparts) do not comprise a majority of
their own gender in Muslim societies, although each may claim to
address the interests of the whole. Doubtless all will contribute to the
future shape of their societies. For the moment, secularists have the
upper hand, since they hold the reins of power in the state. Radicals,
however, appear to articulate the concerns of the masses more
directly. The fate of scholars, as always, will be determined by the
degree of freedom they have to express their views. Given the long
transition upon which the *ummah* has embarked over the past two
centuries, the future configuration of any given society on a spectrum
of modern-secular to modern-Muslim cannot be foretold.

TOWARD THE MILLENNIUM: ISLAM IN THE WEST

When Muhammad al-Saffar visited Paris in the mid nineteenth
century, he and his small party of Moroccans were the only officially
acknowledged Muslim presence in France. Since his day, the era of
imperialism has come and gone and France has witnessed a dramatic
change. Estimates in the mid 1980s suggest that there are over three
million Muslims, or at least people of Muslim cultural background,
living in France. The vast majority are from former French overseas
possessions, Algerians and their French-born children, Moroccans,
and Tunisians, although a substantial number of Turks and West
Africans contribute to the total. The figure also includes an estimated
30,000–50,000 French converts to Islam, possibly the highest figure
for any country in Western Europe.[51]

Britain, France's major rival in the carve-up of the Muslim *ummah*,
experienced a similar pattern of Muslim immigration from territories
of her former empire. As in France, the 1960s marked a point of rapid
increase in the numbers of immigrants from Muslim countries. The

estimated number in Britain by the mid 1980s was just under one million, by far the largest single group coming from Pakistan, with much smaller representations from Bangladesh (the former East Pakistan), India, the Arab world, Iran, Turkey, Cyprus, Malaysia, and East Africa. Conversion to Islam among the British is much lower than in France, estimated at around 5,000.

Germany, although a negligible imperial overseas imperial power, nevertheless has the second largest Muslim population in Western Europe today. The 1960s, too, was a period of rapid growth of "guest-workers," as they are called (rather than immigrants), who settled as cheap labor in the major cities of West Germany. The overwhelming proportion of these workers by the mid 1980s were from Turkey, numbering about a million and a half persons. The conversion of Germans to Islam reaches the British figure of about 5,000. Other countries of Northern and Southern Europe have experienced Muslim immigration as well, possibly adding a further million and a half persons to an uncertain total of seven to eight million by the end of the 1980s.

This phenomenon has been described as "the new Islamic presence" in Europe and North America.[52] The phenomenon represents a mutual challenge, one to the peoples of Europe among whom the newcomers have settled and another among the Muslims themselves. The experience on both sides is novel. For Muslims, at least for those who have taken with them a strong attachment to their religious culture, transplantation has raised the problem of how to be a Muslim in societies where secular norms are deeply rooted and where the traditional religious expression is Christianity. In other words, the immigrant is a Muslim in a non-Muslim environment. It is a thoroughly modern condition, not one envisaged by the jurists of the classical schools, whose world had been neatly divided into two distinct spheres, the *dar al-Islam* and the *dar al-harb*, which did not overlap. A Muslim's true existence, they imagined, was where the *shar'iah* was sovereign. There are, of course, many larger Muslim minorities elsewhere than Western Europe, dispersed throughout Asia, the Pacific, and Africa. The novelty for Muslims of minority status is reflected in the establishment of the Muslim World League (1966) in Saudi Arabia. Part of its work is targeted toward the problems of Muslim minorities, such as those in India, as well as others facing more continuous forms of oppression in Palestine, South Africa, and the Philippines. The League's concern with the Muslim minorities in Western Europe and North America has not been with their oppression but rather with the powerful forces of acculturation, that is, the dangers of their absorption into secular society.

Muslims' search to define their identity and place in Western societies has stimulated debate over the merits and risks of integration and participation as against efforts to build a separate and distinctive community within the host country. The strongest impact upon a minority's options and strategies comes from the day-to-day realities it faces. Access to adequate housing, education, and employment in the host country are important factors in a minority's assessment of its long-term prospects. Another is the presence and degree of racist acts committed against its members. Within the countries of Western Europe there have been differing degrees of accommodation to Muslim ritual practices such as allowing time to perform daily prayers in the workplace; allowing time off for the two major religious festivals associated with the pilgrimage month and Ramadan; and permitting the slaughter of animals in the Muslim (and, incidentally, the Jewish) fashion so that dietary rules may be properly observed in the home, school, or workplace. The degree of adaptability of Muslim immigrants to their host countries is affected, too, by the background from which they come, whether urban or rural, educated or unskilled, Middle Eastern, African, or Asian. Pressures exerted by the dominant host culture upon the minority will always be greater than the reverse so that concessions to the customs of the majority may seem a significant loss of a minority's sense of identity.

To conclude this survey of issues in contemporary Islam, we shall look briefly at two Muslim minority communities in quite distinct contexts. They illustrate contrasting ways religious symbols have been employed in a minority's defense against the dominant culture.

Britain and the "Rushdie Affair"

It has been observed that had *The Satanic Verses* been written, say, by a Moroccan Muslim and published in France, there would have been no controversy. Appeal to the hypothetical is seldom illuminating in understanding events which have taken place. In this instance it serves to focus upon the background of the author, Salman Rushdie, and the particular segment of the Muslim immigrant community in Britain which was most immediately aggrieved by the book's publication. Half of the Muslim population in Britain is from the

Indian sub-continent, the largest groups coming from poor rural areas of Kashmir and the Punjab in Pakistan and from the regions of Sylhet and Chittagong in Bangladesh. Salman Rushdie was born in India. His family later moved to Pakistan and he received his secondary and university education in England. Rushdie was already an established writer when *The Satanic Verses* appeared in September 1988 (indeed he was the recipient of the prestigious Booker McConnell Prize for an earlier novel, *Midnight's Children*), by which time he had also built a solid record of support for anti-racist campaigns in England.

The first notice of the controversial nature of the book was the occasion of its public burning during a demonstration in Bradford, in January 1989. Heated media coverage followed, and the whole "affair" was hijacked by Ayatullah Khumayni the following month when he issued his notorious *fatwa*. It expressed the Ayatullah's view that Rushdie had insulted the Prophet and was therefore an apostate whose life, according to Islamic law, was forfeit. Separate from the principle of the *fatwa*, a reward was offered for whoever carried out Rushdie's execution, and the author in consequence was forced into hiding for his own safety. Doubtless many Muslims in Britain took comfort from the attention given the issue by an international figure like the Ayatullah. More irresponsible elements in the community called publicly for Rushdie's death, deeply damaging the image of Muslims in Britain as an industrious, law-abiding people.

Central to the whole affair, however, was the gulf of misunderstanding which existed between the dominant liberal, secular culture (of which Rushdie was a part) and the Muslim minority. The Muslim population of the northern town of Bradford originates largely from rural parts of the Punjab which brought to Britain a tradition of veneration for the Prophet Muhammad. This tradition is more deeply and emotionally internalized than reverence for the Prophet elsewhere. For example, whereas in Pakistan the Prophet's birthday is celebrated, it is forbidden in Saudi Arabia, since it is not regarded as a genuine part of the prophetic *sunnah*. Photocopies of the book's offending passages depicting the Prophet, his wives and Companions circulated widely in the Muslim community. Muslim revulsion was felt elsewhere in the country at the author's insulting and blasphemous treatment of the Prophet, and there were renewed calls to have the book withdrawn from circulation. Many of Rushdie's supporters, on the other hand, damaged their cause by turning the issue of freedom of speech into a stone-graven commandment of their own secular, liberal "religion," ignoring thereby the obvious fact that free speech is not an absolute moral principle in any Western society.[53] In the end, the Muslim community's vigorous defense of their Prophet was in part a defense of British society's apparent consent to the open denigration of their faith. It was also partly an expression of deeper frustrations stemming from the community's experience of adjustment to the impact of British culture. For example, for some years community leaders have been refused official sanction to establish Muslim schools as a means of protecting and transmitting their religious heritage in the same way British Christians and Jews are allowed the opportunity to run their own schools funded chiefly from public money. At present, community leaders are searching for a fine balance which will avoid total assimilation into British society yet will not result in helpless isolation from it.

The United States and the Nation of Islam

The Muslim population of the United States numbers some two million persons, less than 1 percent of the total population (about the same proportion as in Canada). Immigrants from many Muslim countries form part of the total, but none has achieved the same degree of public notice in the United States as the Nation of Islam. In contrast to the immigrant British Muslim community, the Nation of Islam is a community of black American converts founded in the 1930s. Many at the time had recently performed their own internal migration from the southern States in hope of a better life. During the years of the Great Depression, however, the black American experience in the northern cities of the States was one of poverty, unemployment, and racist degradation. In 1930, the rather shadowy figure of Wallace D. Fard appeared among the black community of Detroit preaching, in the name of Islam, a doctrine of black emancipation and total separation from the heathen white race. In 1934 Fard, who was known as Farad Muhammad, mysteriously disappeared and bequeathed his mission to his close associate Elijah Muhammad.

The son of an itinerant Baptist preacher from Georgia, Elijah Muhammad dominated the Nation of Islam until his death in 1975. His Islam was idiosyncratic. This is nowhere more clearly shown than in the black Muslim witness to faith, the *shahadah*: "In the name of Allah, who came in the person of Master Farad Muhammad, the Beneficent, the Merciful, the One God to whom all things are due, the

Lord of the Worlds, and his Apostle the honorable Elijah Muhammad, the last of the Messengers of Allah." Moreover, the accompanying theology did not fit within the boundaries of normative Islamic thought. God, the creator of the heavens and earth, was black. Although he no longer exists, his descendants, the black race who are called the righteous Originals, share in his divinity. Hence it was possible for a divine presence to continue in the world in the figure of the Supreme One, Farad Muhammad, whose infinite wisdom would raise the condition of the blacks of America. Whites, in contrast to the righteous blacks created by God, were the invention of a black scientist who rebelled against God and created a race of devils. Muhammad of Mecca, however, was acknowledged as a prophet to whom the Qur'an had been sent. Elijah Muhammad accorded the Qur'an a special place in his thought, but he regarded himself as the sole authoritative interpreter of all scriptures. This role was based on his claim to be the last prophet who had been instructed directly by a living deity, Farad Muhammad.

The polarization of American society between the dominant white caste and a black underclass was matched in Elijah Muhammad's ideology by the struggle of righteous blacks against the devil whites. Black salvation meant a separate black nation within the United States. Opponents, white and black, accused him of preaching racism. Muslims who followed normative Islamic teachings and practices found his ideas shocking. Yet his message effectively gave a sense of dignity and purpose to his first converts found among the black slums and ghettos, in prisons, drug-abuse clinics and dole queues, people who "were most battered by racism and stifled by convention, and whose experience of white man's 'invincibility' made the acceptance of Black inferiority seem as reasonable as it was pervasive."[54] Elijah Muhammad's "theology," however bizarre it may appear in normative Islamic terms, can be accommodated nonetheless within one strand of contemporary radical Muslim thought. Qur'anic teachings, it is suggested, can be applied to new situations confronted by Muslims in the West without reference to theological argument developed during the course of Islamic history in its Middle Eastern contexts. In any event, Elijah Muhammad's mission rejuvenated the life of many black urban communities. By the time of his death the Nation is estimated to have grown into a community of one hundred thousand persons. This success owed much to the articulate and charismatic personality of Malcolm X

(1925–65), the Nation's most public figure before his split with Elijah Muhammad and subsequent assassination.

Leadership passed into the hands of Elijah Muhammad's son Wallace Muhammad, and a profound transformation occurred in the movement. First, the Nation was renamed and is now known as the American Muslim Mission. More fundamentally, Wallace (who is now called Warith Deen Muhammad) took the major step of erasing the black nationalist image of the Nation to bring it closer to full association with the rest of the Islamic world. The change toward normative Islam is explained as a natural progression of the teachings and ultimate goal of Elijah Muhammad himself, who had promised his people that they would one day achieve full understanding of the religion of the Qur'an. Warith Deen's new program has led to schism within the movement. A splinter group now follows Minister Louis Farrakhan, who continues to expound the original teachings of Elijah Muhammad's Nation as more relevant to the true condition of the majority of America's black population. The Mission, however, survives as an increasingly respected voice of black Muslims in America and in Muslim countries abroad.

The new Islamic presence in Western Europe and North America is a relatively recent phenomenon of immigration and conversion. The growth or survival of these Muslim communities will depend in the end upon the balance between their adaption to and adoption of the host cultures, a process which should on the whole be a peaceful one. There is, however, another, much older, Islamic presence on the very threshold of Western Europe. Since the collapse of communism in Central and Eastern Europe, the West has been occupied with the tragic consequences of the break-up of Yugoslavia. The fate of the 500-year-old Muslim community of Bosnia has equally been the concern of other Muslims throughout the *ummah*. As the largest minority group in Bosnia, followed by the Serbs and Croats, Bosnian Muslims have fought to preserve the multi-national, multi-religious, secular nature of their newly independent state. Many, if not all, Bosnian Serbs and Croats have supported the same project. The objective of Bosnian pluralism, however, has been thwarted by the policies of Serb irridentism orchestrated from Belgrade which seek to absorb Serbs from all quarters of the former Yugoslav republic into a greater Serbian nation; this explicit political goal has been accompanied by the systematic ethnic cleansing of non-Serbs from areas in Bosnia which have fallen under Serb control. The Bosnians' failure to receive adequate political support from Western governments and the United Nations for their civilized pluralist program has in effect rewarded the Serbs' aggression and their ideology of ethnic purity.[55] Whatever the final outcome of this conflict for the Muslims of Bosnia, the experience of today's tragedy could have repercussions for tomorrow. Muslims elsewhere, whether radical or not, may well ponder whether they are witnessing the slow demise, if not of the Western secular model of society, at least of the alleged moral superiority upon which it rests. From there, an Islamic model of the good society cannot but seem to be a cultural imperative.

Excursus on Islamic origins

The reader who comes fresh to the subject of Islam, with or without a prior interest in any of the great contemporary religious traditions, will find the literature on Islam bewildering in its sheer quantity and varied in its quality and apparent aim. Any casual reader of the daily press, or television viewer for that matter, will realize that Islam plays an important role in many parts of the globe, whether in the trouble-torn former republic of Yugoslavia, in the Muslim states of Pakistan, Iran, Egypt, and Algeria, or even in the (post-Christian?) secular society of modern-day Britain in the aftermath of the so-called Rushdie Affair and the decree of the late Ayatullah Khumayni against the author and the publishers of *The Satanic Verses*. Over the past fifteen years or so, books on Islamic history and thought and on the current phenomenon of Islam in politics have become a growth sector in the publishing world. Only a tiny portion of this output can be cited in the notes and list of further reading below. In this excursus discussion is restricted to a selection of works in English dealing with the question of Islamic origins, since much important, original – and controversial – work has been done in recent years on this subject. However, in addition to new studies with fresh perspectives, there are available, too, numerous reprints of scholarly and popular works on Islam originally published, in some cases, as much as a hundred years ago. It is a discriminating reader today who picks up a book on Islam and looks to see when it was first published. It should be evident, however, that a book on Islam written around 1900 cannot be accepted as a reflection of our understanding of the subject nine or ten decades later. In other words, as obvious as this is, serious studies and popular accounts of the Qur'an and the life of the Prophet Muhammad have a context and a history of their own. The purpose of this excursus is, in a very general way, to bring the reader's attention to this simple but generally unstated fact.

In the West, Islam has been the subject of attention almost since the formation of the community in the seventh century CE. The question of the early Christian perceptions of Islam has been touched upon in Chapter 2 above. Norman Daniel has treated the subject in detail in his *Islam and the West: The Making of an Image* (Edinburgh: Edinburgh University Press, 1958). In his later book, *The Arabs and Medieval Europe* (London: Longman, 2nd ed., 1979), Daniel observes that in medieval Christian accounts of the Prophet, "he was subjected to gross abuse which, however shocking in itself, we must understand as rooted in folk-lore. The Qur'an was seen as the product of the events of the life of the Prophet, but rather as a deliberate contrivance than as God's revelation, in response to particular needs" (p. 234). A briefer account, complementary to Daniel's, is R. W. Southern's *Western Views of Islam in the Middle Ages* (Cambridge, Mass.: Harvard University Press, 1962). Modern Western scholarly endeavor fortunately no longer indulges in crude and fanciful stereotypes of Muhammad and Islamic scripture. Stereotypes of Islam and Muslims generated from the pool of medieval "folklore" survived, however, throughout the nineteenth century in many books of a popular nature. They can also be detected today in so-called "best-sellers," works of "instant analysis" by self-styled experts, and in much of the Euro-American media coverage of current events in the Middle East and other Islamic countries. As a sequel to his first volume, Daniel has covered the nineteenth century in *Islam, Europe and Empire* (Edinburgh: Edinburgh University Press, 1966). To this should be added the important, but controversial, analysis of Western attitudes to Islam by Edward Said in his *Orientalism* (London: Routledge & Kegan Paul, 1978) and his incisive account of Western media treatment of Muslims and Islam in the wake of the of the Iran hostage affair of 1979–1980, in *Covering Islam: How the Media and the Experts Determine how we See the Rest of the World* (London: Routledge & Kegan Paul, 1981). The following articles of Albert Hourani are also recommended: "Islam and the philosophers of history," in his *Europe and the Middle East* (London: Macmillan Press, 1980), and the title essay of his *Islam in European Thought* (Cambridge: Cambridge University Press, 1991).

Scholarly Euro-American inquiry over the past century on the nature and origins of the prophetic-revelatory event (dealt with in Chapter 1 above) has nevertheless resulted in interpretations which contrast with, even contradict, the traditional Muslim interpretation. This is not surprising. In contemporary Western secular societies, matters of faith have been almost entirely consigned to the individual's personal conscience. Therefore, in theory, a scholar's public discourse on faiths other than his or her own should be free of his or her own personal religious predilections. The result is supposed to be an "objective" account. In other words, there apparently exists a secular truth distinct from religious truth. In theory, secular truth is "objective" in a way that religious truth cannot be, because religious truths are embedded in scripture believed to be of divine provenance but which is not subject to rational proof. At one time religious truths prevailed in societies in general, reinforced by an intellectual arrogance which at times resulted in persecution and oppression of those who dissented from the accepted norms. Today, explicit persecutions of this type are fortunately rare. There is nonetheless, today, a form of secular intellectual arrogance which, even while it cannot claim absolute certainty for a particular hypothesis, deems its findings superior to the content of religious truth. The two perspectives are irreconcilable and totally out of touch with each other. This, at least, appears to be the case with a range of writings currently available dealing with the origins of Islam. In the discussion which follows, these writings form two distinct groups. The first is mentioned briefly only in order to draw the necessary contrast between it and the second group.

The first group may be called the Faithful. The Muslim perspective is that of the "insider," as it were, which is held to be true by hundreds of millions of Muslims who have been, and still are, guided in their daily lives by the Qur'an and the example of the Prophet. The integrity of the Qur'anic text, according to the Muslim sources, was spared possible corruption and distortion since the establishment of a reliable and uniform edition within a few years of the Prophet's death. An additional source of knowledge of the content of the divine will and command was the *sunnah* of the Prophet. This was believed to be his words and deeds as transmitted by his Companions which were finally collected, sifted, and recorded in the late third/ninth century. These two sources, scripture and *sunnah*, inform every aspect of subsequent Muslim religious inquiry, whether in law, in theology, or in mystical spirituality. The ultimate source of guidance for Muslims, in this world and in preparation for the next, is therefore divine, whether transmitted by direct revelation or by inspired comment upon revelation reflected in the exemplary life of the Prophet himself. One excellent example of the Muslim perspective is that of the Indian scholar Syed Ameer Ali, who, in his *Spirit of Islam* (London: Methuen, 1965 [1922]) set out to explain his faith to a British public which was either indifferent to or ignorant of Muslim thought and practice. More recently, the late Professor Fazlur Rahman, a Pakistani Muslim scholar who in his lifetime contributed much to a modernist reorientation of Islamic thought, describes the Qur'an as a "document of [Muhammad's] revelatory experiences" in which the central concern is with human conduct, since, he says, "no real morality is possible without the regulative ideas of God and the Last Judgment" (*Islam and Modernity* [Chicago: University of Chicago Press, 1982], pp. 13, 14). Rahman's concern with a proper understanding of scripture for modern Muslim life was urgent owing to the threat of modernity to religious faith. As he observes, "the bane of modernity, in the form of secularism [is that] secularism destroys the sanctity and universality [transcendence] of all moral values" (p. 15).

For modern Western scholars, on the other hand, the sacred sources of Islam are seen in a different light. This is so, in part, because they are simply not Muslims and do not share the commitment of the Faithful. Nevertheless, as "outsiders" they have contributed to an understanding of Islamic origins by bringing to the early extant Arabic sources different concerns, questions, and methods of investigation. Their approach to Islam has, moreover, been profoundly influenced by the new approaches in scholarly research applied to the sources of the Judeo-Christian tradition, the Hebrew Bible, and the New Testament which commenced in European academies in the nineteenth century. Indeed many of these scholars of the early generations (for example Julius Wellhausen, to name but one) were as much at home in biblical studies as they were investigating the origins of the Islamic community. For both these reasons, therefore, Western scholarship approaches the Qur'an, not as revelation, but as a man-made historical source subject to the usual probing methods of modern historical research. The phenomena of revelation and prophethood are not regarded as the proper domains of scientific inquiry. Rather they must remain in the realm of faith, the certain truth of which cannot be rationally demonstrated. In this sense, the earlier, largely negative, European attitudes to the Prophet and the Qur'an have been abandoned for what is, in theory, a more "objective" and "value-free" approach. A useful survey of the various and changing views of Muhammad, for example, will be found in James Royster's article "The study of Muhammad: a survey of approaches from the perspective of the history and phenomenology of religion," *The Muslim World*, 62/1 (1972), 49–70. This second group of writers, the "outsiders," will now be discussed in more detail. Depending upon the degree of reliability with which they view the primary Arabic sources for the study of Islamic origins, this group may be further divided into doves and hawks. We commence with the doves.

At first, it is worth noting that an obsession with origins presents its own pitfalls. The French historian Marc Bloch has reminded us that in the search for origins "there lurks the danger of confusing ancestry with explanation." Two monographs which displayed an obsession with the antecedents of Islam were written by Richard Bell and Charles Torrey. They both accept that the Qur'an was Muhammad's own composition and express confidence in its historicity as the authentic basis for our knowledge of the Prophet's life and thought. The question of whether it is revelation is irrelevant. On the other hand, each regards the material contained in the *sunnah*, the record of the Prophet's words and deeds, as of little use in providing genuine data on the Prophet's life. Therefore, as a historical document, the Qur'an could be examined in order to determine the sources which inspired and influenced Muhammad's own ideas. For Bell and Torrey, the antecedents clearly lay in the Judeo-Christian tradition. Bell, the more cautious of the two, saw Muhammad as "a brooding religious genius and man of great native mental power, but very limited knowledge, striving to find out what others more enlightened than his own Arab people knew, which might be of use to him in his own enterprise" (*The Origin of Islam in its Christian Environment* [London: Frank Cass, 1968 (1926)], p. 111). He was an avid collector of information from whatever quarter he could find it. Bell's deep interest in the history of the Qur'anic text resulted also in his attempt to reconstruct its chronology in order to determine the development of Muhammad's ideas (see his *The Quran Translated with a Critical Re-arrangement of the Surahs* [2 vols., Edinburgh: T. & T. Clark, 1937–1939]). Apart from certain religious vocabulary which he supposes Christians to have introduced into Arabia, Bell observes that it is impossible to determine at the outset of his career any direct Christian or Jewish influence on Muhammad since he himself did not distinguish between the two monotheistic faiths. Only as his career developed and his knowledge increased can such external influence be detected, although the immediate sources of his information and the channels through which they reached him cannot be definitely decided. His conclusion, however, is that the contemporary Christian environment provided the ultimate stimulus to Muhammad's religious ideas.

All things considered ... I think it was the great religion which prevailed in the land round about Arabia, and especially in Syria and the Roman Empire, which had attracted his attention and which occupied in his untutored mind a position of imposing authority. From it he was prepared to borrow, probably assuming that in the Revelation which it cherished were contained those things which by his own reflection he could not reach, but which were as necessary for the true religion as was the truth of God's creative power and bounty, which he had reached by himself, and upon which that religion was also founded. (*Origin of Islam*, pp. 136–137; see also p. 41)

Charles Torrey, on the other hand, is more categorical. For him, Muhammad was a "thoughtful man and, in addition, a man of very unusual originality and energy" (*The Jewish Foundation of Islam* [New York: Jewish Institute of Religion Press, 1933], p. 7). As to the Qur'an, Muhammad's own creation, Torrey states that "there is no clear evidence that [he] has ever received instruction from a Christian teacher while many facts testify emphatically to the contrary; and that, on the other hand, the evidence that he gained his Christian material either from Jews in Mecca, or from what was well known and handed about in the Arabian cities, is clear, consistent and convincing" (ibid.). In general, he concludes, "while Muhammad's Islam was undoubtedly eclectic, yet both in its beginning and in its later development by far the greater part of its essential material came directly from Israelite sources" (ibid., p. 8). To support his position, Torrey goes so far as to postulate the existence in Mecca of an anonymous Jewish teacher of Mesopotamian origin who instructed the Prophet. The problem with the Bell–Torrey approach, as we can now see it, is that the milieu of seventh-century central Arabia is as yet so little known that the Qur'an cannot easily be placed in its historical and cultural context. More recent surveys dealing with some of the problems raised here may be found in Maxime Rodinson, "A critical survey of modern studies of Muhammad," first published in 1963 and translated from the French in Merlin Swartz, *Studies on Islam* (Oxford: Oxford University Press, 1981), pp. 23–85 and the articles on "Muhammad" and the "Kur'an" in the new edition of the authoritative *Encyclopaedia of Islam* (Leiden: E. J. Brill, 1979 in progress). The author-revisor of these articles, A. T. Welch, has also attempted a biographical sketch of Muhammad based on the Qur'an, in his "Muhammad's understanding of himself: the Koranic data," in R. G. Hovannisian and S. Vryonis (eds.), *Islam's Understanding of Itself* (Malibu, Calif.: Undena Publications, 1983), pp. 15–52.

Undoubtedly, the next milestone in the study of the Prophet was erected by William M. Watt, whose two-volume study appeared in the 1950s (*Muhammad at Mecca* [Oxford: Oxford University Press, 1953] and *Muhammad at Medina* [Oxford: Oxford University Press, 1956]). He was influenced by but went significantly beyond the work of Richard Bell. This he accomplished by reconstructing the socio-economic and political context of the central Arabian society in which Muhammad and his community lived. He was less concerned to look for supposed influences upon Muhammad from the earlier religious traditions. In the introduction to the volume on Mecca, Watt states, "I have endeavoured, while remaining faithful to the standards of Western historical scholarship, to say nothing that would entail the rejection of any of the fundamental doctrines of Islam" (*Mecca*, p. x). In his discussion of the Arabic sources, the Qur'an is taken as the record of revelations which Muhammad believed he received from God but which does not, as with Bell and Torrey, provide the fundamental source for the Prophet's life owing to its partial and fragmentary character. He says,

The sounder methodology is to regard the Qur'an and the early traditional accounts as complementary sources, each with a fundamental contribution to make to the history of the period. The Qur'an presents mainly the ideological aspect of a great complex of changes which took place in and around Mecca, but the economic, social and political aspects must also be considered if we are to have a balanced picture and indeed if we are to understand properly the ideological aspect itself. (Ibid., p. xv)

By "traditional accounts" Watt means sources such as the biography of Muhammad by Ibn Ishaq (mentioned in Chapter 1 above), the history of al-Tabari (mentioned in Chapter 2 above), and the collections of the prophetic Traditions (treated in Chapter 3 above), the earliest of these sources being composed more than a century after the Prophet's death. Of this material Watt says, "I have proceeded on the view that the traditional accounts are in general to be accepted, are to be received with care and as far as possible corrected where 'tendential shaping' is suspected, and are only to be rejected outright where there is an internal contradiction" (ibid., p. xiv; see also his discussion in *Medina*, pp. 336–338). In this manner Watt accounts for the beginnings of Muhammad's career against the background of a Meccan transition to a mercantile economy which undermined the traditional tribal order by creating a moral and social malaise. Muhammad's mission, therefore, was a response to these markedly deteriorating conditions.

On the question of influences upon the Prophet's thought and practice, Watt noted that pagan ideas were retained where they were either already deeply rooted in Arab society or else provided a degree of social utility to the new community; these included the belief in angels, jinn, and demons and acceptance of the notion of the sacredness of certain places (*Medina*, pp. 309–315). As for Christianity, he notes that "One of the most remarkable features of the relationship between Muslims and Christians is that neither Muhammad nor any of his Companions seems to have been aware of some of the fundamental Christian doctrines" (ibid., p. 320). Relations with the Jews of Medina were at once closer and more complicated. Muhammad believed that his message was identical with that which had been given to both Jews and Christians and also that the teachings of these two communities were similar to each other. However, after the decision was taken to move from Mecca to Medina, Muhammad "appears to have tried to model Islam on the older religion" of Judaism in instituting Friday worship, praying in the direction of Jerusalem, the institution of the fast, and the introduction of the mid-day prayer (ibid., pp. 198–199). Other gestures of accommodation toward the Jews of Medina were made in order to win over their support and to demonstrate the essential identity between his revelations and theirs. These overtures were rejected by the Medinan Jews, partly from religious, partly from political motives. When Muhammad received a revelation ordering him to change the direction of prayer from Jerusalem to the Ka'bah in Mecca, relations between himself and the Jews soured and finally ended in open hostility. The ideological distinction that Muhammad then drew between himself and both previous monotheistic communities was to make the Muslims followers of the creed of Abraham, who was neither Jew nor Christian. Thus Muslims became adherents of the pure religion of God, since all subsequent prophets, including Moses and Jesus, had received essentially the same message.

For nearly a quarter of a century Watt's attractive "materialist thesis" was universally accepted in its general framework, if not in every detail. To this point, modern Western scholarship on Islamic origins may be said to have been "dovish" in its treatment of the Arabic source material. Now came the turn of the "hawks" to claim revenge. In 1977 a book appeared which its authors calculated would create a storm. The book was *Hagarism: The Making of the Islamic World*, by P. Crone and M. Cook (Cambridge: Cambridge University Press, 1977). In the preface the authors acknowledge that their account is radically new, a "pioneering expedition" (p. vii) "written by infidels for infidels" (p. viii). Readers had been forewarned. The novelty of the work lies in the method adopted toward the primary source material and, of course, in its conclusions. Their method reverses that of Watt. Crone and Cook are Sceptics and argue on the one hand that there is no hard evidence for the existence of the Qur'an until the decade of the 690s CE and, moreover, that Muslim tradition which places the Qur'an in its historical context cannot be attested before about 750 CE. Their attitude toward the entire tradition contained in the Muslim historical sources is that since there are "no cogent internal grounds for rejecting it, there are equally no cogent external grounds for accepting it"; therefore, "the only way out of the dilemma is . . . to step outside the Islamic tradition altogether and start again" (p. 3). Having combed through an impressive array of non-Muslim sources of Greek, Jewish, Armenian, and Syriac provenance, the authors hit upon three meager scraps of testimony which provide the foundation for their novel interpretation. They argue that Muhammad was preaching some form of Judaic messianism and that the earliest stage of the Arab conquests was an irridentist movement in alliance with Jewish refugees from Palestine aimed at the recovery of the Holy Land. Moreover, the invaders were not called Muslims at this stage but rather *muhajirun* or Hagarenes, "those who take part in an exodus." The movement subsequently split and the Arab break with the Jews (which does not occur in Medina according to the Muslim sources, Watt, and everyone else) takes place in Palestine when the Arabs cloak their movement in "Islamic" garb, presumably in an attempt to conceal the movement's true origin in order to gather support from the numerically larger Christian communities.

The Crone–Cook theory has been almost universally rejected. The evidence offered by the authors is far too tentative and conjectural (and possibly contradictory) to conclude that Arab–Jewish relations were as intimate as they would wish them to have been. In addition, the non-Muslim sources themselves would seem to be of equally doubtful historical value since they are all polemical works of one kind or another, a point possibly appreciated by the authors but one they do not trouble to make explicit as a fundamental problem. The Crone–Cook methodology is judged on another point, too, "particularly so because the authors' criticisms of the possibilities of understanding the earliest periods of Islam would seem, if applied as a general method to the sources used by historians of religion, to lead to a kind of historical solipsism" (G. D. Newby, *A History of the Jews in Arabia* [Columbia: University of South Carolina Press, 1988], p. 110). The book, nevertheless, has raised serious and legitimate questions by emphasizing the difficulty in employing the Muslim sources for a reconstruction of Islamic origins. Indirectly, it poses the broader question of how any of the contemporary sources relevant to Islamic origins, Muslim and non-Muslim alike, can be understood and interpreted in a manner which has some hope of securing a consensus, if only among Western scholars. That task awaits completion.

Meanwhile, in a second study Patricia Crone, this time on her own, returned to the question of Islamic origins in her *Meccan Trade and the Rise of Islam* (Princeton: Princeton University Press, 1987). The same hawkish approach to the sources is employed, of which she states, "It is not generally appreciated how much of our information on the rise of Islam, including that on Meccan trade, is derived from exegesis of the Qur'an, nor is it generally admitted that such information is of dubious historical value" (p. 204). The work is directed explicitly against both the method and the reconstruction of Islamic origins proposed by Watt. That method, however, says Crone, rests on a misjudgment of the sources.

The problem is the very mode of origin of the tradition, not some minor distortions subsequently introduced. Allowing for distortions arising from various allegiances within Islam such as those of a particular area, tribe, sect or school does nothing to correct the tendentiousness arising from allegiance to Islam itself. The entire tradition is tendentious, its aim being the elaboration of an Arabian Heilsgeschichte [salvation history], and this tendentiousness has shaped the facts as we have them, not merely added some partisan statements that we can deduct. Without correctives from outside the Islamic tradition, such as papyri, archeological evidence and non-Muslim sources, we have little hope of reconstructing the original shapes of this early period. Spurious information can be rejected, but lost information cannot be regained. (Ibid., p. 230)

On the substance of Watt's reconstruction, she writes that ultimately "the Watt thesis boils down to the proposition that a city in a remote corner of Arabia has some social problems to which a preacher responded by founding a world religion. It sounds like an overreaction" (p. 235). Crone's own alternative hypothesis, tentatively suggested to be sure, is that Islam was a nativist movement, originating somewhere (but not Mecca) in northwestern Arabia as a reaction to foreign, primarily Persian, domination which, in the nature of these movements, invariably took a religious form so as to reaffirm native (i.e. Arab) identity and values (p. 247). The link with the thesis in Hagarism is explicit: "Muhammad mobilized the Jewish version of monotheism against that of dominant Christianity and used it for the self-assertion, both ideological and military, of his own people" (p. 248). The reaction of one Muslim reviewer to the book was that as a refutation of the Watt thesis it was "excellent." Crone's alternative hypothesis, however, was judged much weaker. The reviewer lamented that Western scholars have paid so little heed to the Muslim viewpoint on the question of Islamic origins (M. A. Khan in *Muslim World Book Review*, 8 iv [1988], 15-17). This well illustrates the gulf which exists between the viewpoints of the Faithful and the Sceptics. It would have been appropriate to note that as in the case of *Hagarism*, the alternative hypothesis proposed in *Meccan Trade* rested upon equally conjectural evidence, that acceptance of it was as likely as rejection.

Sceptics, of course, must expect their views to be challenged and ultimately modified or even refuted, regardless of how passionately they advocate their own views and polemically attack those of others. Moreover, scepticism in the Western study of Islam did not begin in the 1970s. Contributions to an understanding of the first Islamic centuries have been made in the following works. There are, for example, the indispensable studies of the Hungarian scholar Ignaz Goldziher, published originally in 1889-1890 and translated into English and edited by S. M. Stern as *Muslim Studies* (2 vols., London: George Allen & Unwin, 1968, 1971). Volume 2 contains his studies of the development of prophetic Tradition (*hadith*). He shows that as a corpus, the Traditions should be understood as a panoramic picture of the first two or three centuries' development of the Islamic community rather than as a faithful depiction of the life and sayings of the Prophet himself.

Building upon Goldziher's insights, Joseph Schacht produced his major study on *The Origins of Muhammadan Jurisprudence* (Oxford:

Clarendon Press, 1950), which was followed by *An Introduction to Islamic Law* (Oxford: Clarendon Press, 1964). Schacht proposed that the authentic legal Traditions contained in the *hadith* corpus cannot be older than the year 100 of the Muslim era or 718 of the Common Era. As a methodological rule, he states that "every legal tradition from the Prophet, until the contrary is proved, must be taken not as an authentic or essentially authentic, even if slightly obscured, statement valid for his time or the time of the Companions, but as the fictitious expression of a legal doctrine formulated at a later date" (*Origins*, p. 149). Extended to the entire corpus of Traditions including the legal, this rule meant that, unless in each instance the contrary could be proven, there existed no genuine record of the Prophet's life. It also implied that Muhammad could not possibly have been regarded by his immediate Companions and their successors as a guide whose life was a religious paradigm and therefore normative for the community as a whole until more than a century after his death. This proposition, if true, held grave consequences for Muslims who have held that the prophetic example, the *sunnah*, is the second pillar of the religious law, the *shar'iah*. One respected Muslim scholar rejected the notion of a total absence of prophetic guidance as a "shallow and irrational 'scientific' myth of contemporary historiography" (Fazlur Rahman, *Islam* [Chicago: Chicago University Press, 1966], p. 52). More recently the Indian scholar Muhammad al-Azami dedicated an entire volume to an attack on Schacht's position. (See his *On Schacht's "Origins of Muhammadan Jurisprudence"* [Chichester: Wiley, 1985]; see also Muhammad Abdul Rauf, "Hadith literature – I: the development of the science of hadith," in A. F. L. Beeston et al. [eds.], *Arabic Literature to the End of the Umayyad Period* [Cambridge: Cambridge University Press, 1983], pp. 271–288.) The Sceptics dismiss these Muslim objections as "unscientific." Certain Western scholars, however, have also suggested modifications to some of Schacht's views. N. J. Coulson, for example, accepts Schacht's thesis in its broad essentials as irrefutable. On the other hand, he observes that Schacht's methodological rule creates a void or vacuum in the development of the law and asserts that a reasonable principle of historical inquiry should be "that an alleged ruling of the Prophet should be tentatively accepted as such unless some reason can be adduced as to why it should be regarded as fictitious" (*A History of Islamic Law* [Edinburgh: Edinburgh University Press, 1964], pp. 64-65). G. H. A. Juynboll, for his part, proposes to push back Schacht's dating of Tradition as a whole by about two decades (see his *Muslim Tradition* [Cambridge: Cambridge University Press, 1983]). And the work of H. Motzki, pursuing investigations into sources of Tradition (*hadith*) earlier than those that had been available to Schacht, may modify further his accepted views on *hadith* transmission (see H. Motzki, 'The *musannaf* of 'Abd al-Razzaq al-San'ani as a source of authentic *ahadith* of the first century AH," *Journal of Near East Studies*, 50 [1991], 1–21). It is just conceivable that in the study of *hadith* some accommodation between Western and Muslim approaches might be possible, since the spurious nature of a large part, but by no means all, of the prophetic Traditions had been acknowledged in certain modernist Muslim circles even before Goldziher's innovative studies in the West. For the moment, however, Michael Cook seems to have struck a properly judicious note saying, "The bottom line in the study of early Islamic traditions may well be that anyone can wriggle out of anything" ("Eschatology and the dating of traditions," *Princeton Papers in Near Eastern Studies*, no. 1 [1992], 23–47).

Finally, the Qur'an has not escaped the scrutiny of the Sceptic's eye. Crone and Cook's mentor, John Wansbrough, produced two monographs in the late 1970s entitled *Quranic Studies: Sources and Methods of Scriptural Interpretation* (Oxford: Oxford University Press, 1977) and *The Sectarian Milieu: Content and Composition of Islamic Salvation History* (Oxford: Oxford University Press, 1978). Wansbrough attempts to assess the sources, the Qur'an, the Prophet's biography, and the Muslim exegetical tradition by the method of literary analysis. These sources must be viewed, in Wansbrough's view, as "Salvation History" (*Heilsgeschichte*). He argues that although these sources purport to record the historical events of the Prophet's time as they actually occurred, in reality the events are described from a later period of time and are simply theological rationalizations of those events. In consequence there is no real possibility of recovering any true kernel of history in the life of the Prophet since, from the very nature of the sources, we can never know what really happened. A second proposition is that the Qur'an was not the product of Muhammad's Mecca but developed over time in a milieu of Judeo-Christian sectarian polemics. It was only at the end of the second/eighth century that the text was set down in the form we have today. This is opposed to the traditional Muslim understanding. That view places the final collection of the Qur'an in the time of the Caliph 'Uthman, less than twenty years after the Prophet's death, and says that it preserved revelations almost precisely as they had come to Muhammad. Owing to Wansbrough's dense and technical style, his books are not for beginners. There is, however, a clear overview of his position by his disciple A. Rippin (see "Literary analysis of the Qur'an, Tafsir and Sira: the methodologies of John Wansbrough," in Richard Martin [ed.], *Approaches to Islam in Religious Studies* [Tucson: University of Arizona Press, 1985], pp. 151–163). By coincidence, one of Wansbrough's former colleagues, John Burton, published another monograph on the Qur'an at the same time as Wansbrough's *Quranic Studies*. Applying his own sceptical methods to the Muslim sources, he concluded in the startling last sentence of his book that "What we have today in our hands is the *musnaf* of Muhammad" (*The Collection of the Qur'an* [Cambridge: Cambridge University Press, 1977]): that is, not the 'Uthmanic edition of Muslim tradition, but the very edition prepared by the Prophet himself. Where Wansbrough saw in the Qur'anic text the activity of later shaping, Burton saw none. Both cannot be correct, and possibly both are wrong; the methods of analysis and interpretation clearly still require refinement. F. E. Peters has outlined some of the problems which scholars have confronted in the study of Islamic origins compared with those who have explored the origins of Christianity. (See his "The quest of the historical Muhammad," *International Journal of Middle East Studies*, 23 [1991], 291–315; contrast Peters's discussion with that of a modernist Muslim scholar, Mohamed al-Nowaihi, "Towards a re-evaluation of Muhammad: Prophet and man," *Muslim World*, 60/4 [1970], 300–313, who seeks to recover the real qualities of the Prophet by shedding the fanciful and picturesque Traditions about his character but who nonetheless employs the Qur'an as an inviolate source of confirmation.)

Finally, it remains to say a word about the approach in the present work. In an introductory book such as this it is not possible to present a detailed argument on the subject of origins. Briefly, therefore, as to the Qur'an itself, I take the text as an integral and authentic document of the Prophet's day. Rather than seeing either a decisive Christian or Jewish influence mirrored in it, I have hinted that the two monotheistic traditions may be read as sub-texts to the Qur'an as a whole, which better reflects a changing pagan environment in which the inhabitants of central Arabia, pagans, Jews, and Christians, shared a common store of religious ideas for which I have used the expression "common Arabian prophetic pool." This description allows for the possible existence of an indigenous monotheistic tradition of Arabian prophets also alluded to in the Qur'an. As for all other non- or extra-Qur'anic sources, I assume that they mirror different stages and varying aspects of the developing Islamic tradition during which Judeo-Christian influence is stronger and more pervasive. In this perspective, the Qur'an is crucially the bed-rock of practically every aspect of Islamic religious culture which I have tried to demonstrate throughout the book. The Sceptics' view that our present assumptions and knowledge about the origins of Islam may indeed rest upon precarious foundations can be taken seriously. It does not follow that their alternative hypotheses need be accepted as well, a cautionary word which naturally applies to my own position as well. It is in the very nature of research that our present state of knowledge is tentative and subject to change should new source material come to light or new interpretations of the existing sources be proposed.

Glossary

'adl: the mean or balance between two extremes, hence "justice" in human affairs; a person who possesses high moral qualities necessary to hold public or juridical office; also refers to the absolute justice of Allah.

al-ahkam al-khamsah: "the five legal values *or* qualifications" applied to individual actions in Islamic law. *See haram, wajib.*

ahl al-bayt: "people of the House," referring to the immediate family of the Prophet.

ahl al-dhimmah: "communities protected by pacts." *See dhimmi.*

ahl al-'ilm: "people of knowledge." *See 'alim, 'ilm.*

'alim: In Islamic society, the word designates a scholar of the religious sciences (pl. *'ulama*). As one of the many epithets for Allah in the Qur'an, it means "(all) knowing." *See hakim.*

'amal: agreed judicial practice; for the Maliki school of law, the practice of Medina; "act" (pl. *a'mal*) in both the mundane and religious sense.

'amal (al-ta'at): act of obedience, good work.

'ammah: the common people. *See khassah.*

Ansar: "helpers." Those inhabitants of Medina who joined Muhammad's mission and supported his efforts to found a community in their midst. *See Muhajirun.*

'ard: one of several methods of transmitting a manuscript. *See mukatabah, munawalah.*

Ashraf: (pl. of *sharif*): "nobles," the descendants of the Prophet.

athar: a report transmitted by a Companion or Successor of the Prophet. *See hadith, hadith nabawi.*

aya (pl. *ayat*): "sign" or "symbol" in the sense that the created order and all it contains are identified as signs of Allah's power and mercy; also refers to a single verse in the Qur'an.

Ayatullah: "sign of Allah." The highest-ranking religious dignitary in the hierarchy of the Imami or Twelver Shi'ah.

baqa': "subsistence," the highest station in Sufism, in which the soul is said to subsist in Allah after experiencing annihilation. *See fana'.*

batin: the "inner" or esoteric aspect of a text, doctrine, or religion; also refers to an inner, spiritual state. *See zahir.*

bid'ah: "innovation" in Muslim ritual practice or beliefs for which there is no authority in the practice of the Prophet. *See sunnah, talaq al-bid'ah.*

bid'ah hasanah: "a good innovation," but one denied as valid by many jurists.

bila kayfa: "without (knowing) how," referring to the doctrine of acceptance of the anthropomorphic terms for Allah in the Qur'an, without questioning what they mean in reality.

Caliph: *see* Khalifah.

dahr: "time," the pre-Islamic notion of an impersonal, preordained fate.

da'if: *see hadith.*

dar al-harb: "abode of war," that is, territory not under Muslim sovereignty.

dar al-islam: "abode of Islam," the Islamic realms, where Islamic law prevails.

dhikr: "remembrance"; applies particularly to the Sufi group practice of invoking or mentioning the name of Allah.

dhimmi: Jews, Christians, and other non-Muslims accepted as subjects of Muslim rule who paid a special tax (*jizyah*) according to a pact or covenant with the Muslim state in return for legal protection of their lives and property.

fana': "annihilation" in Allah, one of the highest stations in Sufism. *See baqa'.*

faqih (pl. *fuqaha'*): a Muslim jurisprudent.

fara'id: rules of inheritance; the portions allotted to heirs.

fard: *see wajib.*

fard 'ayn: a duty incumbent upon an individual according to the religious law.

fard kifaya: a collective duty.

fasiq: grave sinner.

Fatihah: "opening," the first chapter of the Qur'an, which also forms part of the prayer ritual.

fatwa (pl. *fatawa*): an authoritative, advisory legal opinion issued by a specialist (*mufti*) on a point of law but which in itself had no binding force. *See fiqh.*

fiqh: "understanding"; the science of jurisprudence; Islamic religious law, which includes ritual, civil, criminal, and public law.

fitnah: "temptation" or "trial," commonly used in the sense of sedition or political upheaval.

furu' al-fiqh: "branches," positive law as distinct from its theoretical "roots" (*usul*).

ghafur: "(All) Forgiving," one of the epithets for Allah in the Qur'an. *See rahim, hakim, 'alim.*

ghaybah: "occultation" of the twelfth and last Shi'ah Imam.

hadd (pl. *hudud*): fixed punishment for a certain crime/sin as specified in the Qur'an.

hadith (pl. *ahadith*): a report or Tradition of the sayings and deeds of the

Prophet, containing his exemplary practice or *sunnah*, the second source of authority for Muslims after the Qur'an. According to its validity, a Tradition may be classed as *sahih*, "sound," *hasan*, "fair," or *da'if*, "weak." The Shi'ah use the term *hadith* for sayings of the twelve Imams, but they distinguish clearly between the sayings of the Prophet and those of the Imams. *See also athar.*

hadith nabawi (also *hadith al-nabi*): a report transmitted directly from Prophet. *See athar.*

hadith qudsi: "divine saying," a report or saying transmitted by the Prophet in which Allah speaks in the first person. These reports do not form part of the Qur'an.

hajj: pilgrimage to Mecca, held annually and prescribed for all Muslims at least once in a lifetime. A person who has performed the pilgrimage is given the honorific title of Hajj (Hajjah for a woman). *See ihram, Ka'bah.*

hakim: "(All) Wise," one of the many epithets in the Qur'an for Allah. *See 'alim.*

hal (pl. *ahwal*): a spiritual "state" which the disciple experiences on the Sufi path.

halal: lawful, allowable, contrary to *haram*.

halqah: "circle" of students studying in a mosque; applies also to meditating Sufis.

al-hamdu li'-Llah: "praise be to Allah."

hanif: the term in the Qur'an for a true "monotheist," associated with the prophet Abraham and others who lived in pagan times, but followed a belief in one God.

haram: a sacred enclave, where fighting was prohibited during four holy months during which lives were held sacrosanct, for example, the *haram* of Mecca.

haram: "prohibited," "forbidden" action according to the law. *See halal, wajib.*

hasan: *see hadith.*

hijrah: the migration or journey of Muhammad and his Companions from Mecca to Medina in 622 CE, marking the commencement of the Muslim era.

hiyal: legal devices.

hujjah: "proof" from Allah; designation for the Shi'ah Imams; also used by Sunnis to refer to certain great scholars.

hulul: incarnation.

Husayniyyat: places of Shi'ah worship or halls for the performance of religious drama commemorating the death of al-Husayn. *See ta'ziyah.*

'ibadah (pl. *'ibadat*): an act of worship, including prayer, fasting, pilgrimage; one of the two general divisions of the law. *See mu'amalat.*

Iblis: One of the Qur'anic terms for Satan, the devil.

'id al-adha: feast of the sacrifice, celebrated on the tenth of the pilgrimage month, Dhu al-Hijjah.

'id al-fitr: the Muslim festival celebrating breaking the fast of Ramadan.

'iddah: the "waiting period" of a woman after the termination of marriage or death of her husband.

ihram: the Meccan pilgrim's state of ritual purity; the special two-piece white cloth worn by pilgrims.

ihsan: perfection (of belief, faith).

ijazah: a document given by a teacher to a student certifying that he or she is capable of teaching and transmitting a particular work of his or her master.

ijma: "consensus" in Islamic jurisprudence, generally meaning the agreement of legal scholars on a point of law determined explicitly by the Qur'an and the Sunnah.

ijtihad: "effort," "exerting oneself"; the exercise of independent judgment in Islamic law so as to arrive at a fresh interpretation of a point at issue; often used in the sense of *qiyas*, reasoning by analogy. *See mujtahid.*

illah: the common denominator, or "effective cause" shared between two cases in the law.

ilm: "knowledge," "learning," "science"; especially theoretical knowledge of the religious sciences; truths derived from the Qur'an and prophetic Traditions. *See talab al-ilm.*

Imam: "one who stands before"; a leader, especially in prayer and thus by extension the supreme leader of the Muslim community (*see khalifah*); legitimate successor of the Prophet, used by the Shi'ah for 'Ali and his descendants.

imamah: political and/or religious leadership; office of the Imam.

iman: belief, faith.

in sha'a Allah: "If Allah wills."

iqrar (bi'l-lisan): verbal confession of one's faith (in Allah and his Messenger). *See tasdiq.*

islah: reform.

islam: in the religious sense, "the willing and active recognition of and submission to the Command of the One, Allah."

isnad: chain of transmitters or authorities appended to a *hadith* whose names indicate the degree of its validity. *See matn.*

isra': in Islamic tradition, this refers to the night journey by Muhammad from Mecca to Jerusalem. *See mi'raj.*

istihsan: a discretionary decision of "approval" on a point of law, given by a judge where the public interest may be concerned.

istislah: public welfare. *See maslahah.*

ittihad: unitive fusion with Allah.

iwan: rectangular arched façade of a vaulted open hall in a mosque.

jahiliyyah: "time of ignorance," a Qur'anic term, applied by Muslim theologians to the period of paganism prior to the advent of Islam; in modern usage, the term has been applied by radical Muslims to other Muslims whom they regard as having gone astray from the true path, and are therefore unbelievers.

jami: congregational mosque. *See masjid.*

jihad: "striving," "exertion," usually translated as holy war against infidels;

also the effort directed toward overcoming one's inner passions and imperfections of the soul (more specifically called *jihad al-nafs*).

jizyah: see dhimmi.

Ka'bah: the cube-shaped shrine, of pre-Islamic origin, located in the center of the great mosque in Mecca. It is the focal point of Muslims' daily prayers and the annual pilgrimage.

kaffarah: religious expiation.

kafir (pl. *kuffar*): "infidel," "unbeliever"; in its original sense "one who is ungrateful," and by extension, one who is ungrateful for the bounties and mercies of Allah; can also apply to a Muslim whose beliefs or practices are judged to go beyond the permitted limits of variation. *See mu'min.*

kalam: "word"; the term used for the discipline of "dialectical theology," which sought to defend by rational argument Muslim beliefs and provide proofs for many subjects such as the unity of Allah, his attributes, human free will and predetermination.

kanun: state or administrative law.

karamah (pl. *karamat*): "miracle" attributed to the Prophet or a holy person.

kasb (also *iktisab*): the theological doctrine that humans "aquire" their actions from Allah, are therefore responsible for committing them, and can be punished or rewarded accordingly in the afterlife.

Khalifah: "Successor" of the Prophet and head of the Muslim community. *See* Imam.

khanqah: Persian word for a Sufi lodge. *See zawiyah.*

khassah: "elect," "elite." *See 'ammah.*

khatib: see khutbah.

khilafah: office of the Caliphate.

khirqah: patched garment of a Sufi.

al-khulafa' al-rashidun: The Rightly Guided Caliphs, being the first four successors of Muhammad (Abu Bakr, 'Umar, 'Uthman, and 'Ali) to lead the Muslim community. All are accepted by the Sunnis as legitimate leaders; only 'Ali is regarded as legitimate by the Shi'ah.

khulud: "eternity," understood in the pre-Islamic Arab era as the time between birth and death.

khutbah: sermon delivered by the *khatib* in the mosque at the Friday congregational prayer.

kufr: unbelief. *See kafir.*

laylat al-qadar: "the night of power," one of the odd-numbered of the last ten nights of Ramadan when the Qur'an is said to have been first revealed. *See sawm, 'id al-fitr.*

madhhab (pl. *madhahib*): "school" of Muslim religious law; the four Sunni schools are the Maliki, Hanafi, Shafi'i, and Hanbali.

madrasah: in medieval times a college for the study and teaching of the law, often but not necessarily attached to a mosque.

Mahdi: also called *al-Muntazar*, the Expected, Awaited One; in Shi'ah belief, the Twelfth Imam, who is at present hidden but whose return will herald the end of time and the immanence of the Day of Judgment.

mahr: dowry or nuptial gift promised by a prospective husband in a marriage contract.

makruh: "reprehensible" action. *See al-ahkam al-khamsah.*

makruh tahrimi: a reprehensible action, utterly discouraged, but where evidence for its total prohibition is uncertain.

mandub: "commendable" action. *See al-ahkam al-khamsah.*

maqam: "station" on the Sufi path.

ma'rifah: gnosis; experiential knowledge of Allah; mystical knowledge.

masjid: "place of prostration"; a mosque for worship and a center of communal affairs.

maslahah (also *istislah*): "public welfare."

matn: the "body" or substance of a report or *hadith*. *See isnad.*

mawali (s. *mawla*): "clients" or "freedmen," non-Arab converts to Islam in the early Islamic centuries. *Mawla* can also refer to a patron or master, including Allah in this sense as well.

mawdu'at: forged Traditions. *See hadith.*

mawla: *see mawali.*

mawlid: celebration of the Prophet's birthday or the birthdays of Sufi holy persons.

mazalim (pl. of *mazlamah*): the court of complaints where inquiries were conducted, originally by the Caliph in person and later by his officials, into charges brought against government officials.

mihrab: arched concave niche in a mosque, indicating the direction toward Mecca.

minarah: tower, minaret of a mosque.

minbar: pulpit-like structure in a mosque.

mi'raj: "ascension," referring in tradition to the ascent of Muhammad to heaven and into the divine presence. *See isra'.*

mu'abbirun: experts in dream interpretation.

mu'adhdhin: one who calls the faithful to prayer.

mu'amalat: one of the two broad divisions of the law dealing with social relations. *See 'ibadah.*

mubah: "permissible" action, of neutral legal value. *See al-ahkam al-khamsah.*

mudhakkirun: popular preachers. *See qussas.*

mufti: a specialist in Islamic law competent to issue a *fatwa*. Usually a private person whose advice was sought by others owing to the *mufti's* scholarly reputation and piety.

Muhajirun: Muslims who accompanied Muhammad on his migration from Mecca to Medina. *See Ansar.*

muhtasib: market inspector, charged with the detection of false weights and the punishment of public acts of immorality; his task was defined as "commanding the good and preventing evil."

mujaddid: the traditional renewer of religion toward the end of each century.

mujtahid (pl. *mujtahidun*): a jurist qualified to give an independent opinion on the law. Today, the term is used almost exclusively in Imami Shi'ism. *See ijtihad.*

mukallaf: a person of full legal responsibility.

mukatabah: one of several methods of transmitting a manuscript from teacher to student. *See munawalah, 'ard.*

mu'min (pl. *mu'minun*): "believer" in one God, Allah, and one who follows the injunctions of Islam. *See kafir.*

munafiq (pl. *munafiqun*): a hypocrite, one who conceals his true religious beliefs.

munawalah: one of several methods of transmitting a manuscript. *See mukatabah, 'ard.*

muqallad: a jurist who employs *taqlid*, that is, who relies upon the teachings of a master or of a school without question and without employing independent investigation of the reasons for these teachings. *Taqlid al-mayyit*: reliance upon the teachings of deceased religious leaders alone; *marja' al-taqlid*: "source for imitation": a leading religious figure in Shi'ah Islam.

murid: a disciple in a Sufi brotherhood.

mursal: a Tradition lacking a link in the chain of authorities.

murshid: *see pir.*

murtadd: an apostate from Islam.

muruwwah: a central notion of the pre-Islamic value system, understood to mean "virtue" or "manliness," and which included the qualities of loyalty, courage, and hospitality.

musannaf: a collection of Traditions arranged according to subject matter. *See musnad.*

mushrik (pl. *mushrikun*): polytheist, idolater; one who commits the cardinal sin of *shirk*, the association or worship of something other than Allah; one who holds that there are realities independent of Allah.

muslim (pl. *muslimun*): in the religious sense, "one who surrenders himself or herself (to Allah)."

musnad: a collection of Traditions arranged according to their chain of authorities (*isnad*). *See musannaf.*

mut'ah: Shi'ah institution of temporary marriage.

mutakallim: "dialectical theologian." *See kalam.*

mutawatir: a Tradition which has been handed down by a number of different channels of transmitters or authorities, hence supposedly ruling out the possibility of its having been forged.

nabi: "prophet." *See rasul.*

nafs: "soul." Stages of the soul beginning with repentance are *al-ammarah, al-lawwamah, al-mutma'innah.*

nass: the Shi'ah doctrine that each Imam was "designated" by his predecessor, the first Imam, 'Ali, having been designated by Allah through the Prophet.

nawruz: the Persian New Year.

nikah: marriage.

pir: Persian word for spiritual master.

qadar: "power" understood both in the sense of man's free will to act by his own capacity (*qudrah*) and Allah's power over all his creation.

qadi (pl. *qudah*): a judge, appointed by the ruler to settle disputes according to the *shari'ah*.

qiblah: the direction toward Mecca which one faces at prayer.

qiyas: reasoning by analogy in Islamic jurisprudence.

qudrah: see *qadar*.

qur'an: literally, "recitation"; the name given to Muslim scripture.

qussas: "story-tellers" who, in the early days of the Muslim community, transmitted religious knowledge in a popular manner to the general public. *See mudhakkirun*.

qutb: "pole," "axis"; in Sufism, the head of an invisible hierarchy of saints upon whom depends the proper order of the universe.

rahim: "(All) Merciful," one of the many epithets for Allah in the Qur'an. *See ghafur, hakim, 'alim*.

Ramadan: see *sawm*.

rasul: "messenger" (of Allah), one of the designations for the Prophet (*nabi*) Muhammad.

ra'y: a judge's decision based upon his own discretion.

ridwan: Allah's pleasure.

rihlah: "journey" for the purpose of pilgrimage to Mecca, or to study and gather knowledge from scholars elseswhere. *See talab al-'ilm*.

sadaqah: non-obligatory alms.

Sahabah: the Companions of the Prophet. *See Tabi'un*.

sahih: "sound," valid, legally effective, referring to the highest quality of Traditions, deemed absolutely reliable.

sahn: courtyard of a mosque.

salaf: "pious ancestors," referring to the earliest generations of Muslim religious scholars.

salat: canonical prayer, obligatory for Muslims five times daily.

sawm (or *siyam*): fasting, prescribed during the month of Ramadan. *See 'id al-fitr*.

shahadah: "witnessing." The Muslim profession of faith expressed in the words "There is no god but Allah and Muhammad is the Messenger of Allah."

shari'ah: the will of Allah, as expressed in the Qur'an and the *sunnah* of the

Prophet; the sacred law of Islam.

sharif (pl. *shurafa'*): persons claiming descent from the Prophet.

shaykh: an elder, chief, teacher, a learned, pious man, a spiritual master.

Shi'at Ali: "party of Ali," the Shi'ah.

shirk: see mushrik.

shura: consultation, specifically between a ruler and his chief advisers.

silsilah: Sufi chain of spiritual authority.

Sufi: "wearer of wool (*suf*)"; a Muslim mystic.

sunnah: "trodden path." Tribal custom of pre-Islamic Arabs; also refers to Allah in the sense of his commands and prohibitions. It is used in Islamic law to mean the normative practice of the Prophet Muhammad, the authoritative example of the way a Muslim should live. *See hadith.*

surah: a chapter division of the Qur'an, of which there are 114.

Tabi'un: the Successors to the Prophet's Companions; the "second" generation of Muslims after the Prophet. *See Sahabah.*

tafwid: possible stipulation in a marriage contract that the wife may terminate the union herself.

takfir: the action of declaring someone an unbeliever. *See kafir.*

takhayyur: selection of a particular position from a legal school other than the one to which a jurist belongs.

talab al-'ilm: "quest for knowledge," especially religious knowledge in its broadest sense. *See 'ilm, rihlah.*

talaq: legal divorce.

talaq al-bid'ah: the irrevocable triple divorce formula which jurists had traditionally regarded as an innovation but nevertheless supported as valid.

talfiq: the legal device of combining together the views of different schools or of individual scholars.

taqiyah: precautionary dissimulation; in Shi'ah practice, concealing one's true religious beliefs for fear of persecution.

taqlid: see muqallad.

tariqah: the Sufi way or path; a Sufi brotherhood.

tasawwuf: Arabic term for Sufism.

tasdiq (bi'l-qalb): the silent assent to one's belief (in Allah and his Messenger) in the heart. *See iqrar.*

tasmiyah: uttering the expression "In the name of Allah."

tawbah: referring either to a person's "turning" toward Allah in repentance for his or her sins or Allah's "turning" toward his servant in compassionate acceptance.

tawhid: the doctrine of Allah's oneness, uniqueness.

ta'wil: illumination of the inner or esoteric meaning of a text.

ta'ziyah: the Shi'ah performance of a drama commemorating the martyr's death of al-Husayn.

ummah: the world-wide Muslim community; also called *ummat al-islam*.

'umrah: a form of pilgrimage to Mecca outside the pilgrimage season during

which many of the essential pilrimage rituals are not performed.

'urf: "custom."

usul al-fiqh: the "roots" or theoretical bases of Islamic law.

wahdat al-shuhud: unity of vision of Allah.

wahdat al-wujud: unity of being, ontological union with Allah.

wajib: "obligatory" action. Also called *fard*. *See al-ahkam al-khamsah*.

wali Allah (pl. *awliya' Allah*): "friend of Allah" or Sufi holy person, who enjoys a particular relationship (*wilayah*) with Allah.

waqf (pl. *awqaf*): pious foundation or endowment; the income from a property designated by the founder for a specific religious purpose such as the building of a school or mosque or other charity.

wasiyah: "testamentary bequest."

wilayah: *see wali Allah*.

yawm al-qiyamah: the Day of Resurrection.

zahid: an ascetic. *See zuhd*.

zahir: "outward" or "manifest"; the exoteric or literal aspect of a text or doctrine. *See batin*.

zakat: obligatory alms or "purification tax" paid by Muslims, charged upon certain categories of property and assigned to certain specified purposes of benefit to the Muslim community.

zandaqah: free-thinking or heretical beliefs.

zawiyah: Sufi meeting place, lodge. *See khanqah*.

zuhd: asceticism. *See zahid*.

Notes

I "THERE IS NO GOD BUT ALLAH. . ."

1. A. J. Arberry, *The Seven Odes* (London: George Allen & Unwin, 1957), pp. 115–116.
2. Helmer Ringgren, *Studies in Arabian Fatalism* (Wiesbaden: Harrassowitz, 1955), pp. 33–34.
3. *The Book of Idols: Being a Translation from the Arabic of the Kitab al-Asnam by Hisham ibn al-Kalbi*, trans. Nabih Amin Faris (Princeton: Princeton University Press, 1952). On divining arrows, see pp. 23, 41; on avenging murder, p. 41; on violation of sanctity of idol, p. 52.
4. *The Life of Muhammad: A Translation of Ibn Ishaq's Sirat Rasul Allah*, trans. Alfred Guillaume (Oxford: Oxford University Press, 1955), pp. 104–106.
5. Ibid., p. 119.
6. Ibid.
7. R. B. Serjeant, "The *sunnah jami'ah*, pacts with the Yathrib Jews, and the *tahrim* of Yathrib: analysis and translation of the documents comprised in the so-called 'Constitution of Medina,'" *Bulletin of the School of Oriental and African Studies*, 41 (1978), 1–42, especially at pp. 33 and 35.
8. *The Life of Muhammad*, p. 233.
9. Ibid., p. 212.
10. Ibid., p. 651.
11. Ibid., p. 683.
12. Ibid., pp. 71–72.
13. Ibid., pp. 181–186.
14. Wali al-Din Muhammad b. 'Abdallah al-Khatib al-Tabrizi, *Mishkat al-masabih*, trans. James Robson (Lahore: Muhammad Ashraf, reprint, 1990), 1: 465.
15. Ibid., 1: 458.
16. Especially *surah*s 7, 10, 11, and 26.
17. Toshihiko Izutsu, *Ethico-Religious Concepts in the Qur'an* (Montreal: McGill University Press, 1966). Chapter 5 deals with the Islamization of old Arab virtues.
18. Ibid., p. 76.

2 TRADITION IN THE MAKING

1. Modern Spain and Portugal. The region in medieval Islamic times was known as al-Andalus, the term used throughout this book to refer to the area of Muslim presence in the peninsula.

2. See the Excursus on Islamic Origins above.

3. *Al-Muwatta of Imam Malik ibn Anas: The First Formulation of Islamic Law*, trans. Aisha Abdurrahman Bewley (London: Kegan Paul International, 1989), p. 422.

4. *The Life of Muhammad*, pp. 635ff.

5. *Sunan Abi Da'ud*, edition compiled by Muhammad Muhyi al-Din 'Abd al-Hamid (Beirut: Dar Ihya' al-Turath al-'Arabi, n.d.), *hadith* no. 3641. The *dinar* and *dirham* were kinds of currency, the former being a gold coin, the latter silver.

6. The *Muwatta'* of Malik, the recension of al-Shaybani, ed. 'Abd al-Wahhab 'Abd al-Latif (Cairo: Al-Maktabat al-'Ilmiyyah, 1979), *hadith* nos. 555, p. 186, and 883, p. 314.

7. In his treatise on story-tellers, Ibn al-Jawzi (d. 597/1200) defines the function of each as follows: the *qass* tells stories of the past; the *mudhakkir* informs people of Allah's blessings and urges them to render their thanks to him; the *wa'iz* instills a pious awe in people that softens the heart. See Ibn al-Jawzi's *Kitab al-qussas wa'l-mudhakkirin*, ed. and trans. Merlin Swartz (Beirut: Dar al-Machreq, 1986), pp. 96–98.

8. Ibid., p. 181.

9. Ibid., p. 109 English, p. 21 Arabic. The need to make such an observation suggests that Ibn Jawzi was not happy with the state of learning of story-tellers in his day.

10. Ibid., p. 117 English, p. 33 Arabic (my translation). Tamim was a Christian convert from Hebron in Palestine.

11. Ibid., p. 134 English, p. 51 Arabic (my translation).

12. Hamid Enayat, *Modern Islamic Political Thought* (London: Macmillan, 1982), p.19.

13. *Sunan Abi Da'ud*, hadith no. 3592.

14. This and the following paragraphs are based upon the edition, study, and translation of Ibn Waddah's work *Kitab al-bida'* (*Tratado contra las innovaciones*) by M. I. Fierro (Madrid: CSIC, 1988). See the same author's "The treatises against innovations (*kutub al-bida'*)," *Der Islam*, 69/2 (1992), 204–246.

15. See N. J. G. Kaptein, *Muhammad's Birthday Festival* (Leiden: E. J. Brill, 1993).

16. Ibid., p. 63.

17. Jean-Marie Gaudeul, *Encounters and Clashes: Islam and Christianity in History* (2 vols., Rome: Pontificio Istituto di Studi Arabi e Islamici, 1984), II:18. The quotations here and in the preceding paragraphs are taken from this excellent anthology.

18. On this subject see the article from which these details are taken by

David Thomas, "Two Muslim–Christian debates from the early Shi'ite tradition," *Journal of Semitic Studies*, 33/1 (1988), 53–80. On a similar theme of the camel and ass riders see Suliman Bashear, "Riding beasts on divine missions: an examination of the ass and camel traditions," *Journal of Semitic Studies*, 37/1 (1991), 37–75.

19. The complete epistle of Jahiz has been translated into French by I. S. Allouche, "Un traité de polémique Christiano-Musulmane au 9ᵉ siècle," *Hesperis* (1939), 123–155.
20. Tabrizi, *Mishkat*, I: 11.
21. Ibid., I: 20.

3 DIVINE WILL AND THE LAW

1. See Bernard Weiss, "Covenant and law in Islam," in *Religion and Law: Biblical-Judaic and Islamic Perspectives*, ed. E. Firmage, B. Weiss, and J. Welch (Winona Lake: Eisenbrauns, 1990).
2. Ibn Khallikan, *Dictionary*, trans. Mac Guckin de Slane (Paris: Oriental Translation Fund of Great Britain and Ireland, 1868), III: 555–565.
3. Ibid., II: 545–551.
4. Ibid., II: 569–574.
5. Trans. Majid Khadduri, *Islamic Jurisprudence: Shafi'i's Risala* (Baltimore: The Johns Hopkins Press, 1961).
6. Ibid., p. 283.
7. Tabrizi, *Mishkat*, I: 793.
8. Cited in Mohammad Hashim Kamali, *Principles of Islamic Jurisprudence* (Cambridge: Islamic Texts Society, 1992), p. 329.
9. Tabrizi, *Mishkat*, II: 1053.
10. *Sahih Muslim*, trans. 'Abdul Hamid Siddiqi (4 vols., Lahore: Sh. Muhammad Ashraf, 1979), *K. al-libas*, no. 2.
11. Tabrizi, *Mishkat*, I: 771.
12. Ibid., I: 762.
13. Cited in Kamali, *Islamic Jurisprudence*, p. 178.
14. Khadduri, *Shafi'i's Risalah*, p. 205.
15. See the articles by W. B. Hallaq, "On the origins of the controversy about the existence of *mujtahids* and the gate of *ijtihad*," *Studia Islamica* (1986), 129–141 and "Was the gate of *ijtihad* closed?," *International Journal of Middle East Studies*, 16 (1984), 3–41.
16. On this concept, see the discussion in M. Khalid Masud's *Islamic Legal Philosophy* (Islamabad: Islamic Research Institute, 1977), pp. 149–172.
17. George Makdisi, *The Rise of Colleges: Institutions of Learning in Islam and the West* (Edinburgh: Edinburgh University Press, 1981), p. 277.
18. *Watha'iq fi ahkam quda' ahl al-dhimmah fi'al-andalus, mustakhrajah min makhtut al-ahkam al-kubra li'l-qadi Abi al-Asbagh 'Isa b. Sahl*, ed. Muhammad 'Abd al-Wahhab Khallaf (Cairo, 1980), p. 70.
19. Aharon Layish, "The *fatwa* as an instrument of the Islamization of a

tribal society in process of sedentarization," *Bulletin of the School of Oriental and African Studies*, 54/3 (1991), 449–459.

20. Mahmud Shaltut, *al-Fatawa* (Cairo, 1983).
21. On Islamic ritual in general, see William Graham, "Islam in the mirror of ritual," in *Islam's Understanding of Itself*, ed. R. Hovannisian and Speros Vryonis (Malibu, Calif.: Undena Publications, 1983), pp. 53–71.
22. Tabrizi, *Mishkat*, I:115–116.
23. *The Translation of the Meanings of Sahih al-Bukhari*, trans. Muhammad Muhsin Khan (Chicago: Kazi Publications, 1976), I: 102, Book of ablutions.
24. *Al-Muwatta of Imam Malik ibn Anas*, trans. Aisha Abdurrahman Bewley (London: Kegan Paul International, 1989), p. 49.
25. Tabrizi, *Mishkat*, I: 128.
26. *Bukhari*, I: 334, Book of prayer.
27. *Al-Muwatta of Imam Malik*, p. 420.
28. Tabrizi, *Mishkat*, I: 372.
29. *Bukhari*, II: 288, Book of zakat.
30. Tabrizi, *Mishkat*, I: 417.
31. Ibid.
32. *Al-Muwatta of Imam Malik*, p. 42.
33. Ibid., p. 121.
34. Tabrizi, *Mishkat*, I: 538.
35. *The Ma'alim al-Qurba fi Ahkam al-Hisba of Ibn al-Ukhuwwa*, ed. Reuben Levy (London: Luzac, 1938), pp. 31, 33.
36. Emilio Garcia Gomez and E. Levi Provençal, *Sevilla a comienzo del siglo XII: el tratado de Ibn Abdun* (Seville, 1981), paragraph 154.
37. A. L. Udovitch, "Commercial techniques in early medieval Islamic trade," in D. S. Richards (ed.), *Islam and the Trade of Asia* (Oxford: Bruno Cassirer, 1970), p. 62.
38. J. Schacht, *Introduction to Islamic Law* (Oxford: Clarendon Press, 1964), p. 130.

4 THEOLOGY: FAITH, JUSTICE, AND LAST THINGS

1. Toshihiko Izutsu, *The Concept of Belief in Islamic Theology* (Tokyo: The Keio Institute of Cultural and Linguistic Studies, 1965), p. 42, citing the jurist al-Malati (d. 377/987). My italics.
2. Tabrizi, *Mishkat*, I: 19.
3. Ibid., I: 11.
4. Izutsu, *Belief*, p. 164, citing al-Malati.
5. J. A. Williams, *Islam* (New York: Washington Square Press, 1963), pp. 163–164 (quotation modified).
6. A. J. Wensinck, *The Muslim Creed* (London: Frank Cass, 1965), p. 124.
7. *Al-Kashshaf* (Beirut, n.d.), on Chapter of the Cow, verses 2–4.
8. On his work the *Kitab al-Iman* (*The Book of Faith*) see Wilferd Madelung's

"Early Sunni doctrine concerning faith," *Studia Islamica*, 32 (1970), 233–254.

9. Ibn Khallikan, *Dictionary*, i: 370–373.

10. See Julian Obermann, "Political theology in early Islam: Hasan al-Basri's treatise on Qadar," *Journal of the American Oriental Society*, 55 (1955), 138–162; Michael Schwartz, "The letter of al-Hasan al-Basri," *Oriens*, 20 (1967), 15–30.

11. A. Rippin and J. Knappert (eds.), *Textural Sources for the Study of Islam* (Manchester: Manchester University Press, 1986), p. 117.

12. See W. M. Watt, *Formative Period of Islamic Thought* (Edinburgh: Edinburgh University Press, 1973), pp. 209–224 for a survey of some of these problems. A recent view is that of S. Strumsa in *Jerusalim Studies in Arabic and Islam*, 13 (1990), 265–293.

13. Ralph Lerner and Muhsin Mahdi (eds.), *Medieval Political Philosophy* (New York: Macmillan [The Free Press], 1963), p. 27.

14. Michael Cook, "The origins of *kalam*," *Bulletin of the School of Oriental and African Studies*, 43 (1980), 32–43, at p. 37; the quotation above has been altered slightly from the translation in Cook's text. The statement is taken from an anti-Qadarite tract attributed to al-Hasan b. Muhammad al-Hanafiyyah (d. ca. 100/718). On the same subject but from a contrasting viewpoint to Cook's, see Joseph van Ess, "The beginnings of Islamic theology," in J. E. Murdoch and E. D. Sylla (eds.), *The Cultural Context of Medieval Learning* (Dordrecht/Boston: Reidel, 1975), pp. 87–111.

15. Abu 'l-Hasan al-Ash'ari, *Maqalat al-islamiyyin wa' ikhtilaf al-musallin*, ed. Hellmut Ritter, 3rd. ed. (Wiesbaden: Franz Steiner Verlag, 1980), pp. 155–156.

16. al-Ash'ari, *Maqalat*, p. 234.

17. Ibn Khallikan, *Dictionary*, ii: 227–228.

18. R. McCarthy, *Theology of al-Ash'ari* (Beirut: Imprimerie Catholique, 1953), pp. 120–121, 133–134.

19. Al-Ash'ari, *The Elucidation of Islam's Foundations*, trans. Walter Klein (New Haven: American Oriental Society, 1940), p. 89.

20. George Makdisi (ed. and trans.), *Ibn Qudama's Censure of Speculative Theology* (London: Luzac, 1962), p. 22. My italics.

21. Al-Ash'ari, *Elucidation*, p. 80.

22. Ibid., p. 102, translation modified slightly.

23. Ibid., p. 109.

24. McCarthy, *Theology*, chapters 5 and 6 for al-Ash'ari's translated text.

25. Ibn Khaldun, *The Muqaddimah: An Introduction to History*, trans. Franz Rosenthal (New York: Pantheon Books, 1953), iii: 53.

26. Ibn Khallikan, *Dictionary*, ii: 621–624.

27. See W. M. Watt (trans.), *The Faith and Practice of al-Ghazali* (London: George Allen & Unwin, 1953). Watt has also devoted a monograph to al-Ghazali's life and thought in his *Muslim Intellectual* (Edinburgh: Edinburgh University Press, 1963).

28. See I. R. Netton, *Allah Transcendent* (London: Routledge, 1989).

29. See chapter 1 of al-Ghazali's *Tahafut al-falasifah (Incoherence of the Philosophers)*, trans. Sabih Ahmad Kamali (Lahore: Muhammad Ashraf, 1958).

30. Ibid., chapter 13.

31. Ibid., chapter 20, p. 229 (with modification).

32. Ibid., p. 249.

33. Iysa A. Bello, *The Medieval Islamic Controversy between Philosophy and Orthodoxy: Ijma' and Ta'wil in the Conflict between al-Ghazali and Ibn Rushd* (Leiden: E. J. Brill, 1989).

34. Translated by S. van den Bergh (Cambridge: E. J. W. Gibb Memorial Trust, 1987 [1954]).

35. Al-Ghazali, *The Remembrance of Death and the Afterlife*, trans. T. J. Winter (Cambridge: Islamic Texts Society, 1989). See also the excellent study by Jane I. Smith and Yvonne Y. Haddad, *The Islamic Understanding of Death and Resurrection* (Albany: State University of New York Press, 1981).

36. Al-Ghazali, *Remembrance*, p. 179.

37. Ibid., p. 183.

38. Ibid., p. 180.

39. Al-Ash'ari, *Kitab shajarat al-yaqin*, ed. and trans. Concepción Castillo Castillo (Madrid: Instituto Hispano-Arabe de Cultura, 1987), pp. 67–70.

40. Al-Ghazali, *Remembrance*, p. 210 (with modification).

41. Ibid., pp. 250–251.

5 THE WAY OF THE SUFI

1. Lenn Evan Goodman, *Ibn Tufayl's Hayy b. Yazqan* (New York: Twaine Publishers, 1972). The literal meaning of the name in Arabic approximates "Living Being son of Vigilant." Goodman's rendering is "Life Awareson." The introduction and notes accompanying his translation are valuable guides to this unique work.

2. Ibid., p. 142.

3. Ibid., p. 153.

4. Ibid., p. 156.

5. Ibid., p. 160.

6. Ibn Tufayl's relationship to his philosopher predecessors is lucidly discussed by Muhsin Mahdi, "Philosophical literature," in *Religion, Learning and Science in the Abbasid Period* (Cambridge: Cambridge University Press, 1990), pp. 76–105.

7. On these and other stories see Farid al-Din Attar, *Muslim Saints and Mystics*, trans. A. J. Arberry (London: Penguin Arkana, 1990 [1966]). On the nature of the early ascetic movement, see Tor Andrae, *In the Garden of Myrtles* (Albany: State University of New York Press, 1987 [1947]).

8. 'Ali b. 'Uthman al-Hujwiri, *The* Kashf al-mahjub, *the Oldest Persian Treatise on Sufism by al-Hujwiri*, trans. Reynold Nicholson (London:

Luzac, 1911), pp. 33–44, especially at p. 42.

9. Ibid., 48.

10. Abu Bakr Siraj ed-Din, "The nature and origin of Sufism," in *Islamic Spirituality: Foundations*, ed. Seyyed Hossein Nasr (London: SCM Press, 1989), pp. 225–226.

11. See al-Hujwiri, pp. 329, 316, 325, 303 for the examples of each of these rituals.

12. A. J. Arberry, *The Doctrine of the Sufis* (Cambridge: Cambridge University Press, 1935), p. 92.

13. Al-Hujwiri, p. 181.

14. See *Al-Ghazali's Book of Fear and Hope*, trans. William McKane (Leiden: E. J. Brill, 1965).

15. Ibid., p. 245.

16. See Annemarie Schimmel, *And Muhammad is his Messenger* (Chapel Hill: University of North Carolina Press, 1985), especially chapter 9.

17. Al-Hujwiri, p. 152.

18. English translation by Khalil Semaan entitled *Murder in Baghdad* (Leiden: E. J. Brill, 1972). Al-Hallaj's life has also inspired a modern dramatic narrative in English by Herbert Mason, *Death of al-Hallaj* (Notre Dame: Notre Dame University Press, 1979).

19. The quotations in these two paragraphs are taken from R. Nicholson, *The Mystics of Islam* (London: Routledge & Kegan Paul, 1970 [1914]), pp. 157, 159.

20. George Makdisi, "The Hanbali school and Sufism," *Humaniora Islamica*, 2 (1974), 61–72.

21. See the excellent study by G. Bowering, *The Mystical Vision of Existence in Classical Islam: The Qur'anic Hermeneutics of the Sufi Sahl at-Tustari* (Berlin: Walter de Gruyter, 1980). On the subject of these commentaries in general see Abdurrahman Habil, "Traditional esoteric commentaries on the Qur'an," in *Islamic Spirituality: Foundations*, ed. Seyyed Hossein Nasr (London: SCM Press, 1989), pp. 24–47.

22. See Muhammad Abul Quasem, *The Recitation and Interpretation of the Qur'an: Al-Ghazzali's Theory* (London: Kegan Paul International, 1982).

23. See the translation of al-Ghazali's *Mishkat al-anwar (The Niche for Lights)* by W. H. T. Gairdner (Lahore: Muhammad Ashraf, reprint 1952 [1924]). The authenticity of the final part of this work has been questioned.

24. Al-Hujwiri, pp. 212–213.

25. Wilferd Madelung, "Sufism and the Karramiyya," in his *Religious Trends in Early Islamic Iran* (Albany: State University of New York Press), 39–53.

26. P. M. Currie, *The Shrine and Cult of Mu'in al-Din Chishti of Ajmer* (Delhi: Oxford University Press, 1989).

27. See Victor Danner, "The Shadhiliyyah and North African Sufism," in *Islamic Spirituality: Manifestations*, ed. S. H. Nasr (London: SCM Press, 1991), pp. 26–48.

28. *Ibn Ata'Allah, The Book of Wisdom*, translation and introduction by Victor Danner (London: SPCK, 1979), pp. 80, 140–141.
29. Ibid., p. 70.
30. Ibid., p. 121.
31. *Ibn Abbad of Ronda: Letters on the Sufi Path*, translation and introduction by John Renard (New York: Paulist Press, 1986), pp. 157, 73.
32. See p. 139 above.
33. This work has been translated by R. W. J. Austin, *Ibn al-'Arabi: The Bezels of Wisdom* (New York: Paulist Press, 1981).
34. A study of a contemporary offshoot of the Shadhiliyyah "chain" is the important biography of the Algerian mystic Shaykh Ahmad al-'Alawi (d. 1934) by Martin Lings, *A Moslem Saint of the Twentieth Century* (London: George Allen & Unwin, 1961).
35. See J. A. Boyle's translation of his epic mystical poem, *The Ilahi-nama or Book of God of Farid al-Din Attar* (Manchester: Manchester University Press, 1976).
36. Umar ibn al-Farid, *The Mystical Poems*, trans. A. J. Arberry (London: Emery Walker, 1956).
37. *Mystical Poems of Rumi*, trans. A. J. Arberry (Chicago: Chicago University Press, 1968).
38. *The City of the Heart: Yunus Emre's Verses of Wisdom and Love*, trans. Suha Faiz (Shaftesbury, Dorset: Element Books, 1992).

6 THE WAY OF THE IMAMS

1. Tabrizi, *Mishkat*, II: 1343.
2. Martin J. McDermott's *The Theology of al-Shaikh al-Mufid* (Beirut: Dar al-Machreq, 1978) also contains a chapter each on Ibn Babawayhi and al-Sharif al-Murtada.
3. *Kitab al-Irshad (The Book of Guidance into the Lives of the Twelve Imams) by Shaykh al-Mufid*, trans. I. K. A. Howard (London: The Muhammadi Trust, 1981), p. 124.
4. Ibid., pp. 138–139.
5. *The Life of Muhammad*, pp. 79–81.
6. *Kitab al-Irshad*, p. 254.
7. Ibid., p. 263.
8. Ibid., pp. 3–6.
9. *Kitab al-Irshad*, pp. 299–372; the event may also be followed in I. K. A. Howard's translation of volume XIX of *The History of al-Tabari: The Caliphate of Yazid b. Mu'awiyah* (Albany: State University of New York Press, 1990). An absorbing analysis of the tradition of al-Husayn's martyrdom in Shi'ah thought is Mahmoud Ayoub's *Redemptive Suffering in Islam* (The Hague: Mouton, 1978).
10. *Al-Tabari: Caliphate of Yazid*, p. 73.
11. Ibid., p. 90.

12. Ibid., p. 96.

13. Ibid.

14. Cited in Ayoub, *Redemptive Suffering*, p. 132.

15. Ibid., chapter 5.

16. The account, a Persian *ta'ziyah* based upon oral tradition, has been translated by Lewis Pelly, *The Miracle Play of Hasan and Husayn* (2 vols., London: W. H. Allen, 1879), II: 86 (republished, 1970 by Gregg International Publishers, Farnborough). See also Werner Ende's "The flagellations of Muharram and the Shi'ite Ulama,'" *Der Islam*, 55 (1978), 19–36.

17. *The Miracle Play of Hasan and Husayn*, p. 347.

18. Ibid., p. 348.

19. *Kitab al-Irshad*, p. 296.

20. "An-Nawbakhti. Les Sectes si'ites," *Revue de l'Histoire des Religions*, 154 (1958), 146. The French translation of this important early Shi'ah text by Abu Muhammad al-Hasan b. Musa al-Nawbakhti (d. 300–310/912–922) is by M. J. Mashkur. The complete translation is found in parts 153 (1958), 68–78, 176–214; 154 (1958), 67–95, 146–172; 155 (1959), 63–78.

21. *Kitab al-Irshad*, p. 525. See also the translation by A. A. Sachedina of al-Sharif al-Murtada's short work on the Imam's disappearance, "A treatise on the occultation of the Twelfth Imamite Imam," *Studia Islamica*, 48 (1978), 109–124.

22. Asaf F. Fyzee has translated Ibn Babawayhi's *Risalatu'l-I'tiqadat* as *A Shi'ite Creed* (Calcutta: Oxford University Press, 1942), p. 98.

23. Ayoub, *Redemptive Suffering*, p. 54.

24. A bi-lingual, English–Arabic edition of al-Kulayni's collection of Traditions from the Imams entitled *Al-Kafi* is in preparation by the World Organization of Islamic Services, Tehran, dating from 1981. This tradition is taken from vol. I, part 2, p. 83.

25. Ibid., p. 249.

26. Ibid., pp. 36–37.

27. Ibid., p. 142.

28. Mu'tazilite influence on Shi'ah thought is discussed by Wilferd Madelung, "Imamism and Mu'tazilite theology," reprinted in his collected essays, *Religious Schools and Sects in Medieval Islam* (London: Variorum, 1985). The same volume also contains his discussion on "Authority in Twelver Shi'ism in the absence of the Imam."

29. Translated by William Miller, *Al-Babu 'l-Hadi 'Ashar: A Treatise on the Principles of Shi'ite Theology* (London: Luzac, 1958).

30. Wilferd Madelung, "A treatise of the Sharif al-Murtada on the legality of working for the government (*Mas'ala fi'l-'amal ma'a'l-sultan*)," *Bulletin of the School of Oriental and African Studies*, 43 (1980), 18–31, at p. 26.

31. Abu Mansur Abd al-Kahir ibn Tahir al-Baghdadi, *Moslem Schisms and Sects*, trans. Kate Chambers Seelye (New York: AMS Press, 1966 [1920]), p. 30.

32. On this matter, see Joseph Eliash, "The Shi'ite Qur'an," *Arabica*, 16 (1969), 15–24; E. Kohlberg, "Some notes on the Imamite attitude to the Qur'an," in S. M. Stern et al. (eds.), *Islamic Philosophy and the Classical Tradition* (Oxford: Cassirer, 1972), pp. 209–224; B. Todd Lawson, "A note for the study of a Shi'i Qur'an," *Journal of Semitic Studies*, 36 (1991), 279–295.

7 THE HEARTLANDS AND BEYOND

1. The travels have been abridged and translated into English by H. A. R. Gibb, *Ibn Battuta: Travels in Asia and Africa, 1325–1354* (London: Routledge & Kegan Paul, 1963 [1929]). See also the recent study by Ross E. Dunn, *The Adventures of Ibn Battuta: Muslim Traveller of the 14th Century* (Berkeley: University of California Press, 1986).
2. Gibb, *Ibn Battuta*, p. 137.
3. Ibid., p. 238.
4. Ibid., p. 269.
5. Ibid., p. 271.
6. Ibid., p. 242.
7. Ibid., p. 244.
8. Ibid., p. 290.
9. Ibid., p. 292.
10. Ibid., p. 321.
11. See the discussion of Akbar by Aziz Ahmad, *Studies in Islamic Culture in the Indian Environment* (Oxford: Clarendon Press, 1964), pp. 167–181.
12. Ibid., p. 175.
13. Tabrizi, *Mishkat*, I: 152.
14. *Manners and Customs of the Modern Egyptians* (London: Dent, 1954), p. 85.
15. Tabrizi, *Mishkat*, I:142.
16. See the discussion on "Islam and art" by Isma'il Faruqi, *Studia Islamica*, 37 (1973), 81–109.
17. Seyyed Hossein Nasr, *Islamic Art and Spirituality* (Ipswich: Golgonooza Press, 1987), p. 11.
18. See E. Kohlberg, "Aspects of Akhbari thought in the seventeenth and eighteenth centuries," in his *Belief and Law in Imami Shi'ism* (London: Variorum, 1991).
19. On Wali Allah's major work, see M. K. Hermansen, "Shah Wali Allah of Delhi's *Hujjat Allah al-baligha*: tension between the universal and the particular in an 18th century Islamic theory of religious revelation," *Studia Islamica*, 63 (1986), 143–157.
20. See Hafeez Malik's translation of "Shah Wali Allah's last testament," *Muslim World*, 63 (1973), 105–118.
21. Cited in Michael Cook, "On the origins of Wahhabism," *Journal of the Royal Asiatic Society* (July 1992), 191–202, at p. 198, n. 69.

8 ISSUES IN CONTEMPORARY ISLAM

1. Muhammad al-Saffar's travels have been translated, edited, and provided with an excellent introduction by Susan Gilson Miller, *Disorienting Encounters: Travels of a Moroccan Scholar in France in 1845–1846* (Berkeley: University of California Press, 1992).
2. Ibid., pp. 193–194.
3. Ibid., p. 157.
4. Ibid., p. 200.
5. Ibid., p. 215.
6. Ibid., p. 220.
7. Ibid., p. 190.
8. A serious, yet entertaining account of the coffee controversy in the Middle East is by Ralph Hattox, *Coffee and Coffeehouses: The Origins of a Social Beverage in the Medieval Near East* (Seattle: University of Washington Press, 1985).
9. The travels of al-Tahtawi and Muhammad al-Saffar reflect many of the same concerns, admiration tempered with criticism, as those shown by an even earlier traveler to Europe from India. Mirza Abu Talib Khan left his impressions of Britain in his *Travels in Asia, Africa and Europe*, trans. C. Stewart (London, 1814). He traveled in Europe during the years 1799–1803.
10. Cited in Ibrahim Abu Lughod, *Arab Rediscovery of Europe: A Study in Cultural Encounters* (Princeton: Princeton University Press, 1963), p. 94. See also on al-Tahtawi, Albert Hourani, *Arabic Thought in the Liberal Age, 1798–1939* (London: Royal Institute of International Affairs/Oxford University Press, 1962), pp. 69–83.
11. Cited in Hourani, *Arabic Thought*, p. 88. My italics.
12. See Amedeo Maiello, "Sir Sayyid Ahmad Khan and the Christian challenge," *Annali* (Naples), 36 (1976), 85–102.
13. Fazlur Rahman, *Islam and Modernity* (Chicago: University of Chicago Press, 1982), p. 74. Less critical of Sayyid Ahmad Khan's educational program is the assessment of Aziz Ahmad, *Islamic Modernism in India and Pakistan, 1857–1964* (London: Oxford University Press/Royal Institute of International Affairs, 1967), chapter 2.
14. An extract from this lecture is reproduced in the anthology edited by John Donohue and John Esposito, *Islam in Transition: Muslim Perspectives* (Oxford: Oxford University Press, 1982), p. 42.
15. Ibid.
16. See Hourani, *Arabic Thought*, chapters 6 and 7.
17. See ibid., chapter 5 and *An Islamic Response to Imperialism: Political and Religious Writings of Sayyid Jamal al-Din al-Afghani*, trans. and ed. Nikki Keddie (Berkeley: University of California Press, 1968).
18. Keddie, *An Islamic Response*, p. 179.
19. Cited in Hourani, *Arabic Thought*, p. 141.
20. Donald Reid, *Cairo University and the Making of Modern Egypt* (Cambridge:

Cambridge University Press, 1990), p. 18.

21. Translated by Ishaq Musa'ad and Kenneth Craig, as *The Theology of Unity* (London: George Allen & Unwin, 1966).
22. Ibid., p. 31. My italics.
23. Ibid., p. 119. Elsewhere, p. 79, he says "The revelatory wonder is not rationally to be classified as an impossibility. For the contravening of the familiar, natural pattern of things is not something susceptible of proof as to its impossibility."
24. G. H. A. Juynboll, *The Authenticity of the Tradition Literature* (Leiden: E. J. Brill, 1969), p. 32. See also Abduh, *Theology of Unity*, p. 156 and the full discussion of the reform movement by Ali Merad in the *Encyclopaedia of Islam*, 2nd ed. (Leiden: E. J. Brill, 1965–), s.v. *Islah*.
25. Abduh, *Theology of Unity*, p. 39. My italics.
26. Ibid., p. 115.
27. For an extensive discussion of this subject, see J. Esposito, *Women in Muslim Family Law* (Syracuse: Syracuse University Press, 1982).
28. For a discussion defending the analytical use of the term "fundamentalism" in the contexts of contemporary Christianity, Judaism, and Islam, see Bruce Lawrence, *Defenders of God: The Fundamentalist Revolt against the Modern Age* (London: I. B. Tauris, 1990). A contrasting use of the term in a broader and longer historical setting is John O. Voll's *Islam: Continuity and Change in the Modern World* (Boulder: Westview, 1982). A perceptive discussion of the label is William Shepherd, "Fundamentalism Christian and Islamic," *Religion*, 17 (1987) 355–378.
29. See John O. Voll, "Renewal and reform in Islamic history: *tajdid* and *islah*," in J. Esposito (ed.), *Voices of Resurgent Islam* (Oxford: Oxford University Press, 1983), pp. 32–47.
30. On their history, organization, and ideology, see Richard P. Mitchell, *The Society of the Muslim Brothers* (Oxford: Oxford University Press, 1969).
31. Ibid., p. 230.
32. See ibid., p. 274 and chapter 10 for details of their reform program.
33. Ibid., p. 244.
34. See Charles J. Adams, "Mawdudi and the Islamic state," in Esposito, *Resurgent Islam*, pp. 99–133.
35. Ibid., p. 113.
36. Rahman, *Islam and Modernity*, p. 15.
37. See the articles of Charles J. Adams, "The authority of the Prophetic *hadith* in the eyes of some modern Muslims," in D. Little (ed.), *Essays on Islamic Civilization* (Leiden: E. J. Brill, 1976), pp. 25–47 and "Abu'l-Ala Mawdudi's *Tafhim al-Qur'an*," in A. Rippin (ed.), *Approaches to the History of Interpretation of the Qur'an* (Oxford: Oxford University Press, 1988), pp. 307–323, and the discussion in Mitchell, *Muslim Brothers*, chapter 10.
38. On the Party's position with regard to the Palestine problem, see Suha Taji-Farouki, "A case study in contemporary Islam and the Palestine

Question: the perspective of the *Hizb al-tahrir al-islami*," *Studies in Muslim–Jewish Relations*, 2 (1993).

39. *Modern Islamic Political Thought* (London: Macmillan Press, 1982), p. 104.
40. On this theme, see John O. Voll, "Islamic renewal and the 'Failure of the West,'" in R. T. Antoun and M. E. Hegland (eds.), *Religious Resurgence: Contemporary Cases in Islam, Christianity and Judaism* (Syracuse: Syracuse University Press, 1987).
41. See Y. Y. Haddad, "The Qur'anic justification for an Islamic revolution: the view of Sayyid Qutb," *The Middle East Journal*, 37/1 (1983), 14–29.
42. See Hamid Enayat, "Iran: Khumayni's concept of the 'Guardianship of the jurisconsult,'" in James Piscatori, *Islam in the Political Process* (Cambridge: Cambridge University Press, 1983).
43. Michael M. J. Fischer, "Imam Khumayni: four levels of understanding," in Esposito, *Resurgent Islam*, p. 162.
44. Said Amir Arjomand, *The Turban for the Crown: The Islamic Revolution in Iran* (Oxford: Oxford University Press, 1988), p. 114.
45. Ibid., p. 210.
46. See David Pearl, "Executive and legislative amendments to Islamic family law in India and Pakistan," in Nicholas Heer (ed.), *Islamic Law and Jurisprudence* (Seattle: University of Washington Press, 1990).
47. On classical patriarchy, see Deniz Kandiyoti, "Islam and patriarchy: a comparative perspective," in N. Keddie and B. Baron (eds.), *Women in Middle Eastern History: Shifting Boundaries in Sex and Gender* (New Haven: Yale University Press, 1991), pp. 23–42; neopatriarchy has been analyzed by Hisham Sharabi in his *Neopatriarchy: A Theory of Distorted Change in Arab Society* (Oxford: Oxford University Press, 1988).
48. "Islam and patriarchy," pp. 32–33.
49. Cited in Y. Y. Haddad, *Contemporary Islam and the Challenge of History* (Albany: State University of New York Press, 1982), p. 63.
50. *Women and Islam: An Historical and Theological Enquiry* (Oxford: Basil Blackwell, 1991), p. ix.
51. The figures in this and the following paragraphs are taken from the excellent study by J. Nielsen, *Muslims in Western Europe* (Edinburgh: Edinburgh University Press, 1992). Note the author's word of caution concerning the estimated numbers of Muslims, pp. 167–168.
52. See Tomas Gerholm and Yngve Georg Lithman (eds.), *The New Islamic Presence in Western Europe* (London: Mansell, 1988).
53. On this point see the remarks by Gavin D'Costa, "Secular discourse and the clash of faiths: 'The Satanic Verses' in British society," *New Blackfriars* (October 1990), 418–431; also the incisive analysis in Richard Webster's *A Brief History of Blasphemy* (London: Orwell Press, 1992).
54. C. Eric Lincoln, "The American Muslim Mission in the context of American social history," in E. H. Waugh et al. (eds.), *The Muslim Community in North America* (Edmonton: Edmonton University Press,

1983), p. 222; see also the article in the same volume by Lawrence Mamiya, "Minister Louis Farrakhan and the final call: schism in the Muslim movement"; on Elijah Muhammad's thought, see Z. I. Ansari, "Aspects of black Muslim theology," *Studia Islamica*, 53 (1981), 137–176.

55. A recent, excellent treatment of the historical background and current events in Bosnia is Noel Malcolm, *Bosnia: A Short History* (London: Macmillan, 1994).

Further reading

1 "THERE IS NO GOD BUT ALLAH. . ."

Apart from the works cited in the Excursus on Islamic Origins, the following are suggested for the pre-Islamic background, the Qur'an, and the life of the Prophet. There are now available collections of studies relevant to the pre- and early-Islamic periods which are indispensable but display different approaches and methods. These include M. M. Bravmann, *The Spiritual Background of Early Islam* (Leiden: E. J. Brill, 1972); M. J. Kister, *Studies on Jahiliyyah and Early Islam* (London: Variorum, 1980); R. B. Serjeant, *Studies in Arabian History and Civilization* (London: Variorum, 1981). Some of the translated articles by French and German scholars in M. Swartz, *Studies on Islam* (New York, Oxford University Press, 1981), deal with the pre-Islamic period and the Prophet.

On the Qur'an, the best introduction in English remains Bell's *Introduction to the Koran*, revised and enlarged by W. M. Watt (Edinburgh: Edinburgh University Press, 1990 [1970]). A systematic, modern Muslim introduction is Fazlur Rahman, *Major Themes of the Qur'an* (Minneapolis: Bibliotheca Islamica, 1980). For the treatment of a specific but central theme in the Qur'an, see T. Izutsu, *God and Man in the Koran* (Tokyo, 1964). A study of this theme as reflected in the everyday speech of Arabs is M. Piamenta, *The Muslim Conception of God and Human Welfare* (Leiden: E. J. Brill, 1983). See also W. M. Watt, *Early Islam: Collected Articles* (Edinburgh: Edinburgh University Press, 1990), part 1 of which deals with Muhammad and the Qur'an. Watt presents his early views and methods in a more recent introduction to Islamic origins in *Muhammad's Mecca: History in the Qur'an* (Edinburgh: Edinburgh University Press, 1988). Mahmoud Ayoub has commenced a projected multi-volumed work on *The Qur'an and its Interpreters* (Albany: State University of New York Press, 1984), 1, which presents the Muslim scripture as Muslims themselves have seen it over the centuries. There is the single volume of brief translated passages from the Muslim exegetes, arranged thematically and prepared by Helmut Gatje, *The Qur'an and its Exegesis: Selected Texts with Classical and Modern Muslim Interpretations*, trans. from the German by Alford T. Welch (London: Routledge & Kegan Paul, 1976). Jane Dammen McAuliffe's *Qur'anic Christians: An Analysis of*

Classical and Modern Exegesis (Cambridge: Cambridge University Press, 1991) is a study of Muslim understanding of Christians as expressed in their interpretation of certain key Qur'anic verses. A collection of essays on the history of Qur'anic exegesis is A. Rippin (ed.), *Approaches to the History of the Interpretation of the Qur'an* (Oxford: Clarendon Press, 1988).

On the pre-Islamic material in Ibn Ishaq's biography of the Prophet, see Gordon D. Newby, *The Making of the Last Prophet: A Reconstruction of the Earliest Biography of Muhammad* (Columbia: University of South Carolina Press, 1989). It is useful to compare and contrast the biography of Muhammad from the point of view of an "insider" and an "outsider." For the former, see Muhammad Husayn Haykal, *The Life of Muhammad*, trans. I. R. al-Faruqi (London: Shorouk International, 1983); the latter is represented by Maxime Rodinson's *Muhammad* (Harmondsworth: Penguin, 1976). Another "insider's" view which attempts to capture the atmosphere of the original Arabic sources is Martin Lings, *Muhammad* (London: George Allen & Unwin, 1983).

2 TRADITION IN THE MAKING

A recent book on the socio-political history of the formative period of Islamic culture is Hugh Kennedy's *The Prophet and the Age of the Caliphs* (London: Longman, 1986), which covers the first five centuries of the developments of the community. Kennedy does not, however, touch upon North Africa west of Egypt, or the Islamic presence in the Iberian peninsula. These regions are covered by Jamil Abun-Nasr's *A History of the Maghrib* (Cambridge: Cambridge University Press, 1975) and the shorter survey on al-Andalus by W. M. Watt and P. Cachia, *Islamic Spain* (Edinburgh: Edinburgh University Press, 1965). Gerald Hawting's *The First Dynasty of Islam* (London: Croom Helm, 1986) provides an excellent survey of the first century and the historical and historiographical problems it involves. For a work more focused upon the making of the religious community of Islam, see the treatment in the first and second volumes of Marshall G. S. Hodgson's brilliant *The Venture of Islam* (Chicago: Chicago University Press, 1974). Two works covering different aspects of the Muslim conquests are Fred Donner, *The Early Islamic Conquests* (Princeton: Princeton University Press, 1984) and Michael Morony, *Iraq after the Muslim Conquests* (Princeton: Princeton University Press, 1984). Morony discusses the various ethnic, religious communities in Iraq and the cultural interchange between them and the invading Arabs from the peninsula. See also the collection of articles in G. H. A. Juynboll (ed.), *Studies on the First Century of Islamic Society* (Carbondale, Ill., 1982). The reader now has access to an English translation of the most important work on early Islamic history down to the end of the third/ninth century written by al-Tabari, *History of al-Tabari* (Albany: State University of New York Press) to be completed in thirty-eight volumes.

Franz Rosenthal's *Knowledge Triumphant: The Concept of Knowledge in Medieval Islam* (Leiden: E. J. Brill, 1970) is exhaustive in its coverage.

Stephen Humphries has dedicated a chapter to the *'ulama'* (with a useful discussion of the secondary sources in European languages) in his *Islamic History: A Framework for Inquiry* (London: I. B. Taurus, 1991). A collection of essays dealing with traveling scholars and other pilgrims has been edited by Dale Eickelman and James Piscatori, *Muslim Travellers: Pilgrimage, Migration and the Religious Imagination* (London: Routledge, 1990). Two monographs which treat the scholarly community quite differently are Muhsin Mahdi's essay on the thought of the eighth-/fourteenth-century scholar Ibn Khaldun, *Ibn Khaldun's Philosophy of History* (Chicago: University of Chicago Press, 1957), and R. W. Bulliet's study of a whole segment of religious notables, *The Patricians of Nishapur* (Cambridge, Mass.: Harvard University Press, 1972). Essays devoted to an assessment and appreciation of the enormously varied output of the *'ulama'* will be found in two volumes of the *Cambridge History of Arabic Literature*. These are entitled *Arabic Literature to the end of the Umayyad Period* (Cambridge: Cambridge University Press, 1983) and *Abbasid Belles Lettres* (1990). G. H. A. Juynboll's *Muslim Tradition* (Cambridge: Cambridge University Press, 1983) is a recent attempt to lay bare some of the mysteries of the origins and development of *hadith* material. An excellent study of the *hadith qudsi* is William Graham's *Divine Word and Prophetic Word in Early Islam* (The Hague: Mouton and Co., 1977). Two other collections of essays by eminent scholars on different subjects dealing with the formation of the Islamic world are C. E. Bosworth, *Medieval Arabic Culture and Administration* (London: Variorum, 1982) and Wilferd Madelung, *Religious Trends in Early Islamic Iran* (Albany, N.Y.: Bibliotheca Persica, 1982).

The subject of conversion has been tackled in R. W. Bulliet's imaginative *Conversion to Islam in the Medieval Period: An Essay in Quantitative History* (Cambridge, Mass.: Harvard University Press, 1979), and, on the same theme, covering different regions and periods, the papers in Nehemiah Levtzion's edited volume *Conversion to Islam* (New York: Holmes & Meier, 1979) are helpful. There is also the excellent collection of essays dealing with Christian conversion and Christian–Muslim relations edited by M. Gervers and R. Bikhazi, *Conversion and Continuity: Indigenous Christian Communities in Islamic Lands: Eighth to Eighteenth Centuries* (Toronto: Pontifical Institute of Mediaeval Studies, 1990). For the status of the non-Muslim in Muslim society, there is the somewhat outdated but still useful work by A. S. Tritton, *The Caliphs and their non-Muslim Subjects* (London: Oxford University Press, 1930, reprinted London: Frank Cass, 1970); see also Bernard Lewis, *The Jews of Islam* (Princeton: Princeton University Press, 1984), and Norman Stillman, *The Jews of Arab Lands: A History and Source Book* (Philadelphia: Jewish Publication Society of America, 1979).

The text and translation of an early Muslim polemical work has been edited by David Thomas, *Anti-Christian Polemic in Early Islam: Abu 'Isa al-Warraq's "Against the Trinity"* (Cambridge: Cambridge University Press, 1992).

3 DIVINE WILL AND THE LAW

The reader is reminded to consult the Excursus for references to works on the law. In addition to these, the following general and more specialized works can be recommended. P. Crone continues her controversial explorations into Islamic origins in *Roman, Provincial and Islamic Law: The Origins of the Islamic Patronate* (Cambridge: Cambridge University Press, 1987). Still useful is Goldziher's chapter on law in his *Introduction to Islamic Theology and Law*, trans. A. and R. Hamori (Princeton: Princeton University Press, 1980). Schacht's views are set forth in two essays (which are a good introduction to his more detailed monographs mentioned in the Excursus) in *Law in the Middle East*, ed. M. Khadduri and H. Liebesny (Washington: The Middle East Institute, 1984 [1955]); the volume also contains useful articles by other Muslim, Sunni and Shi'ah, and Western scholars. A Muslim treatment of the law is A. Hasan's *The Early Development of Islamic Jurisprudence* (Islamabad: Islamic Research Institute, 1970) and his more specialized *Analogical Reasoning in Islamic Jurisprudence: A Study of the Juridical Principle of Qiyas* (Islamabad: Islamic Research Institute, 1986). Farhat Ziadeh has translated into English a general introduction to the law by the Lebanese scholar S. R. Mahmassani, as *Falsafat al-tashri' fi al-Islam* (Leiden: E.J. Brill, 1961). For Shi'ah law there is Hossein M. Tabatabai, *An Introduction to Shi'a Law: A Bibliographical Study* (London: Ithaca Press, 1984).

Majid Khadduri has translated an early legal text into English in his *The Islamic Law of Nations: Shaybani's Siyar* (Baltimore: Johns Hopkins Press, 1966); see also his *War and Peace in the Law of Islam* (Baltimore: Johns Hopkins Press, 1955), which deals with the status of the *dhimmi*s, or non-Muslims in the Muslim polity. An introduction to Islamic political theory, including that of the Shi'ah, is A. K. S. Lambton's *State and Government in Medieval Islam* (Oxford: Oxford University Press, 1981). A modern Muslim treatment of the law of the state is Muhammad Hamidullah, *Muslim Conduct of State* (Lahore: Sh. Muhammad Ashraf, 1977).

Three collections of essays on various aspects of the law, classical and modern, are Nicholas Heer (ed.), *Islamic Law and Jurisprudence* (Seattle: University of Washingtom Press, 1990); R. B. Serjeant, *Customary and Shari'ah Law in Arabian Society* (London: Variorum, 1991); and Aziz al-Azmeh (ed.), *Islamic Law: Social and Historical Contexts* (London: Routledge, 1988).

The following monographs deal with more specialized legal topics within the broad scope of the *shari'ah*. The list is very selective, intended only to show the range of material that is becoming available. On commercial law, see Abraham Udovitch, *Partnership and Profit in Medieval Islam* (Princeton: Princeton University Press, 1970); Jeanette Wakin, *The Function of Documents in Islamic Law* (Albany: State University of New York Press, 1972); Farishta Zayas, *The Law and Philosophy of Zakat* (Beirut, 1962); Jamal J. Nasir, *The Islamic Law of Personal Status* (London: Graham and Trotman, 1986); David Powers, *Studies in Qur'an and Hadith: The Formation of the Islamic Law of Inheritance* (Berkeley: University of California Press, 1986); Franz Rosenthal,

Gambling in Islam (Leiden: E. J. Brill, 1975); Baber Johansen, *The Islamic Law on Land and Rent* (London: Croom Helm, 1988); A. M. A. Maktari, *Water Rights and Irrigation Practices in Lahj: A Study of the Application of Customary and Shari'ah Law in South-west Arabia* (Cambridge: Cambridge University Press, 1971); on the question of birth control, see B. F. Musallam, *Sex and Society in Islam* (Cambridge: Cambridge University Press, 1983); a detailed historical study of a religious endowment, or *waqf*, is R. D. McChesney, *Waqf in Central Asia: Four Hundred Years in the History of a Muslim Shrine, 1480–1889* (Princeton: Princeton University Press, 1991). Finally, the concept of *jihad* or holy war is discussed by several contibutors to the volume *Just War and Jihad: Historical and Theoretical Perspectives on War and Peace in Western and Islamic Traditions*, ed. John Kelsay and James Turner Johson (Westport, Conn.: Greenwood Press, 1991).

4 THEOLOGY: FAITH, JUSTICE, AND LAST THINGS

The best general introduction to the subject is still W. M. Watt, *The Formative Period of Islamic Thought* (Edinburgh: Edinburgh University Press, 1973). The important work of the German scholar Josef van Ess is not available in English, but there is his very useful essay "Early development of *kalam*" in G. H. A. Juynboll, *Studies in the First Century of Islamic Society* (Carbondale: Southern Illinois University Press, 1982), pp. 109–124. H. A. Wolfson's detailed treatment of Muslim discussions of God's attributes, the creation of the world, causality, freedom, and predestination appears in his *The Philosophy of the Kalam* (Cambridge, Mass.: Harvard University Press, 1976). A rather technical discussion of sources for the reconstruction of early theological questions in Islam is Michael Cook, *Early Muslim Dogma: A Source-critical Study* (Cambridge: Cambridge University Press, 1981). Mu'tazilite thought concerning one topic of the *kalam* discussions is examined by Richard Frank, *Beings and their Attributes: The Teaching of the Basrian School of the Mu'tazila in the Classical Period* (Albany: State University of New York Press, 1978). The Mu'tazilite position on the nature of the Qur'an is treated by J. R. T. M. Peters, *God's Created Speech* (Leiden: E. J. Brill, 1976).

A translation of a portion of a fifth-/twelfth-century work on "heresies" which deals with the Mu'tazilites, Kharijites, and the Shi'ah is *Muslim Sects and Divisions*, trans. A. K. Kazi and J. G. Flynn (London: Kegan Paul International, 1984). Modern studies dealing with these and other groups are the essays of Wilferd Madelung, *Religious Schools and Sects in Medieval Islam* (London: Variorum, 1985) and George Makdisi, *Religion, Law and Learning in Classical Islam* (London: Variorum, 1991). Essays related to Mu'tazilite thought and other topics are found in George Hourani, *Reason and Tradition in Islamic Ethics* (Cambridge: Cambridge University Press, 1985). Other collections grouping together articles of varying focus are G. E. von Grunebaum (ed.), *Theology and Law in Islam* (Wiesbaden: Harrassowitz, 1971); P. Morewedge (ed.), *Islamic Philosophical Theology* (Albany: State University of New York Press, 1979); M. Marmurra (ed.), *Islamic Theology and Philosophy* (Albany: State University of New York Press, 1984). A study which borders the concerns of theologians and philosophers is F. Shehadi, *Metaphysics in Islamic Philosophy* (Delmar N.Y.: Caravan Books, 1983). The work of the great French scholar Henry Corbin is now available in translation as *The History of Islamic Philosophy* (London: Kegan Paul International, 1993 [1964]).

Eric Ormsby has examined an important aspect of al-Ghazali's thought in *Theodicy in Islamic Thought: The Dispute over al-Ghazali's "Best of all Possible Worlds"* (Princeton: Princeton University Press, 1984). Translation of his "spiritual" autobiography and other important, short works are included in R. J. McCarthy, *Freedom and Fulfillment: An Annotated Translation of al-Ghazali's* Munqidh min al-Dalal *and Other Relevant Works of al-Ghazali* (Boston, Mass.: Twayne, 1980).

J. N. Bell's *Love Theory in Later Hanbalite Islam* (Albany: State University of New York Press, 1979) is an interesting study of an aspect of Ibn Taymiyyah's thought. A translation of Ibn Taymiyyah's attack on certain Sufi practices is in M. U. Memon, *Ibn Taimiya's Struggle Against Popular Religion: With an Annotated Translation of his* Kitab al-iqtida as-sirat al-mustaqim mukhalafat ashab al-jahim (The Hague: Mouton, 1976).

5 THE WAY OF THE SUFI

The literature on Sufism is more extensive than almost any other aspect of Islam. The two volumes devoted to Islam in the series entitled World Spirituality: An Encyclopedic History of the Religious Quest provide the most recent collection of essays on Islamic spirituality. Both volumes are edited by Seyyed Hossein Nasr. The first volume, *Islamic Spirituality: Foundations* (London: SCM Press, 1989 [1985]), includes, among others, articles on the Qur'an and Tradition, the spiritual dimension of Islamic rituals, the origins of Sufism, Sufi practices and Islamic understanding of God, the angels, the cosmos, and eschatology. The second volume, *Islamic Spirituality: Manifestations* (London: SCM Press, 1991), treats the main Sufi brotherhoods and the role of Sufism in the different regions of the Islamic world, together with essays on various Sufi literatures, music, dance, and art. As with any large collection of essays (there are forty-five in the two volumes), quality is not uniform, but it is the most ambitious and comprehensive enterprise on the subject to date. Both volumes contain good bibliographies and a glossary. J. Spencer Trimingham's *The Sufi Orders in Islam* (Oxford: Clarendon Press, 1971) contains much useful material to supplement that contained in vol. II of this series. An older but still useful work on Sufi origins is Tor Andrae, *In the Garden of Myrtles: Studies in Early Mysticism* (Albany: State University of New York Press, 1987 [1947]).

The most readable and authorative single-authored account of Sufism remains Annemarie Schimmel's *Mystical Dimensions of Islam* (Chapel Hill: University of North Carolina Press, 1975). Schimmel has also devoted a study to Sufi poetry, *As Through a Veil: Mystical Poetry in Islam* (New York: Columbia University Press, 1982). Julian Baldick's more recent introduction, *Mystical Islam* (London: I.B. Tauris, 1989), attempts a "history of religion" approach to the same subject. The major work on Sufism by the German scholar Fritz Meier is not available in English, although his useful survey "The mystic path" is included in *The World of Islam* edited by Bernard Lewis (London: Thames & Hudson, 1976). Whereas both Schimmel or Baldick may be read with profit by someone seeking a straightforward introduction to Sufism, other works which appear to appeal to the same audience are less helpful. Titus Burckhardt's *An Introduction to Sufism* (Wellingborough: Crucible, 1990 [1976]), Martin Lings's (Abu Bakr Siraj al-Din) *What is Sufism?* (London: Unwin Hyman, 1981), and S. H. Nasr's *Living Sufism* (London: Unwin Paperbacks, 1980 [1972]) are all authoritative in the sense that the authors write from *within* the Sufi tradition, but they each represent a modern expression of Ibn al-'Arabi's thought which does not present an easy entry into Sufism. A necessary beginning to Ibn al'Arabi, however, is provided by William Chittick's *The Sufi Path of Knowledge: Ibn al-Arabi's Metaphysics of Imagination* (Albany: State University of New York Press, 1989). There is also the volume of essays edited by S. Hirtenstein and M. Tiernan, *Muhyiddin Ibn Arabi: A Commemorative Volume* (Shaftesbury: Element Books, 1993). The work most likely to become the standard work of reference, however, is the French scholar Claude Addas's *Quest for the Red Sulphur: The Life of Ibn Arabi* (Cambridge: Islamic Texts Society, 1993). William Chittick's study of Rumi contains much material translated from his works, *The Sufi Path of Love: The Spiritual Teachings of Rumi* (Albany: State University of New York Press, 1983). The work on al-Hallaj by the famous French scholar Louis Massignon has been translated by H. Mason, *The Passion of al-Hallaj: Mystic and Martyr of Islam* (4 vols., Princeton: Princeton University Press, 1982).

A monograph based on field work among Egyptian singers and performers of *dhikr* rituals is E. H. Waugh, *The* Munshidin *of Egypt: Their World and their Song* (Columbia: University of South Carolina Press, 1989).

6 THE WAY OF THE IMAMS

More attention has been given to the Shi'ah in recent years, and works are now available by both Shi'ah and Western scholars. A general political history of the pre-Safavid and Safavid periods is David Morgan, *Medieval Persia 1040–1797* (London: Longman, 1988). Moojan Momen, *An Introduction to Shi'i Islam. The History and Doctrine of Twelver Shi'ism* (New Haven and London: Yale University Press, 1985), provides much detail, useful appendices containing a chronology, a list of Shi'ah dynasties, and brief biographies of famous '*ulama*' as well as a good bibliography. There is now the indispensable survey by Heinz Halm, translated from the German, *Shi'ism* (Edinburgh: Edinburgh University Press, 1991 [1987]), with extensive bibliographies.

This may be read together with S. A. Arjomand, *The Shadow of God and the Hidden Imam: Religion, Political Order and Social Change in Shi'ite Iran from the Beginnings to 1890* (Chicago/London: Chicago University Press, 1984).

Valuable studies on early Shi'ah themes by Etan Kohlberg have been collected together in his *Belief and Law in Imami Shi'ism* (Aldershot: Variorum, 1991). Covering the history of the period down to the sixth Imam, Ja'far al-Sadiq, is S. Husain M. Jafri, *Origins and Early Development of Shi'a Islam* (London: Longman, 1979). History and thought are combined in the work of the renowned late Iranian scholar Allamah Sayyid Muhammad Husayn Tabataba'i, *Shi'ite Islam* (Albany: State University of New York Press, 1975).

Two anthologies of selections from the writings of chiefly modern (but also classical) authors, annotated and introduced by Seyyed Hossein Nasr, Hamid Dabashi, and Seyyed Vali Reza Nasr, are *Shi'ism: Doctrines, Thought and Spirituality* (Albany: State University of New York Press, 1988) and *Expectations of the Millennium: Shi'ism in History* (Albany: State University of New York Press, 1989). To these may be added William Chittik's *A Shi'ite Anthology* (Albany: State University of New York Press, 1980).

Abdulaziz Abdulhussein Sachedina has written monographs on two important aspects of the Shi'ah tradition, *Islamic Messianism: The Idea of the Mahdi in Twelver Shi'ism* (Albany: State University of New York Press, 1981) and *The Just Ruler in Shi'ite Islam: The Comprehensive Authority of the Jurist in Imamite Jurisprudence* (Oxford: Oxford University Press, 1988). J. M. Hussain's *The Occultation of the Twelfth Imam: A Historical Background* (London: Muhammadi Trust, 1982) is a portrayal of current "official" Shi'ah doctrine. Another work published by the same trust is a fine translation by William Chittick of supplications attributed to 'Ali's grandson, the Imam Zayn al-'Abidin, *The Psalms of Islam* (London, 1988).

A collection of essays on the performance of the al-Husayn passion is edited by P. J. Chelkowski, *Ta'ziyeh. Ritual and Drama in Iran* (New York: New York University Press, 1979). A study of Shi'ah temporary marriage is by Shahla Haeri, *Law of Desire: Temporary Marriage in Shi'i Iran* (Syracuse: Syracuse University Press, 1989).

7 THE HEARTLANDS AND BEYOND

The period of the "gunpowder" empires, the Ottoman, Mughal, and Safavid, is covered by Marshall Hodgson in vol. III of his *Venture of Islam* (Chicago: Chicago University Press, 1974). Essays by H. Inalcik and R. Savory in the *Cambridge History of Islam* (Cambridge, 1970), vol. IA, deal with the Ottomans and Safavids, and I. H. Qureshi writes on the Mughals in vol. 2A. For more detailed coverage of the Ottoman period there is H. Inalcik, *The Ottoman Empire: The Classical Age, 1300–1600*, trans. N. Itzkowitz and C. Imber (London: Weidenfeld & Nicolson, 1973); for the Safavids, see R. Savory, *Iran under the Safavids* (Cambridge: Cambridge University Press, 1980), and the articles in the *Cambridge History of Iran*, vol. VI, *The Timurid and*

Safavid Periods, ed. P. Jackson and L. Lockhart (Cambridge: Cambridge University Press, 1986), which contains essays on the history of the period (H. Roemer), religion and spirituality (B. S. Amoretti and S. H. Nasr), and architecture (R. Hillenbrand); Annemarie Schimmel's *Islam in the Indian Subcontinent* (Leiden: E. J. Brill, 1980) includes the Mughal period. For the architecture of the empires of the sultans, see also G. Goodwin, *A History of Ottoman Architecture* (Baltimore: Johns Hopkins University Press, 1971) and *Cities of Mughal India* (New Delhi, 1977).

For the region of southeast Asia down to the eighteenth century, there is the brief essay by H. J. de Graaf, also in vol. 2A of the *Cambridge History of Islam*. For the same period covering northwest Africa and the Islamic expansion southward, see the articles by H. J. Fisher and N. Levtzion in the *Cambridge History of Africa* (Cambridge: Cambridge University Press, 1977, 1975), in vols. III and IV respectively. To this may be added *Studies in West African Islamic History*, vol. I, *The Cultivators of Islam*, ed. John Ralph Willis (London: Frank Cass, 1979), and E. N. Saad, *Social History of Timbuktu: The Role of Muslim Scholars and Notables 1400–1900* (Cambridge: Cambridge University Press, 1983).

The central Islamic lands in the eighteenth century are dealt with in the collection of essays edited by T. Naff and R. Owen, *Studies in Eighteenth Century Islamic History* (Carbondale: Southern Illinois University Press, 1977). Society and social change in Iran in the nineteenth century are the subjects of A. K. S. Lambton's *Qajar Iran: Eleven Studies* (London: I. B. Tauris, 1987). The renewal movement in India is the background to S. A. A. Rizvi's *Shah Wali-Allah and his Times* (Canberra: Ma'rifat Publishing House, 1980). A translation of a work on Sufism by Shah Wali Allah is *Sufism and the Islamic Tradition: the Lamahat and Sata'at of Shah Waliallah*, trans. G. N. Jalbani (London, 1980). A full-scale study of Ibn Abd al-Wahhab has yet to appear in English, but there is the short article by G. Rentz, "Wahhabism and Saudi Arabia," in *The Arabian Peninsula: Society and Politics*, ed. D. Hopwood (London: George Allen & Unwin, 1972).

Monographs on eighteenth- and nineteenth-century Islamic renewal movements in different regions include: M. Hiskett, *The Sword of Truth: The Life and Times of Shehu Usuman Dan Fodio* (New York: Oxford University Press, 1973); C. Dobbin, *Islamic Revivalism in a Changing Peasant Economy: Central Sumatra, 1784–1847* (London: Curzon Press, 1983); R. S. O'Fahey, *Enigmatic Saint: Ahmad ibn Idris and the Idrisi Tradition* (London: Hurst, 1990); and B. G. Martin, *Muslim Brotherhoods in Nineteenth-Century Africa* (Cambridge: Cambridge University Press, 1976).

8 ISSUES IN CONTEMPORARY ISLAM

An excellent overview of the premodern and contemporary Islamic world is in John O. Voll's *Islam: Continuity and Change in the Modern World* (Boulder: Westview Press, 1982).

For different regions in the reform period from roughly the late nineteenth to mid twentieth centuries see on *India*: Christian Troll, *Sayyid Ahmad Khan: A Reinterpretation of Muslim Theology* (Delhi: Vikas Publishing, 1977); P. Hardy, *The Muslims of British India* (Cambridge: Cambridge University Press, 1972), which covers the period from the Mutiny in 1957 to partition in 1947. *Indonesia*: Deliar Noer, *The Modernist Muslim Movement in Indonesia, 1900–1942* (Kuala Lumpur: Oxford University Press, 1978); B. J. Boland, *The Struggle of Islam in Modern Indonesia* (The Hague: Nijhoff, 1971). *China*: R. Israeli, *Muslims in China: A Study in Cultural Confrontation* (London: Curzon Press, 1980). *The Arab World*: Hisham Sharabi, *Arab Intellectuals and the West: The Formative Years, 1875–1914* (Baltimore: Johns Hopkins Press, 1970); Abdallah Laroui, *The Crisis of the Arab Intellectual: Traditionalism or Historicism?*, trans. D. Cammell (Berkeley: University of California Press, 1976); C. D. Smith, *Islam and the Search for Social Order in Egypt* (Albany: State University of New York Press, 1983); A. L. al-Sayyid Marsot, *Egypt's Liberal Experiment, 1922–1936* (Berkeley: University of California Press, 1977). *Iran*: H. Algar, *Religion and the State in Iran, 1785–1906* (Berkeley: University of California Press, 1969); S. Bakhash, *Iran: Monarchy, Bureaucracy and Reform under the Qajars: 1858–1896* (London: Ithaca Press, 1978). *Turkey*: D. Kushner, *The Rise of Turkish Nationalism, 1876–1908* (London: Frank Cass, 1977). Islam across Asia major is the subject of a dozen essays in R. Israeli, *The Crescent in the East* (London: Curzon Press, 1982).

On the radical movements, there is the very helpful bibliographical introduction by Y. Haddad et al. (eds.), *The Contemporary Islamic Revival: A Critical Survey and Bibliography* (Westport, Conn.: Greenwood Press, 1991); see also Y. Choueiri, *Islamic Fundamentalism* (London: Pinter, 1990) (on Mawdudi and Sayyid Qutb); G. Kepel, *The Prophet and Pharaoh: Muslim Extremism in Egypt* (Berkeley: University of California Press, 1985). On Iran and Khumayni: N. Keddie, *Religion and Politics in Iran: Shi'ism from Quietism to Revolution* (New Haven: Yale University Press, 1983); S. Bakhash, *The Reign of the Ayatollah* (New York: Basic Books, 1984); Roy Mottahedeh, *The Mantle of the Prophet: Religion and Politics in Iran* (Harmondsworth: Penguin, 1987); Ayatollah Khomeini, *Islam and Revolution: Writings and Declarations of Imam Khomeini*, trans. H. Algar (Berkeley: Mizan Press, 1981) (contains his text on the Islamic State); J. J. G. Jansen, *The Neglected Duty: The Creed of Sadat's Assassins and Islamic Resurgence in the Middle East* (London: Macmillan, 1986); Olivier Roy, *Islam and Resistance in Afghanistan*, 2nd ed. (Cambridge: Cambridge University Press, 1990).

Works on the role of Islam in contemporary societies include: R. Peters, *Islam and Colonialism: The Doctrine of Jihad in Modern History* (The Hague: Mouton, 1979); S. A. Arjomand (ed.), *From Nationalism to Revolutionary Islam* (London: Macmillan, 1984); M. Gilsenan, *Recognizing Islam: Religion and Society in the Modern Arab World* (London: Croom Helm, 1982); B. Tibi, *Islam and the Cultural Accommodation of Social Change*, trans. C. Krojzl (Boulder: Westview Press, 1990); J. R. Cole and N. Keddie, *Shi'ism and Social Protest*

(New Haven: Yale University Press, 1986); J. Esposito et al. (eds.), *Islam and Development: Religion and Socio-political Change* (Syracuse: Syracuse University Press, 1980); Richard Antoun, *Muslim Preacher in the Modern World* (Princeton: Princeton University Press, 1989).

The literature on women increases rapidly. A good introduction with bibliography is V. M. Moghadam, *Modernizing Women: Gender and Social Change in the Middle East* (Boulder: Lynne Rienner Publishers, 1993). A historical treatment of the subject is Leila Ahmad, *Women and Gender in Islam* (New Haven: Yale University Press, 1992).

Other books on the subject of Islam in the West include: W. A. R. Shadid and P. S. van Koningsveld (eds.), *The Integration of Islam and Hinduism in Western Europe* (Kampen, Netherlands: Kok Pharos Publishing House, 1991); Larry Poston, *Islamic Da'wah in the West: Muslim Missionary Activity and the Dynamics of Conversion to Islam* (Oxford: Oxford University Press, 1992); E. H. Waugh et al. (eds.), *Muslim Families in North America* (Edmonton: University of Alberta Press, 1991).

Index

315